Travels with Pookie

A humorous e-mail diary of RV travels to National Parks and other attractions in the US & Canada

By

Evan Davis

ISBN: 1-4107-0046-1 (e-book)
ISBN: 1-4107-0047-X (Paperback)

Library of Congress Control Number: 2002096323

This book is printed on acid free paper.

Printed in the United States of America
Bloomington, IN

1stBooks - rev. 03/11/03

Table of Contents

Introduction

Naaah, that's not Pookie on the cover. That's Winston. But like most of the fun things in my life, Pookie is responsible for Winston. She talked me into buying him from our friends, Nora and Harbert.

Pookie is my girlfriend, lover, spouse and life partner. She's also my seamstress, laundress, cook, maid, social secretary, and companion. At times she acts like my supervisor, my chief critic or my Mother, but those times are minimal. Perhaps most importantly, Pookie is my best friend and I love her totally. This book is dedicated to her.

This book did not start out as a work to be published. It began in 1998 as a series of e-mails to friends and family as we began a post-retirement series of travels, originally intended to take us by travel trailer to all of the Scenic National Parks in the United States. It was really a means to stay in contact during some rather lengthy trips all over North America, north of Mexico. We ended up with a list of eighty odd members in our Travelogue group after five years of RV trips and frequent requests to add additional recipients. A significant number of the recipients of those e-mails suggested that I publish the combined travels, as they thought it might be of interest to others. I added the chapter about Duke's acquisition, as I sent those e-mails to the Travelogue group also, when they were first written, although we were not on the road.

I alone have served as the editor of this work, and that was intentional. I wanted the published version to retain the feel of the original, which was written as an informative and often humorous e-mail and not as a grammatically correct, polished work. I wanted it to retain the immediacy, authenticity and style of e-mails, rather than appear as a traditional book, and therefore chose not to use the services of a professional editor. The format contains sentence fragments, my own personal abbreviations or emphasis, and other shortcuts customarily placed in e-mails by writers who are not the world's best typist and are not particularly concerned with correctness of form.

The book is primarily my observations about the people, places and things we see on these trips plus my intentional efforts to make the e-mails funny, entertaining and informative. I also inject some of my rather conservative political philosophy, along with Pookie's comments and observations. Parts of it are tongue-in-cheek, exaggerated or sarcastic, and I think you'll recognize those. I alone am responsible for the errors or mistakes. Thanks to all the people who encouraged me to publish.

Chapter 1. Notes From the Road, Trip to the Southwest —1998

Date: Thursday, March 19, 1998 3:21 PM
Subject: Day 1

We're in Vicksburg and doing O.K. so far. Our leader miscalculated mileage by 4 miles and had to walk for gas on the Natchez Trace yesterday. The damn thing gets 2 miles per gallon less with all the added weight of Pookie's nesting materials. Fortunately, a guy gave me a ride to a gas station and a Park Ranger gave me a lift back and I only walked 3/4 mile. The worst part was listening to Pookie about running out of gas. The last time I did that, Doyle was 2 months old (I have received a detailed account of a 33 year old event in the last 24 hours—several times). Winston is doing better than we expected. After 3 or 4 hours, he figured out we weren't going to the vet, and likes the traveling life. He slept in the trailer last nite and we stayed in Ena's house. He is a little anxious about being left somewhere and sticks to me like glue. If I start up the Blazer without putting him in it, he tries to get in. Maybe he's figured out my hemlock plan for him! Obie doing well and still has a tongue. Said something about her son having more money than sense when she heard about me running out of gas. She got in the trailer today with a little help and was impressed. Of course, she can't see too well. Took her to lunch today and she ate like a horse and then asked what time I would pick her up for dinner tonite. After my screw up of yesterday, I looked up a place to stay tomorrow night on the way to Austin and actually called and made a reservation at a Texas State Park (don't need any more criticism for a day or so). More later.
Evan

Date: Saturday, March 21, 1998 6:06 PM
Subject: Day 2 of Odyssey

Well, our Hero made another mistake today, but as usual, it was Pookie's fault. We left Ena's house about 9 a.m. and went to the HOME to tell Obie goodbye. Got away around 9:30 and crossed the Miss. River headed west into the Louisiana Delta with a strong headwind. I commented that the trailer was really pulling hard, compared to our previous day on the

Trace. The response from my favorite traveling companion was the same I have heard since I bought the Blazer in 92—You should have bought a bigger tow truck! To make up for the insult, I started to pass the slowest doublewide in America. Most of them travel at 70 and this one was poking along at 55. The Blazer was really struggling, but now I was pissed! For the last 5 miles, the cruise control wouldn't hold our speed and I attributed it to the head wind. By flooring it, I could pass the doublewide on a 2 lane Interstate (I-20) and show my butt and my truck to the critic in the front seat! After I passed the rear escort vehicle and pulled even with the double-wide, the escort vehicle pulled up beside us and gestured frantically Not knowing what he meant, I put down the front window and heard him shout, "You've got a flat"!

After I pulled over and stopped, I discovered that not only did I have a flat, I had no tire left and the wheel was all bent up. The trailer is a tandem axle and has 4 wheels with 2 on each side. I had pulled it about 7 miles at 60 mph on I-20 which is horrible in LA with only 1 tire on 1 side. (Criticism about the towing capacity of the Blazer should slowly decrease over time with my help reminding the critic of it's excess—$125 tire replacement cost— capacity.) It will ride on 1 tire inflated, but when you hit a bump, the tire not inflated hits the pavement and shreds. I could blame this on Louisiana politicians who never let a free dollar get to the highway system, but everybody knows that already. Went back to Vicksburg and called Louis who took us to his tire dealer who sent a truck to get the wheel and straightened it and sold me the expensive replacement tire and asked me to return for more business in the future.

I am now convinced that we are going to learn everything about this RV the hard way. Stopped for lunch today at a rest stop and Pookie insisted on lighting the stove to brown some pimento cheese (Allene's pimento cheese) sandwiches. Ever had pimento cheese soup? The damn oven works!

Winston is a very happy camper! He gets anxious when I'm out of his sight (and he's blind!) and he can't hear either. On the other hand, if I had to depend on me for my survival and I was 13 (91 in people years?), I'd be anxious too. He sleeps in the back of the Blazer since he snores worse than either of us. We're in Rusk/Palestine State Park in Texas now and head to Austin tomorrow to see David and Margaret and Holly. After that, we're free to destroy the RV on our own schedule.
More Later. Evan

(PS. this is from me-the companion) He accuses me of complaining when actually I am laughing and being a pretty good sport, I think! More later from the Clampetts!!!

Date: Sunday, March 22, 1998 10:12 AM
Subject: Truth

Saw where my sole remaining dependent added a false postscript to my message of last nite. We don't have access to a phone, so these messages will be sent later and I'm not responsible for superfluous comments added in the dark of the nite.

We've learned several other things on this trip, besides how to run out of gas and how to tell when you're driving with a flat. We now know how to light the stove and how to burn food. Also, we have christened the toilet—that's the only part of the user manual I read before trying to use something (for obvious reasons). The user manual is 6 inches thick and the first 50 pages are safety tips—boring as Al Gore. Our patented trial and error system has worked for years and is being retained. Occasionally my "companion" isn't entertained enough with our natural screw ups and goes outside the required effort to find new ways to screw up. For example, in Vicksburg she found time to go shopping and bought some incensed candles. One is named Happy Camper and she had to try it last nite. Ena guessed it might smell like sweat or something. I really can't describe the odor, but Pookie lit it and put it on the dinette. When the smoke alarm went off, I turned over the dog's water when I leaped to my feet in sheer terror! It is LOUD! She hasn't tried the other candle named Romantic.

Last nite it got down to near freezing but we were warm and cozy in our toy home on wheels while the poor dog shivered in the back of the Blazer. On the other hand he wasn't waked up by his companion going to the indoor facility during the nite who announced that there was a lightning bug under the dinette. I told her it wasn't a bug and was some kind of electronic gizmo. She agreed that it was too regular to be a bug and what did it do? I told her I remembered the salesman showing it to me, but didn't remember what it did. Her comment was that it was probably O.K. as long as it blinked green. This morning I crawled up under the dinette and read L P Gas Detector on the light that blinks. My conclusion is that if it changes to red or yellow, we have 3 choices. We can:

1. Read the manual, or
2. Evacuate the premises, or
3. Die.

On to Austin today where we'll be able to use a phone to send and receive. We have extra time for repairs scheduled for the first time. Evan

Date: Sunday, March 22, 1998 10:12 AM
Subject: Austin

Spent last nite with Margaret and David in their new (to us) house. It really is nice with an open and bright layout. Too bad we're running out of relatives to leech from. Only have Pam and Jerry in Albuquerque and Mary Nelson and Jim in Hot Springs left to free load from on this trip. We downloaded some rather cryptic responses to my previous trip e-mails yesterday and sent out a few new ones. There seems to be a common and mistaken opinion that it's hard to run out of gas. Actually, it's quite easy since the gauge reads differently with the trailer weight sitting on the rear end and you can't fill the thing all the way up and each fill-up is different depending on type of pump and how much gas you can cram in before the pump cuts off. Enough about that. I'm carrying 2 6 gal. gas cans to extend our range out in west Texas where stations are few and I guess I'll start filling them up now.

Yesterday was quite uneventful in comparative terms. We only had 1 Pookie Navigational Correctional Fix (that's called a U-Turn by other people) to deal with. She denied responsibility by claiming to be asleep when I took the wrong turn, but when you've been assigned the task of navigating; sleeping on the job is not an acceptable excuse. I figured it out when we began to see signs pointing to the Bush Presidential Library, and nobody goes to Texas A & M on purpose.

Yesterday morning as I was unhooking the electricity to the camper I noticed a sticker over the wheels, which says to check the lug nuts on the wheels after the first 50, 200, 500 and 1000 miles. After considering the matter all morning, I checked them when we stopped for lunch. Since I've towed this thing from Pennsylvania to central Texas, I did all 4 checks in one, and they were O.K.

Paula, we brought our NCAA score sheets along and Pookie had 42 points after the 1st 2 rounds and I had 38. You need to Get Right With Jesus before we call in the Congressional Budget Office to do an audit. I also remember that last year we bet $20 per person instead of per couple. Are you trying to reduce Sue's income? Let's raise the ante to last year's level and do away with the 2nd place winner (which Pookie won last year) since I have KY to go all the way. What do you think? Plan to spend tonite near the LBJ Ranch and see if they really did have to screw him into the ground. Evan

Thursday, March 26
Subject: 1st Dump

Pookie stood close by this a.m. with her camera at the ready to record my first dump of the "black" and "gray" water into a sanitary dump station. I know she was hoping to immortalize on film a screw up, but it worked perfectly and I didn't even get a drop of anything on me (forgetting to put the cap back on the trailer and driving off without it doesn't count as a screw up since it has a safety cord on it and I heard it dragging and picked it up). Thank God we didn't bring the video camera for her to tape the crisis moments!

We had a nice visit with Holly in Austin and took her to brunch. Spent the next nite at another Texas State Park after doing LBJ National Historic Park for the best part of a day and the Chester A. Nimitz Museum in Fredericksburg, TX. Spent last nite in our 3rd Texas State Park. They really are nice. The first had a narrow gauge railroad that gives a 60 mile round-trip ride, but too many kids and we've done that on much more scenic routes. Pedermales Falls State Park near the LBJ ranch has gorgeous waterfalls and we took a couple of hikes near the river.

We're already at 3300 feet and Big Bend NP is 127 miles away and up another 2,000 feet. So far, the Blazer has laughed at the load and chugs along even on long upgrades at about 50 and 60 on level ground. I ordered it from the factory with a towing package that includes a transmission fluid cooler, lower rear end gear ratio, positraction rear-end and extra large radiator. Finally got the temperature up to 200 today on a 3 mile upgrade, but it cools down to 180 on the flat. It redlines at 260, so I should be O.K. since the temperature today was 85 at noon and we were running the AC. It's only a 4.3 liter V-6, but sure has a lot of torque since I'm now pulling nearly 5500 pounds. Now to con the lady at this KOA park into letting me download e-mail and send the stuff in the Outbox. More later.
Evan

Thursday March 26
Subject: Wetback

For some reason, the Ft. Stockton message didn't go out, so we'll try again if we ever get to a place where I can use a phone. The Nat. Parks are NOT accommodating. They could make a few bucks if they would require a $2 or $3 donation to use the phone for e-mail, but I don't think they understand. I'll help them if I ever get somewhere to send a suggestion to their bosses. They all act afraid to make a decision and don't know anything about computers. More Clinton work?

We got here in time to get the LAST spot in the only trailer park in Big Bend with electricity and water and sewer hookups. I had told Pookie that we would not have them, but I relented because of Winston. Today it was 102 and yesterday 98. My dog needed air conditioning! We leave him in the trailer when we're out cruising around the Park (so far 200 miles IN the Park) and he sleeps in the Blazer, but it gets down to 55 or 60 at nite. When I walked him this a.m. we passed some guy with 2 young dogs and Winston couldn't see or hear them. He walks with a slow, awkward gait and it's obvious that he's very old. When we passed, the guy said, "He's in a world of his own" and I had to agree.

This is the 2nd or 3rd biggest Nat. Park outside of Alaska and is the only one, including Alaska to have an entire mountain range inside the Park. Yesterday, I waded across the Rio Grande into Mexico and back, so I'm a certified wetback. Pookie watched thru the camera lens hoping for a Kodak moment, but I lived up to my nickname of Flawless and didn't get wet above the knees. Today she tried it in a different spot and gave up claiming it was too deep. I watched thru the lens this time and was equally disappointed.

We put the awning down today for the first time and naturally, a windstorm came up. We can't get it back up correctly in the dark, but will try again in the a.m. It's easier to read the instructions when we have light outside and the guy across from us gave up too. Tomorrow we have an all day scenic rafting trip thru Colorado Canyon on the Rio Grande. I'm paying $236 for the 2 of us (lied and told them Pookie was 55 to get her the discount too) so maybe they'll let me send and receive e-mail. Pookie wants to know if she can retire too at 55, but the answer is obvious and negative. We ate lunch today in The Basin Lodge and tomorrow the rafting company provides lunch with wine. Am I spoiling her or what? She hasn't even done laundry yet! Tonite is spinach salad and I better eat before she reads this!

This Park is really beautiful. The scenery changes every mile or two and with the light. At 5500 feet, there are trees and grass and on the desert floor there is a lot of variety. At a spring in the desert, it's totally different and each spring is different. El Nino caused a drought here and it's not as colorful as usual. There are 3 mountain ranges here and all are different. I may come back sometime when it's wetter to see what that looks like. The air quality was rated poor today; we could only see 31 miles. On a good day they say you can see up to 200 miles, like we did one day in New Hampshire when we could see the Atlantic Ocean from the top of a mountain. The day after tomorrow, we'll take a boat across to a small Mexican village and rent a burro to ride into town and see the sights, but I ain't gonna eat or drink nothing. I'll take pictures of Pookie on the ass! Boy, I could think of a lot of captions for those pictures, but I better not!

Asked Pookie what she wanted me to say and she replied, "Tell them we're still on the first roll of single ply toilet paper!" Is this girl basic or what? Actually, I've been using other facilities for the big job, but then I have to empty it and she doesn't. She said to tell Sue their gift of Scott tissue will last many miles. Want to travel with my girl?

The 8 Wheeler (And don't get in my way on the downhill side!)

Date: Saturday, March 28, 1998 8:52 PM
Subject: Cool Down

Well, the raft trip was just about perfect, and it really was all day. We left the campground at 6:30 a.m. and got back at 6:30 p.m. We had to drive 50 miles across the park to get to the pickup point and then they took us another 40 miles toward Presidio, TX to launch us. On the way they told me not to come this way in the RV as there was a hill with a 17% grade for a mile and RV's were not recommended, as the road wouldn't meet modern day standards. We climbed this hill to get to the launch point and floating back we went thru the canyon beside it and they pointed out the wrecks of 2 cars, an 18-wheeler and a pickup who didn't make a turn slow enough. They also told us how each person died, except for the drunken teenagers who survived. I was coming that way exiting the Park but have decided to take their advice.

The dust storm the day before cleared the air and visibility was up to at least 100 miles and it cooled down to 80 and we had a tail wind all thru the canyons—in the shade it was a little chilly with the wind blowing. Pookie and I shared a river guide with a woman doing her own thing while her husband took their boys fishing. Our guide was a young single female, husky, and a little bit of an Amazon with blisters on her hands cause she wouldn't wear gloves while rowing the raft. She was very nice, but the type you sprinkled your conversation to with Yes Ma'am and No Ma'am every now and then so she knew you understood that you understood. Her best line of the day was "This ain't no oar, this is my seester". She did say it was nice to have guests in the raft that entertained her instead of vice versa. We ate lunch on a sandbar with a tablecloth and too much to eat. In honor of Tommy, I took and drank a 6 pack during the trip. On the way over and back, we saw coyotes up close and personal and damn near hit a mule deer that ran in front of the Blazer. They are a lot bigger than whitetails and would have hurt. We saw a lot of birds and the other raft had a pair of dedicated birders from NJ. I told them they didn't have to apologize for being from NJ and damn near told them they looked like birds, but held my tongue (it was hard to do).

Most of the guys you meet in these RV Parks are wanna be mechanics or truck drivers. I feel like a Lilliputian among the giants in most of these parks. A majority of the rigs are as big as or bigger than a Greyhound bus.

Those that aren't self-propelled mostly have muscle trucks pulling them with a lot of them diesels and nearly all have dual cabs and dual rear wheels. I'm tired of being asked if the Blazer will really pull this thing. I told the last guy that it pulled it here from PA, but might not pull it out and he sadly agreed. My Blazer, which is 6 years old with 83,000 miles, did cry a little when we saw a big motor home towing a new Blazer as an extra. One guy told me his carbon monoxide warning device went off the other nite when nothing (meaning his engine, generator, AC, furnace, etc.) was running. Said he tried to figure it out for an hour and when he couldn't nor could he find the fuse, he cut the wires leading to the thing (my kind of guy)! Another guy told me that he downshifted into 6th on a hill the other day and his rig wouldn't slow down so he was going to add some Banks exhaust brakes. No, I don't know what that is, but if it involves using exhaust to slow down, my theory after seeing the size of his rig is that whatever it is will be like farting into the wind. I called the salesman today about getting the awning down. Would you believe we did it right the first time and it's not supposed to latch at the back of the trailer and needs that free play it has?

We did Bouquillas, Mexico today and yes; I have pictures of Pookie riding her ass into town. She has a picture or two of what some would call an asshole riding an ass. Pookie couldn't get the burro to stop nor could she get her left foot in the stirrup, so I hired a 10 year old named Adrian as my Main Man and burro assistant, cum tour guide. He walked behind and whipped the burros to get them going and would run up front and yank them to a halt if needed. He has 3 brothers and 2 seesters (no, he didn't try to sell me the seesters). He also is a little con artist who started out working for $2 and ended up with $3 plus a coke in the cantina from the Senora Pookie who thought he was cute. He wanted to take us to his house, but I figured that would cost more. He did warn the Senora NOT to pay the old beggar who wanted to have her take his picture for $1 in the local church, but to no avail. In honor of Tommy (he's good for something), I drank a Mexican beer in the cantina, but no tacos or burritos, although Pookie got some to go. If I'm not nice, she may put them in my food.

Tomorrow we say goodbye to Big Bend and drive to Ft. Davis thru Alpine, TX instead of Presidio. The main thing Pookie is looking for is an RV Park with cable TV for the finals of the NCAA Mon. nite. Here we don't have ANY radio, TV, newspaper or cell phone service. Have no idea how the semi-finals went today, but am confident that if not cheated, I will win the pool!

Your Tutor!

Date: Monday, March 30, 1998 4:46 PM
Subject: Davis,Davis,Davis

We're in the Davis Mountains at Ft. Davis in Jeff Davis County and all of them are named for my ancestor cousin who was Secretary of War when they got named. Some insensitive, damnyankee tourist asked the ranger today why didn't they change the name after he served as president of the Confederacy. His answer was that they wanted to pacify the South. I don't think it worked.

We did the McDonald Observatory this a.m. on the top of a 6800-foot mountain and it was snowing when we finished our guided tour. They have a 107-inch telescope, an 82-inch, and a 360-inch and it was a very informative hour long tour by an actual astronomer, viewing the 2 biggest telescopes and having them actually rotate. About 6 universities and NASA fund the thing with UT (where the T means Texas) being the primary player although the University of Chicago and Penn and Boston U. are big players. Ft. Davis is at 5300 feet and it's cold today after being hot yesterday. We did the Fort this p.m., but the wind is blowing hard and it's cold so we didn't stay outside too long.

On the way here, I considered the fact that everywhere we go in this desert, we see turkey vultures. There's always a few circling in sight and every 5 or 6 miles there are from 1 to 6 sitting in the highway having a meal. The birds won't get up and fly off until you're practically on top of them and then they lumber into the air and you sometimes have to dodge them to keep from breaking a windshield. On the other hand, you can drive an hour and not see another car. How does the roadkill occur? There doesn't seem to be enough traffic to generate the volume of roadkill, and at night with the tourists not on the road there must be practically no traffic. Most of the roadkill seems to be rabbits, but you can't identify some of it. Are the roadkill victims suicidal and hurl themselves into the path of the only available vehicle? If so, why don't they take advantage of daylight and do it when you can see them? Do they all go there to die of natural causes? Do the vultures find them elsewhere and bring them to the road to use it as a warming plate and lunch table? If so, why don't you ever see a vulture flying with lunch in its talons? You would think that a federal government that can fund research to see if men and women think differently could fund some valuable research like finding out how the roadkill originates. I can see it now—video cameras and infrared cameras strung out alongside the road for miles to record how it happens. Write your congressman and let's waste our tax dollars learning a deep mystery!

When we got here, we used our cable TV hookup for the 1st time and it works! Pookie played with the remote for about 1/2 hour to see if she still retained her eye-hand coordination and was successful. We watched the women's NCAA final last nite and will catch my victory in the men's tonite. Tomorrow it's on to Carlsbad, NM to another commercial campground. There are no hookups at Carlsbad Caverns or at Guadalupe Mountains National Parks so we'll home base in Carlsbad and do day trips. Buzzard Benefactor

Date: Friday, April 03, 1998 7:25 AM
Subject: Shopping/Guadalupe Mountains

We got to Carlsbad early yesterday, but by the time we got nested, downloaded and read 38 e-mails and walked Winston, it was too late to go to a Park. Therefore, we fell back to Plan B—shopping. I learned about 35 years ago (we will have been married 35 years in Sept.) that to keep my girlfriend happy and content in her current status as Wife # 1, it is necessary to let her go shopping every few days. Luckily for me, she isn't too picky (some would say that is obvious by who she married) and it doesn't have to be an upscale store. In a crunch, a gift shop, Wal-Mart or even a grocery store will do. After 5 days and 4 nites in Big Bend with only the campground store and the Visitor Center available, she had gotten the shakes and needed a fix, so we did Wal-Mart yesterday. She had a list and after I got my assignment of a longer cable TV hookup cable, a new camera battery (the previous one was bought in England when we rented the narrow boat with Heidi and Bob, and was a camera cell in their terms), a gizmo to fix the 25 foot telephone wire for the computer, and a replacement mirror for the towing mirror we broke, I was dismissed. I really think this shopping need is a learned instinct for all women. My theory is that it goes back to the time when we were hunter/gatherers in caveman times. If the women didn't go out and get berries or nuts or roots or something to eat, they didn't get to eat any of the meat from the hunt. We would all have been better off to let them have meat, without any pre-conditions. Now they have to have their own kind of kill and bring the trophies home every few days or they get difficult to live with. Anyway, I waited in the Blazer till she was satisfied and now we're both happy, although she had to do another grocery store this p.m. I really believe we're going to get home with more food than we left with and then we'll have 3 full refrigerators

We did Guadalupe Mountains Nat. Park today and it didn't take too long. You do have to re-enter Texas, but then you get a 70mph speed limit. It's a lot like Big Bend, except made from limestone instead of lava. It's really for backpackers and hikers and doesn't even have a driving trail. We did 1 short (.3 mile) walking trail and then did one of my patented shortcuts back (.6 mile, uphill into a 35mph wind). Now Pookie appreciates what the Blazer has to do. We ate a picnic lunch at the Frijole Ranch in the Park. It has a large spring, which was running, all over the ground and the picnic table was actually in a little water. It was cold with the wind blowing in the shade and I heard a little under—the—breath muttering that sounded like this, "It doesn't get any better than this" and "Who else would picnic in a damn lake?" Later we stopped at Rattlesnake Springs and saw a lot of wild turkeys doing mating displays. That is a lot more moving than driving thru real ranching country and seeing stock tanks pumped by solar panels instead of windmills. Even the Mexicans in Boquillas had solar panels, but for what I don't know since there is no electronic communication of any type available, including satellite dishes. Pookie thinks it's for cooking, but then she's always been biased on that subject.

Listening to Mark Russell on the Paula Jones case, so I'll sign off.
Evan

Date: Friday, April 03, 1998 7:26 AM
Subject: Whole 9 Yards

We did the whole 9 yards at Carlsbad Caverns today. If you don't know where that expression originated, you're about to learn. Everybody needs a little trivia knowledge and I've got a lot. It originated in WW II with the pilots of fighter planes and fighter-bombers. The standard ammunition belt for a .50 caliber machine gun in a fighter plane was 27 feet long. If a pilot shot the whole belt at a single target he said, "I gave it the whole 9 yards". You're welcome.

We walked down the natural entrance to the Cave, which is about 1 1/4 miles long and descends 750 feet. It's a little strenuous and after about 3/4 of the trail I was ready to walk backwards. When we got to the bottom, we did the Big Room, which is another 1 1/4 miles, but mostly flat and covers 14 acres. This is a National Park worth seeing and is quite majestic in it's beauty and formations. All this took about 2 1/2 hours with stops to see the various formations. The temperature is a constant 56 and the humidity is 90 %, so it's cool. We took the elevator back up and ate lunch in the restaurant in the Visitor Center since the food in the underground restaurant looked like it had been there since the Park opened in the 1920s. After lunch, we went back down to the Big Room level and took a ranger guided tour for 1 1/2 hours that cost extra and went down another 100 feet. Ranger Bob was pathetic! Pookie said he was the worst tour guide she had ever seen. We know all his bad jokes and how he met his wife (I bet she's a piece of work), but not much about what we saw. The highpoint of this guy's life has been to meet the star of "Dukes of Hazzard" on one of his tours. I thought the star of "Dukes of Hazzard" was the car! This guy knew his (the star's) real name and had met his father who is a retired airline pilot. Go figure! After that, we did the Visitor Center and all the exhibits and then took a 10-mile desert loop road tour. Actually, they've discovered another cave that's bigger and more beautiful, but much more fragile. It's closed to the public and used for research only and is named Lechuguilla and is the only known all gypsum cave. Photos are available in the Visitors Center and you could buy picture books, but we didn't, but we did buy a CD ROM on Guadalupe and Carlsbad National Parks.

Tomorrow we travel to Alamogordo where we'll park the trailer for a few more days. We're booked for a tour to the Trinity site on Sat. where the 1st Atomic bomb was exploded. You can only enter the site on the 1st Sat. in April and Oct. as it's in the White Sands missile range and closed to the public the rest of the year. I think it's closed to limit exposure to radiation too. We'll go in a caravan in our own vehicle and have to take our own food and water and it's 85 miles from Alamogordo. Pookie says I can have sardines and radiation for lunch. I'm really curious what it looks like. You know there was a small body of scientific opinion that the 1st A-bomb explosion might set off an uncontrolled chain reaction that would destroy the entire atmosphere. The really bright guys said no, that wouldn't happen, but the decision was important enough to go to Truman. He said, "somebody will try it at sometime and it might as well be us". He was something else. To be continued Evan

Date: Monday, April 06, 1998 9:20 AM
Subject: Deception Revealed

Driving here (Alamogordo) from Carlsbad, Pookie figured it out. She said I had planned this whole trip around being here on April 4 when the Trinity site would be open. Well, it had crossed my mind that if we were coming this way anyway, why not? She also wanted to know why I didn't write another episode Sat. or Sun. That's easy—those are my days off.

We drove here on highway 82 which also goes thru my hometown of Greenville, MS. I've nearly been killed several times on this highway before, so the odds are in our favor. We climbed for about an hour while Pookie read a magazine. I told her to look up when the snow got pretty deep and we were passing ski lifts. We crossed the pass thru the Sacramento Mountains at Cloudcroft, elevation 8650 feet. The Blazer thought it was a piece of cake.

The descent was 4300 feet in 12 miles and I don't yet trust the electric brakes on the trailer. There is a gorgeous view coming down with Alamogordo in the foreground and what I first thought were clouds in the background. Pookie deduced that it was the White Sands Nat. Monument after awhile. We didn't do much Fri. afternoon except go by the Visitor Center and get the scoop on the caravan to Trinity.

About 200 vehicles of all types left at 8 the next a.m. Pookie said it was like going to Woodstock or a "trekkie" group as we left with sirens flashing from the escort cops and military police. The White Sands Missile Range doesn't show any roads on the map, but it has better and more paved roads than the state. The signs encourage you not to leave the road, such as "Danger—Unexploded Munitions" or "Missile Impact Zone" or something about lasers, but my favorite was "Zurf Area" (I didn't make that up)! They say no pictures till you get to Trinity and Pookie wouldn't let me take any. We did see a herd of Oryx or Gemsbok up close. That's a very large antelope with 2 huge horns like unicorns that's native to the Kalahari desert in southern Africa. They are a pest that thrives like kudzu and should not have been introduced here. This place is so remote, that we could set off a few more bombs here and nobody would notice.

When we got to the site, it was overrun with people who came on their own or in caravans from other locations. T-shirts, books, postcards etc. were available as well as about 50 porta-pots. The actual site is fenced in and we got to ground zero just as a tour guide with a large bus group was finishing his talk. This is where "Fat Man" the plutonium bomb was tested. The uranium bomb was a much simpler design and didn't need testing. Fat Man was dropped on Nagasaki and "Little Boy" on Hiroshima. Talk about bad luck, Nagasaki was a secondary target and the bomb was diverted there because of bad weather over the primary target. The tower here (100 feet tall) was vaporized and the crater was only about 6 feet deep, but it's almost unrecognizable now. The Army cleaned up the site a number of years ago and it's different than the old pictures. The explosion did create a few acres of green glass fused from the sand. The stuff is called "Trinitite" and most of it is gone, but Pookie and I managed to collect about 10 small pieces. It's only mildly radioactive and Pookie smuggled it out undetected. We let her carry the contraband for several reasons:

1. I've got a long enough rap sheet already and this has to be a federal offense.
2. She didn't object and looks better wearing orange than I do.
3. She's already sterile.
4. That stuff looks like (and may be) kryptonite and might negatively affect some of my extraordinary powers.

The Army provides buses at the site that take you 2 miles to the McDonald house, an old ranch house where the bomb was assembled. Only the roof was blown off in the explosion and it's been restored to 1945 condition. It was originally called the Schmidt house for the original owners. You may know some of their children, Aw Schmidt, Tough Schmidt or No Schmidt.

We ate a true sand—wich off the hood of the Blazer during a duststorm (Pookie's idea) and came back the long way thru Carrizozo. I hate riding in a caravan where you're always speeding up and slowing down. We stopped at 3 Rivers Petroglyph site where there are 21,000 designs carved into rocks by natives 1,000 years ago. We ended the day by seeing "Antarctica" at the local Imax Theatre. That's appropriate since Antarctica is the only place on earth more arid than the desert. There's plenty of water there, but it's all frozen. The guy operating the movie had a captive audience and at the end showed the night sky and gave a lecture on the constellations. Heard a lot more than I want to know about the big and little dippers, Orion, the dog star, the great bear, etc. This guy was the polar opposite of Ranger Bob and almost as boring.

Sun. my laundress did the wash and provided me with clean underwear! In her honor, I treated us to lunch at the Golden Corral which is like a self-serve cafeteria. Pookie's buddies call it "The Golden Trough". Got my veggies at last. We also did a sunset walk through the sand dunes at White Sands Monument with an excellent tour-guide ranger who is an ex-schoolteacher. Best guide we've had yet. Tomorrow, we're going back through Cloudcroft to Sunspot, NM to a solar observatory on top of another mountain.
Evan

Date: Wednesday, April 08, 1998 6:21 PM
Subject: Sun/NOT

I demonstrated my keen sense of timing and my impeccable judgment yesterday by scheduling and then doing a tour of a solar observatory on the only day since we left Louisiana that there was no sun. It was probably the only day this year that there's been no sun in New Mexico. We went to Sunspot, altitude 9700 feet, for this event. The snow was melting when we started up the mountain, but by the time we got to the top, it was coming down again and freezing on the road. When we got out at the Visitor Center it was snowing hard. Pookie was putting on her parka hood while snow blew in the Blazer when she made the semi-mutinous and sarcastic comment that "It's sooooo much fun to travel with you". I'm used to a little criticism from that source, so I ignored it. Reminded me of the trip to Alaska last year when Mt. McKinley successfully hid in the clouds till we left. Saw the same # of moose here as we saw in Denali Nat. Park in Alaska—zippo. We were the 1st visitors to sign the guest book today although another idiot showed up later. There was a frozen pond outside the Visitor Center and the wind chill must have been about 15 degrees.

It's a self-guided tour thru the various buildings and quite interesting. In one building there's a TV monitor you can cut on and watch the current observation of the sun—except on cloudy days. One of the telescopes weighs 200 tons and is supported on a rotating platform by 3 bolts and 3 mercury bearings. The whole platform rotates at the speed of the earth to keep the sun in constant view and the whole thing is balanced so well that a 1/4 horsepower electric motor turns it. All the astronomers can do their work from their homes by computer, so there's nobody there to give tours. After freezing between buildings, I took my sweetheart to lunch in Cloudcroft to improve her attitude and it worked.

By the time we got back to the basin floor, the sun was out, but the visibility was terrible because of a duststorm. We went back to White Sands to do the Visitor Center and exhibits and movie since they were closed the previous day when we did the dunewalk. We took the boys to the Monument in 1976 and came up from El Paso when we had the pop-top camper, but we never got to Alamogordo. Then we left the camper in El Paso and just came up for the day. The Monument is 14 miles west of the Sacramento Mountains and the dust was so bad you couldn't see them from the Monument. Then I gave the Blazer a kwik lube and wash since it's been such a good boy. Forgot to mention that Holloman AFB is next to the Monument and is mostly a Luftwaffe base for training German pilots—you see a lot of car tags in Alamogordo that are German with the German flag on them.

This a.m. it was cloudy again, but the sky was clear to the northwest, so we are now in Socorro, NM. There's a radio observatory near here and we might as well do all 3 kinds. Probably have enough sunspots and sun flares tomorrow to wipe out all radio traffic for the day. There's also a NWRA (national wildlife reservation area) near here with a driving tour that we might do tomorrow too. Getting here thru Las Cruces was the hardest pull yet for the Blazer. Uphill into a 35/40mph headwind. When we turned north on I-25, they became cross winds and even more dangerous. Wind advisories on the radio and warning signs everywhere for "high profile" vehicles and trailers. They close highway 70/82 west out of Alamogordo sometimes for missile tests or high winds. When you can't even speed up going downhill, the wind is tough. Passed a motorhome stuck in the median on I-25 with several troopers trying to get it out and I think the wind blew it off the road. We must be 100 miles west of the Sacramento Mtns. today, but the air is so much clearer that we could see them through passes in the San Andres Mtns. today.

The dog is still on central time instead of mountain daylight although they are supposed to be the same. He starts barking for supper a lot earlier than at home, or he's afraid that each meal will be his last. Pookie keeps talking about the "Big Shot" every time we pass a veterinary clinic and mumbling that we need a new dog. When I went to our vet at home to buy the $1.35 per can special diet dogfood for dogs that have kidney stones, the receptionist said, "Mrs. Davis wants a King Charles V Spaniel when Winston goes". I told Pookie she could have a new carpet in the den when Winston dies, and his popularity has declined since then. His increasing incontinence doesn't help either.

Evan

P.S. Ena, don't show the last paragraph to Obie. When we called her last week, all she could talk about was how was Winston doing? Fortunately, Obie raised a masterful liar, and I snowed her.

Date: Friday, April 10, 1998 7:07 PM
Subject: Turnaround

Wed. a.m. we got up and went about 50 miles west of Socorro to the VLA (Very Large Array) Radio Telescope. It's also called the National Radio Astronomy Observatory and is FASCINATING! It consists of 27— 225 ton radio telescopes that each has a huge dish. They are totally computer controlled (eat your heart out Louis— 750 billion computations per second) and movable on a double railroad track. They are arranged in a Y and each leg of the Y is 13 miles long at maximum. They can all be put together, or extended the full 13 miles, which gives them a zoom effect. When extended, it is the equivalent of a single dish antenna with a receiver 27 miles wide. I always wondered why we did radio astronomy, but it's really just a different form of light that is invisible to the human eye, but very visible to our tools. When fully extended, the VLA can focus on an object much, much smaller than the most powerful optical scope, and can give a much better perspective of it. Even more impressive is that we can hook it up to other radio telescopes from Puerto Rico and the Virgin Islands to Hawaii and make a REALLY big dish. Unlike solar and optical telescopes, they aren't limited to night or daytime hours and observe 24 hours per day, 362 days per year. The tour is self guided and took us a couple of hours and is really well done with a great slide show at the start. The movie "Contact" with Jodie Foster was filmed here. If you're interested the web site is http://www.nrao.edu although I haven't been to it.

This is as far west as we are going on this trip, hence the subject. When we left the observatory, we went to the Bosque del Apache National Wildlife Refuge. Got some great views of wildlife including sandhill cranes, ducks and geese, beaver, hawks, turkeys, pheasant, etc. This Refuge is very aggressively managed with crops, burning, irrigation, etc. It hosts 30,000 snow geese, 13,000 sandhill cranes and a few very confused whooping cranes in Dec.-Feb. They've started a 2nd flock of whooping cranes by stealing eggs from the Aransas Refuge in TX and putting them on sandhill crane nests. The whoopers imprint with the sandhills and migrate with them to a safer and less distant summer area than Canada in a different flyway, but they are having trouble getting the whoopers to mate and breed. They think they can breed with the sandhills, and since there are a lot more sandhills they almost never find another whooper. I'd whoop too if I thought I had a few thousand new chances, but what does one do when rejected a few thousand times?

Woke up Thurs. a.m. and it was quiet, no wind! Put on my shorts and sandals for the first time in several days and we gave the trailer a bath in one of those 18-wheeler wash things before we left for Albuquerque. Passed a doublewide in the ditch on the way from previous day's wind. Remember when NC State won the Final 4 in Albuquerque over Houston with that last second fluke/pass that ended up in a stuff? I remember Jimmy Valvano being interviewed on national TV. He was so excited he said, "I love this town. We've had a lot of fun! My wife doesn't know it yet, but she's got to be pregnant and we're going to name this kid Al B. Querque".

This is our 3rd time here and we've done all the museums, Sandia Peak Tramway, scenic drives etc. I did promise Aunt Lib to look up Jerry and Pam, so we made contact and took them to a great northern Italian restaurant on old route 66 in the university area. The food would have tasted even better if I wasn't buying. Pam is my first cousin on my father's side and was raised in MS too. She's a few years younger than me and grew up in Clarksdale. She took off for San Francisco after college and ended up here where she met Jerry who's from Kingsport, TN. Jerry's surname is Allgood, so you know instantly that he's no blood kin.

Pookie did see in USA Today on Thurs. an article about Bruce Springsteen that mentioned my nephew Will Percy's first cousin, also named Will Percy. It seems that Walker Percy, the author of "The Moviegoer" and other works wrote a fan letter to Bruce in 1989. Bruce never answered and Walker died in 1990, but Bruce did get interested enough to read "The Moviegoer". Then in 1995, Bruce met Will Percy after a concert in VA. Will is Walker's great nephew and Bruce told him how he regretted not responding to Walker's letter. Will talked Bruce into writing Walker's widow (her name is Bunt) and he wrote her a 4 page letter describing how "the toughness and beauty of The Moviegoer have stayed with me". Now, the spring issue of "Double Take", a quarterly from The Center for Documentary Studies at Duke University has a lengthy interview between Will Percy and Springsteen, titled "Rock and Read".

We left NM today and now are in Amarillo, TX. Saw the Cadillac Ranch on the outskirts and took a few pictures. That's where a rich Texan has buried 10 Cadillacs nose down in the ground along Route 66/I-40. There are no signs, and most people don't even see them in a field 150 yards off the interstate, but our eagle-eyed leader saw them and stopped. May spend a few nites here. It sure has grown since we were here last as all I remember from 25 years ago is grain elevators, cattle feed lots and railroad yards. Pookie picked out our campground, which advertised "No noise from I-40" since its several miles away from I-40. I call it creative advertising since we're 1/2 mile from the airport at runway 27 and you can't hear the 18-wheelers for the jets. Close to the railroad too, and the whistles sometimes drown out the planes.

Eastbound and Down

Date: Monday, April 13, 1998 6:58 PM
Subject: Tailwind!

Sat. we did the Panhandle Plains Historical Museum on the campus of West Texas A & M in Canyon, TX. Only an Aggie (in a rare moment of enlightenment) would describe something in North Texas as being in West Texas and then permanently display the error in a formal name. It took us over 3 hours to see it all and it's quite well done. The petroleum part is the most interesting with actual size derricks, tanks, drills, etc. They have old movies about the oil boom days and actually demonstrate how they were dug or more appropriately pounded and blasted out of the rock. They didn't use rotary drills till the late 30's and the early cable and bit drills were lifted and dropped and blasted with nitro till they crashed into a pool and hit oil.

Pookie called Alicia to find out when she thought Will would be home from Turkey and ended up talking to Catherine, Alicia's mother, as Alicia was out. Pookie told her we were going to Palo Duro Canyon that afternoon and locate the spot where we found Will sitting on the top of a cliff 100 feet above us when he was about 8. She told Catherine that we lost Will all over the United States when we were traveling in the pop-top camper. Catherine said she believed her as he still wanders off by himself from time to time. Palo Duro is one of the larger canyons in the U.S., but a lot smaller than Grand Canyon. It's 20 miles south of Amarillo and if you're ever here in mid-summer, go see the huge extravaganza production of "Texas" performed in an outdoor amphitheatre on the floor of the canyon. It's done for 10 weeks from mid-June to the end of August. They drive cattle and trains across the stage, and have a stampede sparked by lightning, which is really gunpowder in cracks in the cliff face. It's the history of Texas and lasts 3 or 4 hours. We saw it with the kids long ago and it's now hard to get a ticket. We did find our old campsite where I looked up and saw Will standing on the edge of the cliff yelling down at me to look at him. I remember going into the camper and getting the camera while Pookie had a fit and said DO SOMETHING. I told her I was going to take a picture first and then I was going to climb up there and whip his butt. Actually, I took 2 beers with me, yelled at him to sit down and stay put or I'd kill him and climbed up and sat beside him while I drank the beers. We had a helluva view. Actually, it was better than our view Sat. as another duststorm came up and except on the canyon floor, it was very poor visibility.

Sun. a.m. the forecast was for 30-35 mph. winds and gusts up to 45 and hazardous driving for trailers, BUT IT WAS FROM THE WEST and we're going east. We left the campground with the owner saying we should stay put (and pay him for another day). Pulling was a dream. For the first time since I got the trailer I could pull in 4th gear—even up hills. I normally pull in 3rd and it downshifts to 2nd on a long steep hill. I was reminded of that old song from the late fifties, "Maybelline" by Chuck Berry. You don't remember it? Well, fortunately dear reader, you have me to demonstrate my "selective total recall, modified by genius". In the song, Chuck's girlfriend Maybelline tries to run away in her Cadillac, but "nothin outrun my V-8 Ford". In the original version, at first the Ford overheats and can't catch up, but then a thunderstorm hits and "rainwater rollin all under my hood, I knew that was doing my motor good". Well, the Blazer can handle the heat, but these headwinds we've had since crossing the MS River have made it work hard and sucked up the gas, so in my version it's wind, not heat. "The wind died down and then it shifted around, and that's when I heard the highway sound. 5th wheeler lookin like a ton of lead, 60 miles per hour half a mile ahead. 5th wheeler lookin like it's sittin still, and I caught that dude at the top of the hill. Oh Maybelline, why can't you be true, you've started back doing the things you used to do." (This is where you may applaud.) I told Pookie we might overshoot Tennessee and end up in Carolina somewhere if the tailwind kept up. It only lasted for about 75 miles though and then it shifted to the south and became a vicious crosswind. It later shifted to the southeast and became a quartering headwind again.

Mel and Elaine passed us just inside OK in their rental motorhome. We had met them in Alamogordo in a RV park and seen them at the Trinity site. They were looking for a place to retire and I met them while walking Winston by their 2 Shi Tzu (sp) dogs. I caught up and pulled up beside them on I-40 and waved. Elaine went to the back of their motorhome and put up a sign "next rest stop". Pookie checked her 20 pounds of reference material and saw there were no more rest stops on I-40 in OK, so we pulled ahead again and yelled Clinton, the name of our next stop about 25 miles ahead. We pulled off there in front of the Route 66 Museum and visited. They had been all the way to Phoenix and Tucson since Alamogordo and had decided to sell their house and get a big slideout 5th wheel and become "full-timers". We toured the Museum (O.K., but not 5 stars) with them and agreed on the same RV park for Sun. nite in the eastern part of OK City and met them there a few hours later. We got sites next door to each other and Pookie made spaghetti while Elaine did a salad and we ate supper together. Mel has been retired for several years and Elaine retires soon. (I've tried that idea on Pookie several times and it hasn't worked yet. She's depriving me of the dream of all red-blooded American men—to be a KEPT man.) We plan to stop in St. Louis and see Mel and Elaine either on our way or returning from the next trip to the upper peninsula of Michigan, Canada and Minnesota.

The TV just said tomorrow nite's special news was on new discoveries about the danger of stress. I commented that stress was your wife giving the wrong directions a nano second before you committed to a left turn in front of an 18 wheeler while pulling 5,500 pounds, and then screaming that she changed her mind. She sweetly replied that her definition of stress was traveling with your husband to Timbuktu accompanied by a nearly dead dog. Evan

Date: Wednesday, April 15, 1998 6:31 PM
Subject: End of the Trail

Mon. we did the Myriad Botanical Gardens and Crystal Bridge in OK City in the a.m. I left my camera in the Blazer and Pookie took hers, so I'm sure we'll have a number of really good shots of her finger in front of the lens. The Crystal Bridge is a 3-story (vertically) aluminum and glass cylinder lying on its side and forming a bridge over a man-made pond in the gardens. Inside is a rainforest and desert co-existing side by side. The gardens outside are very well done also.

Mon. p.m. we visited an island oasis of common sense in a sea of political correctness—The National Cowboy Hall of Fame. No women here, much less Blacks, Hispanics, Asians, etc. This is a refuge for all the white Anglo-Saxon males who have been driven to near extinction by the political idiots and their media. Imagine, a huge TV monitor continuously playing clips from all the John Wayne movies, and the Duke didn't take any Schmidt. Here we can continue to extol the grand American tradition of screwing the Indians that goes back to Manhattan Island without any wimps apologizing to the world at large. Yes, they did have a picture of Barbara Stanwyck on one wall for her role in "The Big Valley", but that's only because the show took its name from the cleavage she displayed in the TV series. The only other females displayed were 2 national champion women rodeo performers, and they were tastefully hidden in a back corner. The only US Presidents who made the museum were Thomas Jefferson who bought the West, Andrew Jackson who sent the Indians on the Trail of Tears, Abraham Lincoln who encouraged the settlement of the West and Ronnie Reagan who played all of them at one time or another. Even the rodeo horses and bulls buried on the site are all male and not a single mention of Annie Oakley or Calamity Jane. Here is pure unadulterated TRUTH for all to see. I may even give them a donation—well, maybe that's going a little too far.

Tues. we drove all the way to Petit Jean State Park in AR. We stopped in Ft. Smith for an hour or so and toured the National Historic Site of the old fort and courthouse where Judge Parker sentenced 79 bad guys to hanging. Saw the gallows and considered what would happen now if these kids who take guns to school and kill their schoolmates and teachers were hanged about 3 days later on the courthouse square with national TV coverage. I bet it wouldn't take but 1 or 2 hangings and it would stop permanently. Judge Parker said, "It's not the severity of punishment that deters crime, but the certainty of punishment promptly received".

We also stopped at the welcome to AR center on I-40 so Pookie could take my picture giving the finger to the "Home of Pres. Bill Clinton" sign. I-40 across AR must have the same contractor as I-20 in LA. All concrete, which pounds you to death as it deteriorates. I did discover that the Blazer will stop the trailer without the electric trailer brakes, but you need a lot of stopping room. The pounding finally separated the electric plug-in to the trailer and I drove about 50 miles before getting out and plugging in again. Hey, you've got to test these things so you'll know in the future.

We did the state park today. It's the oldest state park in AR but nice. Of course the public servants who operate it won't let me send e-mail since they don't have a policy on it. Would I like to send a fax? Yes, may I do it with my computer? No, we don't do that. Tomorrow we go see my cousin Mary Nelson and her husband Jim in Hot Springs Village. We haven't seen their digs since they retired here a short time ago. We'll do Hot Springs Nat. Park the next day and then go to Heber Springs and Eden Isle (the Red Apple Inn community on a peninsula in Greer's Ferry Lake) where Pookie's sister and brother-in-law, Barbara and Gene, have a condo. While we've been gone, they've bought a house there and sold theirs in Greenville so we must inspect. No, we ain't gonna buy their condo. We'll stop in Crawfordsville, AR and see Doyle's fiancée's mother and then on home. I'll send 1 more message, but it'll be a little different and will call for a response. I've had several people mention that their e-mail from this trip has been readable, but a little garbled. Apparently it's only happening to users of Eudora programs and when returned to me, the errors disappear. I use Internet Explorer 4.0 Outlook Express and when a Eudora user switched to that, it was received clearly. I use the same program on my desktop machine and have received no complaints on it, although that machine has a newer version of WIN 95 than the laptop. I am sending in plain text and not in HTML and USIT is upgrading their e-mail servers over a 4 or 5-week period on Mondays, but I don't know why some of you get garbled mail. Let's blame it on Bill Gates. Evan

P.S. "End of the Trail" is the name of a famous sculpture of an Indian finally giving up the fight against the white man

Date: Saturday, April 18, 1998 11:03 AM
Subject: Copyright!

Yep, ole Gene was the 1st one to figure it out. This has been a sample to gain an opinion from an eclectic group (that means weird assortment of folks) to help me make a decision. Now sports fans, you need to respond with your opinions. I've been toying with the idea of writing a book entitled "Fun with Pookie" for a couple of years. It would be a story of my 37 years of fun with my girlfriend. It would have a little bit of philosophy and some unhappy events, but mostly humorous stories. This series of e-mails could be edited and make up 1 chapter. What I want from you in exchange for this vicarious enjoyment of our trip is your opinion, based on this sample, of whether or not it would sell. I'm not in the least interested in fame or notoriety or celebrity status. I would refuse to do book tours or TV (reserving the right to do Leno or Letterman only if the other guests are supermodels). What I am interested in is cold, hard cash—moola, shekels, wampum or whatever you call it. Could I get some cash? Son Will has already e-mailed from Turkey that he's worried about me saving enough for the HOME, and subtly hinted that I should try to leave a little inheritance. Another relative has suggested that I might not get a fair opinion from a group of friends and relatives. Who wants a fair sampling? Hell, I've learned from Bill that it's the economy, stupid.

Now for the warning. I've been sending copies to my 2 attorney/snake associates, Bob and Phil. Actually; Phil is an attorney/CPA/snake, which is a subspecies with more fangs and venom. (Neither of these 2 subspecies is as gifted as an attorney/retired banker/snake, which is usually referred to as a king snake.) Now, my 2 attorney/snake friends probably don't know Jack Schmitt about copyright law, but I am supremely confident in their ability to make any attempt to infringe on my rights so extremely cost prohibitive that all resistance would melt away. (Incidentally, Jack Schmitt is a cousin of the Schmidt children and the most famous of the group, probably because his father couldn't spell his own name.) Therefore, take heed about republishing my art before I have gleaned all the material value from it. I've considered trying to sell the e-mails to "Trailer Life", but I'm not sure those wrench-heads have enough of a warped sense of humor to appreciate it. It may be a bit too irreverent and graphic for them.

To resume our tale, the last nite at Petit Jean State Park it rained about an inch with wind while Pookie watched the TV threaten us with tornados and I slept. Actually, we found out later that tornados did hit AR and TN with considerable loss of life. Apparently the trailer doesn't leak, and on my command the next a.m. it stopped so I could hook up the trailer without getting wet. We do need, however, to add poncho to the list of things to put in the trailer.

Friday we moved south to Hot Springs Village and mooched off Jim and Mary Nelson. They only had to buy 4 sacks of groceries. Jim already had a superb selection of single malt scotches. Winston loves it when we do this cause he gets to sleep in the trailer when we're mooching off relatives. We really like their house on a lakefront lot, but MN couldn't talk us into retiring there so she gets no commission. We did get a tour of the development (couldn't see much because of speed blur—MN drives faster than the trailer trash are used to) and it seems very nice. Definitely put it on our schedule for a return mooch.

Friday we toured Hot Springs Nat. Park for several hours, but no baths were consumed. It's the only Nat. Park that is also a city since most of the town is inside the Park. They have big signs claiming to be the boyhood home of Bill Clinton who moved there from Hope at a young age. I tried to get Winston to pee on the plaque in the sidewalk about Bill, but he wouldn't cooperate. He waited till a cop on foot patrol came along and then wet the whole sidewalk in front of the cop, but not on the plaque. I just shrugged at the cop and some lady who couldn't get her car started intervened at the perfect time to divert his attention so we could make our getaway. Treated Pookie to lunch at the 3 Monkeys restaurant/bar/nightclub and then we moved to Heber Springs. We're on a lakefront site with a gorgeous view and a cold wind with clouds. Ate dinner last nite at a new place with Gene, Barbara, Holly, Bill and Martha. I broke a front tooth at dinner and really look nice.

Our only remaining scheduled stop is Crawfordsville, AR to meet Jean, the mother of Diana, Doyle's fiancée. Pookie's gray roots are showing, I've got a broken front tooth, Winston is pitiful and when we show up in a trailer, it may not give the best impression. I told Pookie we could play a Mozart CD on the sound system in the trailer when we show it to Jean. Pookie thinks the best thing I can do is keep my mouth shut and I don't think she's talking about the tooth. This ends the tale of this trip.

Now remember to send your comments. If you feel compelled to say it's the most scintillating thing you've ever read, it's O.K. If you feel compelled to say they'll puke after the 1st paragraph, just say not recommended. Evan

Chapter 2. Midwestern Trip—1998

Date: Saturday, June 20, 1998 7:19 AM
Subject: Manistee, MI

Well, this trip started a lot worse than the last and that one had running out of gas and a flat. Mon. late p.m. while we were loading the trailer to leave Tues., Winston had a seizure while walking across the driveway. He fell and whimpered and couldn't get up for a few minutes. When he did get up, he was partially paralyzed on the left side and couldn't walk. Tues. a.m. he still couldn't walk very well and would fall every few feet but was as hungry as usual. We took him to the vet who did an exam and said he could give him something for the pain, but not really improve his quality of life. The vet guessed he had suffered a stroke. We reluctantly gave him the Big Shot while we were petting him and took him home and buried him in the back yard. Sort of puts a damper on the whole trip. We still expect to have him greet us after a day of sightseeing or demand to go for a walk when we stop for gas. Heidi said she was sorry, but I really don't believe that. Faye said we had the dog on life support for 2 years and she was surprised we didn't take oxygen with us for the dog. I think Faye was more honest this time.

To continue our good luck, it's rained every day but 1 and I scratched up the side of the trailer against a stone wall. On the other hand, we're finally far enough north to escape the heat and humidity. We did the Speedway in Indianapolis and an IMax movie and a museum on the 2nd day. The Speedway is interesting with a museum of its own and a tour of the infield in a narrated bus. We couldn't go on the track as 2 Indy and 1 Nascar cars were doing practice laps. The Indy cars were running above 200mph and the Nascar around 150mph. A real blur when they pass you. Indiana is the crossroads of America and the worst signed and advertised place I've ever been. No brochures or roadside signs about attractions and you really have to hunt for them. Indiana lost more killed in the War of Northern Aggression than in WWI, WWII, Korea and Vietnam combined and they had fewer troops than Delaware! I think I know why. The hayseeds were too dumb not to make good targets (Gene, do you agree?). We also toured the Indiana State Capitol, which is gorgeous with a tour guide who knew her stuff. We've been in most of the state capitols and this is in the top 5.

On day 3 we did the Studebaker museum and the mansion of George Oliver in South Bend and then walked around the campus of Notre Dame. Oliver was the inventor of the chilled plow, which led to the Oliver Tractor Co. and the tour of his home was very interesting. I even liked it, but made the mistake of telling Pookie who picked out a loser to tour the next day. The Notre Dame campus is signed like the rest of Indiana and the map is wrong too but the campus is pretty. Still hot in South Bend where temp was above 90 and humidity high. Day four was another travel day but only a few hundred miles. We stopped in Holland, MI for Pookie to tour Windmill Island—rip,rip,rip. It's a park with a 200-year-old 12 story high windmill actually grinding grain. It was disassembled in Holland and reassembled here. Local school girls do a Dutch dance in wooden shoes and there is a slide show on Holland, and you get to climb up to the top of the windmill and see how it works. The Nazis used it as an observation tower in WWII and there are bullet holes in one of the blades where our troops shot at them. The park also has a simulated Dutch village full of stores. We also had to do the Delft factory and the wooden shoe factory.

Today its on to the Upper Peninsula of MI, or at least to the top of the Lower Peninsula. When we lived in WI, the story was that WI and MI had a fight over who got the Upper Peninsula and MI lost. Sort of like the story that the best thing that ever happened to VA was when West VA seceded during the War of Northern Aggression. Evan

Date: Sunday, June 21, 1998 7:54 PM
Subject: Feeling Better

Don't know if it's the passage of time or me skipping a shower yesterday and getting all good and smelly, but I'm beginning to feel better. Yesterday we did Sleeping Bear Dunes National Seashore on the west coast of Michigan. The Indian legend is that a mother bear and her cubs were swimming the lake from Wisconsin to Michigan and the cubs drowned and the mother bear slept on the side of the lake waiting on them. Bet most of you thought all Indians did was run casinos! Actually, they spend a good bit of time making up dream stories involving animals. Having lived in Wisconsin, I would believe that the inhabitants are dumb enough to try and swim the lake. (Thoeny is from there.) Anyway, on the driving tour (they made me leave the trailer in a parking lot but the big self propelled guys can go—is that justice?) we ran into a bunch of real Indians—the kind from India—and Pookie asked them if they wanted her to take a picture of them all together. Of course they did and she did. (I suggested that she ask her new buddies if they like their new atomic bomb, but she refused.) One stop was right on the edge of the lake on top of dunes 450 feet high that sloped at about a 75 degree slope right into the lake. 2 young couples had ignored the signs and climbed down the dunes to the lake and were trying to climb back up. They looked like ants down below and were using hands and feet trying to get back up sliding backward for every foot forward. Pookie commented that it WAS fun to be young and stupid. I agreed, but said that at that age I was young and stupid and absolutely certain that I wasn't stupid since I knew everything back then. I think the young part was the best. I also enjoyed overhearing the following conversation between a mother and 5-6 year old daughter. "You can't ever travel with us again and from now on you'll have to stay with aunt Amy or Susan!"

After the park, we traveled to St. Ignace, MI right across the bridge over the straits of Mackinac on the UP. Pookie picked out this campground, so it has no flaws like mine. We do have a view of the bridge, the longest suspension bridge in the world, from the campground. St Ignace is named for the latest of the 3 Saints Ignatius (not your book, Michael). Today we did Mackinac Island, which is a 30-minute boat ride from here. The carriage ride around the island was the best part—except Pookie made me tip the driver. No autos allowed on the island and everybody walks, rides a bike or rents a horse carriage or a saddle horse. Really a pretty place and nicer than Gatlinburg, but full of tourists. Some local adopted us and told us the shortcuts and where to rent a carriage and where to eat. I told Pookie not to trust a guy who said the best place to eat was "Little Bob's, but he went out of business", but to no avail. We ate at the Village Square, which wasn't too bad. Avoided the Grand Hotel where lunch was $30, and Pookie didn't even buy too much (she reads my e-mail, and I'm horny).

Tomorrow it's off to Sault Ste. Marie to view the Soo Locks and then we head back west toward MN. I've decided not to go around Lake Superior on the north shore, but to do the south shore in the U.S. and turn back north at Duluth, MN to International Falls, MN. Evan

Date: Wednesday, June 24, 1998 11:50 AM
Subject: Observations

O.K., to please Pookie, I'm sending blind carbon copies instead of listing the addressees. She has a lot of weird hang-ups and one is seeing all the addressees.

Time to pass along a few of my observations on this trip.

1. Horse pollution. On Mackinac Island they employ a small army of people with large pooper scoopers, little wagons and brooms and shovels to clean up after the horses. The pollution is in the air, visual and physical. My carriage driver couldn't explain why they don't make the carriage horses and work horses pulling various wagons wear diapers like they do in New Orleans, but he did have a point when he said the stuff did serve one useful purpose— it tends to gum up the roller blades. I couldn't help but

wonder how bad it was in the major cities 100 years ago. Had to be worse than diesel fumes.

2.   Porcupines. These things have to be a northern relative of the possum. I think their sole purpose in life is to be roadkill. One of the travel books says they seek the highways to get salt from the winter road salting and they like automobile solvents and paints for the same reason. Saw 3 in a single 1/2 mile stretch, but the quills seem to keep the vultures away.

3.   UP. I asked a native Michigander if the story they tell in WI about the Upper Peninsula is true. He laughed derisively and said of course not. He said the truth is that MI and OH had a territorial dispute and MI got the UP while OH got Toledo. He said it's called the Toledo War and nobody knows yet who won or lost. I think I remember something like that from an old history class.

Monday we did a narrated tour of both Sault Ste. Marie's with an hour on each side of the border. It was on a silly little train on rubber tires, but well done and we got to see a lot more than the boat tours that just go thru the locks and up and down the St. Mary River. Got to watch a large ore carrier pass thru the Soo locks and did the Tower of History, which gives good views of both cities. The Canadian city is much larger, but the U.S. side is prettier. It was 1 city till the Treaty of Ghent that ended the Revolutionary War and divided it. It claims to be the 3rd oldest city in America behind Santa Fe and St. Augustine. All the big locks are on the American side and both countries generate a lot of hydropower from the 21-foot fall of the water from Lake Superior to Lake Huron. Almost all the rapids are gone with the diversion of most of the water to hydro plants and the locks. Yesterday we traveled about 115 miles west to Munising, MI where we unloaded the trailer in a campground and then did a glass bottom boat tour of 3 shipwrecks in Munising Bay for 2 hours. The water is very clear and you can see down about 30 feet. The oldest wreck is from the 19th century and about 200 feet long. The best preserved is a schooner about 140 feet long and only about 10 feet under water. Scuba divers have stripped them pretty clean. It was cold on the water with a lot of wind and we wore windbreakers and still got chilly. Lake Superior has 10% of the world's fresh water and its level has fluctuated over 100 feet in the last 5,000 years. The water is so clean and cold that the wooden wrecks are projected to be preserved for 2,000 years.

After short hikes to a couple of small waterfalls and doing the Pictured Rocks National Seashore visitor center, we chartered a 4 passenger plane to do a 1 hour tour of the Pictured Rocks and Grand Island which is a nature preserve in the Bay. I didn't have Tommy or Gene to split the cost of the plane and had to buy the empty seat, but then without them to nag me, I got away with no tip for the pilot. We didn't go up till 7:30 p.m. and the sun was behind us to view the rocks, which are several different colors and average 200 feet in height. You get to see the whole coast versus a smaller part of it by boat and there is 1 waterfall into the lake past the boat range plus the lakes and rivers behind the rocks. Over Grand Island we flew past the highest elevation lighthouse in the US at 1000 feet above sea level. Lake Superior is at 603 feet and this lighthouse sits on a bluff 350 feet above the lake and is about 50 feet tall. A really pretty view of the whole area and we went up to 3,000 feet and could see Lake Michigan also. Absolutely a gorgeous day. We could see the shallow shipwreck almost as well as from the tour boat and got a view of the entire wreck at once.

Today, my laundress is doing her slave work and we'll stay in Munising till tomorrow. Might even treat her to dinner tonite, but then again she made me take the more expensive air tour.

Evan

Date: Saturday, June 27, 1998 8:55 PM
Subject: Moose Sighting!

Yes, dear reader, our leader, a.k.a. the Great White Hunter, found real live moose—actually 3, a cow and 2 calves, for us this a.m. after failing to see any on the trails on Isle Royale that the rangers recommend—but that tale comes later in this episode.

Some of you are reporting garbled e-mail again. On our first trip this year we had many complaints which turned out to be punctuation symbols that come out as capital letters, plus or minus signs and the word ACE or AC or CI or something that is nonsense. I used a Norton Uninstall program on this laptop last spring and it deleted some files that it said were fragments or unnecessary and screwed up the e-mail program. I use Outlook Express in Internet Explorer 4.0 and deleted it and reinstalled it from my desktop machine, which never had the Norton program. I then sent myself an e-mail over the Internet to my desktop using all the punctuation marks on the keyboard and it was received normally, so I thought the problem had been fixed. Apparently it still affects some users of Eudora or Netscape e-mail programs. Sorry, but I can't fix on the road.

We spent Thursday traveling from Munising to Copper Harbor, MI with a few roadside stops. Got in early and a good thing since we had a big-time thunderstorm early in the p.m. which spawned a tornado in Alger County where Munising is and which we had just left. Hard to hit a moving target. It rained cats and dogs, but the trailer doesn't leak. Fri. a.m. we boarded a 100 passenger boat for Isle Royale, the National Park on an island in Lake Superior. It's a 56-mile ride to the island and we got there about 12:30 p.m. after a 4 1/2 hour boat ride. $160 boat ride and $226 per nite in the Lodge on the Island. 1 nite and we were history at those prices, although 3 meals are included in the Lodge rate. Isle Royale is a large series of islands actually, with a very large main island. It has no roads, just hiking trails and canoe and kayak portages and some guest cabins with no TV, radio or phone service (yep, none of that stuff in the Lodge and no air conditioning either, but you don't need AC). It's a wilderness park with moose and wolves and is not open or even inhabited in the winter and is kept that way intentionally. It has 165 miles of hiking trails and you can bring your own canoe or kayak or rent them. It's served by boat from MI and MN and by seaplane or you can come in your own boat or seaplane. They advertise that nearly every visitor sees moose, (reputedly 700 on the islands) but they lie. This leads me to Pookie's comment that we did the A tier National Parks with the kids (Yellowstone, Grand Canyon, Smokies, etc.) and now are doing the B and C tier on our own. Actually, Isle Royale brags that it gets fewer visitors in 1 year than Yellowstone gets in 1 day.

I have observed that the most important thing to do in becoming a tourist attraction is to put out a lot of propaganda promising a bunch of stuff that can't be delivered and then blame it's absence on the "season" that the visitor arrived. For example, we did Alaska in July last year and hit the absolute PEAK of ground squirrel season at Denali Nat. Park since that's all the animals we saw. The brochures promise you'll see all kinds of wildlife, but we never even saw Mt. McKinley. The "Large Wild Animals Will Run Over You" season occurred either before or after we were there. Big Bend promised abundant wildflowers in the spring, but when we got there they blamed El Nino for a poor season of wildflowers. A trail in Pictured Rocks Nat. Seashore had a pamphlet that said, "If you had been here in May, the woodland floor would have been covered in wildflowers and the forest would have smelled like a perfumery." Whoever wrote that missed his calling. He or she could make a helluva lot more money writing speeches for that other great BS speaker, Bill Clinton.

After checking into the Lodge, we took a 5-mile hike on a trail to Scoville Point on the northeast side of the big island. The trail brochure says if you have to do the big job, to go off the trail at least 100 feet and dig a shallow hole and cover up your deposit with your camping trowel. (That's the only tool Pookie doesn't carry in her purse.) Actually, we saw bogs, forest and rocky shore and 13 piles of moose droppings, but no moose. ALL the moose deposits were in the center of the trail, but humans can't do that, which led me to 4 possible conclusions:

1. The moose don't read the trail brochures, or
2. The moose don't give a damn about being politically correct, or
3. The moose have been oppressed by evil white males and therefore are not responsible for their own actions or,
4. The moose don't have camping trowels either.

After dinner we did the nature program on wildflowers with a lady ranger—I slept thru most of it-and then crashed. It doesn't get dark till 10 p.m. but I can sleep in the daylight if necessary.

This a.m. we got up early and ate breakfast and then rented an outboard motor and boat. I had read about another trail, 10 1/2 miles long by land, that went by Hidden Lake, a small lake in the interior of an island that was only a few hundred feet from the big lake and had a salt lick at one end of the small lake. We found the trail and walked up on the cow and twin calves about 60—75 yards in front of us at about 8:30 in the a.m. The calves were still trying to nurse, but the mother wasn't too interested as they are old enough to be weaned and she discouraged them. We watched for a few minutes and I tried my "Here Moosey, Moosey, Moosey call" which only made them look up. All the wildlife on this island is tolerant of humans and not the least afraid. Ducks and squirrels and rabbits will walk up to you, even with offspring. We toured an old fish factory and a lighthouse in the outboard and then went back and ate lunch and came back to Copper Harbor. On to Voyageurs Nat. Park in MN tomorrow. I just got up the nerve to tell Pookie that it has no roads either and must be toured by boat. She's getting used to this airplane bit and asked about seaplanes. I countered by offering to do the 2 Nat. Parks in Hawaii by cruise ship and bought a few days of happiness.
Who wants to go? Evan

Date: Thursday, July 02, 1998 8:51 AM
Subject: Land of Sky-Blue Waters

Yep, that's what Minnesota means in Indian according to the natives, or at least the docent in the Depot in Duluth. We spent a night in Bayfield, WI on the way here. Bayfield is a quaint little town that serves as the headquarters for the Apostle Islands Nat. Seashore. Actually, there are 21 islands, but the fur traders only counted 12 when they named them. We skipped the cruise around the islands and just walked around the small harbor and watched a few boats leave and enter. It's quite pretty, but we're about to get our fill of Lake Superior. I used to think there was no more reasonably priced real estate with a water view left in America, but alas, that was my 2nd mistake. Actually there are a few thousand miles of it around Lake Superior if you're tolerant of cool weather, and for no extra charge you can walk on the water for about 1/3 of the year.

We arrived in Duluth in mid afternoon and left the trailer in a campground and went downtown and toured the Depot. It's an old RR Station that's been made into a group of museums and a performing arts center. Really well done with a history, railroad, children's, art and lumbering museums plus the ballet and theatre and symphony. Downtown Duluth is neat and refurbished and concentrated on the waterfront. The city is 85,000 and lots of blonde people as it was settled mostly by Scandinavians—they think it's warm here. The forecast for the whole week is for a high of 76 and a low of 52. We haven't used the AC in the Blazer or the trailer for at least a week. We took several tours the next day starting with Glensheen, a 39-room mansion built by a snake/businessman who became a millionaire buying iron ore real estate and selling it to US Steel. We then did a narrated lunch cruise of the harbor, except we were too late to get lunch and we did Subway while most of the folks got a seated luncheon—but 2nd class is cheaper. Very interesting ride around the harbor which is ringed by grain elevators, coal docks and iron ore loading docks. Saw a "saltie" or ocean going freighter get loaded with 3/4 million bushels of grain, which only takes 3 hours. It was headed to Casablanca down the 2400 mile St. Lawrence Seaway. The twin ports of Superior, WI and Duluth, MN are treated as 1 port and rank in the top 10 US ports and are closed 1/3 of the year. The harbor averages 3 to 5 feet of ice in winter. The newer lake freighters are 1000 feet long and 105 feet wide and can carry 60,000 tons. Duluth actually was cut off from the lake by a sandbar 6 miles long deposited by the St. Louis River that forms the boundary between MN and WI. The cities sued each other with Superior having the natural harbor entrance and trying to freeze Duluth out of the shipping trade. The Supreme Court sided with Superior and issued an order to prohibit Duluth from cutting a canal thru the sandbar and opening the Duluth side of the harbor to lake traffic, but Duluth dug the canal before the decision was issued, making the order moot and they now operate as 1 harbor by order of Congress. Another way to skin the cat.

We then toured a 610 foot retired lake carrier that serves as a maritime museum. It was the flagship of the US Steel fleet and carried guests in guest cabins with their own dining and sleeping rooms. It's now too small to be efficient as the newer lake carriers carry 3 times the cargo with less crew. At 1 time US Steel had the largest privately owned fleet in the world. Even if small now, the hold is huge. Next we did an Omnimax movie on Mt. Everest and finished the day by touring a Corps of Engineers tugboat and the Corps museum and public park on the shipping canal. We had gone under the bridge that lifts its span to 140 feet over the canal on the cruise boat and watched a small freighter go under it at sunset. Nice day.

Yesterday we dropped the trailer in a campground half way up the north shore of MN and toured our 5th or 6th lighthouse. Pookie's developed a fetish for lighthouses and bought 2 books on them. Maybe it's a phallic symbol? We also did some scenic view stops and walked to some waterfalls at a state park. We also went all the way to Canada and did the Nat. Monument at Grand Portage, MN although it had closed by the time we got there. We did walk to the falls at a state park on the international border of the Pigeon River and they are impressive. I even went into Canada for a few minutes to see if they had a duty free store to try and buy some Cuban cigars for my snake associates, Bob and Phil. No shop at this port of entry but I did learn that it's illegal to bring Cuban cigars back to the US. Can you believe that these snakes—sworn officers of the courts— would ask me to perform an illegal act to gratify themselves? Alas, they are typical of the breed I fear. Fortunately, I am above reproach myself.

Today we move on to Ely, MN and then go to Voyageurs Nat. Park near International Falls, MN. We are continuing to slowly destroy the trailer. I reported my brushing up against a stone wall and scratching off the gizmo that holds the door open. We now use a bungee cord to hold the door open and look more like Tennessee Trailer Trash if you look at that side. We've also busted the igniter that lights the stovetop, torn the cover on the couch, broken the TV antenna gizmo that rotates the antenna although the antenna still works, blown the light on the range top hood and to top it all off, Pookie set off the LP gas detector the other day. LP gas is heavier that air and it's located on the floor. "Off", or whatever insect repellant she was using must be heavier than air too. The damn thing does turn into a red blinking light, but you don't notice that till you get over the terror of the foghorn noise. To reset it, you have to set it off again and it took 2 tries to keep from flinching when it goes off. Pookie just returned from the showers in this campground, the 1st one we've had that didn't have a water connection, and reported that it took quarters and stops in the middle of the hot water when the quarter runs out and is replaced by cold water. I may skip a shower today. Onward. Evan

Date: Friday, July 03, 1998 6:05 PM
Subject: Random Ruminations

1. I Haven't kept you informed about my navigator/co-pilot. She's been a pretty good girl, but can get testy when tired, hungry or cooped up too long in the Blazer. Rough roads also seem to hack her off. She does give off clues when it's time to back off. Usually, the first clue is something like an instruction to drive thru a concrete building or off a cliff or something like that. If you respond negatively to her suggestion with something like, "Are you crazy" or "What the hell do you mean?" you usually get the 2nd subtle hint which is a really dirty look accompanied by the finger with no verbal response. It is best to remember then that the alpha female in the wolf pack will sometimes attack her mate. I sometimes have trouble with the next part, but it's best to respond with submissive behavior like asking if she would like to have dinner or lunch out. If I'm really tired too, I am in danger of not being responsive appropriately and the next step is that she emulates that famous Indian squaw, No Nooky of the North. Usually, she backs down after being fed and always cools off after a day of rest. I wouldn't trade her.

2. Tannic Acid. All the rivers and streams that feed Lake Superior from Minnesota are the color of coffee. I mean really dark brown and almost black. The waterfalls are brown too. However, the water is 99.5% clean and after it's in the lake, the lake a few miles away from the source is crystal clear. They explain it by telling you that the water flows thru forests with decaying vegetation that creates huge amounts of tannic acid, the iron ore in the soil makes it dark colored and there is red clay in the soil. They can't explain why it clears up so fast.

3. The road from Finland, MN to Ely, MN is the worst I've ever been on with the trailer and 1 of the worst I've ever been on. It curves constantly, is rough as a cob and goes up and down every 75 feet. The speed limits posted are 55 and 50, but every 200 feet is a curve sign that says 15, 20 or 30. After 10 miles I told Pookie I had never been on such a bad road and then a sign appeared that said BUMPS—NEXT 25 MILES. That guy had to be a humor nut, but it was a MN DOT sign in orange. It took us 1 1/2 hours to go 45 miles. Navigator does not sleep on this type road.

4. Why do mosquitoes get bigger in the NAWTH? We've killed a few 100, but there are plenty left. Out West this spring it was often too cold to leave the trailer for too long, but here it's mosquitoes. Pookie gets bitten a lot more than me, but it's not cause she's sweeter. She just tastes better. Would you rather eat cow or bull? A few days ago, I killed 15 in the bathroom and at least 10 were full of blood. Pookie had a lot of bites and me none. Looking out the windows in the trailer we can see them trying to get in the screens. They all come in when we open the door and I get criticized if I leave it open for 5 seconds or leave the screen door closure—4 square inches—open when hooking up or unhooking the trailer. Did you know that only the female mosquito bites you? The males are all off chasing females to mate with and in the process pollinating flowers and other plants. Pookie set off the LP Gas Detector again today even though she went in the bathroom to put on her "Off"—she'll eventually go outside to do it unless she really loves the adrenalin rush one gets when the alarm goes.

5. Passed a sign yesterday going into Voyageurs Nat. Park that said, "Last Chance Liquor Store". I've always been opposed to marketing that uses fear as a motivator, but I did feel a little, and checked my supply. Did the American Express ads that threatened you with disaster from Karl Malden if you didn't buy

traveler's checks hack you off too? That's when I quit buying traveler's checks.

6. Wolf International Center—Ely, MN. A really neat place with their own wolf pack of 4 neutered and spayed wolves. The naturalist gave a talk on wolves and their behavior that was quite interesting. A wolf can bite with a force of 1500 pounds with its molar teeth vs. 800 pounds for a German Shepherd or 300 pounds for a human. Can open a moose femur with a density and size of a Louisville slugger baseball bat in less than a minute and only 6 bites in order to get to the bone marrow. They've also discovered that wolves do not suffer from genetic defects if inbreeding occurs. Must be related to rednecks.

7. Minnesota doesn't have a helmet law for motorcycles and scooters. Pookie has suggested that I might want to ride some up here. Wonder what that means. Over and Out

Date: Monday, July 06, 1998 5:40 PM
Subject: Been There—Done That

Got to Voyageurs Nat. Park Thurs. p.m. just in time to sign up for the concessionaire provided all day boat cruise on a large float—pontoon—boat to Kettle Falls the next a.m. The boat had mosquito screens and was covered in case of rain since it is cool here. This Park is only 23 years old and is a disappointment. The good news is that the govt. didn't give away the store on this one. When they bought the land in 75 when the Park was established they gave 25-year leases to the people who wouldn't sell at then fair market values to reduce the acquisition cost and they expire in 2000. Until then, we have seadoos (no offense Tommy), lots of private cabins and all kinds of private boats in the Park. It's kind of like Center Hill Lake in TN with more wildlife.

The Voyageurs were the French-Canadians who paddled the 26-foot canoes from Montreal to the Pacific carrying trade goods to get furs from the Indians and this was a central location on the route. Voyageur means traveler in French and the primary cause of premature death among them was from hernias from carrying all the freight on portages. Kettle Falls is one of the few points where you look south into Canada from the US. Actually, there are no more falls at Kettle Falls cause Boise Cascade has dammed up the falls to generate hydropower to run their huge paper mill in International Falls. The same is true of International Falls where the bridge to Canada goes thru the Boise Cascade Plant that sits astride the Rainy River on top of another dam that generates more hydropower for the mill. We did see pictures of the falls in both places before the dams and in fairness, the dams do provide for more wildlife by keeping the water levels at higher levels in the Park. I did get hacked at the toll into Canada when I asked the girl if the US and Canada split the toll proceeds and she said no, the money actually went to Boise Cascade since it was their dam the road was on. There is a strike on in Canada against Boise, but the people are working in the US. How do they do that, when it's all 1 plant even if it is huge? They even have their own railroad to bring logs to the plant and their own RR rolling stock. Came back on a free bridge over the Rainy River 70 miles to the west. It's obvious crossing the border that economically Canada is not on our level. Of course it's much, much better than Mexico, but still too socialistic to achieve what the US does.

We saw a few eagles in the Park and there are reputed to be moose there but they have brainworm, which makes them do crazy things—kind of like snakes (a test to see if they are paying attention). We even did 2 of the naturalist programs at nite in the Park. One on Black Bears and one on Wetlands. On the 4th we went to the parade in International Falls, a town of 8300 people. Not many parades have bagpipers from across the border and it was really a neat day. Also had a cement truck and lumbering truck—free advertising I guess. Had a bratwurst in Smokey Bear Park for lunch and it was full of people—kind of like Italian Street Fair in Nashville, except not an Italian within 500 miles. The people are friendly, but no southerners here except for a few from GA we met today in Ft. Frances across the border. We also met a lonely black guy from Chicago who was very friendly and didn't have a northern accent so I guess he's not originally from there. He let us download e-mail at the Visitor Center where he moonlights from his job managing the Holiday Inn. Sent every tourist who asked for a lodging reference to the Holiday Inn.

Now for the part you've been waiting for—what did I do with the snake associates and their request for illegal goods. Well, I considered it for a while and decided it wasn't totally their fault. After—all, they were only asking me to subborn perjury by lying to the customs inspectors, and our president—with a little p in his case since he's a prick too—has been lying for years and teaching everyone what it means to subborn perjury. The question became, would I get the REAL Cuban cigars, or get the imitation ones made with Cuban seed, of tobacco grown in Honduras or the Dominican Republic and called Cuban—which are legal to bring back. Knowing how slimy the snakes really are, I concluded that anything but the real stuff would not be acceptable. I mean, they had promised to spring me from incarceration for no cost (anyone believe that?) if I was interdicted by the border patrol. Pookie refused to hide the contraband in her blouse, so I was left with the sole option of my slick tongue and clever mind. YES, they are now indebted to me again! We await their humble thanks and salutations for a successful scam on the feds. Of course, their reply will determine whether this acquisition is a gift, a purchase to be repaid or the cause of an auction to interested parties. Southbound and Down

Date: Tuesday, July 07, 1998 7:38 PM
Subject: Heater

Yep, I did it. Driving from International Falls to St. Paul yesterday I cut on the heater in the Blazer. It never got above 67, I had on shorts and I tried not to for all you poor slobs in the South, but I got cold. It's only July and my perception is that it heats up here in August for 2 weeks. Plan to be home then cause I'm a little bit tired of these damnyankees. The 1st Minnesota suffered 82% casualties at Gettysburg, but it wasn't enough. The tour guide at the State Capitol today did a bit on the Civil War and then asked where we were from. I said the bad guys won and it is really The War of Northern Aggression, which gave her the correct impression of our origin. The Capitol is absolutely gorgeous. I think it's better than Indiana. Why are all the Midwestern capitols the most attractive? They were all built around the same time. WI, MN, IA, and NB are the prettiest we have seen—and I'm including MS, the home state.

After the Capitol tour with a really good lady tour guide, we did St. Paul Cathedral, which is almost as impressive as some of them in Europe. It's better than Notre Dame in Paris, but not as good as Chartres or Cologne. It seats 3,000 and sits on a hill so you can see it all over the city. I really think it has the best stained glass of all of them, but probably better technology than the European ones had.

Next we did a sternwheeler riverboat tour on the MS River. The boat was about 1/3 the size of the General Jackson at Opryland. The MS River is not navigable for big boats above Minneapolis, which was originally named St. Anthony's Falls. The original name for St. Paul was "Pig's Eye" after a whiskey trader who sold to the Indians. Once again we were unable to get the luncheon cruise, so we did Subway. They really do save you a lot of money. After the boat tour, we did the MN History Center which is FREE— THE 1st FREE THING WE'VE HAD! It is very well done and by the MN Historical Society. I got so enraptured at the low cost that we stayed too long and the parking fee was $3.00. Ruined my enjoyment of the cheap cost. After that we went to THE MALL OF AMERICA! Pookie had to have something to compare the Opryland Mall to. I forgot to mention that we are in a campground that Pookie picked out 1/4 mile from an outlet mall that she toured last nite. She said we did The Mall of America in 15 minutes, but she fudges. She didn't score off of Sir at the Mall Of America, but Rachel did. They have kiddie rides galore and a lot of daddies are on them too. A roller coaster, log flume ride, Ferris wheel, and some new ones we can't name. They even issue their own credit card that gives you points instead of frequent flier miles.

Tomorrow we do the Great River Road in WI on our way to Monroe and then to St. Louis and home. I've about decided to buy another set of tires for the Blazer and keep it for a few more years. I'm just getting it broken in to towing all this weight and nothing has ever broken on it. What's wrong with 91,000 miles? Evan

P.S. Have heard nothing from the snake/associates, so I assume they are laying low till they get the ill-gotten goods at which point I expect a scurrilous attack, which may be sent to you too. I apologize in advance for their lack of class.

Saturday, July 11 1998 9:36 p.m.
Home Again

We got home this afternoon. Sorry I haven't written for a few days, but I didn't feel like it. Lots of bad news on this trip. It started with the dog dying, and then I heard my stepbrother had lymphoma again and then my good friend Tommy had a stroke. It's hard to be very entertaining when you keep getting that kind of info. My friend Bill in Monroe, WI said that "Murphy was an optimist" and I think he's right. To demonstrate his point, he told me a story about the woman who moved to the West Coast and flew out there with her pet skunk. She had to provide the airline with a certificate from the vet certifying that the skunk had been descented, which she did. She presented the pet skunk in a pet carrier and the certificate to the airline and got on the plane. The problem arose when the skunk had a litter of young on the trip in the carrier and the babies were definitely NOT de-scented.

We did the Great River Road, Highway 35 in WI, from Prescott outside of St. Paul to Prairie du Chien. It's billed as 1 or the top 25 scenic drives in America and they told the truth this time. About 150 miles along the Miss. River with a lot of wetlands and great views of the river and marshes and the WI countryside. We stopped for an hour and watched a tug split its barges in half to transit one of the locks on the upper Mississippi. Most people don't understand that the upper MS River is a baby compared to the lower MS. 2/3 of the water that flows past New Orleans enters the river from the Ohio and although the upper MS is much longer, it doesn't carry much water. To give you an idea of the difference, on the upper MS they measure the flow in gallons per second past a given point. On the lower MS, they use acre-feet per second. An acre-foot is 1 acre of water, 1 foot deep. Gallons would give you such a large #, it would be meaningless. I grew up on the lower MS where it's 300 feet deep in places and a mile wide. At La Crosse, WI its 3 miles wide, but only a few feet deep in most places.

An absolutely gorgeous day with sun, scattered clouds and cool. I had almost forgotten how pretty WI is in summer. We spent 2 nites in Monroe, WI with the Bakers and we got to renew acquaintances with a lot of friends we hadn't seen in 16 years. We lived in Monroe from 78 to 81 and were last there in 82. Monroe still has a 1-cent parking meter on the square, but they've gotten extravagant and raised the ticket for over parking from 50 cents to $1.00. It's a Swiss community and they are a bit frugal. I fit in well at the bank there and some of them thought I was Swiss too, but it's Scotch, both the bottled and inherited kind, and the Swiss are really pikers compared to my bloodlines.

We drove to St. Louis on Fri. and stopped in Springfield, IL and did the IL Capitol. Like all the Midwestern Capitols, it's absolutely magnificent. The Dome is much higher than the US Capitol in DC and the stained glass is better than most cathedrals. We spent Fri. nite with the Tenhulas and met the Seichkos for dinner. Yep, if you'll make friends with damnyankees, you get names like that. The Tenhulas (Finnish, but I tell him he looks like an Indian) are old friends from Jackson, TN and the Seichkos are new friends we met on the trip out west this spring. Elaine got us in this fancy restaurant that Tenhula said we couldn't get in on a Fri. nite, but we did have to use an alias from some guy in the Russian Mafia named Gusnik. It worked like a charm. I misread the check and tipped too little, so we probably can't go back. Drove home thru KY and got in about 6 p.m. Hope the next trip brings less bad news. Evan

Chapter3. We Acquire Duke!—1998

Subject: Dog
Date: Sunday, July 19, 1998 9:16 PM

We have a new dog! Name is Duke—he came with a name that I couldn't improve upon—pure male dog. A Jack Russell Terrier, $300, but cheaper than a new rug. Bought him from the wife of my state representative, a democrat, but not too bad a guy, for a snake—dog will be trained as a Republican. He's 7 months old and has already climbed the fence in the backyard twice in 1 day. Rode in a car for the first time today and had on his first leash, not to mention first exposure to air conditioning, which he loves! Next I have to buy an electric fence to put on top of the wood fence, or he'll end up as roadkill. He's smart—sucked up to Pookie right away and ensured his acceptance when he licked her all over the face. Peed on the rug, and has taste—picked out the oriental instead of the one we want to replace—may have been frustrated at the democrat's house where he had to share quarters with a Vietnamese pig, goats, horses, rabbits, ponies and a lot of other dogs. Is now asleep at my feet and appropriately enraptured with me, as are all dogs, women and small children—smart dog! Evan

Reply to Dog from Snake Henry: (he can't spell or type, but he's a democrat/snake too!)

It the early days, before Duke's eyes opened it would be easy to confuse him with a Republican. Later as Duke craps on everyone else things, chews up the property of others and issues nothing but sound bites (barks), his behavior may be confused with the demeanor of a Republican. While living in his enclosed compound, he will mature and will probably have no hope— although it is the demeanor of the Jack Russell breed (Republican) to be a one family (single issue) in their behavior. The carpet disdain may be his disdain for the laborers who worked hard to complete the carpet. Clearly, I had hoped to tell you that Duke has hoped growing up in Giles County to be a Democrat, but, you are right, Duke must be raised as a Republican with all the natural tools he has at his disposal.

Subject; Dog Part 2
Date: Monday, July 20, 1998 8:45 PM

I see where the snake/democrat that smokes illegal cigars has replied to all of you about my purchase of a democrat dog that I will attempt to makeover into a sensitive, caring Republican. It will be quite a feat if I can achieve this transformation into an outstanding member of the community, but then, most of us, including myself, have made this leap from the depths of society (born of democratic parents) to the pinnacle of achievement, membership into the fold of the honest, hardworking Republican Party. First, I must relate the events of the last 24 hours. Duke made another mistake on the carpet about 9:30 p.m. After rubbing his nose in it, I put him out into the fenced yard to repent his ways. He howled miserably for a few minutes while he anguished at the back door begging to be forgiven for his error. When I went out a few minutes later to see if he was adequately remorseful, he was gone. He had climbed the fence again—the first time without me being outside the fence to tempt him—and disappeared. I immediately leaped into the Blazer and began a search of the neighborhood in the fog and heat where the AC caused condensation on the windshield and I had to run the wipers intermittently to see more than a few feet. At 11:15 p.m., I gave up and returned home with never a sight or sound of Duke. It was like he had said,"Up yours", as many democrats do. Pookie too had gone on a search in her car and was even willing to let the dog get in her car if she found him, but to no avail.

This a.m., I got up at 6 and went on another 2-hour search while Pookie called the local vets to report a missing Jack Russell Terrier. No luck again and I called the paper and placed a lost dog ad in the classifieds. I also called the local humane society and pound and put a blurb on the local radio station. Finally, I took a shower and got dressed to go to Rotary on my scooter. For the 3rd time I rode over to the Country Club across the street, only this time, I rode out on the course and found the cute little blonde female greens keeper. She reported no dog on the course all morning. As I was riding away, she yelled at me to stop and I turned around and looked over my shoulder. Coming over the crest of a knoll 100 yards away was a golf cart with the young male greens keeper and sitting on the seat beside him was Duke! There is obvious hope that he may yet learn to like the Republican lifestyle, as he seemed to enjoy the golf cart ride and atmosphere of the course.

My guess is that he was wooed away by the passage of an unattended female dog through the neighborhood, sort of like the snake/democrat/philanderer-in-chief in Washington who sets the standards for all other democrats. Pookie had already discussed having Duke neutered, to reduce his tendency to roam, with one of the vet assistants she had talked to that morning. Like Hillary, all women consider this from time to time, and it may be near the time to do Duke and Bill, or at least Bill. The vet assistant told Pookie that; "a few snips will make him into a totally different dog!" Duke deserves another chance or 2, but Bill has proved repeatedly that he's incorrigible.

This p.m. we went to the local Co-op and bought a pet carrier and one of those electric invisible fences (running total up to $500 and climbing—with no new rug). We came home and watched the video that comes with the invisible fence. We let Duke watch too, and he paid attention till it got to the part where it said, "without proper training of your pet, the fence won't work". Duke lost interest then and went to sleep knowing he could win again.

I took that fence back and got a K-9 electric fence and a $95 rebate on the credit card. Not going to let Duke see the directions on this one and am resorting to brute force. He's gonna fry if he climbs that fence again. The only way to get the attention of most democrats is with a shock. Pookie said the only thing he's learned yet is to sleep in my lap. Well, what other skill could be so central to his acceptance other than to ingratiate himself with me? I mean, he ain't dumb, just boisterous. Actually, he figured out the pet door in a few seconds and almost made another escape through the pet door after I thought I had locked him in the storeroom. So far, the score is democrats 1, Republicans 0, but I don't have the electric fence plugged in yet.

If you receive anymore slimy comments from the snake, consider the source.
Evan

Another Snake Reply:

Date: Monday, July 20, 1998 11:30 PM
Subject: Re: Dog Part 2

I promise I did not attempt to kidnap him to place Duke in a good home. I will contact human resources to report you if you persist in parental mismanagement.
Honest, Christian democrat,
Bob

Date: Wednesday, July 22, 1998 9:09 PM
Subject: Stressful Day for Duke

Duke had a rough day. It started with Pookie running the vacuum cleaner around 8 a.m. Duke never wore a collar or leash till Sun. p.m. and had trouble adjusting to the vacuum. He seemed to think his job was to defend the household against it. After a few false attacks and a lot of barks, he compromised by getting the hell out of the way while complaining loudly. When Pookie got ready to leave for Nashville and got all dressed and cleaned up, Duke still blamed her for the vacuum and barked at her like she was still running it.

Poor Duke, he has learned an enormous amount in a few days. He likes air conditioning and my lap, but is not sure about TV or radio—smart dog! He does like riding in the Blazer, but doesn't know my plans to teach him to ride behind me on the scooter in the basket. After Pookie left for the day, I put him in the pet carrier while I went out to electrify his fence. I can't leave him alone in the house, or he will trash the place. He whined and cried for 3 hours while I set up the fence, charger, ground pole, etc. He kept hearing me hammering or drilling a hole thru the wall from the storeroom to the backyard for the wiring or pounding the 8-foot grounding pole into the ground, and knew I was still here. After nearly 3 hours, I was thru and invited Duke to roam the backyard on his own. He tried the fence in about 2 minutes and got fried. I left him out there for 2 hours and heard a few more yelps. He has decided now that he doesn't want to climb the fence to express his displeasure with me. I left him out for 2 hours this p.m. while I ran some errands and he stayed home! Score is now democrats 1, Republicans 1.

Then, I invited Leigh, age 7 to go wading in Pigeon Roost Creek with me and Duke. I figure Duke is about 7 age equivalent and having Leigh yank him around on a leash is giving him a dose of his own medicine. Duke likes the water almost as much as a spaniel and got to swim and splash more than he can do in his water bowl at home on the kitchen floor, but had to put up with Leigh loving him all the time—JUSTICE! Poor dog is learning fast, but has trouble keeping up. Next, I have to train him to poop in the neighbor's yard instead of mine, a true Republican talent. I'm beginning to think he may make the cut and get to stay—I shrewdly bought him on approval and can take him back if he flunks, or outsmarts me.
Evan

Sent: Saturday, August 01, 1998 7:47 PM
Subject: Duke da Dog Part IV

Can you believe it! August 17 is my birthday and my present will be the Philanderer-in-Chief finally having to testify under oath! This guy has made a living by lying and being rewarded for it and now there is a remote possibility he may have to pay a small price for lying. Tough to criticize the tobacco companies—who have had warning labels for years— for lying when he's done it constantly. Duke and I may watch as a way of adding to Duke's education about democrats.

Well, I'm still ahead, but only barely. Duke in 2nd week of potty training and still making mistakes, but not as often. I think he loses focus on the subject while scheming up new ways to get his way. We went to a party Sun. p.m. and when we got home, he was playing with the grandkids next door instead of in the back yard. An examination revealed a hole in the bottom of the fence and a hole dug in the ground under the hole Duke had eaten out of the fence. He didn't run away this time and I now walk him in the yard without the leash. He's just now learning to chase the cows in the pasture.

My next trip to the Co-op was entertaining. All the salesmen out there want to meet Duke. They say he is responsible for me becoming their best customer. I bought more wire, insulators etc. to electrify the bottom of the fence. One of the guys offered to sell me a new electric collar that is supposed to shock the dog if he barks too much. I told him we don't have that problem yet—and ruined his day since he wants to find out if it works.

After wiring the bottom of the fence, I intentionally walked away on the outside and watched Duke get fried when he tried to crawl through his hole—yelp, yelp! He hasn't figured out another escape route yet, but complains wholeheartedly when left alone in the back yard. Score is now democrats 3-Republicans 2 1/2.

We went to Nashville yesterday and left Duke in the back (read electrified) yard. He trashed the storeroom which he can go into and out of through the doggie door. Broke some of Pookie's stuff and is now on the endangered species list. He should be in the Flying Wallenda family since he can leap small buildings without a cape. Alicia says he's the Velcro dog cause he can't be separated from me without a tearing sound and pain. He's also mastered the art of getting on our bed and it's at least 4 feet high. Good thing he adores me as the local supervisor is losing her infatuation, although she took him to the Post Office at midnight the other nite—one of her normal times to go. Maybe she needs a subject to smother. Evan

Date: Tuesday, August 04, 1998 1:58 AM
Subject: Duked Again

This is one for the books. Duke enlisted allies from the animal world. It's an old democratic tradition to enlist slime ball help if you can't win honestly. The most damaging recent use of this tactic by democrats was to induce Ross Perot to enter the presidential race TWICE so they could elect a scumbag as a minority president and make all the rest of us suffer from their scheme to control. It's rained so much lately that I never went outside to inspect the bottom electrified wire on the fence. Turns out that I have electrocuted a number of birds during all the rain lately. They now fall underneath the wires and cannot be cleaned up in the normal fashion by

Duke or his allies. Saturday night I was awakened about 1 a.m. by a horrible smell in the house. It persisted all the rest of the night, and I knew from past experience what it was. An inspection Sunday revealed the cause and result. The dead birds were all on the north side of the house, inside the fence and near the air conditioning unit for the downstairs. They had begun to decompose and smelled a little, but not so much that you could tell from inside the house. They were now carrion, and what animals are attracted to carrion? SKUNKS! (More symbolic of democrats than even the ass!)

The skunk or skunks were apparently fried when they tried to get the dead birds and then turned loose. One or more hit the AC dead center and the aroma was spread throughout the house by electricity, one of the works of modern man. By 7 a.m., I had to get up and go outside for fresh air and discovered the problem. It's all Duke's fault. If he wouldn't climb and dig under the fence, I wouldn't have to electrify it. That's the bad news. The good news is he hasn't peed or pooped in the house for 3 days. I'd rather have the bathroom problems. You never can tell with democrats who tend to publicize their most intimate bodily events worldwide—like their Leader. At least no one will want Duke's DNA.

By Sun. p.m., Betty next door said she could no longer smell the skunk when she came inside our house. I can still smell it outside by the AC, but we must have a helluva filter since it has gone away inside. I even opened the crawl space underneath the house and it smells O.K. The saga continues. I threw the dead birds over the barbwire fence into the pasture and Duke immediately went out in the pasture and rubbed in them since he thought they were sooo attractive. He is still a democrat in spite of all my training to date. Score now is democrats 4, Republicans 3. Evan

Sent: Saturday, October 24, 1998 2:44 PM
Subject: Duke Report

Pookie has chastised me for not sending out a Duke Report lately, so I shall report briefly on several aspects of his life and educational achievements:

1. Potty. Training I now pronounce Duke house trained, since he hasn't screwed up in our house, the bank, the liquor store or Betty's house in the last month. He also has learned at long last how to hike his leg properly when performing # 1. His development in this area was retarded by him spending the first 7 1/2 months of his life in a kennel run with his mother and not having a proper male figure to emulate. Actually, it was kind of funny to watch him develop this skill on his own. At first, he would hike the leg too low and pee on his front leg. Then, in an

over compensation, he would hike his leg too high and fall over on the opposite side. Fortunately he is ambidextrous and learned to fall on both sides till he got it right.

2. Hunting. The Dukester is rapidly becoming a lethal killer of various forms of wildlife and a harasser of others. His first conquests were small, but led to diarrhea after he ingested them. They were various forms of flying insects like flies, moths, etc. Next he dug up moles in my yard and Betty's and played with them like a cat with a mouse till they were totally expired. The yards looked better with the moles alive. I took him with us to Lawrenceburg for Rachel to feed the geese at a lake in the state park and found he would chase the geese, even out in the water, and completely ignores the hissing and honking. Next, he discovered what a cat was when a stray tried to take up residence under a car a visitor had parked in Betty's yard. When barking didn't intimidate it, he bit it and discovered what cat claws are, but also discovered that the cat would run from him, which led to the cat spending a night up a tree. Next he chased a skunk away with only a near miss scored by the skunk, which resulted in Duke having a bath and me buying a live animal trap to catch the skunk. So far I've caught Duke one night and a feral cat another that was the biggest I ever saw, but no skunk. The cat wasn't a lynx or wildcat, but was huge and fortunately for Duke he didn't meet up with the cat except when it was in the cage since it outweighed him by at least 5 pounds. Several weeks ago he chased a deer for 20 minutes in the pasture behind the house, but finally came home. Speaking of pastures, he is becoming quite good at herding cows. He prefers to chase the calves, but has learned the mama cows will chase him back. When this occurs, he runs back under the barbed wire and tries to goad the cow into getting stuck by the barbs in the wire. He also enjoys catching them lying down chewing cuds when he can run up within a foot or so and bark and nip till they stand up. Last night we were taking a walk about 8:30 when he found a possum and I had to carry Duke home to keep him from killing the possum. He even chases birds and I think he'll catch one someday. For a 16-pound dog, he surely isn't afraid of other animals.

3. Chewing. Pookie says he has a mouth like an alligator and just as many teeth, and she may be right. We give him chew toys, but they ain't good enough. When we left him for a few days while we were in AR, he chewed up 2 screen doors on the backyard patio to pay us back for leaving him alone. He gets Rachel's stuffed animals from upstairs and brings them downstairs to devour at his leisure if we turn our backs. Betty

feeds him when we're out of town and she has scratches all over her arms from his rough play and love bites, even though she tells him she's his only friend and he better be nice to her. We left him with Barbara this week while we went to a funeral visitation and I told Barbara to scream NO every now and then and she'd be correct even if she couldn't see him. I told Pookie this is the first dog we've ever had that we did NOT give the run of the house to when we left for a short time. She replied that this was the first dog we've ever had who COULD run. Pookie says he'll never make a trailer dog cause he would eat it up if we left him alone in it. Of course, Pookie said he'd never get house trained also and she's had to admit that he is. End of Report

Evan

Chapter 4. Southern California Trip—1999

Sent: Friday, May 14, 1999 3:47 AM
Subject: WaKeeney, Kansas

Yep, we're on the road again, and for the first time with Duke! Marguerite, call Betty Jo and tell her we still have Duke, but we're still in Kansas, so he can't relax yet, and still has a chance of getting left behind. We got off about 9 a.m. on Tues and made it to St. Louis by around 5:30 p.m. Duke has to ride in the front most of the time and sits on the bench between the 2 front bucket seats. Pookie has fixed a towel there to give him better traction and they have developed a better relationship. Duke now sucks up to her and pays her some attention—smart dog!

We parked next to Mel and Elaine, our RV friends from St. Louis, in a trailer park off I-44 in southwest St. Louis. Mel and Elaine are now full timers in a big 5th wheel and are in St. Louis for a month seeing their daughter and Morgan and Bennett, the grandkids. We enjoyed meeting Jennifer, their daughter and the kids. Bennett will be christened soon and then Mel and Elaine are off for the Dakotas and then Arizona for the winter. They fed us steak and we had a nice visit. Duke was so well behaved that we were stunned. He made up for it later that nite when I tried to put him in his pet taxi in the back of the Blazer. He cried and whined till he woke up the neighbors and I let him in the trailer to sleep. Going to be a long trip, but he sleeps on the couch and we close the door to our room and it's not a problem till about 6:30 in the a.m. when he wants to play.

I can't believe how stupid I was the next morning when I opened the box containing his citronella collar to control barking and whining. I tried to inject the citronella spray into the collar by inserting the gas under pressure (like a butane cigarette lighter refill) into the microphone on the collar instead of the citronella container. Ruined the $156 bark control collar and now it's worthless as it sprays the gas whenever the battery is put in. I think Duke knew I would screw it up.

We left late Wed. a.m. and since we were so far southwest of St. Louis and didn't want to backtrack to get to I-70, I decided to go to Jefferson City to see the state capitol on the way to I-70. Bad idea! 2 lane hilly roads and it started to pour rain when we could see the state capitol from about 5 miles away. There's nothing else in Jefferson City and we couldn't park within 1/2 mile of the capitol as I think everybody in town works there. Decided I didn't want to see it that badly and my traveling companion agreed she didn't want to get wet either.

Drove on to Kansas and spent the nite in a trailer park in Lawrence. I'm firmly convinced that there is a twisted, psychotic engineer (probably a Miss. State graduate) who designs all these trailer parks and the access roads. You never see or cross railroad tracks driving into them and the directory never mentions it, but they all have a train in close proximity which you discover after you have checked in, paid and unhooked and set up for the nite. Here we heard the Atchison, Topeka and Santa Fe all night long as the engineer blew his horn for some road crossing nearby. Since the horn always sounded the same and it sounded about every 20 minutes, I figured that the damn thing went in an elliptical circle around us all nite till the guy driving got tired about 5 a.m.

Drove on to Topeka Thurs. and toured the Kansas state capitol with a tour guide named Bob and Mrs. Steed and her 3rd grade class. The kids asked some interesting questions and for the first time on any state capitol tour, they let us go up to the top of the dome—I guess there are some benefits to being with a bunch of 9 year olds. Very interesting tour, but the capitol is not as pretty as many others. Went to the Kansas State Museum of History in Topeka next, as recommended by Bob. It's quite well done, but we've seen so many museums about Great Plains history that we didn't stay too long.

Next stop was Dillard's for some therapy shopping by Pookie and then a Pet Smart for Duke. Got another $90 worth of toys, stake out chains and an electric anti-bark collar. He believes in electricity and this might work. Patty and Shawn said I could return it to any Pet Smart if it fails. Drove on here for the nite and passed thru Russell, Kansas, home of the 1st husband, Bob Dole. I know my left wing, liberal democratic friends will be pleased to know that Russell is in the middle of an oilfield and is surrounded by pumping wells—I can see them smirking and saying they aren't surprised. 300 miles to Denver and our 1st Nat Park, Rocky Mountain isn't too much further. Kansas is still as boring as our last drive thru it and we haven't seen any sign of Dorothy, although the girl at the toll-booth grinned when I called her Dorothy. Evan

Sent: Sunday, May 16, 1999 2:43 PM
Subject: Rocky Mountain Nat. Park

Well, we're in Estes Park, CO right outside the gates of the Nat. Park. Estes Park is a city, not a park and is named for the original settler who decided to park here. The campgrounds in the park don't have hookups so we're in a KOA with cable TV and all hookups. Drove here direct from Kansas and it's a tough uphill pull all the way. We're at 7500 feet now and the Blazer is resting, but got us here by late afternoon on Fri. We have a gorgeous view out the trailer windows of snow-covered peaks in the distance and it's very cool, even in the sun and down to low 40's at nite. There are elk and mule deer everywhere and they wander thru the streets of Estes Park and are a hazard when driving.

Saturday we did the Park all day and I'm glad we did since it's raining today and we can't even see the mountaintops. Absolutely fantastic views and scenery, but as usual, we aren't here at the correct season. The highway thru the Park to the other side is still closed by snow and they are still plowing and hope to have it open by May 28. It's the highest continuous road in the US, but we could only go to 11,000 feet. Higher up, it's thru alpine tundra with no trees according to the propaganda they give out. We were able to tour about 1/3 of the Park, but saw the most impressive views. We stopped at a Park Museum and the flag was at half-staff and I asked why. The lady behind the desk said it was National Slain Peace Officers day, or something like that. I responded that I had hoped that Hillary had finally shot Bill and everyone laughed. Saw huge herds of elk, beaver and other small mammals and found out that the elk were reintroduced to the Park in the 1930s from Yellowstone. Lots of horseback riding, fishing and tons of hikers. There are 3,000,000 visitors each year and I'm glad I'm here now instead of the peak of summer. It's crowded to me now. Estes Park is a lot like Gatlinburg, only smaller and not as developed. Pets aren't allowed on the trails, so we left Duke in the Blazer and did some short trails, but there's too much snow to hike the long ones and we get winded fairly easily at these altitudes. We went back to the Visitor Center at 7 p.m. and heard a very interesting 1- hour presentation on the elk-3200 in the Park— by ranger Dick with slides and other exhibits.

Duke Report—I decided not to use the electric collar. Wondered what would happen if a car parked next to us with a dog who barked and his barking caused Duke to get shocked (lots of people traveling with dogs in the car) or what if a car alarm went off and set off Duke's collar. Everybody who sees Duke wants to pet him and says he's adorable or cute or something like that. When I offer to let them have him, they back up and Pookie says it's obvious they don't know him. He's behaving much better that we expected and getting better daily—may learn the meaning of "NO" yet. The only real problem is we can't leave him alone in the trailer or he would tear it to pieces trying to get out, so we have to leave him in the Blazer with windows cracked for ventilation and he whines and cries when we leave. Not a big problem while it's cool, and he calms down after awhile, but what about Death Valley? Do I have to leave the Blazer running and the AC on? Hell, he might drive off! Pookie says she wanted a Bulldog and it isn't her fault, but she is getting more and more attached to him. Going back to Denver and try to find a citronella collar tomorrow on our way to Utah. Pookie says I have to pick up after him when he poops in the pet walk area in these campgrounds—female brain. When the ground in the pet walk is covered with elk poop, why not leave the Duke poop?

Today it's rained most of the day so we've eaten out and read and rested. Took Pookie to see "Entrapment" at the local movie this afternoon. Onward to where it isn't raining. Evan

Sent: Wednesday, May 19, 1999 9:24 PM
Subject: Estes Park Forever

Well, we're still in Estes Park, CO, but hopefully will get to leave Fri. a.m. When I last wrote, it was raining hard and getting cold. That was the good news. As soon as I finished the e-mail, the rain turned to snow and then to ice. When we got up Mon. a.m., there was ice all over the Blazer and trailer and the temperature was about 28.

After we unhooked the trailer when we got here, I noticed a rubbing, roaring sound in the rear end of the Blazer while we rode around the Nat Park. The Blazer ran fine and shifted fine and climbed the mountains like normal, but the sound continued even when coasting downhill, so out of an abundance of caution I took it to the only car dealer in town, a Ford/Chrysler dealer at 7:30 a.m. when he opened for the day. He said he'd work me in, but was booked up for the day. About 2 pm, I called back and got the good news that the differential in the rear end was shot. When they opened the access plate, which is a magnet to attract any loose metal that grinds off the gears, they found it covered in metal shards. He said I needed new carriage bearings, pinion bearings and maybe some other stuff, or needed complete rebuilding. The Ford dealer said he couldn't fix it, but he had called the Chevy dealer in Loveland—23 miles away—and had gotten me an appointment for Mon., the 24th, or a week before they would even look at it. I told him thanks, but no thanks and started calling Chevy dealers all over central CO. Found one in Boulder—35 miles away—who would take me right away if I could get it there. I had the Ford guy put the access plate back on and drove it to Boulder, Mon. p.m. We're now in a bright red 4x4 Jeep Classic SUV rented from Enterprise for $25 per day while the Blazer is in the shop. It rides rougher than the Blazer and burns more gas, but beats the hell out of not having any transportation. The bench between the front seats is too small for Duke. Conned the girl at Enterprise into the dealer's rate for a subcompact, but got a jeep SUV for Duke for the same rate. Hope to get the Blazer back Thurs. p.m., but will have to come back to Estes Park to get the trailer, so won't get out of here before Fri. am at the best.

Tues. we went to Loveland/Ft. Collins as that area just received the #1 place to retire from one of these rating services that doesn't mean it is, just that it might be. We walked around Old Town with Duke, and it really is nice—an old 1870's area redone into shops, nightclubs, restaurants and sidewalk cafes. Then we rode around the campus of CO State Univ., which is rather new, but big and nice. The trip over and back follows the Big Thompson River thru the mountains and is very, very scenic. Went to the Stanley Hotel in Estes Park when we got back and walked around the grounds and public areas. It was founded by F.O. Stanley, the inventor of the Stanley Steamer auto, and was the setting for the movie "The Shining" by Stephen King who wrote the book and movie after staying here at the Stanley. An original Stanley Steamer car is in the lobby, and a small museum is on the ground or basement floor.

Today, Pookie said she was treating me to lunch, cause she felt sorry for me with the Blazer being sick—it just turned 99,000 miles and I've never spent any money on it except for tires, a headlight and a new battery and normal maintenance—estimated cost for the differential is $1300 plus some other stuff that gets the total to $1850— and we went to the local micro brewery/beer garden/cafe/gift shop for lunch. I had a "Staggering Elk" organic lager that was so good; I had to have a refill. After that and some piddling around, we went to "Star Wars—The Phantom Menace" at the local theater for $4 each and no waiting lines for the matinee—eat your heart out Kenny—I saw it before you.

Everybody in this little town is as nice as they can be and very helpful. Today, I sent some e-mail to the local library to have it printed out so I could mail hard copies off by regular mail for some stuff we needed to do—no problem. Duke is getting easier and easier to handle and is beginning to like the stakeout chain in the trailer parks. Even Pookie is getting attached to him, but still no offers to adopt!

Tomorrow we'll go south on a highway we haven't tried yet and end up in Boulder to hopefully get the Blazer back. Utah here we come!

Sent: Sunday, May 23, 1999 6:24 PM
Subject: Man Defeats Dog! —Blazer Next?

I decided I wasn't going to write again till I had at least some small victory to report. The Blazer is still winning and we're still in CO, but I finally defeated Duke! Like my first success against him, I had to use electricity, but at least I won.

Yesterday we left him in the Blazer with the windows down about 3 inches so he couldn't get out, for about 20 minutes, parked under a tree with the temperature about 70 degrees, while we were in a Wal-Mart. When we came out there was a note on the windshield telling me that dogs can't sweat, overheating can cause them to have brain damage (which might be O.K.) and I should leave the dog at home. I spent part of the rest of the day making various size swivel chain outs from coated 1/8 inch wire cable with swivels and hooks on the ends. I made 1 36 inches long, measured so we could chain him to a cabinet door in the trailer and he couldn't reach any of the windows or screens with his teeth. This campground, called Denver North, serves cooked breakfasts, so we left him on that chain while we went to breakfast today. When we came back, we could hear him whining and crying and barking from 100 yards away with the trailer closed up, the TV on and the fan on the air conditioner running. When we went in the trailer, he was still chained up, but had reached the Venetian blinds on 1 window with his front paws and had bent them all up and pulled down the curtain, attached with Velcro, also with his front paws. I decided to use the juice. Yesterday we also had fitted the electric collar and watched the video about the electric collar—we even let Duke watch it. The video said use 3 days to train the dog to wear it and another 2 days wearing it without the juice being turned on. I decided Duke was smarter than the dogs in the video and was going to enroll, learn and graduate in the same session.

I put the battery in the collar, put it on Duke, put Duke in the pet taxi, closed up the trailer with the TV and AC on and we sat outside on the picnic table to listen. The collar gives a free bark and static shock on successive barks for 30 seconds and then cuts off for 3 minutes—if the dog continues to resist, it then repeats the cycle. The first bark was normal and Pookie said, "it isn't working" and then the barks became much more anguished, more quickly repeated and we could hear the pet taxi thrashing around as Duke continued to bark for the full 30 seconds of shocks. You could tell when the juice turned off and then he barked intermittently for the next 3 minutes and Pookie kept saying it wasn't working (I had left the TV on a baseball game for noise and she also said maybe Duke didn't like baseball) and then Duke went thru cycle 2. After another 30 seconds of shocks while Pookie pleaded his case, he shut up. We walked around the trailer park twice and then visited with the people next door who had told us to leave—they had used a similar collar to train their dog—and they reported Duke hadn't barked a single time. We continued to visit with them for about 30 minutes and the AC cut off on our trailer. Duke probably then heard us outside, and went thru another cycle and then was quiet. Finally I told Pookie I was going to let him out and she said she hoped he bit me.

It was almost a carbon copy of teaching Doyle not to stand in his baby bed and scream, cry and yell when we put him to bed at nite. Back then; I made Pookie sit on the front porch of our apt. with the door shut and I took Doyle out of the bed—so he wouldn't be afraid of the bed—spanked him and then put him back. I told Pookie in advance it would take 2 spankings and not one and she was flipping thru the pages of Dr. Spock and yelling at me that she knew he was too young to spank and it was in the book somewhere. I guess Doyle is quicker to learn or maybe less stubborn than Duke since Doyle stopped his act after 2 spankings while Duke took 3 sets of shocks. Now we can leave Duke in the trailer in the pet taxi while we go places and do things if it's too hot to leave him in the Blazer, without getting kicked out of a campground for a barking dog. So far, all we've been able to use the pet taxi for is to put the groceries or doggie bags in it for us, till we get back to the trailer so Duke can't get at them in the Blazer. Of course, it might come in handy if we decide to airmail Duke home.

I'll report on the Blazer when we finally get it fixed, or I give up and buy a new tow vehicle. I've already thought about getting Bettye Jo to go in the house and get the Blazer's title and mail it to some car dealer out here. The problem is you have to break in a new tow vehicle before you tow with it and I'm ready to leave CO. I've already received comments that "You have a Ford in your Future", "sounds like the trip from Hell" and "sorry about the Blazer". So far the sympathy responses are ahead of the smart ass ones by 1 vote. That's a lot better than my score against Duke on this trip which currently is Duke 6—Evan1, although I did win one at home by bolting clear 1/8 inch Plexiglas to both sides of the screen door so he couldn't tear it up— glad I did. Maybe we can leave for Utah tomorrow.

Evan

Sent: Tuesday, May 25, 1999 11:42 AM
Subject: Blazer's Last Chance

To continue our tale of woe, we got the Blazer back last Thurs. late and drove it to Estes Park where the trailer was parked. Thurs. during the day we had driven south next to the Nat. Park on a scenic drive to view the scenery and to check out the road which I was thinking about taking to I-70 as it was shorter than back thru Denver. It climbed several times above 9,000 feet and then down again and I decided not to come that way with the trailer. It turned cold and rainy shortly after we hit the road and the ceiling descended so we couldn't see the mountains anyway. We ate lunch in Nederland and drove back to Boulder following Boulder Creek, while it snowed all over the road. The next morning we got up early to leave and ran out of propane gas when Pookie lit the stove to heat water for my hot tea. It was only about 40 degrees, but no problem, the campground sold propane and I filled both tanks (Pookie thought it was a little problem when she got in the shower in the trailer and I suggested that if the stove wouldn't work, neither would the hot water heater—we could microwave my hot water). I had filled both tanks last summer after our 1st trip southwest, but forgot to fill them after the trip to the Midwest.

Well, we hooked up and left and about noon stopped on I-70 about 40 miles west of Denver after climbing over the Front Range at about 8,000 feet. As I turned left into the service station I heard this LOUD clank, clank from under the rear end. Yep, the differential had been severely wounded again, after being completely replaced with a new gear set. I called the dealer who repaired it and he said for me to try and make it back to Boulder and if we broke down to call him on the cell phone and he'd send a tow truck to get us. We left the trailer next to an empty building next to the gas station and headed back in the Blazer. The damn thing heals itself or at least runs O.K. without the trailer and after a few clanks as we started off, did fine all 70 miles back to Boulder. They put the Blazer up on a lift and drained the differential fluid, which was boiling. It was now about 3:30 p.m. and the mechanic replaced the fluid and we went for a test drive. It ran fine and would not repeat the clanking sound of course. At 4 p.m. he decided he didn't have time to get another gear set, or even tear it down to inspect what was wrong. Since it was Fri. p.m. and they were going to close for the weekend we had a conference with the service dept. people who said they could fix it next week, but I shouldn't leave the area. I decided to go back and get the trailer and pull it to a park closer to Boulder since it was downhill most of the way anyway and we didn't want to leave it out on the interstate for 3 or 4 nites, and the Blazer seemed to be running fine. We made a reservation at Denver North Campground and headed out.

When we got back to the trailer and hooked up, the brakes were locked on the trailer and I couldn't pull it. They were even locked when I disconnected the Blazer's electricity from the trailer and I tried for an hour to get them to unlock by doing different things. Finally we called the campground and canceled our reservation and got ready to find a nearby motel. By now, I'm a little teed off and wonder what else can go wrong—and then discover Duke has broken out from the Blazer while we're fooling with the trailer and is gone. I start out calling for him and he shows up at full speed from somewhere within hearing range and leaps into my arms with a lot of licks. I put him back in the Blazer and walk around the trailer 1 more time before we leave—this is a routine whenever I move it or leave it and you'd be amazed at the things you can discover by walking and looking to see if everything is O.K. before you drive off. I notice the breakaway cable, which is set to turn on the electric brakes using power from the trailer battery if the trailer breaks loose from the Blazer, is hanging loosely from the frame of the trailer. Yep, someone has pulled it out while we were gone and after putting it back in, the brakes release. We call the campground again and get to it at dark. Good thing I already drink as I would whether I did or not by the time we get unhooked, and I enjoyed the hell out of the booze that nite. I did crawl up under the Blazer and put my finger on the differential and it's hot, but not as hot as the tailpipe and I can hold my finger on it for about 5 seconds vs. 1 second for the tailpipe. I also notice the tailpipe has several holes in it and needs replacing. Of course, it is made in 1 piece with the muffler, so it'll have to be replaced too. Back to the bottle.

Sat. we piddle around in Boulder and walk along Boulder Creek thru the campus of the University of CO, which Duke really enjoys. I've never seen so many bicyclists, which are all over CO. The football stadium is like the 1 at LSU with dorm rooms or classrooms all underneath it. Sat nite there is a tornado warning and the wind is blowing like crazy in the campground and the TV says cars are hiding under the overpasses to avoid the 1 1/2 inch hail that is falling. It's raining hard in the campground and I figure we'll miss the hail since I don't have the rental car anymore to get ruined and our luck has to change soon. No hail, but it rains hard all nite. Sun. we don't do much except make the obligatory trip by Pookie to the grocery store and Wal-Mart.

Mon. I get up bright and early and am the 1st one in line at the dealer's service dept., 15 miles from the campground at 7:30 a.m. Naturally, my technician/mechanic doesn't arrive till 9 a.m. At 11, I get the dealership to take me about 3 miles away and drop me off a block away from the local Dodge dealer since I already know I want a 2-wheel drive Dodge Durango with a towing package, 3rd seat to hold 7 passengers and the small V-8. I've already priced it on the web and know as much about it as the salespeople. Discover that nobody in CO orders or stocks the 2-wheel drive as everybody out here wants 4-wheel for the snow. The 2-wheel will tow more and gets a lot better mileage so I walk back to the dealership and get there about 5 seconds ahead of the rain—a good sign—I could have been soaked. At noon the mechanic has torn down the differential and yep, it needs another gear set as some bearings are scorched by heat and already worn too much. You have to set some torque on a differential to keep it together and I'm suspicious that he set too much and made it overheat, but he denies this. We do notice a hole in the tailpipe facing the differential and maybe the hot exhaust is helping heat it up. Newest plan is to replace the gear set again, replace tailpipe and muffler and drive it 200 miles before towing to get it broken in. Parts won't arrive till 3:30, so I rent another car and go back to the campground. Tues. I'm to pick it up early afternoon and drive 200 miles and Wed. am we try again to leave. If the damn thing breaks again, I'm buying whatever I can find that will tow the trailer.

Evan

Sent: Thursday, May 27, 1999 8:34 PM
Subject: Blazer Sacrificed—Literally!

Well, I didn't leave ALL my money in Colorado, just the part my kids were going to inherit. Sorry boys. Pookie really likes my new wheels, a 99 Dodge Durango, bright red with all the gizmos and stuff. It has 4 wheel drive, which I didn't want, the big V-8, which I didn't think I wanted and the 3rd seat that folds down like the 2nd seat, which I did want. It also was a demo and had 5900 miles on it which I craved, but told the dealer I didn't want as a negotiating tool—already broken in and could tow immediately. I had them backed into a corner and told Pookie I was getting it for $2000 less than I expected to pay till they drove the Blazer and came back and said, "it doesn't have 4-wheel drive"! I said yep, and I really don't want it on the Durango. They said they had to raise the difference we agreed on by $4,000 since nobody in CO would buy an SUV without 4-wheel drive with all the snow and they'd have to wholesale it. They made some calls at my request and couldn't get a local Chevy dealer to take it. I know when to surrender and gave up, but got them to switch all the towing gear and electric brake controllers at no charge. Betty Jo mailed the Blazer title to them and faxed a copy and we drove off. They wanted me to leave a signed check in case the title didn't show up, but I told them that was a deal killer and they backed off.

Pookie was playing the CD player and telling me how much she liked it and she would have to write Dot a postcard and tell her we now had a "movie car" that would take 7 women shopping and to the movies. Actually, it will take 8 if 1 in the 3rd seat doesn't have a seat belt and the 3 in the back aren't as big as Kenny and can fit into a small space. I said something about the fact that Pookie wouldn't let me use her car very often, and why should she get to use mine? She replied sweetly that I could use her car whenever I wanted, but Duke couldn't ride in her car.

Durango also has an extra air conditioner unit in the top of the roof for the rear seat passengers to control—or maybe it's for Duke. The tow rating is 7400 pounds vs. 6000 for the Blazer, but climbing over the Rockies today I discovered that it really doesn't climb up the 4 mile 9% grades much better than the Blazer, but it does have a lot more spare capacity at less steep grades and rides a lot better. Duke and Pookie are satisfied.

We're now in Moab, Utah about 5 miles from the entrance to Arches Nat. Park and 25 from the entrance to Canyonlands Nat Park. I grew up on the King James version and don't remember anything about Moab, but I'm terrified that he's a big deal in The Book of Mormon. With my luck, he's a close relative of Job and I'm gonna get more bad news—but maybe not.

The clincher on the Blazer was after I put 200 miles on it and the differential was still too hot to hold your hand on and the tech called Detroit and then told me the new gear set would have to be broken in for 500 miles and 1,000 for towing. I decided to trade it and never looked back, till last nite when I was reading the maintenance schedule on the new SUV and saw the part that said, "Always remember that when changing the lubricant in a limited slip differential, you must add anti-friction additive". Naaaaahh, I don't really want to know! Water under the bridge.

We haven't been here since 1976 when we took the boys to Yellowstone and did Arches Nat Park on the way home. I had forgotten how pretty the drive is and especially the part thru Glenwood Canyon along the path and side of the Colorado River. I-70 actually goes right beside the river and in a lot of places; the east and westbound lanes are on top of each other like in a cramped city because of the limited space. They now have a paved walking path next to the river and we stopped in a rest area and walked Duke along the river. About 5 or 6 tunnels and you cross the river 3 or 4 times. The headwaters of the river are actually in Rocky Mt. Nat Park and you can step over it if the alpine drive is open. I remember breaking the leaf spring on the poptop camper in Arches and towing it at 15-20 miles an hour on gravel roads and 40-45 on I-70 into Grand Junction, CO to repair. That's when I discovered that they didn't sell my brand of poptop west of the Rockies and I couldn't get a spare part. I found a snowmobile dealer in Grand Junction with a welding shop and he took off the good spring and made me a new one with it as a pattern. Funny how things repeat. Back then I had the most expensive spring in America and now I have the most expensive tow vehicle I could find when you include the Blazer's sacrifice. We spent the whole day in the Colorado Nat. Monument while the guy fixed the poptop, so we rode thru today without stopping.

I heard on the news this a.m. that some crazy in Wisconsin tried to kill 2 boys with his car. That makes 2 in the last few weeks as some nut in CA tried to kill a few children on a playground with his car a few weeks ago. It's obvious to me that the democrats in Congress need to try and ban the use of cars. Alternative measures could be to encourage civil litigation against the manufacturers of cars or at least to pillory the NADA, the dealer's association. Maybe we need background checks at auto shows or used car dealers. Snake Henry, I think you should draft some legislation for your fellow liberal democrats and e-mail it to Washington. I would suggest that you start with Al Gore—he needs a good campaign issue.

Only 10 days late, we start our tour of some additional parks tomorrow.
Evan

Sent: Sunday, May 30, 1999 6:28 PM
Subject: Durango Loses Virginity—Duke Loses Freedom

Well, we slept late Fri. (Duke now lets us sleep till 8 a.m.) and piddled around in the campground till almost noon. We're 200 yards from the Colorado River and it's very high from all the snowmelt this year. Cataract Canyon, the stretch after the Green River joins it, is considered a Class V or whatever is the toughest whitewater in the world and equal to the Grand Canyon rapids, but I can't believe it's that good this year. Seems like the rapids would be flooded or at least have a lot of boulders under water. Decided to skip trying to get a raft trip as this place is packed solid with Memorial Day campers and not a single motel room available. We got the last spot in this RV park and it's the only one with cable TV. I never saw this many Germans in Germany. A group of 23 rented motorhomes, all

Germans, pulled out of this Park Fri. early and we had to move to one of their vacated spots to stay the weekend. We've met Germans everywhere we've been and all are very friendly. Most couples have a least 1 spouse who is fluent in English, but we did meet a young couple in Denver who could read English, but only speak it very broken. They were standing outside the restrooms and bathhouse trying to figure out how to get in. I said number and pointed to the coded lock and showed them how to work it while the female kept her legs crossed and hopped around.

We did Arches Nat. Park Fri. p.m. with Duke in the Durango. Left it running and the AC on for 30 minutes while we did the video in the Visitor Center and looked at the exhibits and it was hot when we returned. Decided not to do that again when the heat is above 80 and no breeze to cool it down. Arches is one of those Parks that can be seen almost entirely from your vehicle—like Glacier Bay in Alaska is seen from the deck of a cruise ship. Other Parks like Mammoth Cave or Carlsbad Cavern can't be seen fully unless you walk a few miles. Since we were here before, they have added some roads and now you only have to walk 100 yards to get a view of Delicate Arch while on our previous trip it was a pretty good hike. It's pretty, but was packed with tour coaches as well as cars. Good thing its car friendly, as Duke is not allowed on any of the trails and can only be walked in the parking areas. Arches is a small Park and only took a few hours to drive around. Decided to board Duke for a few days and went into Moab to find a kennel. Found one that would take him for Sat. and Sun. and made arrangements to drop him off Sat. a.m. The lady vet was cute and gave me a whole sheet of paper to fill out on Duke and us.

Sat we got up early and dropped Duke off. The lady vet asked if I had done my paperwork and I said my supervisor had completed it. She said she used to be a supervisor herself and told me about doing the paperwork on her ex to check him in the hospital once. Said the Dr. asked her husband if his wife had done the paperwork and he responded with how did you know? Said the Dr. replied that the paperwork said he was female. I said that Duke was a neutered male like me and she laughed. She gave me a phone # to call when we wanted to pick Duke up and I couldn't read the #s and told her she wasn't a real Doc and should be able to write better than that. She said she was studying to be a real Dr.

We drove to the southern entrance to Canyonlands Nat Park, called The Needles, which is 65 miles from Moab and well off the beaten track. You enter thru a state park along a stream and at first I thought it resembled Palo Duro Canyon in TX, but it soon became apparent that you could put 10 Palo Duro Canyons in it and have a lot of room left. We stopped at Newspaper Rock, a state monument and looked at the Petroglyphs that have been there since B.C. The NP is a lot like The Grand Canyon and absolutely gorgeous with magnificent views and a lot of variety. Overlooks abound and there are a lot of short hikes to other overlooks and attractions. After the visitor center and orientation, we went on a 7-mile, 4-wheel drive only, track to an overlook over the Colorado River that the ranger recommended. He said the last mile was a little rough. Hell, the last mile and more could have been a commercial for Dodge if we'd had the camcorder. Pookie became a little mutinous and a good bit verbal. "You're going to tear it up! "Honey, I didn't buy it to park in the garage and look at it", "Well, why destroy it in 3 days! Let's go back!"

After my companion for life began to offer constructive criticisms, I decided that silence was appropriate since there are certain times when whatever you say can and will be used against you. Finally we came to a series of mini-cliffs that you have to drive off of, or climb over. I would get out to see what seemed to be the least bad decision and walk ahead a few yards to make a good guess. Other comments include, "If you go down that, the front bumper will hit the ground and the airbags will go off!" "Have you ever driven a 4-wheel before?" "Our wheelbase is too long and we're going to get hung up on a cliff!" "We're not a little jeep—are we a high clearance vehicle?" and my personal favorite, "I'm sure glad we brought a picnic lunch so we can eat when we get there and then barf on the way back!" Finally, we reached the overlook and the view was terrific. There were no other views that actually included the water in the river, as the canyons are very deep. There were 3 young girls on mountain bikes there and nobody else. While we were eating, a convoy of 3 jeeps and a 4-wheel drive pickup with the big tires drove up. They had stopped at the worst part and yelled at me to ask how bad it looked. I had yelled back that it was bad and I think they waited to see if we came back before attempting the last mile. This is big jeep rental country and they're all over the place and now I know why. Pookie now reverts to the tour guide and is telling them that the river is over here and over there is just a dry canyon and of course the Durango could make it.

The trip back was a lot quicker as I now knew the way better and we only scraped the skid plates a few times. Spent the rest of the day in the Park and did a few trails. We got caught a few hundred yards from the Durango when a thunderstorm blew up and Pookie was ahead of me running to the Durango. When she got there she screamed and didn't get in right away and I asked why. She pointed at the ground by her side of the Durango and there was a beautiful gopher snake about 5 feet long slithering away. She jumped in and we drove home in the rain. Do you know anyone else who could bring rain to the desert?

Today, we went back to Canyonlands thru the northern entrance about 35 miles north of Moab. This part is called Island in the Sky as it's on a 6000 foot high mesa eroded down to the rivers on all sides and joined to the rest of the plateau by only a 40 foot part called the neck. The access road crosses the neck, which is eroding away too and someday it'll be a real island. More gorgeous views and a lot of short trails. We've been to 21 Parks and I would put this one in the top 5. I haven't been to Yosemite and Glacier/Waterton yet, but I would put this one up there after Yellowstone, Grand Canyon, Teton and Big Bend. Canyonlands is a big Park where the Green and Colorado Rivers meet and has been carved by both rivers. Saw the Green River from an overlook and it's not nearly as full of silt as the Colorado, but carries almost as much water.

Went back to Moab about 3 p.m. and went to the local arts and crafts festival—read hippie flea market for my description—and then picked up Duke who was delighted to see us. Tomorrow we leave here for Capitol Reef Nat. Park., which isn't too far away. Pookie told me I needed a haircut the other day and I agreed, but told her the 10-day Blazer delay had screwed up my plan about a haircut. She asked what had been my plan and I told her I had it cut before we left and had planned on getting it cut again when we got to Las Vegas. The plan was to find a single-mom showgirl working a second job in a hair salon. Pookie laughed for 5 minutes and said to put that in the next e-mail. Evan

Sent: Tuesday, June 01, 1999 7:38 PM
Subject: Torrey, Utah

We drove here from Moab on Mon. and got here about 1 p.m. It's uphill the last 50 miles and into a hard headwind. We actually drove thru Capitol Reef Nat. Park and are in a campground about 10 miles west of the Park. We were both tired and took a nap and read after we unhooked the trailer. I actually finished a book I started on the airplane flying back from Germany on April 30. The wind was blowing so hard and steady that we didn't feel like getting out and it got cold early in the afternoon with little sun. I took Duke for his last walk of the day about 9:15 p.m. and it was bitterly cold with the wind still at 40 mph. Of course, he jumped a rabbit and yanked the leash out of my hands as I didn't see the rabbit till he hit the end of the leash at 25mph. Good thing the rabbit didn't run in a straight line and the leash got caught on brush as I'm too old to be running thru the sagebrush at nite. I came back bleeding from the thorns, but Duke wasn't scratched.

Got up this morning and it was 39 degrees but no wind. I started out with long pants, which guaranteed that it would get hot later in the day and by 9 a.m. it was warm enough to change to my uniform of sandals and shorts. We put the shock collar on Duke and put him in the pet taxi and left the AC on and the fan on the AC blowing to drown out noise from outside. This dog knows after 1 session not to make a peep when the shock collar is on and we cranked up and rode around the campground and stopped by our trailer and still no noise from Duke, so we left him for the day.

Capitol Reef is neither a capitol nor a reef. It's an upward fold of sedimentary rock that has been eroded by nature to it's present shape and is about 100 miles long from northwest to southeast, but only about 12 miles wide. Capitol comes from domes of petrified sand dunes that look like domes over state or national capitol buildings and reef comes from the early pioneers who were often mariners and called anything that blocked their passage a reef. It was a formidable barrier to early travelers and wasn't settled till the late 1800's and then by Mormons. It's called a Waterpocket Fold because the rocks often contain holes or pockets that hold water for months after a thunderstorm. Most of it is red rock, but there are different layers of sedimentary deposits in colors from yellow to green and gray.

We did the Visitor Center and the video giving the geological and historic background and then took the scenic drives and some short trails to overlooks and then took a 3 mile roundtrip hike up a dry wash to Pioneer Rock, which has names carved in the rock with dates by the early settlers which range from 1871 to the early 1900's. Ate another picnic lunch and the wind picked up in the canyon to the point that it blew the pickles off my ham sandwich while I was making it. Then we rode some more to view Petroglyphs and then to another trailhead to Hickman Bridge, a natural bridge. The trail guide said 2 miles roundtrip to the natural bridge and a moderate hike. If that's moderate, we aren't ever going to take a strenuous hike. We climbed and descended about 700 feet during the roundtrip and my traveling companion wasn't too pleased. It was now about 85 degrees and the footing varied from sand to rock to loose rock. When we finally got to the natural bridge, my first thought was that there is no difference between a natural bridge and an arch and we've already seen a bunch of arches that are a lot prettier. On the way back I told Pookie, who was puffing and groaning, that it was good practice for her walking Duke when we got back to the trailer. Her answer is universally understood by the initials BS! She also made some comment to the effect that my next wife would make me carry my own water bottle. We rode some more and then did a short 2/3-mile hike roundtrip to Sunset Point for some pictures, even though it was only 4 p.m. The ultimatum then came in the form of a very quiet wish to go see Duke—the kind you don't dare ignore. I guess we walked about 6 1/2 miles today and climbed maybe 900 feet in the process. Capitol Reef is pretty, but doesn't need to be on your must see list. Tomorrow it's on to Bryce Canyon Nat. Park, which again is fairly close by.

Miscellaneous comments:

1. Pookie says she is going to report me to The Good Sam Club if I don't start picking up the Duke poop in the pet walk areas of these campgrounds. She's going to think we have a very constipated dog when I start lying and tell her he didn't poop. You'd think that after 35 years of marriage, she'd give up on

reforming me. Somewhere along the way I must have given her reason for hope, but for the life of me I don't remember it.

2. Duke doesn't act any differently, but I wonder if the Mormons tried to convert him when he was in that kennel. They try everybody else.

3. I wonder if all these young kids on bikes are training to be Mormon Missionaries and that's why they ride bicycles.

4. Canyonlands had a 100-mile 4-wheel drive loop trail called The White Rim Road that takes 2 to 4 days to drive. When I mentioned it to Pookie, she said Duke and I could go, but leave her in Moab near the gift shops. I figured I couldn't afford it.

5. I left out one of Pookie's best remarks while we were doing the 4-wheel drive rough part in Canyonlands. Between clenched teeth while bouncing around in her seat and holding on for dear life she said with a glare, "You're enjoying this, aren't you?". No way to answer that and not get in trouble. Sort of like the question, "When did you stop beating your wife?" that all the law schools use as an example of an unanswerable question.

6. On the showgirl part, I've refined my idea some. I need some investors to back me with their money, but we could make a trade name license agreement and set up franchises all over the country called Hooter's Haircuts using well endowed gals and skimpy costumes. Hell, we'd have bald guys coming in 2 or 3 times a week. I should retain 50% for the idea and we would need to maintain tight quality control, so I would do the interviewing for all the girls at all the franchises, but are any of you interested in putting up the money? David J. once told me I needed to come up with an idea for us to jointly make some money. Here it is David!

I should report that I took Pookie to dinner in a very nice restaurant in Moab our last nite there. She had salmon and I had halibut, so I'm not all bad. Evan

Sent: Saturday, June 05, 1999 5:44 PM
Subject: Duke's Revenge

We continue to make the weather uncomfortable for the locals. We left Capitol Reef early on Wed. and drove thru the Dixie Nat. Forest and Grand Staircase-Escalante Nat. Monument to Bryce Canyon. It's a secondary road and climbs to 9100 feet in the forest. At about 8000 feet we entered the fog or clouds and visibility dropped from 1/2 mile to maybe 40 yards in a short distance. Then it began to sleet and the Durango was reading 37 degrees. By now I'm going about 20mph as it's difficult to see the road and it constantly twists and turns with occasional steep cliffs on one side or the other. The sleet begins to pile up in the road and Duke is afraid to look out. The outside mirrors fog up and then we discover we have mirror defrosters that actually work. The trip computer says I'm getting 2 miles per gallon on the steep upgrades and 46 miles per gallon coasting downhill. We finally crest the mountain and as we descend the visibility improves and the sleet turns to rain and then to a carwash rain. We ate lunch at a local restaurant in the town of Escalante and overhear the locals saying the weathermen are always wrong and the 3 days of rain in the forecast will probably only be 1 day—they don't know us. The road thru the monument has 14% grades on a hogback with sheer drops on each side and Pookie won't look out now. The views would be spectacular if it weren't raining and I could look at anything besides the road. German tourists are stopping at the overlooks and getting out in ponchos to look at the mountains in the rain and mist.

We stay in a campground 1 mile from the entrance to Bryce Canyon Nat. Park and it stops raining long enough for me to unhook the trailer and then resumes with a cold wind. It's a really nice campground and we're at 8000 feet and at least 80% of the people speak German. The campground general store has a bulletin board that offers to exchange marks for dollars at 48 cents for a mark. I look in USA Today and the exchange rate that day is 53 cents for a mark. It warms my heart, as a retired moneychanger, to see my Mormon brethren following the golden rule—he who has the gold makes the rules. Do unto them what they did to me in Germany! There is even a group of 6 Germans on motorcycles—I guess they are rented. I'm reminded of our trip to Paris in 75 when at least 80% of the tourists were Japanese, but you don't see many of them anymore.

The next morning the high for the day is predicted to be 50 degrees so I decide to take Duke with us and put the shock collar on him in the Durango if he whines and cries when we leave him to walk on the trails. The sun comes out about 9 a.m. and it turns out to be an absolutely gorgeous day, though cool and windy. We go to Bryce Point for the first overlook and the view is magnificent. Lots of hoodoos or vertical spires of eroded rock. Duke whines like crazy so I go back to the Durango and put the shock collar on him and we walk away. When we're out of sight, he starts really tuning up and then when the shocks start, he shifts to overdrive. Pookie says she's not going back to the Durango and be accused of torturing the dog and I can pick her up down the road. We stay out on the overlook and after the 30 seconds of shocks, Duke shuts up. We wait till we think everybody in the parking lot when we left are gone and then go back. Duke hasn't made anymore sound and I remove the shock collar. At the next overlook, I walk him in the parking lot and then put the shock collar back on and we leave and scene 1 is repeated. He must have associated the shock collar with the pet taxi rather than the collar, but after 2 series of shocks, he shuts up again and doesn't do any more whining and barking when we leave him after that. We visit several more overlooks and are impressed with the views and shapes and colors, although the colors aren't as varied as Capitol Reef or Canyonlands. I offer to do lunch at the Lodge and Pookie quickly accepts. We leave Duke with the shock collar on and not a peep. Very nice lunch.

After lunch I tell Pookie I'll walk Duke on the Lodge grounds before we resume sightseeing. I jump in the driver's seat and take off the shock collar and put on his regular collar and leash and jump out with him and start out in front of the Durango. Pookie yells at me to wait and I turn around. She's laughing and says for me not to reach for my wallet as Duke has pooped in my seat in the Durango and I sat in it and it's on the seat of my pants. I think she said something about me shocking the s—t out of Duke. I failed to see as much humor in the situation as she did. We clean up the Durango and go back to the trailer and I change pants and put Duke back in the pet taxi and leave him with the shock collar on. He's gonna regret this—no more Nat. Parks for him, even if it is cool enough to leave him in the Durango. I'm convinced he did it on purpose as he hates to be left alone and gets mad and then tries to get even. He pulls that kind of stunt at home too and although he's never pooped to get even, he does tear up stuff if you leave him too long alone.

We finish touring all over Bryce Canyon and take the walk between Sunrise and Sunset Points alongside the amphitheater, which is what they call the main canyon. We think the overlooks on the scenic drive and at Fairyland Point are superior to the amphitheater. Bryce Canyon has 1 million visitors a year and it is different from the other parks we've seen and is 9100 feet at the south end. It has bristlecone pines, the longest living thing on earth. One was cut down here in 1964 that was over 5000 years old. From the south end you can see the plateau that has the Grand Canyon and the visibility is 200 miles on a clear day, but only about 110 when we were there.

The next morning I'm walking Duke about 300 yards from our campsite when an ambulance pulls in with its lights flashing, but no siren. I follow it to where it stops and join a small crowd that's standing around. It's cold, about 40 degrees and windy with no sun and the talk is subdued. It seems that a guy in a big motorhome has altitude sickness and can't breathe, but didn't have a heart attack as his wife thought. The paramedics give him some oxygen and tell him he shouldn't be at this altitude as he has had several heart attacks in the past. The forecast is for snow above 7000 feet today, so we leave for Zion Nat. Park, which is at about 4000 feet.

We don't get 4 miles from the campground when it starts to snow as thick as I've ever seen it, but doesn't stick as the temp is up to 42 now. It snows for an hour before we get down low enough for it to stop and then turns to driving rain again. We drive in the east entrance to Zion NP and go through the park to right beyond the south entrance where we get a campground for 2 nites. The road drops 2000 feet inside the park in a series of switchbacks and sharp turns and goes thru a 1 mile long, unlighted tunnel built in 1930. I have to pay $10 and get them to turn the tunnel into a 1-way highway for me alone and drive in the middle of the road as the trailer exceeds the width and length limitations of the tunnel and the height limitations if I drive on the right side only. Makes you very popular with the people driving cars. The trailer brakes are soaked and grab and screech as we try to slow down in the tunnel which is downhill too, with a rough surface and idling in 1st gear won't slow the trailer down enough. I don't check my blood pressure when we get to the campground, and it again stops raining long enough for me to unhook the trailer and hook up the sewer, cable, electricity and water. After an hour, the rain lets up a little and Pookie tries to take Duke for a walk. It starts again and now we have a wet dog with us too. Duke and I watch an old John Wayne movie on the AMC channel while Pookie takes a nap. The furnace runs constantly and the local newspaper headlines say that the weather record for coldness in the month of June has been broken and it hasn't been this cold since they started recording the weather 65 years ago. Right.

Today we did Zion and the Visitor Center says the normal high for June is 93 degrees. We did reach 62 as the sun came out after lunch for a few hours. We left Duke in the trailer and walked the Narrows along the side of the Virgin River, which carved Zion Canyon over the last 14 million years. We also went back to the east entrance and through the tunnel 2 more times. Definitely easier without the trailer. Zion has 3 million visitors a year and is different too, with sheer canyon walls, weeping rock where water seeps out high on the cliff sides and a lot of hanging gardens, or plant life high on the rock where there is water available. There are 10 Nat. Parks on the Colorado Plateau, more than any other section of the country except east of the Miss. River where there are 11, and we've now done 9. I've decided to go to the 10th, Great Basin in east central Nevada and then come back to Vegas so when we do the Northwest next year we can come home on I-80 instead of I-70. Besides, I'm getting tired of Colorado Plateau parks and want to finish the group. Refilled 1 of the propane tanks today so we're ready for more cold weather, but I can't wait to see if we can make it turn wet and cold at Death Valley. Evan

Sent: Tuesday, June 08, 1999 9:25 PM
Subject: Viva Las Vegas

Did you know Las Vegas means "the meadows"? That's where we are now, but 1st, how we got here. We drove from Zion to Great Basin Nat. Park and gained an hour as we are now on Pacific time (except for Duke, who doesn't wear a watch, or give a damn). There are no commercial campgrounds within 60 miles of the Park, so we "dry camped" in the park campgrounds with no hookups, within 15 feet of a mountain stream that sounded great all night long. We haven't dry camped since the poptop, but it sure is nicer in the trailer. Everything works off of propane or the trailer battery except for the microwave oven and the AC. Since we have fresh, gray and black water tanks and an electric water pump, you can even take a shower in the trailer and of course we have running water for the commode. The fridge converts to propane too so there's ice for whiskey. I finally today found Ushers Green Stripe in Vegas and can quit drinking that really cheap stuff like Thoeny buys such as Crawford's or Scoresby. We got here in time to sign up for a ranger-guided tour of Lehman Cave. It's a small cave compared to Carlsbad, but chock full of formations in a small space and lighted with trails of concrete and steps and handrails. I think it is more impressive than Carlsbad. Ranger Stuart was a young man in his 20's who loves his job and gave a terrific tour. He told a story about being forced to go to Acadia Nat. Park in Maine every year for his family vacation and hating the 10 hour car ride with his sisters while all his friends got to go to Disney or somewhere like that on vacation, but when he grew up he decided to be a park ranger because he enjoyed the outdoors experience so much.

After dinner, we went to a ranger talk in the campground by Ranger Darryl (nope, I didn't ask about his other brother Darryl) on fire in the forest and it's beneficial effects. It was pretty good, till the inevitable rain started, but we were prepared and stayed till he finished. Duke went with us to the fire talk and behaved even though another dog was there too. Pookie and Duke had walked up on 2 mule deer in the campground earlier and he enjoyed that. It only got down to 45 that nite, but our trusty little furnace kept us warm. I talked Pookie out of running the TV on the battery to be sure we didn't run it down—we were so far in the sticks that I'm sure there was no reception on the antenna anyway even though we were camped at 7200 feet. Great Basin is a new park created in 86 and very limited in facilities. The alpine drive to Wheeler Peak at 11,000 feet had been opened on Memorial Day, but they had 22 inches of snow since Memorial Day and it was now closed at 9500 feet. Wheeler Peak is 13,000 feet and was named Jeff Davis Peak till the War of Northern Aggression when they renamed it. We drove up it the next morning and the view was spectacular. Great Basin is named for the 1/12th of the lower US it occupies which includes all of Nevada except the southern tip, most of Utah and parts of CA, WY, OR, NM and AZ. No precipitation that falls in the Great Basin ever ends up in any ocean as there is no outlet to the sea and not enough rain or snow to create one. I learned that the bristlecone pine which lives so long as a gnarled and deformed small tree on the exposed slopes of high mountains above the normal tree line in rocks and very shallow soil is the exact same species which only lives 2 to 300 years in the upper spruce forest and grows to 40 or 50 feet in the spruce forest lower down. What does that say about facing adversity to be long lived?

This Park only has 90,000 visitors a year and there are no services nearby. We had to detour leaving to get some gas and went east instead of west to fill up and then backtracked. The trip back south to Vegas was one of the most scenic yet for the first 100 miles as you are in a series of valleys between snow-covered peaks. It finally got hot and the temp was 96 as we entered Vegas. We're now on Leaping Lizard Lane in a nice campground with shuttle service to the casinos.

This morning Duke got up at 6 and sealed his fate. Nobody should feel as good as he does when they get up in the morning. It's disgusting to be so happy at the dawn of a new day and so full of energy and playfulness. He's now in a kennel till Thurs. a.m. Pookie signed him up for an extra 1/2 hour of personal playtime with the kennel staff plus 2 walks per day. When I asked what the kennel cost she said, "I didn't ask, does it matter"? Translation— whatever it costs, you're going to pay it willingly and gladly—I need the R & R. I did take her to a hair salon and went in with her. No showgirls in sight, so I left. Filled up the Durango and took it to Jiffy Lube for an oil and filter change and then went to get my haircut. It was like Delilah cutting Sampson's hair. She rubbed all over me, stuck a big one in each ear and got a big tip. I was so weak afterwards that I needed a Guinness for strength.

Actually, I did have a female barber at the barbershop that advertised in the campground newsletter, but no showgirl. I did get a discount price from the ad in the campground letter and hey, money is important too. Besides, I never heard from any of you who wanted to invest in my haircutting chain, so do your own research.

Took Pookie to see "Notting Hill" this afternoon. Trouble is the movie was in a casino and we got there an hour early. Pookie won $35 and I lost $40 on the slots waiting for the movie to start. We usually avoid the middleman when transferring money from me to Pookie, although there is often that much leakage in the transfer. The movie is really cute and especially the dialogue. The script is as entertaining as a Neil Simon play and the characters are hilarious.

Feedback Time—I'm not hearing much response. Where are all the bible scholars to tell me that Moab is a place and not a person? Why didn't I get a rise out of Snake Henry about his liberal- democrat, simpleminded friends? Linda writes often, Dudley wished me luck with the showgirl, Tenhula said pick up the poop (and Pookie now thinks it's cute to call Duke my "poopy dog"), the Seichkos write often, Arlin sends jokes, but not a lot from the rest of you. What's going on? Evan

Sent: Friday, June 11, 1999 5:21 PM
Subject: Death Valley Days

Yep, we're here in Ronnie Reagan country. Not many democrats here except for the 20 mule team mules and they're sterile, so they can't reproduce like other democrats. Of course, it's really 18 mules to a mule train pulling the borax wagons as they need 2 Republican horses at the front to show them where to go and when to stop and start. Some things never change.

On our 2nd day in Vegas, we slept late and then went downtown and got tickets to the musical "Chicago" for Wed. nite. It was playing in a 1700 seat theater at the Mandalay Bay Casino which is one of the huge new resort casinos with 3300 rooms, acres of gambling machines plus a full arena for sporting events, etc. Got the 7 p.m. show so I could stay awake to enjoy it. We had tried to get tickets to "Chicago" last Dec. in New York, but it was sold out. Funny how we couldn't get in "Lion King", "Beauty and the Beast" or "Chicago" which are all more traditional Broadway fare, but could get tickets to "Ragtime" and "Rent", the "cutting edge" stuff which had plenty of tickets available and turned out to be awful and boring and loud. Our last trip to Vegas was in 80 and then we stayed at Caesar's Palace in a small suite with a mirror on the ceiling over the bed. I'm trying to remember why the mirror was there.

We drove down to Boulder to see Hoover Dam. If you're in Vegas and have a 1/2-day available, take this tour as it's well worth your time and fascinating. We ate lunch in Boulder at Bob's Family Restaurant which advertised "best food by a dam site", but wasn't. It took an hour to drive 5 miles from Boulder to the dam as traffic is horrible, but the ride back is very quick. Lots of tour buses from Vegas and other places. They get 1.2 million visitors every year and I think they were all there that day. It's a first class tour and starts with a 36 minute set of 3 films in a revolving theater where the seats turn in a circle at the end of each movie to the next screen and show films about water, the history of the region and the construction of the dam. Then you get a tour guide and go down 550 feet in an elevator to the powerhouse, walk along the bottom of the dam and cross into AZ inside the dam. The penstock pipes, which feed water to the turbines, could hold 2 Greyhound buses side by side. The facts about construction are mind boggling like 4 million cubic yards of concrete, 96 men killed during construction and a dam 720 feet tall. Remember this was built in the early

30's and done with pencils and paper and slide rules—not computers. Average wage was $4 per day and 10,000 men working 3 shifts for 4 1/2 years. A team of experts was called in a few years ago to estimate the useful life of the dam. They concluded that it was 80% overbuilt and should last 1800 years. The whole thing was financed by bonds and paid off early from power sales. Not a typical government job. After the tour, there are interactive exhibits, movies, etc. to take up more time if you're interested. Herbert Hoover was Sec. of Commerce when it was authorized and came up with the compromise between the 7 states claiming the water and power that permitted it to be built politically, and it was named for Hoover. FDR's Sec. of Commerce, Harry Ickes (yes, the grandfather of Harold Ickes, Clinton's onetime chief of staff) detested Hoover and kept calling it Boulder Dam which became the popular name until an act of congress was passed in 1947 officially restoring the correct name. Those slimy democrats will stoop to any level.

"Chicago" starred Ben Vereen and Chita Rivera and was quite good. Chita debuted in "West Side Story" in 1957, so she's getting a little long in the tooth, but she sure was peppy in the performance. A black girl named Stephanie Pope played the part of Velma and stole the show. I bet we hear more about her later. After the show we ate the buffet dinner, which is like Opryland Sunday brunch and includes anything you can think of for $14 per head.

Drove to Death Valley Thurs. am and got in about 1 p.m. as it's not too far from Vegas. It's beautiful in a surreal kind of way. Got an RV spot with full hookups and the AC hasn't cut off since. Had to leave Duke in the trailer yesterday and today in the pet taxi with AC going, but he really doesn't seem to mind too much—anything to avoid the kennel and being left in a strange place. High temp we read in the Durango has been 109, but it's totally dry—10% max humidity—and I guaran-damn-tee (that's a Mississippi word) that it's not as hot as the Mississippi Delta in July and August. The view from Dante's View is worth the trip. It's at 5400 feet and the temp drops 5 1/2 degrees for each 1,000 feet above the desert floor. Saltpans in the valley and sand dunes, volcano craters, weird rock formations, a spot called "artist's palette" with multicolored rocks and Scotty's Castle. A Chicago millionaire couple built the castle and Scotty was a con man, gold prospector, wild west cowboy in Buffalo Bill's Rodeo and storyteller whom the millionaire became best friends with. The tour of the castle was by a ranger lady who wears 1930s dress and talks as if it is 1939 throughout the tour. She was superb and fooled some of the people on our tour who couldn't catch on. Scotty used to tell everyone that it was his castle and hence the name. He actually sold a bunch of investors interests in non-existent gold mines and was a card. Albert Johnson, the millionaire, understood the whole thing and was 100% opposite of Scotty, but put up with him for laughs and entertainment and didn't mind being taken by Scotty.

When the tour guide asked for questions I asked if this was the original site of that famous expression. She said what expression and I replied, "Beam me up, Scotty". Everyone else laughed, but she just got a quizzical look on her face and said she had never heard of that expression—she was very good at staying in character for the period piece stuff.

The lady vet in Vegas said Duke might have a very slight heart murmur. Said it was high on the left chest and she couldn't hear it all the time, so maybe not. Pookie said maybe the shock collar got him—anything to try and make me feel guilty, but it rarely works. When we parked here, there was a coyote 50 yards away sizing Duke up for dinner. The coyote won't leave and isn't at all afraid of me, so we don't leave Duke out on his stakeout cable. When I walk Duke, the coyote stays about 75 yards away, just out of rock throwing range, which just makes Duke go crazy. If the leash breaks, Duke is gonna be history.

Off to Yosemite tomorrow. This is our 27th Park and there are 54. Pookie wants to know when we're going to the one in American Samoa, 2300 miles from Hawaii. I guess we'll do that when we do the 2 in Hawaii on the big island and Maui. Evan

Sent: Monday, June 14, 1999 7:27 PM
Subject: Yosemite Yes!

O.K., this Park is in the top 5 and as of now is #3 behind only Yellowstone and The Grand Canyon. Getting here from Death Valley was a good test for the Durango. We left Stovepipe Wells in Death Valley, elevation -5 feet, and after 1 mile passed a sign saying, "Turn off AC—avoid overheating—steep grade next 20 miles". Pookie looked at me and said, "You're going to ignore that aren't you?" I cheerfully replied that I would ignore it until the engine started to overheat and then would turn off the AC, as there couldn't possibly be a 20-mile upgrade without any level area. Eight miles later, I turned off the AC. After 12 miles, I parked on the side of the road with the engine idling and the gearshift in park while bells and chimes went off and I read thru the owner's manual and ran the heater full speed (running the heater adds another small radiator to your cooling system). On the dashboard one message read Check your Gauges in bright red letters and kept flashing while another said Transmission Overheating in red that stayed on. It was 8:40 a.m. when we left Stovepipe Wells and already reading 98 degrees and now was down to 91 as we had climbed a few thousand feet. The bells quit ringing in a few minutes and the red lights went out after 5 minutes or so and the water temperature gauge went down to 225 degrees. The owner's manual didn't say a damn thing about the transmission overheating so I concluded that it was all the gear shifting between 1st and 2nd gears that had caused the overheating as we tried to climb. I locked the gearshift in 1st so it couldn't shift anymore and we climbed over the pass at 25 mph about 8 miles later and at 5900 feet with no recurrence of the problem. Another clue that it's going to be a long grade is when you see signs reading "Radiator water alongside road next X miles".

We descended to a valley floor again and then had to do the same climb to get over the next range of mountains. We then went north up the Owens Valley still on the east side of the Sierra Nevada. The City of L.A. bought up most of the water rights in the Owens Valley years ago and there is an aqueduct that flows from it all the way to L.A. It's an open ditch most of the way and has signs saying no fishing allowed—wonder how they enforce that? You sure can tell the difference in green vs. brown between the ranches with water rights and those without. We stopped and called a campground around noon as we were afraid none would be available near Yosemite when we got there as we had to drive thru the park from the east entrance to the west entrance on a road only open in the summer (73 miles across) and then 23 more miles to a commercial campground and you never know how busy the NP roads will be, how much construction you'll hit and what the speed limit is in the park. Money talks and for a non-refundable deposit by credit card at an extra high rate, we got a spot for 3 days. I'm a little tired of getting ripped off by these gas stations in out of the way locations, but hit a new record that day at $1.90 per gallon for 87 octane unleaded regular. There are usually 2 stations to choose from, even in remote areas, but they are always in collusion and both overcharge the same. As an ex small town banker who wrote the book on cooperation with your competitors to charge high interest rates and pay low ones, I guess I shouldn't complain.

When we finally turned west to approach the park the sign said "Difficult Road—Steep Grades and Sharp Curves—Not Recommended for Trailers". What else could I expect? After only a 10-mile climb in 1st gear at 25mph, we topped the pass at 9945 feet and entered the Park. It is absolutely beautiful and we stopped several times at overlooks and even at the eastern visitor center, which hadn't opened for the season yet. The speed limit in the park is 35mph, but the roads are so curvy that I couldn't go that fast sometimes and there were 7 miles of construction at 20mph. Only a 330 mile drive that day, but 6:30 when we got into the campground. Only Duke enjoyed the whole day, as he didn't get left anywhere or have to spend any time in the pet taxi.

The next day we went to the Valley part of the Park, which is all that 90% of the 4 million annual visitors see. After touring the main visitor center and exhibits and letting Pookie check out all the stores, we ate lunch near Curry Village at a hamburger stand. Pookie asked what I wanted to do after lunch and I said let's rent a rubber raft and float on the Merced River back thru the Valley past the waterfalls and El Capitan. We got a rubber raft, paddles and lifejackets and entered the river. It averages maybe 5 feet deep and is so clear that you can see the big trout resting on the bottom awaiting their next meal. The current was about 5 or 6 mph, but no white water and a cool breeze about 10mph blowing upstream so we traveled at maybe 3 mph. A gorgeous day with sun and no clouds, shade under the trees and we only paddled to avoid snags or get around sharp bends or pass under the 5 or 6 bridges on the indicated side. An hour and 1/2 of perfection amid spectacular scenery before we came to the takeout point. If there had not been a heavy rope supported on buoys stretched across the river about 1 foot above the water, I would have ignored the takeout signs and kept going a few more miles and I don't even think Pookie would have objected—I had paid cash for the raft and they had no credit card # or other records.

We finished touring the sights on the Valley floor and walking the trails to Yosemite Falls— 2400 feet high— and Bridal Veil Falls and then took the road to Glacier Point. The view here is down into the Valley from 8800 feet looking across the Valley at Yosemite Falls, Vernal Falls and Clark Falls. The view is awesome—and even without the cute young German blonde in the tight fitting sun suit—would still have been spectacular. We drove back to the campground stopping at Wawona Tunnel for the most photographed view in Yosemite, having covered 90 miles in the Park that day and heard on the late news that a rock slide from Glacier Point at 9:30 p.m. had killed a rock climber and forced the evacuation of 1400 campers from Curry Village Campground Lightning killed a Tennessee man while we were at Canyonlands, so we haven't had all the bad luck.

Today we did the Mariposa Grove of giant sequoias near the southern entrance to the Park. They are said to be the largest living thing by volume on earth and live to be 3200 years old. Their roots are only 3 to 6 feet deep and they grow to 270 feet in height with massive trunks. They grow in groves and at 6 to 7,000 feet altitude on the western side of the Sierra Nevada's and this is the northernmost extent of their range. When the roots meet the roots of other sequoias, they fuse together and then share the same food sources and help support the massive trunks against wind and snow weight. Each tree can consume 1,000 gallons of water per day and they never release their cones on their own. It takes a squirrel or a wood-boring beetle to force them to drop cones and spread their seeds. Without frequent fires, they cannot reproduce, as other trees must be removed by fire to let them reproduce and they are very fire resistant. When we protected them from fire for 100 years out of ignorance, no seedlings took root. Now the park sets controlled fires and the ground is covered with young trees. They are a variety of redwood and not as tall by 100 feet as the coastal redwood, but much larger in volume. We took a narrated tour on a tram and it was fascinating. When they fall, it takes 300 years for decay to set in as their bark is so full of tannin that they don't rot—I need more tannin! Lots of tunnels created naturally by fire and trees you can walk through. What do we have left to do at Sequoia Nat. Park?

Clarification Point! —I said a few episodes back that Pookie rarely could make me feel guilty. [You remember she suggested the shock collar might have caused Duke's heart murmur.] Actually, my Mother deserves all the credit for that. By the age of 6, she had tried to lay so many guilt trips on me that I was sort of super—inoculated against feeling guilty. Come to think if it, that was also about the age that the daily or bi-daily or tri-daily spankings began to lose their effect as well. After that she only had 1 really effective technique of behavior modification that still worked on me, and it still does to this day. It was a tool that her generation revered and consequently my generation abhorred. A literally correct, true weapon of mass destruction— the enema! If I thought there was even the hint of an enema in my immediate future, I could clean up my act quicker than you could say Jack Schmitt and still can. A few years ago, Harwell (my Dr.) thought I might have a lower intestinal or colon problem and prescribed a barium enema and x-rays. I begged for another solution, but he wouldn't relent. There turned out to be no medical problem, but my psyche was damaged again and it took me a full week to recover. I would still prefer 100 prostate exams to 1 enema. I think Harwell pulls that kind of stunt to show his power.

Kings Canyon and Sequoia are next. They are 2 separate parks, but adjoin and are administered jointly, so they only count as 1 park in the official list. Evan

Sent: Thursday, June 17, 1999 8:49 PM
Subject: Lemon Cove, CA

This town has everything needed to survive. 191 people, a deli/market, a Presbyterian Church, a gas station and most importantly, 2 liquor stores. My theory is that the whole town is Presbyterian and that's why 2 liquor stores. Somebody tell Brownie we went to the church and let her figure out what I mean.

We did Kings Canyon and Sequoia Nat. Parks yesterday and today. They are mainly Parks for backpackers and boast that by taking certain trails from certain points one can get further from human civilization than anywhere else in the lower 48 states. Whoever wrote that hasn't been to west Texas or even to parts of TN or GA or MS where civilization can end in 100 feet—remember the movie "Deliverance"—it could have been filmed in a lot of places.

Yesterday we did Kings Canyon and went the wrong way as usual. The map showed a much shorter route to the Park by a straight hi-way vs. the park road, but didn't mention the switchbacks, no banked turns or absolute max speed of 15 mph. One and 1/2 hours to get 45 miles. A guy from TX told me that in advance, but I usually ignore signs and people if possible. We stopped at the Grant Grove of Sequoia trees to see the Gen. Grant tree that is the 3rd largest in the world and about 2700 years old. The good news is that 150 yards downhill from the Gen. Grant is the Gen. Robert E. Lee tree that is younger and almost as big. Hang in there, guys. The Marse Robert tree looks more virile and vigorous and in a few thousand years may be the only survivor for a few more thousand years. The SOUTH will win in the end! Just in case, there's a TN tree a few yards away to help out and the only surviving yankee tree is the OR tree and they weren't even in the war.

We ate lunch in the Lodge and then went on to the end of the road in Kings Canyon at Cedar Grove, after stopping at Panoramic Point for the view. Kings Canyon is over 7000 feet deep, deeper than the Grand Canyon, but green all year round and not nearly as impressive or as vast. The Kings River is pure whitewater, but not raftable or kayakable as it's too shallow, at least in the canyon. We had left Duke in the pet taxi in the trailer with the AC on and got back at 6:30 pm, so he had a cool, but miserable day.

Today, I decided to take Duke with us and put him in the pet taxi when we left for a few hours as it's cool in Sequoia at 6,000 feet and never gets over 70 degrees. He did great and is back in the parking business! We've been leaving him without the shock collar in the trailer as he's learned to not whine when we leave and he doesn't whine in the pet taxi in the Durango if we put the shock collar on him. I really think I could throw away the batteries to the shock collar as just putting it on him makes him quiet.

Giant Forest in Sequoia is really impressive with tons of huge trees. Tried to get Duke to pee on one, but he wasn't interested. We did drive thru Tunnel Tree and get on Auto Log which is a downed sequoia 300 years old that you can actually drive inside. The Gen Sherman tree is reputed to be the largest living thing by volume on earth, but if you read James Michener (sp), he says the largest living organism is an aspen grove on a mountain in CO because aspen groves all have 1 originator and spread underground by roots and all trees in a grove are 1 organism. Who knows or cares. Sequoias were really saved from extinction because the wood is too brittle for good lumber and always shatters when the tree is felled. Old pictures of logging show the loggers spending days building pine bough blankets for the trees to fall on so the wood won't splinter, but it didn't work. We ended today at Moro Rock, a granite dome almost 8000 feet high. I climbed up 400+ steps carved from the rock and over 300 feet to the summit, but Pookie took the opportunity to sit with Duke, as he didn't want to be left alone. She wouldn't have finished the climb anyway as in places it is a sheer drop on each side of the steps and it's easy to get vertigo or sheer terror. Gorgeous view from the top.

Miscellaneous Observations:

1. In Vegas we discovered that the University of Nevada at Las Vegas commissioned a local artist years ago to design a work of art to represent the university's search for wisdom and gave him an unrestricted grant. After a few years of work, the artist unveiled a 34-ton chrome and steel flashlight on campus, which was titled, "The Beacon of Knowledge". Pookie said that at UNLV it would be more appropriate to call it "Searching in the Dark".

2. Snake Henry wrote that A. He would give Pookie a cheap—read he gets 2/3 and she gets 1/3 of my assets—divorce. B. He would represent Duke in a claim before the SPCA. C. That Moab was both a place and a people—he obviously got hold of a bible thesaurus and read it upside down as he confused it with Saul and Philistines, and he's a Methodist who wouldn't know Jack Schmitt. He also implied that because Gov. Fordice in MS has run off with some woman, he is as feckless as Clinton. Only a democrat would confuse amorality with immorality, or worse yet, not know the difference, but then again, he's a Methodist, so who knows.

3. Another sicko liberal democrat who shall go nameless, but whose initials are MAM offered Pookie a case of Fleets to help keep me under control. These people are really psychos.

4. Our next Nat. Park is The Channel Islands off the coast of CA accessible only by boat and plane. Duke just got rehabilitated, but will have to spend the time in a kennel when we are on the islands and there are no roads there. Pookie says she brought a backpack, as we have to carry our water and food. She has at least 1 of everything, but she has spent 1/4 of the trip losing, searching for, finding and rearranging her stuff. I bet I have the only wife in America with a color-coded calendar and appointment book, but we never miss having the right equipment. The other day I said I wished we had fingernail scissors and she pulled out 3 different kinds. Onward!

Evan

Sent: Tuesday, June 22, 1999 8:30 PM
Subject: Sacred Soil!

Yes, we went to the sacred ground. We went on Sun. in order to show proper reverence and also because that was Father's Day and I got in free. We were staying in Ventura, CA and it was only a 25-mile drive to the east.

The last few miles are on the Ronald Reagan Freeway, which cheered me up, and the sun came out as we drove east from the coast. Yes dear reader, we spent all afternoon in The Ronald Reagan Presidential Library and Center for Public Affairs at Simi Valley, CA. If only the Snake and MAM could come here and soak up some of the aura and essence of The Great Communicator, maybe they would outgrow their intellectual limitations—but I doubt it. It really is a great exhibit of Ronnie and his ideas and implementations. I've done the LBJ Library and Harry Truman's, but they don't hold a candle to this one. Harry exemplified maybe the best of the democratic reliance on government to accomplish things and LBJ exemplified the excesses to which it led. Reagan exemplifies the turnaround that was overdue and still needs to continue. The multimedia exhibits, which show Reagan himself speaking and his ideas, are the best. The main criticism I have is that the touch screen technology that lets you choose from multiple categories to watch his humor, ideas on taxes or national defense, or politics or charity or civil rights or a host of other subjects are at too low a height and the kids come in and touch the screens at random which then selects that topic next and interrupts your selections. The movie stuff is minimized, but shown and he himself tells about his conscious choice to be an actor and how he got there. His essay on how to be important should be shown to every kid. In addition to all the biographical data and history there is a section of the Berlin Wall that he brought down and an exact duplicate of The Oval Office with him narrating how he felt while in it. He rarely took off his suit coat while there as he felt the need to maintain the dignity of the Office, although he was often shown in jeans and boots while at his ranch. Contrast that with the "blue dress" mentality of Clinton and his total lack of shame or propriety. "White Trash" vs. decency. Truth in labeling like "The Evil Empire" quote about the Soviet Union and a single-minded focus on defeating it by whatever means necessary vs. "that depends on the meaning of the word "is". We stayed till the Library closed at 5 p.m. and thoroughly enjoyed it. What could you really expect from Reagan? After all, he did marry a Davis.

After leaving Lemon Cove, CA, we drove across the San Joaquin Valley to the coast. The Valley reminded me a lot of the Mississippi Delta. Flat, sandy soil, total sunshine and agriculture is king. A lot of cotton and we even saw several hoe gangs chopping cotton—I haven't seen that in the Delta in years and they only use chemicals now in the Delta. The difference is that everything is irrigated in the Valley and the variety of crops is enormous. Citrus of all kinds (how many of you know that cotton is a citrus fruit and it's nearest relatives, okra and tomatoes are citrus fruits as well), vegetables, corn and soybeans, olive trees, alfalfa, wheat, cattle and feedlots, just about any crop you can think of. The water is all from the Sierra Nevada and we even saw a few catfish ponds.

We hit the coast at Oceana and the fog immediately descended and the temperature dropped from the 90s to the low 60s. They call it June gloom along the coast. We stayed in a campground at Ventura about 100 yards from the beach and the sun came out at 7 p.m. every day for 10 minutes over a 4- day period. It never got over 65 degrees and would go down to 54 every nite with the wind constantly blowing and constant overcast. I was reminded of Mark Twain's comment that the coldest winter he ever spent was a summer in San Francisco. The campground was the worst organized I've ever seen and the only place we've stayed on this trip that wouldn't let us send or receive e-mail. They lied about the cable TV in their ads and didn't have a clue as to who was staying there or for how long. The reason is they have no competition and are the only commercial campground within 40 miles and the only one near the Channel Islands Nat. Park. We finally talked the Convention and Visitors Bureau into letting us download and send e-mail, but we couldn't find a kennel to board Duke and had to leave him in the trailer in the pet taxi while we toured and did the park. We did discover that Kinko's, public libraries and cyber cafes all require you to use their computers and systems and aren't even compatible with ordinary telephone lines in most cases. All kennels were booked for the weekend or restricted their services to their "patients". To top it off, the concessionaire that does the boat trips to the Islands limits visitors and although we got to Ventura where the park Headquarters is on Fri., we couldn't get a boat trip till Mon. I had planned to do the boat 1 day and fly out on another day to 2 other islands, but the air charter concessionaire for the park made the boat people look absolutely customer friendly. The air people said to leave a phone # and they'd get back to us if they had time—I left a message, but not about calling me.

Mon. afternoon we did take the boat trip to East Anacapa Island leaving at 1p.m and returning at 6:30. Again no sun, overcast and cold, but an interesting trip. Eleven miles from the coast and 15 from Ventura and we couldn't see it till we were 3 or 4 miles away with all the fog. There are 8 Channel Islands and 5 are in the park. All are joined together and part of a single mountain range submerged by the sea. At low tide, Anacapa is 1 island and at high tide is 3 islands. Santa Catalina Island is the southernmost island and not part of the Park and actually contains Avalon, a city. Anacapa is only 1 square mile, but hosts the largest rookery of CA pelicans and Western Gulls in the world plus sea lions and seals. We did a 1 mile hike with a naturalist and the gulls were raising their chicks and very aggressive about us getting close. The island base is all cliffs and the boat has to back into a pier and then hold itself there by idling in reverse while we climb off in 3-foot swells and go up 153 steps to the cliff top. This is the least visited Nat. Park in the lower 48 and will stay that way till they get new concessionaires. The Chumash Indians inhabited the islands for 11,000 years and paddled canoes to the mainland. Malibu is a Chumash word meaning "noisy waters", or "expensive homes" in modern vernacular. We didn't see any whales or dolphins, but did see a thresher shark leap out of the water 4 or 5 times.

I did let Duke run in the Pacific twice and he didn't care if it was cold. The first time he lapped up a little salt water, but the 2nd time he didn't. We're now in 29 Palms outside Joshua Tree Nat. Park and doing our last desert park tomorrow and maybe the next day. We drove thru L.A. today and I didn't see another RV of any kind on the freeways—think everybody else goes around? As we passed Beverly Hills, I did wonder what that other unimpeachable, innocent, democrat, O. J. was doing today. Probably out on some nearby golf course looking for Nicole's killer. We've decided to go back to San Diego when we leave here and spend some time sightseeing. We may detour to Sedona, AZ on the way home to see if we can find Uncle Bill's grave and to see how Sedona's changed since 75, when we were last there.
Evan

Sent: Saturday, June 26, 1999 8:02 PM
Subject: Joshua Tree Nat. Park

Actually, it's not a tree, but an overgrown agave plant that gets to 40 feet or more in height. Named by the original settlers who wandered into this place and thought it's shape reminded them of the biblical supplicant (Snake Henry will, in all probability need to look him up too) praying to his God. You can stand to miss it if you want. The Park covers both the high or Mojave desert and the low or Colorado desert, but the Joshua trees only grow in the Mojave part above 3,000 feet where it is relatively cooler and wetter (7 to 10 inches of annual rain vs. 2 to 5 in the Colorado desert part of the park). Actually, it's the least pretty of the desert parks as the scenery doesn't change much either at different elevations or in different light, and it's hot, even in the morning and at nite. The view from Key's View at about 5500 feet is quite good as it overlooks The Salton Sea and the Imperial Valley to the west, but the air pollution is significant. You can actually see the smog entering the valley through a pass in the mountains to the north and coming directly from L.A. We got there about 11a.m. and it was already hazy so the view was maybe 35 miles vs. over 100 on a clear winter day. Probably the most impressive thing in the park was the fire sites where 14,000 acres burned over Memorial Day this year and cleaned up all the ground vegetation. No spectacular mountain ranges in the park and just a lot of rocks piled up here and there.

We stayed in a combination RV park and golf course that was very nice and had a lot of permanent residents with cottonwood trees and landscaping. We did e-mail from the golf course clubhouse and it reminded Pookie of the curling club we used to belong to in Wisconsin. Nice little place with friendly people. We did the Visitor Center and a trail around an oasis for a mile or so and then went and got Duke out of his pet taxi and let him go thru the Park with us as it was too hot to do anymore trails and not that much to see anyway. We did a picnic under shade trees with Duke tied to the table while trying to kill every lizard that came close, which is against park regulations, but he doesn't seem to care. The Indians must have had dogs too and I'm sure they wiped out a few lizards.

One of my female correspondents who claims to be an independent, but is married to a liberal democrat and is easily influenced by him, responded to my sacred soil message with the comment that Reagan had Alzheimer's for a year before he left the presidency. Tacky and tasteless, but a typical democrat response. Actually, the democrats should be grateful that he developed Alzheimer's as that makes him fully qualified and eligible to be a democrat again. I think brain impairment is required to be a really sincere democrat. Look at Jim Brady, Reagan's former press secretary. After John Hinckley shot out half of his brain, he became a democrat too (we Republicans can be tasteless too, when provoked). I rest my case.

We left Joshua Tree by driving across the park to the south entrance, which comes out near I-10 and then detoured east for 5 miles to the Gen. George Patton Museum. If you have the chance, skip this too. Rip, rip, rip is the best description and we stayed only a few minutes. We then headed back west and south to the Salton Sea, driving across the Imperial Valley. Again, I was surprised to see how much the terrain resembled the Miss. Delta in visual appearance. We drove down the north shore of the Salton Sea and ate lunch in a state park on the shoreline. Duke didn't touch the water with his tongue and now must know what salt water smells and tastes like. It's 25% more salty than the ocean and the fish are dying. Duke did enjoy rolling in a dead fish before I could drag him away.

The Salton Sea was created in 1905 when the Colorado River broke thru a man-made diversionary channel and reacquired a different, but historical outlet to the sea. A year and one half later it was redirected to the old course. It's 360 square miles and the biggest body of water wholly inside CA. Each year it absorbs 4.1 million tons of additional salt from Imperial Valley irrigation run-off and rainfall and will die soon. The only fish left in large populations were imported from South Africa and have a high tolerance for salt.

That afternoon we headed back west toward San Diego on I-8 and the Durango recorded a temperature of 112 crossing the Imperial Valley on the interstate. This time as we climbed out of the Valley, which is below sea level, as is the Salton Sea, I cut off the AC when the sign said 10 miles of steep grade. After 8 miles we had to pull over again as the transmission overheated light and bells came on again. I had it locked in 2nd gear and it never got below 35mph or shifted on its own and the engine didn't overheat, but the transmission did. After a 5 minute wait, the light went out and we finished the climb in 1st gear at 25mph with no recurrence of the problem and this time I didn't run the heater at all. I need a transmission cooler on this thing.

We're now in Chula Vista, a suburb of San Diego south of the city a few miles in a combination RV Resort and Marina right on the Bay with a gorgeous view and city parks and seafood restaurants. The ads say it's the place to park all your toys—boats, RVs and cars. It's the nicest campground yet and has tours to Mexico as well as to San Diego. I think I'll skip Mexico.

Evan

Sent: Monday, June 28, 1999 7:02 PM
Subject: San Diego Si!

Well, San Francisco used to be my favorite American city to visit, but no longer. San Diego just took its place. I didn't realize it, but San Diego is larger than Frisco and CA's 2nd largest city. It has just as many gorgeous water views and the flowers are everywhere. They modestly claim to have the finest city park in America in Balboa Park, and I agree. In addition to the world famous San Diego Zoo, it has 12 museums, concerts, exhibits, lectures and 2 theaters, and an IMAX theater plus the organ pavilion with a 4500 pipe organ and amphitheater, and a lot of the stuff is free. We spent 1 whole day at Balboa Park and only did 4 museums, the IMAX Theater and the botanical garden, but we did do 2 extra exhibits at 2 of the museums. "Diamonds" on the formation, discovery, mining and setting of diamonds was at the natural history museum and included world famous diamonds and jewelry and "Ringing Thunder"; a Chinese exhibit was at the museum of art. It sounds like an exhibit of their stolen A-bombs, but is an exhibit of artifacts from a nobleman's grave buried during the "Warring States" period of their history about 3000 years ago. He was buried like a pharaoh with 8 wives and several concubines and slaves and the name "Ringing Thunder" comes from the complete orchestra of bells and drums that was buried with him and would completely fill a large sized room. The 3rd exhibit currently showing is "World War II Through Russian Eyes", but we had seen it in Memphis this spring. We saw "Mysteries of Egypt" and "Island of the Sharks" about Co Cos Island off the west coast of Costa Rica at the IMAX. We also got to hear a 1 hour recital on the organ by a guest organist, and since it was Sunday, 30 small houses were open representing 30 nations and offering their native dress and foods.

The weather was perfect. Everyday the night fog and overcast would burn off by 9 a.m. and then sunshine all day long with cool temperatures up in the mid 70's and then down in the 60's and more overcast at nite. No need for AC as a cool breeze was always blowing and a perfect blue sky.

The city is easy to get around, has well marked signage and has good public transportation and tons of bike paths. I now understand why so many people live here.

Our first morning we put Duke in a kennel and then I took Pookie to Coronado, the peninsula in the harbor, to the Hotel Del Coronado. I told her that was where we would have stayed if we had flown out here and after she saw it she said very sweetly, "We can come back sometime soon". After 1 day in San Diego she said, "I'll even come back in the trailer if you can do it without crossing any deserts". The Del as they call the hotel is fantastic, but as we were looking at a bougainvillea plant that looked like a tree in the courtyard I overheard another tourist saying, "This is nice, but not as nice as that Grand Ole Opry hotel in Nashville—you can ride a boat around the lobby in that one". He obviously wasn't impressed with the Pacific Ocean, beaches and views at the Del, but I am. We ate lunch on the sun deck at the Del and Pookie just cooed, "We could charge it to the room if we were staying here". I suggested it might be a nice place for her tennis bunch to come for a tennis vacation, so she went and got some promotional material on the hotel. The cheapest room is $205 per nite and has a view of a closet and will sleep 1 in a closet.

After lunch we went to the Zoo, and it isn't over rated. We didn't see Joan Embry or Johnny Carson interviewing her. We got to see a sea lion show and another show called "The Wild Ones" starring a cheetah and some powdered leopards from Vietnam and did the narrated tour around the zoo and the sky ride over the zoo. To do the whole zoo would take a full day. As we were leaving around 6:30 p.m. we walked by a country and western band on a flatbed truck playing "God Bless Texas", but as we stood there and watched they switched to "Rocky Top" and I got sick at my stomach.

On our 2nd day we went to Old Town, which is a tourist trap, and then to The Cabrillo Nat. Monument on Point Loma overlooking the bay. It matches the view from the Presidio overlooking the Golden Gate in Frisco. We stopped and had a superb crab sandwich on the way after a dinner the nite before at a really good seafood restaurant. We then rode thru the Gas Light District, which is renovated Victorian, but couldn't find a parking place and Pookie can't have any alcohol and said, "We can't stop and drink wine in an outdoor cafe, so keep going!" I think she's feeling cheated by her liver problem which prohibits alcohol. Out of sympathy, I'm doing her part for her. After that we rode by the harbor and then went to Balboa Park to see the shark movie at IMAX.

Sun. we did Balboa Park and left on Mon. a.m. I wanted to go to Sea World and the Wild Animal Park, but we have to save some stuff to do on return trips. I really do like this place and plan to come back. We're now in

Newport Beach, CA in another resort park (that means it costs as much as a hotel room, but has all kinds of stuff and Pookie likes it). I bought her a t-shirt at the Del that has a picture of dollar bills on the front and a caption underneath that reads, "Expert at Pissing Off Money". Tomorrow we take a ferry to Catalina Island and poor Duke gets to stay in his pet taxi all day in the trailer. He'd much rather do that than go to a kennel where he has to stay all day in a cage too, and now he has learned to not whine and cry without the shock collar. No cars on Catalina, but you can get a golf cart to tour around, or take some planned tours.

Master Curler

Sent: Thursday, July 01, 1999 7:07 PM
Subject: Catalina & Cousin Paul

Catalina was a fun day. We took the Catalina Flyer from Newport Beach to Avalon along with maybe 250 other people leaving Newport at 9 a.m. & returning at 6 p.m. The Flyer is the largest catamaran operating solely in the USA and cruises at about 30 knots and can carry maybe 450 people. It's an hour and 1/4 trip and they serve beer, cocktails, wine and useless stuff. Cool and overcast when we left and too cool to do the whole trip from the open top deck, but the sun came out and ole eagle eye Davis spotted some dolphins about 1/2 mile away and everybody on the boat began to look and take pictures. Cars & trucks on Catalina are limited to 700 and you must have a permit to bring one over which costs $800, but the waiting list is 18 years, so everybody drives a golf cart which has no waiting list and no permit. Of course, 1 guy has the exclusive monopoly on renting golf carts and charges $30 per hour. Only 1 grocery store and 1 gas station too, so cost of living is high unless you own the monopoly. 3000 people permanent residents and 700 kids in the local school system. Electricity and water are high too and the smallest houses go for 1/2 million or more. William Wrigley, the chewing gum magnate, bought the island in 1917 and the family still controls 1/2 of the local real estate and guess who gets the monopolies? I think the electric system is a Wrigley subsidiary too. 88% of the island is now in a Nature Conservancy set up by Wrigley when L.A. County raised the assessment from agricultural to commercial and made the real estate taxes about $50 million per year. Ole Bill outfoxed them as he got a huge tax write-off and still controls the Conservancy Board and only kept the true commercial and residential property.

We took a narrated tour of Avalon on a bus by a guy who had failed as a stand-up comedian for 15 years, but kept trying as a tour guide. He was funny at first, but the sound effects and jokes got stale after a while. The setting is gorgeous and the color of the water is aquamarine where it's shallow and it's very clear. Lots of yachts and sailboats and the L.A. Yacht Club leases 1 harbor we rode by. After the tour we did lunch in what was supposed to be a 5 star restaurant, but I would only give it a 2. We then did a 2 hour additional tour in another narrated bus by a local driver who had grown up in Catalina and really knew the history and heritage of the island and contradicted about 1/2 the stuff the comedian had told us. This bus took us inland to the Island in the Sky airport, which is on top of a 1700-foot hill and about 15 miles inland, and we got a few glimpses of the Pacific side of the island. The municipality owns the airport and 2 DC-3s that fly cargo back and forth to the island. Saw a lot of bison which were released on the island by some movie company after filming a movie here a # of years ago. The climate is semi-arid and not a lot of water on the island, but enough for the bison to survive. After that we only had about 45 minutes to kill before the boat left, so Pookie managed to find some stuff to buy in the local gift shops. Catalina is worth a day trip if you ever get a chance to go and they do glass bottom boat tours and botanical tours too.

Wed. a.m. we left Newport Beach and drove thru L.A. toward Barstow, CA, our next scheduled stop. We passed right by the entrance to the Nixon Library at Yorba Linda, but I have no desire to see it. That scumbag violated every Republican principle that exists and then stole and lied to everybody. I still can't believe he cooperated with the democrats to put in price controls, which is insanity except in a full-blown war economy. Read in the paper today that Clinton lied to us about the severity of the atrocities and transgressions of the Serbs in Kosovo———AMAZING that Slick Willie would lie to the American people!

Now for the reason for our trip to Barstow, CA. Pookie has a cousin named Paul who lives in Barstow that she hasn't seen since he was 15 years old and she was 18 and he's now 52. Every time I asked about him I was told he was a gay veterinarian who used to live in Santa Monica, CA where he was "Veterinarian to the Stars". My boys are going to enjoy getting this e-mail, as they don't know he exists. They know all about the weirdos in my family as we talk openly about each other but they know very little about Pookie's family. The truth is that my family characters are staid and dull compared to Pookie's. Well, Pookie asked if we could go see Paul while we were in CA and I said sure. While we were in San Diego, Pookie called Paul to make sure he would be there. Wrong #, so she called Paul's mother, Billie in Biloxi, MS, who is nearly 80, to get a current #. I met Billie and her husband Elliott in 1975 when we visited them in Houston, TX with our boys in the poptop camper. Elliott Sr. is retired Air Force and was working as an accountant for a retail store then. We did the town and I got a little tight as they drank more than I did. The next morning I was in their oversized walk-in shower trying to clear my head when the shower door opened and Billie walked in with a "Bloody Bull" for me and said drink this for your hangover— ignoring the fact that I was butt naked. They had 2 sons and Elliott Jr. is the older of the 2 boys. Elliott Jr. started doing taxidermy while in high school and liked it so much he became a plastic surgeon and now lives in New Orleans. I've met Elliott Jr. at 2 funerals, but never met Paul. Billie tells

Pookie the current phone # and Pookie calls Paul who is delighted to hear from her. I don't know what that phone call cost me, but she must have talked a long time. She comes back to the trailer and says I'm not going to believe what she learned. It seems that Paul had a fling with a girl at an Everly Brothers Concert in Sioux City, Iowa when he was 18 and his father was stationed there at an air base. Well, the girl got pregnant and had a baby girl, and Paul cut and ran and left the girl high and dry. The girl had the baby, and put it up for adoption, when neither Paul nor his family would help out or even acknowledge that the girl was Paul's. Paul went to LSU and became a veterinarian and never married, but knew he had a daughter somewhere. The adopted daughter had tracked down Elliott Jr. in New Orleans as he still lived in Louisiana and he had called Paul in March of this year and Paul gave him the O.K. to give out his current phone # and address. The daughter and Paul had reconciled over the phone and by mail with pictures exchanged and 2 weeks before Pookie called Paul; the daughter had flown out from Minnesota, where she lives in a suburb of Minneapolis. She's now married and 33 years old and brought her 2 kids with her. Her mother had re-married and had 3 more kids and is doing fine also. Paul just found out he's a grandfather to a 9 year old boy and a 5 year old girl at age 52. Pookie says, "What do you think"? I say, "Either he's not gay or he's AC/DC or was at one time".

Pookie says he's really looking forward to seeing us, and she has directions to his house and a time for us to meet for lunch on June 30 and will I please be nice. I say O.K. and then she said he has 6 dogs and 10 cats and said something about having a fenced front yard and 20 odd old cars in the front yard and will I really promise to be nice. I once met Aunt Dolly (another of Pookie's relatives) living in an old farm house out in the country from Black Earth, Wisconsin and supporting a commune of hippie artist kids and a mean as hell German Shepherd that tried to take off my leg, so I say O.K, but with reservations.

Well, we arrive at Paul's house around noon on the 30th and it's a one bedroom shack surrounded by a head-high chain link fence with at least 20 something old junked cars in the front yard in the middle of the Mojave Desert with very few neighbors and a lot of sand and scrub brush and it's 100 degrees in the sun. Paul is standing out front waving and happy to see us. He's smaller than me, but with a physique like one of those exercise gurus on TV that women watch. Well-developed upper torso and dyed blonde wavy shoulder length hair. We shake hands and he hugs Pookie and I begin to wonder where we're going to leave Duke while we do lunch. He shows us some of his old junk cars, which are mostly Hudsons and Packards with a few others. He points out a Jaguar and a black Cadillac that he says was in the final scene of "The Godfather". Pookie tells him that our poptop trailer was in the movie "Walking Tall" and Paul exclaims that he spayed his dog! I ask whose dog and Paul names the actor who originally played Buford Pusser in the original movie. "Vet to the Stars" may have some validity I surmise. It's hot as hell, but I don't think we're going to be invited into the house (and I'm not sure I want to go) so I ask if I can plug the trailer into his house and cut on the AC so we can leave Duke in the trailer. I've got a heavy duty 100 foot electric cord and he has one too, so he goes to get his and I tell Pookie that we need to get some pictures as nobody is going to believe this. She pulls out her Canon Elph that is about the size of a cigarette pack and says she's been taking pictures since we got here. She tells me to be nice, and she's sneaking around like a Russian spy at a NATO base taking secret pictures.

I go get my electric cord out of a trailer outside locker and you really need to get the whole picture. Here we are, the former president of The Bachelor's Club (me), and the former secretary of The Delta Debutante Club (Pookie), standing in front of the debutante's cousin's shack in the damn desert with a yard full of junked cars. There's no porch on the shack, so there is no washing machine on display, but there are 6 junkyard dogs (He's already told me one is a mastiff and he can't leave home, as everybody except his policeman friend is afraid to feed his dogs.) and 10 cats locked in the house so they won't kill Duke. Then we try the power and it will run the AC fan, but not the compressor, so it's probably 20 amp and not 30, as I run the AC in my yard at home with long power cords, so I know it works at my house. Paul rigs up a plastic covered chain to tie Duke in shade under a bush in the yard, with some water in a bowl, and we get in his operating car, a 1965 Buick hardtop convertible with no AC and the ignition hot wired with wires running everywhere under the dash. The upholstery is hanging out everywhere, but it runs and has Hollywood mufflers. Paul takes us to The Burger Bun, which is a meat and three, and the waitress welcomes him like an old friend and asks if he wants a Bud Lite. I get liver and onions, Pookie gets meatloaf and Paul gets a Denver omelet.

Paul says his daughter has a good job and I ask what she does. He replies that she works in a psychiatric hospital. (By now, Tenhula is convinced that I'm making this up, but I'm not that good. I've already whispered to Pookie that this is a better story than I could ever invent.) I ask if she's a nurse and Paul says no, she's a psychologist who interviews all new patients to determine who needs to be restrained. I'm pinching myself under the table so I can keep a straight face. Pookie and Paul talk a long time and I ask a question every now and then. Paul has brought a scrapbook he has made since March of 99, with pictures of his daughter, her adoptive family, the girl's mother and her family and his grandchildren. All of these pictures had been mailed to him before their visit in June or brought on the trip and he's put them in a scrapbook with children's art and paintings like we hang on our refrigerator from our grandchildren. Both his daughter and her mother are attractive and the families seem to be middle class, nice folks. He seems to be a decent, nice guy who got dealt a hand in life that he couldn't figure out how to play. He mentions several other girl friends during the conversation and I don't think he's gay. He was in the Army for almost 20 years as a veterinarian and not in private practice very long and gets a small pension and sells an old car every now and then and does some backup vet work for local vets from time to time, but has very little money and doesn't seem to care. He's kind of estranged from his parents and brother, who can't understand his choice in lifestyle, but at least verbally seems satisfied with his lot in life. Pookie goes to the restroom and I tell him that everybody on this planet who breathes air has some types of problems, we just don't know what they are and he agrees wholeheartedly. I go to the restroom and pick up the check on the way and then announce that we need to go see how Duke is doing, as he gets separation anxiety every time I leave him. Paul has had some copies made of pictures of his daughter and kids and he gives them to Pookie. I take a picture of Paul and Pookie and his car and we go back and rescue Duke who has opened the car door of the junk he's chained to and gotten all tangled up in the chain and turned over his water, but is under a car out of the direct sun, and it is now 106 according to the Durango. Paul puts some water on Duke to cool him off and checks his gum color to make sure he's not in shock and he's fine. We drive off and I'm a little sad about Paul. He's got the pictures and scrapbook, but not the people or the memories.

We drive to Needles, CA and the Durango reads 119 around 5 pm and 117 when we check into the campground and a local radio station gives the same reading. On to Sedona, AZ on the 1st. Evan

Sent: Friday, July 02, 1999 5:55 PM
Subject: Sedona & Uncle Bill

Well, I wish we had skipped Sedona. We were last here in 75 to see Uncle Bill, or more accurately, to get even with Uncle Bill, and it was a delightful little town with only 1 red light and a few artists and almost no tourists. Uncle Bill had said that if it ever got another red light, he was going to move. He died in 82 at age 78 and Sedona now has 9 red lights and about 16,000 residents in the area vs. 1500 in 75. The traffic is horrendous and it's all plastic now, like most of the rest of America. Most of the new buildings are adobe style and McDonald's doesn't have arches, but it is no longer a unique spot. It still has the beautiful red rock scenery and Oak Creek Canyon, but the traffic makes you keep your eyes on the road so much you can't enjoy the scenery and there are tons of gift shops, helicopter rides, hot air balloon rides, airplane rides to see The Grand Canyon, jeep rentals and jeep tours of the canyon country and tourists galore.

Uncle Bill was another of Pookie's relatives, her father's brother. I first met Uncle Bill in Jackson, TN when we lived there. Pookie called me up at the bank early one afternoon and said I needed to come home early as

Uncle Bill was there. I said who is Uncle Bill; you've never mentioned an uncle Bill before. She told me and I asked if she was sure who this guy was and she said yes. Well, I was suspicious, so I did go home right away and there was a 10-year-old Cadillac parked in front of the house with AZ plates. Pookie had never mentioned having any relatives in AZ either. When I went in the den, there sat Uncle Bill, drinking a beer and with one of my boys on each side of him sitting on the sofa. He asked if I would like a beer and when I replied yes, he said, "They're in the refrigerator". He was offering me one of my own beers! He was telling the boys stories and they were enthralled. It turned out that he was on his way to NYC to spend the winter with some relatives and had talked to Pookie's mother who told him to stop and see us. He had recently buried his 2nd wife in Sedona where they lived. He was a colorful character and I can't remember all the occupations he had tried but he had thoroughly enjoyed life. He stayed about 3 or 4 days with us and drank up a lot of beer. In the spring, he came back through on his way back to AZ and stayed another few days and we enjoyed his visits.

Well, when we went out West in the poptop in 75 to see the Grand Canyon among other things, we stopped at Meteor Crater and the Petrified Forest first and as I was looking at the map, I asked Pookie where Uncle Bill lived. I found Sedona on the map and said we were going there to see Uncle Bill so I could get even and drink some of his beer. We drove into town and I stopped at the first gas station and looked him up in the phone book and called. I had refused to call in advance as he never called us in advance and I thought it was only fair to surprise him. Uncle Bill was delighted to hear from us and told me how to get to his apt., so we drove over there. He greeted us and introduced us to his 30 something year old girl friend who was living with him. Yep, at age 72 he still enjoyed life.

He moved out of his apt. and into hers and let us use his apt. for a few days. We used Sedona as a base to explore the country around here for a few days and went to dinner with Uncle Bill every nite. One night after a few too many drinks, he insisted on taking us up to the local airport on top of a nearby mesa to see the stars at nite as there was no light interference there and the airport was closed at nite. He drove the 4 of us in his old Cadillac at breakneck speed up a winding, twisting road with sheer drops on each side. I rode shotgun and Pookie hugged both boys in the back seat with her eyes shut while she prayed. He showed us where his 2nd wife was buried in the Sedona Cemetery and had his uncut stone next to hers. He lived on his social security check for the most part, but insisted on buying his own dinner every nite. We never saw him again, but we did find his grave this morning after an hour-long search. The only local funeral home had no record of where he was buried and it's a community cemetery and no one had a plat of where each grave was located, and there are maybe 250 graves to search. We divided up the Cemetery and I took Duke with me. After an hour we met at the end of the Cemetery and no Uncle Bill found. Since we trust each other implicitly, I started going back over Pookie's part and she went over mine. I found Uncle Bill in Pookie's part.

I may send another epistle about a few things I've left out, but this is the end of the sightseeing. We've seen everything else we want to visit between here and home and have decided to head home early. My 40th high school reunion is July 17 in Greenville, MS and I want to go home and dump the trailer and Duke before the reunion. We'll stop and visit relatives in Austin and Vicksburg, but travel pretty constantly otherwise. We will continue to download every few days if anyone wants to communicate. Adios. Evan

Sent: Thursday, July 08, 1999 8:55 AM
Subject: Addendum & Potpourri

Well, I said we were thru touring, but the distaff side objected. We did 1200 miles in 3 days and Pookie said she and Duke were going to get out and walk. Duke has sucked up to her so much that she's beginning to think he's part hers. The crowning blow was when she started letting him sleep with us and he chose her side of the bed. At Needles, it got so hot that it took the trailer 2 hours to cool off when we got in the campground. That nite, I said we would leave the bedroom door open as the bedroom gets about 1/3 of the AC and when the door is closed to keep Duke out, the circulation slows down as the return vent is in the living room, and Duke stays cooler than we do and has the thermostat in his room too. Well, he came in with us of course, so I put him back out till he tried Pookie's side of the bed and she let him stay. Took only once for him to learn that trick.

After visiting relatives on my side of the family (by definition they're quasi-normal) in Austin and Pookie's niece, we went to College Station, TX to tour the Bush Presidential Library. It's impressive, not as good as Reagan's, but better than LBJ and less than Truman's. Comparing it to Reagan's I was reminded of the biblical quote, "Be ye hot or cold, for if ye be lukewarm, I will spew thee out of my mouth". (Snake Henry, that's in the Book of Revelation—with no s on the end. I taught that in Sunday School to adults and it's a safe subject as nobody understands the book anyway and even your brother Joe could con his way thru that.) Bush was a good, decent man, but too moderate in all things to be great. Pookie commented that the childhood home movies of him playing in the snow with a tie on revealed a lot about his background and class status. Even so, his accomplishments and class values stood him well in life and benefited our society. We stayed 3 and 1/2 hours and were not bored. I didn't remember all the positive things he did in a quiet way for civil and human rights. Well worth a visit if you get the chance.

Potpourri:

1. Kathy Grizzard, the 1st wife of the humorist Lewis Grizzard, wrote a book that was funnier than any of the books Lewis wrote. It was titled "From Debutante to Double-Wide" and told about her transition from an Atlanta debutante to living in a double-wide in Montana. It's hilarious and may be out of print, but we have a copy if anybody in Pulaski wants to borrow it. It's occurred to me that Pookie has been living the title, except that my trailer is a single-wide. She's really been a good sport most of the time until she gets tired and then I have to be careful.

2. Isn't there a country song titled "Cousin-in-law"? (I expect Doyle to answer that for me, but it may just be a refrain or chorus or maybe I'm confusing it with "Mother-in-law".) If there is not, there should be. I could probably write some lyrics if someone would write the music.

3. The tour guide at Hoover Dam said I was right not to waste my money on a white-water rafting trip thru Cataract Canyon this year. Since Hoover Dam was finished in 1936, water has only flowed thru the spillways in the year 1983 when it ran over them for 2 weeks. This year the snow pack was so deep that the melt came within 1 foot of entering the spillways and all the good white-water upstream was flooded out.

4. On Anacapa Island in the Channel Islands Nat. Park there is no natural fresh water supply so the Park Service built two 50,000-gallon redwood water tanks to supply the 2 ranger families that are there full time and the small visitor center. Sailors on passing ships used to shoot holes in the tanks with high powered rifles for sport while passing offshore, so the Park Service built walls around the tanks with a roof and steeple to make them look like a church. No rifle shots since.

5. I forgot to mention the other characteristic that is required to be a sincere democrat, in addition to a mushy brain. You have to have a strong wish and desire to believe in fairy tales, as that is what democrats sell to the public about 1/2 the time. That's why there are more women than men democrats. (That's a generalization and doesn't apply to all women, so hold off Pamela Sue.)

6. All the signage at Texas A & M spells out University after the A & M. I consider that to be false advertising almost on the same scale as calling Tennessee the University of Tennessee. The

only University in Tennessee is Vanderbilt and in Knoxville I bet there aren't 15 people who know the definition of University.

7. Pookie got tired of Duke getting in the front seat while riding and attempting to ride in her lap so in Moab I bought 2 36-inch bungee cords and hooked them together around the headrests above our heads. Pookie hung a towel from them to separate the front from back seats and Duke now rides in the back on top of the folded down seats. Looks a little like Tennessee Trash, but cousin Paul didn't comment.

Finis—Home Sat. nite

Chapter 5. Nova Scotia, P.E.I. and New Brunswick Trip—1999

Sent: Thursday, September 16, 1999 8:22 PM
Subject: Natural Bridge, VA

Yep, we're on the road again and in VA, dodging Hurricane Floyd. Our hero forgot the charger cord for the laptop and our battery doesn't last too long, so we just downloaded messages this a.m. Got several asking how we were and what about the storm from all kinds of places, which were appreciated. We stayed west of the Blue Ridge and got a lot of rain yesterday (Wed.), but no really high winds or other problems. We leave in the a.m. for Shenandoah Nat. Park and will plan on getting to D.C. on the nite of the 19th or morning of the 20th, depending on what we do in the meantime.

Our 1st day out was a lot of travel and we covered 425 miles to a state park about 50 miles into VA near Marion, VA. It is named Hungry Mother State Park and is really pretty. It's at 2300 feet and has a damned up creek that makes a pretty lake. We stayed in the campground next to the creek about 100 yards from where the lake begins. Nope, the park is not named for my daughter-in-law when she is breast-feeding. The legend is that Indians stole a woman and her young daughter in a raid on the New River settlements and the woman and daughter were later released or escaped from the Indians and wandered in the woods for some time. The 3 or 4-year-old daughter stumbled into a white settlement and the only words she could say were "hungry mother". A search party found the woman, but she was dead. It's in Smyth County—pronounced Smith—so Pookie says we're really in VA. There were several people in the campground that had fled Floyd and were from all kinds of places, but had been in the Carolinas on vacation.

Yesterday we drove up to Natural Bridge, and the rain started around noon and was constant till this a.m. Duke got loose in this campground and ran around while I hooked up the trailer in the rain and then when he ignored me, I blew the horn and started up the Durango and he came running and jumped in. Terrified he'll get left, but won't mind unless he's threatened. Pookie says she doesn't think there is another Jack Russell RV dog in America and she has a list of reasons why. Most of the reasons start with hyper. Duke loves you unconditionally—unless there is something else going on which needs his attention, and the subject matter could be an insect or a mammal or the wind— he's interested in everything.

Today we went to the site where the Jeddi Knight of the 19th century, Gen. Robert E. Lee, surrendered his valiant but starving army to the Darth Vader of the Evil Empire of yankeedom. Yep, Appomattox Courthouse National Historic Park. It really is done nicely and recreates the scene very well. The site was abandoned after the war and the courthouse burned to the ground in the late 1800's so when the Park Service decided to recreate the site, it had been saved by neglect and was available. The town of Appomattox moved about 3 miles away so the site has really been reconstructed in great detail. The McLean House where Grant dictated the terms of surrender was not destroyed and has been relocated to its original site and a duplicate of the Courthouse has been rebuilt on its original site along with the other buildings. McLean was the guy who was the alpha and the omega of the War of Northern Aggression. He owned the house on Bull Run at the Manassas Junction,,which was the site of the first 2 large battles and got shot up by cannon. He moved to Appomattox to get out of the war and bought the house where the surrender took place. The Courthouse was in the center of Appomattox County and was never a freestanding town, just an administrative center. Of course, it did have the lawyer scum offices and the jail and 1 store. The power was out due to the storm, so we didn't get to see the slide show or exhibits in the Visitor Center, but we did get an excellent living history interpretation from a Park Ranger who played the part of a yankee soldier who was there and later reposted to provost duty there after the surrender. He was excellent and recounted the retreat and pursuit from Petersburg and Richmond to Appomattox (about 100 miles) while dressed in a yankee uniform and with all the period accents and phrases. He answered questions in the time period and did a super job. He did admit that he was from a western PA regiment that had been decimated by the Confederates and had to be merged with a Philadelphia regiment when it was reduced to less than 100 men at Cold Harbor. We missed the Confederate soldier who does the same thing from the Southern viewpoint, but I'm sure it was superior to the yankee lies.

We came back to Natural Bridge and did the rip off bit. The Bridge was surveyed by George Washington who left his initials (or somebody did) in the granite and it was owned by Thomas Jefferson and his descendants till recently, if you believe the propaganda put out by the current, private owner who charges $8 to walk downhill 137 steps and 1/2 mile to see it. Got a really huge gift shop, or shoppe and parking for tour buses.

We called Betty Jo last nite and she is sending by overnite mail the charging cord for the laptop to Will's hotel room in Annandale, VA so we can pick it up when we stop there later this week. I bought a replacement that doesn't fit right today at Radio Shack, but it does charge the battery so I can send this e-mail if I hold my finger on the charger part of the time. We spend the first few days of each trip replacing and remembering what we forgot to do or did on the last trip. We also left my paperbacks and the Fodor's Guide to Nova Scotia, but I'm sure we'll find substitutes.

Evan

Sent: Saturday, September 18, 1999 5:54 PM
Subject: Shenandoah Nat. Park

Friday we drove up to the southern entrance to Shenandoah and entered on Skyline Drive. It's 105 miles to the exit at Front Royal and has several visitor centers, gasoline stations and campground stores plus campgrounds, picnic areas and a lot of trails to hike. I couldn't find a single trail that didn't have the word "steep" in the description, so we stayed close to the highway. The Appalachian Trail crosses Skyline Drive 28 times in the Park and you see a few hikers doing the whole trail. One was in a Visitor Center and you could smell him from 20 feet away. A sign describing the Appalachian Trail at one of the intersections said the northern terminus was 3 million steps to the right in Maine, and the southern terminus was 2 million steps to the left in Georgia. Lots of deer and birds of all kinds. They say 60-100 deer are killed on Skyline Drive each year by autos—almost like home except I think I see more dead ones in the road at home each year.

This park is unique among the US parks in that nearly all of it was in cultivation or logging or mining for 200 years or more and it has all been reclaimed by nature in the time since it was established in 1935. Virginia bought up the private tracts of land and donated them to the US for an eastern Nat. Park after Congress passed enabling legislation in 1926. About 400 families were displaced and a few stayed till they died off. The weather has been gorgeous since the storm passed and the visibility is unimpaired from the myriad of overlooks. The views to the east are the prettiest to me and in a few places you can see the Piedmont for miles. Piedmont is derived from the Italian word "piemonte" which means "at the foot of the mountains" and describes the plain, with a few hills, between the mountains and the coastal plain. In the US, Piedmont covers parts of 10 states from Alabama to New York, east of the Appalachians and covers almost all of New Jersey. To the west, most of the views are of the Shenandoah Valley and it was so clear we could see the main ridge of the Appalachians, 4 or 5 mountain ridges away, or about 50 miles at times. They've spent some money clearing the brush and small trees away from the overlooks so you can see much better than I remember as a child. The road is still curvy and up and down and the speed limit is 35 most of the time, but you couldn't go much faster anyway. At times the compass says north and at times south and all points in-between as it curves so much. We did the Big Meadows Visitor

Center and the power went off again, so we missed the slide show, which is becoming standard. Duke loves the ride along the Skyline as he gets to hang out the window at slow speeds and goes nuts when we pass a deer or squirrel. He's freely allowed to hunt both species at home in our yard or in the pasture behind the house and doesn't understand why he can't hunt them on the road.

We spent Fri. nite at a campground on a dairy farm near Luray, VA. A very nice couple that emigrated from Switzerland 2 years ago and still speak with an accent. I told them we used to live in a Swiss community in Monroe, Wisconsin and asked what canton they were from in Switzerland. He was shocked when I knew where his canton was located. There was a splendid view of the Shenandoah Valley from the campsite atop a hill on the farm. I did notice however that his cows were Jewish and not Brown Swiss. If they are Hol—steins, they're Jewish aren't they?

Today we finished the northern part of Skyline Drive and then came into the DC area. The power stayed on at the northern Visitor Center and we finally got to see the slide show. We're now in a regional park operated by the State of VA called Bull Run State Park and it's on the bank of Bull Run Creek very near the Manassas Battlefield. It's a huge park covering several square miles with a lot of facilities and we have an electricity hookup.

We met 3 couples on Honda Gold Wing motorcycles pulling the small 2 wheel trailers behind, which were loaded with extra stuff. Pookie asked if that was our next great adventure and I told her it was a distinct possibility, but where would we put Duke? She then wished Duke a long life for the first time. I was feeling cheerful and told her we wouldn't stay in tents and could afford motels if we did this on bikes. I can't wait to unload this stuff we've brought Will, Alicia & kids to deliver to them in DC. A lot of it is piled up on the floor on my side of the bed where I step on it every time I try to get in or out of bed. Pookie thought my side of the bed was expendable and Duke doesn't mind since he sleeps on her side of the bed anyway.

We now plan to stop and spend a day in Annapolis on the way nawth. Pookie loved it when we were there before and this time we don't have to tour the Naval Academy. We have a reservation at a campground in North Bergen, New Jersey near the George Washington Bridge into Manhattan. I bet that site is sort of like the Love Canal with pollution everywhere, but I have an appointment the 23rd to get a botox shot at Mount Sinai Hospital in Manhattan and can't find another campground as close to the city as that one. Several of you have asked where we're going on this trip. Maine, Nova Scotia and Prince Edward Island are on the list and New Brunswick on the way home.
Evan

Sent: Wednesday, September 22, 1999 6:39 PM
Subject: North Bergen, NJ

Lovely spot. Between a railroad yard and a slum, but surrounded by a chain link fence. Have everything locked up, including Duke. Wish the chain link fence had razor wire on top. Actually, it's only a few miles from the Red Roof Inn where I've stayed for 11 years while getting botox shots for my spasmodic dystonia, and we can go in thru the Lincoln Tunnel in the morning and not have to take the George Washington Bridge till we leave tomorrow with the trailer. They actually have tent campers here who take the bus to tour NYC. Can't wait to get to Maine and away from the cities. Washington, DC traffic is a lot worse than L.A. or NYC. I used to say that if I was young again, I'd like to live in DC, but no longer. You can't get anywhere with the traffic gridlocks.

Don't know when we'll get to send these messages, but we had a nice time in DC and Annapolis. Took Will, Alicia & kids to see the Korean Memorial. It's quite well done with a rifle platoon advancing across a rice paddy in combat gear with ponchos on. Will said he felt sorry for the point man who had a short life expectancy. It has a circular pool of water a few inches deep flowing over black marble at the end of the troopers and is almost as impressive as the Vietnam War Memorial, which is close by. Took them to the Vietnam Memorial too, and I found Pookie's cousin Rocky on the first panel. He was a Green Beret advisor and was executed in 1965 after capture in 1963 before we got deeply involved. Pookie gave up looking for him and headed back to the directory before I found him and called her back—don't know why I always have to find her dead relatives. After that we did the Lincoln Memorial which is between the 2 war memorials and then did the highlight of the day, according to Rachel, as we sat on the bank of the Potomac under the willow trees while she played in the river and got her feet soaked. Gorgeous day and a lot of water skiers and boats and airplanes passing overhead low as they descended to Reagan National Airport a few miles away. Rachel had such a good time that she asked Sir to go back the next afternoon, which we did. The next day, Mon., Rachel got out of school at 12:45 and we went to Bolling Air Force base where Will is taking his Masters in Strategic Intelligence for the next year. His classes are in the Defense Intelligence Agency building on the base and he can't tell us what he learns or he'd have to kill us. The base is on the north side of the Potomac only a few miles east of the Mall and is very nice.

We spent another few hours on a ground cover on the bank of the Potomac where Rachel wanted to play and then took them home and went back to the trailer to free Duke from the pet taxi. Letting him out of the trailer was a mistake as there were 2 deer standing by the trailer when we got out and he went crazy trying to get off the leash. It started raining early p.m. and kept it up for 34 hours. We left DC the next a.m. and drove to MD, a little northeast of DC and parked for the nite in a huge campground with 350 sites. We went to Annapolis for the afternoon as we had really enjoyed it on previous visits. We took an escorted tour of the State House with a lady tour guide who was quite good, but in a hurry. It's the oldest constantly used State House in the US and was the scene of George Washington resigning his commission as General of the Army to Congress, which met in the building for a year at the end of the Revolutionary War. It has 2 domes as when it was expanded in the 60s they kept the original and added another on the annex, that was built like a condo with adjoining walls to the original.

The lady tour guide was funny and told about the contractor for the wooden dome, which covers the original dome and was added in the early 1800s. He was on a scaffolding 90 feet high when he stepped back to admire his work and made a mess on the marble floor below. His widow was never paid for his work, as the MD legislature was a cheap bunch. She also said the state legislature would have seceded from the Union at the beginning of the War of Northern Aggression if they had not been kidnapped by federal troops and held at Frederick, MD till they agreed not to secede.

Tues. nite we met Vivian & Walter for dinner at a restaurant northeast of DC. Had a super time visiting with them. They are a black couple we met in Nashville more than 15 years ago. Walter is a medical doctor and was dean of Meharry Medical College back then and we've kept in touch ever since. Walter is a consultant to Howard University now and they've lived in DC for years. I used to come here twice a year as a lobbyist for Third Nat. Corp and later for SunTrust and usually brought Pookie and we would visit with them each trip. We've toured everything in DC, most several times, and weren't interested in doing more tours. Vivian & Walter have twin boys about the same age as ours and Walter told a hilarious story about when the boys were small and Vivian was a bridesmaid in the wedding of a white friend, in fact, she was the only black attendant. Walter didn't pay too much attention to the address of the church and Vivian left the motel early to go get dressed at the wedding while Walter would bring the boys later. Walter finished dressing the boys and left for the church. He knew the name of the street the church was on and stopped at the first church which had a lot of cars parked nearby. They went in and the usher asked did he want the bride's side or the groom's? Walter answered the bride, and they were seated down front. He got a little nervous when he saw no other blacks and he knew the bride had other black friends. After all the bridesmaids walked down the aisle, Walter figured he was in trouble when Vivian wasn't there, but he decided it was too late to leave as they were at the front of the church. All during the ceremony Walter was seeing (or imagining) everybody asking behind closed hands, "Who are those black people"? At the end of the ceremony, they made a quick escape and drove rapidly down the road to the next and correct church. Walter said the whole way to the next church he was coaching the kids (who were very young) to not tell anyone where they had been during the correct ceremony as he was totally embarrassed. I could hear the kids asking, "Why can't we tell about the wedding, Dad?" He said it was 2 years before he told Vivian the true story. Needless to say, Vivian wasn't too pleased either. I couldn't stop laughing at Walter, who was more relaxed than I've ever seen him, as he told us the story.

Don't know where we'll spend tomorrow nite as our reservations at Acadia Nat. Park aren't till Fri., but it will be out of the masses of people.
Evan

Sent: Friday, September 24, 1999 7:51 PM
Subject: Change of Seasons-To top off the perfect day

Well, the 1st day of autumn was not a success. We got up early (6:30) to make my 8:45 appointment at Mount Sinai and got there on time thru the Lincoln Tunnel and then to the east side and up to block 100 where the hospital is located, and then the day went downhill. My doctor didn't show up till 10:00 a.m. and then the FDA (Food and Drug Czars) showed up at the same time. They can't stop the inflow of illegal drugs, but can totally destroy any time schedule for doctors and their patients. Brin (my neurologist since 88 for spasmodic dystonia) apologized for being late and then said he had to spend whatever time it took to get the feds to leave as it was very bad policy to ask them to come back tomorrow—they get suspicious. I could overhear the conversation with the FDA minions and it sounded almost like a banker talking to the bank examiners. FDA has unlimited resources and no common sense, so they suggested every stupid thing they could think of to increase the security over botox—like audible alarms and electronic automatic radio transmitters if the drug vault was opened—in spite of the fact that they said the hospital was doing everything required by law and more controls would require more personnel to implement and botox is not a public danger, as it is anaerobic and is quickly reduced to impotency if exposed to air or oxygen. (All botox patients must come in on the same day as the vials containing the toxin quickly become impotent once they are opened to air.) I told the 2 female intern/fellows from Romania and Holland who were with Brin that I had spent 11 years training him, but we still needed to work on time management—he responded that he had too many patients and I offered to trim some other people from his list if needed.

Finally got my shot at 11:15 and left Manhattan as quickly as possible. I've been driving a car thru Manhattan from Harlem to the Battery and both eastside and westside since 88 on 3 or 4 occasions each year, and I saw a first time event on our way back to the Lincoln Tunnel. Some idiot was trying to deliver cargo in a full size 18-wheeler—everybody else uses smaller trucks, as the streets are so jammed and narrow in width. He was turning onto 57th Street, one of very few 2-way streets in Manhattan, and hung up on a parked car making the turn. A lead car and a trail car like an oversize load use wouldn't work in NYC. This moron must have had testicles the size of grapefruit or a brain the size of a pea, or both.

Next we left the campground and stopped at a service area to eat lunch late and I discovered that my sweetheart, who has a checklist to go over before we leave each time, had forgotten to latch the sliding door between our bedroom and the living room in the trailer and the rough streets of NJ and NY on the interstate had caused the door to slide and jam shut and I couldn't open it.

Ignored that problem for the present and decided to deal with it later. Then as we drove thru CT, Pookie found a scenic route, limited access, 4 lane, blue road on the map parallel to I-95 only 10 miles north of it and said we ought to take it as it wouldn't have all the trucks, so we headed toward it. Had to go thru a lot of construction, but got there in 15 minutes. Trouble is, it said no vehicles over 8 feet in height and the trailer is 9 1/2 feet high. Took another 20 minutes to get back to I-95.

Finally, we got to the campground northwest of Boston in the pine trees and very nice until, unhooking the trailer, I discovered I had left the electric jack post down too low and had hit it on the I-95 potholes in NYC and the bottom was all warped and the base wouldn't fit on it. Decided the best course of action was to have a few drinks and worry about the problems the next day as I lowered the trailer onto the bent post on top of a board. Actually, the bedroom door opened after I bent all the rollers it slides on by brute force and the only real problem was Duke coming into the bedroom when we got up to pee during the nite and couldn't keep him out. To top off the perfect day, we got to spend the nite in the Peoples Democratic Republic of Massachusetts.

This morning I fixed the bent electric jack post by getting the file out of my toolbox and filing off the warped part and the base now fits again. I knew the day would be better when we hit the NH state line and found the state liquor store on the side of I-95. They had so many brands of cheap scotch that Thoeny would have gone crazy. Pookie said I could even afford some of the single malts as they were so cheap, but I deferred as I may need to give her a liver transplant later and mine isn't used to good stuff—no sacrifice is too much for my honey. The little Maine towns along the coast are gorgeous; except we've only seen 1 red tree and we are definitely ahead of the Fall colors. I even managed to fix the door on the bedroom tonite when we parked in a campground near Bar Harbor on the fringe of Acadia Nat. Park. Duke and I watched the sunset over a bay to the west of us at about 6:30 and it was a beautiful sight. Duke played in the seaweed and surf and has now been in the Atlantic and Pacific, but not the Gulf. Will have to go to Key West this winter and fix that. Master Repairman

Sent: Monday, September 27, 1999 9:28 AM
Subject: Acadia Nat. Park

I'm not sure why, but some correspondents have been receiving blank pages of my travelogue on this trip. My sister-in-law, Sara, was the 1st to mention this, and having known her for over 25 years and being aware of her level of competence, I wrote back a smart ass note telling her she was doing something wrong. Then I heard from another correspondent saying the same thing and it hurt like hell, but I had to apologize to Sara. One of them said the message would appear when she hit the reply button, but the other apparently didn't try that tactic. The only thing I can figure is that the travelogue list is in my address book is a group and it has become quite long as additional people keep asking to be added. I've taken the last 15 names on the list and put them in a travelogue group 2 list and I'll send to the first group and cc the 2nd group and see if that works. Anyone who wishes the 1st 4 tomes of this trip let me know and I'll forward them. Incidentally, I don't know if the USIT watt line works in Canada, and if it doesn't, there won't be any more transmissions till we get back in the States. We leave for Nova Scotia tomorrow early. I've got to pay my credit card bill by computer today, just in case.

Duke really loves this Park. They let dogs go on all the trails if on a leash and he's getting his way far too often. Yesterday we met a couple with 3 dachshunds on a leash on a trail and Pookie said, "God, I'd HATE to have 3 Jack Russell's". When we got here, I discovered I had allowed 2 nights between here and NYC and we were a day ahead of our reservations. They had mailed me a confirmation, but I shrewdly left it on my desk at home with the Nova Scotia travel guide and couldn't remember the exact arrival date. Pookie noted that I rushed her thru southern Maine and didn't let her shop at L.L. Bean so we have to stop coming back.

Our 1st day here we awoke to the patter of raindrops on the roof. We're parked only a few feet from a bay, on Mt. Desert Island, with a gorgeous view over the water, but when everything is gray, who cares. The lady at the campground office said it was supposed to clear up after lunch and since she used "yall" in her speech and turned out to be from South Georgia, we decided to trust her. Went to Wal-Mart for Pookie's bi-weekly fix of shopping and I found a pair of moccasins they've started carrying. My toes are getting cold some mornings from wearing the sandals all the time. We did the Visitor Center with Duke left in the pet taxi in the Durango and managed not to knock out their power supply. The video is quite good for a national park and was provided by Ford Motor Co. Then we went up to the summit of Cadillac Mountain where the visibility was maybe 40 yards. The sun started to peek out about half way down on the way back. It's the highest point on the east coast of this hemisphere till you get to Brazil, and it's only 1536 feet high. Kenny said to get up before daybreak and take pictures of the sun rising on the first point it touches on the US mainland. He didn't get up at 4:30 every morning in the summer to go check cotton as an entomologist for 15 years. I've seen all the sunrises I need to see.

The rain did stop around noon and we ate lunch in Bar Harbor and walked Duke around the town a little. Gordon was right and it is a little like Gatlinburg with all the tourists. Then we went on the loop road and stopped at Sand Beach, the only natural sand beach in Maine. Duke really enjoyed running in the surf and there were a # of dogs there for him to smell and sniff. Thunder Hole was next and the tide was about 1/2 in and it was thundering fairly loud. It's a cleft in granite where the waves get trapped and make a thundering sound and throw spray way up in the air. Duke was standing next to the hole when it first went off and jumped up in the air when it scared him. We finished the loop road about 4 p.m. and it started pouring again so we went back to the trailer. Could only get the Michigan/Wisconsin game on TV and didn't get any scores from the South. Heard all the scores from these Podunk schools up nawth who think they play football. Got a USA Today this morning and found out Vandy won again and UT barely beat Memphis.

Yesterday the sun came up at dawn for a delightful day, cool and very clear. Linda and Gordon were here a few weeks ago and had e-mailed us from Prince Edward Island and given us their impressions of Maine and PEI. Acting on their advice, we did the western part of the island, which they had said was not as touristy as the east. We stopped at several overlooks and at Southwest Harbor which is a little fishing village and much more authentic. Gordon may not be able to read the LORAN when he is captaining a sailboat, but he does understand food and directed us to Thurston's Lobster Pound for lunch. It's at the end of a road in Bernard, another fishing village and according to Gordon has the best lobster in Maine. Linda must have found it for him like she reads the LORAN for him, as it is really out of the way with no advertising.

You have to pay before you get a table, so I selected Louie the lobster for Pookie and I got Harry with both about 1 & 3/4 pounds. The girl let me hold Louie while Pookie took his picture. We also got cole slaw and scallop chowder and iced tea, while Louie and Harry took a bath in boiling water. When I picked them up, I couldn't tell Louie from Harry, as both were now bright red and wearing identical rubber bands. They are served in paper bowls, which soon begin to leak thru the table and get lobster juice on your legs. You get no tools to use except a plastic fork and pick, so you get a little messy eating them. Pookie asked what was the yellow stuff she was eating that was attached to the meat. I told her it was vitamins, so she asked what was the green stuff. I told her it was vegetables just as we overheard the woman at the next table tell her companion not to eat that green crap. I received a dirty look. Both of us used the bathroom to wash off after lunch, but not much luck. I thought it was delicious, but Pookie's comment was; "Now we can say we ate lobster in Maine". Duke loves to roll over on his back and rub in dead fish, and he was really jealous of how we smelled when we got back to the Durango.

We went back to see the Bass Harbor Head Lighthouse and then did the Ship Harbor Nature Trail which is a 1 1/2 mile trail with half thru the woods and half along the rocky coast with splendid views over the water. We watched some fishermen work their lobster pots about 100 yards from us in a little cove and sat on the rocks and just looked at the views. Duke and I walked over the rocks to investigate a small tidal pool while Pookie watched from about 35 yards away. Duke saw something move in the tidal pool and launched himself from the edge of the cliff about 6 feet above the pool. He thinks nothing about leaping from heights of 15 feet, so this was not totally unexpected. Fortunately, I had the leash tight and short and I yanked him back as he leaped. The result was a mid air somersault and a perfect upright landing back on the edge of the cliff. Pookie laughed and asked what kind of trick was that. I replied that it was the known as the "I'm not going to have a wet dog in the Durango trick".

We finished the west side of the island and then went back to Jordan Pond on the loop road. I wanted to take the loop trail around it the day before and Pookie wanted to do the gift shop at the restaurant there, but it had been raining hard. Pookie did her thing and then we left for the trail, which my navigator said, was easy and 1.3 miles on a paved surface. The first part was easy or as Pookie calls it, "the suck you in" part. Then it changed to rocks and then large tree roots across the trail and then boulders as large as small cars. I walk almost 4 miles per hour and even with the uneven surface I had the Iditarod sled dog pulling on the leash all the time, so I wasn't going too much slower than normal. After 1/2 hour we weren't to the halfway point around the pond and it was getting darker and colder. We passed a lot of hikers early on the trail, but only 2 couples half way around and they weren't wearing sandals. As we started on the return part of the loop after 45 minutes of steady hiking over constant obstructions we came to a part where the trail was impossible to see and for as far ahead as we could see it was large boulders. Duke shifted to his mountain goat routine and leaped over the boulders like he knew where the trail went. We followed and after maybe 300 yards we came to a visible trail again and a boardwalk over a marshy area. A sign said the forest floor was a fragile ecosystem and to stay on the boardwalks. Duke didn't read it. The only word he fully understands is "eat" and the word "no" is not part of his vocabulary, or at least he refuses to recognize it. We had boardwalks for a few hundred yards and then back to boulders and tree roots. The next time we found boardwalks, I heard Pookie say, "Thank God for the ecosystem"! The end finally came into view about 1/2 mile ahead and Pookie said she knew the last few hundred yards would be "suck you in" with smooth surface and level. She was right. When we finally got back to the Durango she read the trail guide again and it said the trail from the parking area to the restaurant was 1.3 miles and paved and easy. The loop trail was 3.5 miles and ranked moderate. Another small error. We'll never do a strenuous trail, at least not knowingly.

I am continuously amazed at Pookie's ability to awaken from a deep sleep in the Durango while I'm driving and grab her map and give directional instructions with the bark of authority and then crash back into dreamland, leaving me and Duke to figure out what she might have said if she had known where the hell we were when she looked at the map. The words, "I don't know" are beyond her comprehension. I used to think this talent might be unique to Pookie and my Mother, but I now think it may be a sexually inherited trait common to most women.

I made a reservation on the ferry to Yarmouth, Nova Scotia yesterday for us and we have to be there at 7 a.m. The guy said the fare was $234 and I said no, I just want one-way. He said that was the one-way off-season rate. It's a 3 hour crossing and I'll have to invite my lady friend into the bedroom of the trailer while we're on the ferry so I'll be closer to getting my money's worth. Then he asked how long the total was for the trailer when hooked to the Durango. I said 42 feet like I actually knew, when it was really a wild ass guess. Then he said how high was the trailer and I said 9 1/2 feet, when I really don't know. He said he hoped I was correct, as there was a 9 foot 9 inch limitation. I'm gonna measure the damn thing now. Then we're off to see the Schoodic Peninsula, which is a separate part of the park about 45 miles away. Adios.

Sent: Sunday, October 03, 1999 6:42 PM
Subject: Nova Scotia

Well, I guess somebody has to be perfect and it must be me. It's a tough assignment, but I've struggled with it for a long time and still manage to cope. Of course, Pookie expects me to fix all problems, and I usually do. Yep, I just figured out this morning how to communicate again by e-mail while in Canada. The USIT watt line doesn't work here as you've probably guessed by now. When I called them the guy said they were working on it and expected to have the watt line working in Canada in 60 days. Sounds like a bank saying they are going to fix your statement soon. I tried for several days to do a telephone credit card hookup and got the Pulaski USIT connection to talk to my laptop and they were beeping and honking and growling at each other, but the Pulaski connection server would never answer my laptop and would ultimately disconnect. Of course, I blamed USIT for the problem and kept assuming they would correct it in a few days. Turns out that my El Cheapo telephone credit card, Voice Net, which is the cheapest telephone credit card around, will not carry data quality transmissions—it only has microwave towers and has no landlines, but costs less than 1/2 as much as MCI. I'm now using MCI and doing an MCI credit card dialup with country code and it works. Have no idea what it costs, but it ain't cheap. Hold off on the pictures and long multi media files if possible, but I got one today that is so cute, I may send it out anyway. Took 12 minutes today to send 8 messages and receive 80 and download our bank statements.

We did do Schoodic Point our last afternoon in Maine. Absolutely beautiful and a terrific afternoon with waves breaking on the rocks and Duke behaving for once, as we sat on the point for an hour or so. Sunshine, a cool but mild breeze and a spectacular view of the Atlantic. I kept seeing a flash like a semaphore signal with a mirror, which appeared to come from over the horizon out at sea, but nothing would be in sight after the flash. As we left the Point, we drove by a US Navy station that said Group Security Site, No Admittance without DOD Security clearance. I had thought it might be a reflection off a periscope lens and wonder if it was.

The 29th, we got up early and went to the ferry for the trip to Nova Scotia. I was a few minutes late getting there and the guy said was I Mr. Davis when I drove up. I responded affirmatively and he told me to park the trailer and Durango at the front of lane 10 and come back and break in line to buy my ticket using him as authority as I would be one of the first to board the ferry. I instantly recognized true genius and told him I would do as instructed—he had perfect taste and manners. Only a few minutes after I got my ticket and customs form and we put Duke in the pet taxi in the trailer, a guy walked up and said drive forward and enter the ferry. Duke has never ridden in the pet taxi in the trailer when it is moving and immediately began to whine and cry when it moved, but we had been told we had to ride in the passenger section of the ferry and couldn't ride in the car and Duke wasn't welcome in the passenger section. Pookie was delighted to be free of me and Duke for the ferry ride. As I drove forward with a big grin on my face, a guy in a ferry uniform walked up and said, "I hope you can back this thing up". I said sure and he said turn it around and back onto the ferry—250 yards away downhill around a curve with a chain link fence on each side of the road and then up a ramp into a dark hold, with a 6 inch clearance between steel posts on each side, into a parking space, while Duke cries all the time. After he got over laughing at my comment about his ability to excrete solid waste product, he said he would walk beside the trailer and tell me when I did wrong. About half way down the road, when my neck was cramping from trying to see around the trailer, Pookie said very sweetly that everyone was waiting on us to board the ferry and they were all watching me to see if I screwed up. Her way of checking my ability to handle stress!

Naturally we made it perfectly and all 140 other vehicles got to board the ferry on time. The ferry is a catamaran and very fast. It cruised at 39 knots—

45 mph—with 400 passengers and would carry 900. We rode in oversized cushioned seats like 1st class airplane seats, only larger, with a table in front and views out the windows, which were floor length picture windows. There was a full size cafeteria and we ate a big breakfast. The ferry could do 51 knots or 60 mph at full speed and was very interesting. A full casino in operation too, with a whole deck of slot machines. 4 big marine diesels generating 38,000 horsepower (the Titanic only generated 50,000) with each slaved to a 1000-kilowatt generator to power 4 huge turbine pumps. No screws on the ship (literally) as it sucked in water at the front and expelled it at the back at the rate of 2 full-sized Olympic swimming pools per second. Must be very inefficient, but fast as can be, and I guess that's the point for a long distance ferry. It's called "The Black Cat".

When we got to Yarmouth, Nova Scotia we were the first off as everybody else had driven their cars around a semi-circle like in a parking garage and was behind us, but there wasn't enough room for the trailer to turn the corners, hence the backing on. Incidentally, the rig hooked up is 42 feet long exactly—that perfect part again. We stopped in Yarmouth to free Duke and let him ride in the Durango again and to exchange money at a bank. $1.44 Canadian for $1 American with a charge of $1.73 Canadian to exchange $500. If I ran the Royal Bank of Canada, the charge for money changing would go up.

We stopped in a Provincial Park for lunch and drove all the way to a campground outside Halifax for the nite. We did do a detour for an hour or so to Mahone Bay, a picture postcard fishing town on my list to visit. In fact, a lot of Nova Scotia along the coast is like a postcard. Mahone Bay was having a scarecrow festival and the whole town was decorated with scarecrows and was cute as can be. Found a campground with cable TV to suit Pookie and only a few kilometers from Halifax. Discovered my trip computer in the Durango will do statistics in kilometers as well as in miles and will do temperature in Celsius as well as Fahrenheit.

I'm a few days behind in writing as I lost interest when we couldn't transmit, but I'll catch up in the next few days. Have heard from Snake Henry who is in Atlanta with Tax Snake Baddour and their wives at the Marriott. Apparently all their clients will have to pick up the tab as they are going to some kind of school on stealing from the government, which is a relief from their usual practice of stealing from clients exclusively. Snake says they are eating like Epicureans and living in the Marriott with views of the Atlanta skyline and room service and booze whenever they want. He said he couldn't find a porter to carry his laptop from class to class and he really wanted to repair or fix something to equal my skill, but had no tools and nothing had broken yet that servants couldn't fix, but he was on the lookout for opportunities. See why they're Snakes?

Bon Jour

Sent: Tuesday, October 05, 1999 6:47 PM
Subject: Come Back List

Nova Scotia is on my revisit list already. Along the seacoast it's beautiful and cool and very picturesque and everybody is friendly as can be. We did Halifax on the 29th and it's a delightful city. The harbor is one of the world's best and largest. Halifax was the only colony in the Western Hemisphere that was settled and authorized by an Act of Parliament. It was established when England decided once and forever to kick the French out of North America after a series of wars and changes in their relative positions in North America. Of course, the first requirement if you're a maritime power is a first class harbor. Halifax harbor has a narrow entrance, which can be easily defended, is very deep for all size ships and is huge, and could hold the entire Royal Navy at anytime in the Navy's existence. We went to the Citadel for our first stop. It's a fort overlooking the city and harbor and was built to protect the city from a land-based attack, not from the sea. It's actually the 4th fort to occupy the site and was finished in 1865, mainly to protect against the Americans—read that as yankees—who had rough relations with the British during the War of Northern Aggression. We spent several hours there and even ate lunch at the fort. Superb seafood chowder and a quite good sandwich. Watched the firing of the noon signal gun from the fort with a gunnery crew in 19th Century dress and a black powder charge from an old cannon. Also watched bagpipers and soldiers drill and play and fire their black powder rifles. Lots of exhibits and history of the area and of Nova Scotia. Well worth the visit.

Next we did the Maritime Museum of the Atlantic, which took several hours too. They had a 3D movie of the expedition that re-discovered the wreck of the Titanic and their dives to the site filmed under water and covering the wreck. Fascinating and full of surprises. No jewels, but the bow of the ship is just like the movie with the rail where our hero and heroine stood. A lot of history of WWI and II and the role Halifax played in both wars as the convoy departure point for all convoys to Europe. Lots of marine exhibits, but maybe the most interesting is the Halifax Explosion in 1917 that was the largest release of energy at one time prior to the A bomb at Hiroshima. A French munitions ship was hit in the harbor by a Norwegian relief ship for Belgium and the French ship caught fire, was abandoned by its crew and drifted up to a Halifax pier before it exploded. The explosion was heard 200 miles away and the harbor beneath the hull was emptied of water by the force of the blast, which created a tidal wave as it refilled. All buildings within 1/2 mile were eradicated and a lot of people died immediately and a lot later from wounds. Flying glass blinded over 200 survivors and fires were started that burned down most of the rest of the city. The pictures looked just like Hiroshima after the A-bomb. They had a lot of pictures and interviews from survivors. To finish the day, we walked Duke around the Historic District and I went to a memorial for Canadian sailors who died in the Battle of the Atlantic fighting against U Boats and the memorial featured a video about the Canadian Navy in WWII.

The next day we did the southeast coast near Halifax to visit some towns we had bypassed driving up from Yarmouth. Peggy's Cove was our first stop and it is very scenic. It's a fishing village of 60 souls on a bleak and severe coast with rock and grass and no trees, but terrific views of the sea and a lighthouse showing the entrance to Mahone Bay—not the town, but the bay. Looks a lot like Scotland in the North where there is very little vegetation. Even though we are out of season, there were a lot of tour buses at Peggy's Cove. Duke and I walked out on the granite rocks past the signs that said at least 1 or 2 tourists are washed out to sea every year, but most are rescued and they only lose 1 every few years.

Our next stop was Chester, a town where rich yankees from New England have built huge summer homes and where a lot of loyalists from New England resettled during the Revolutionary War. We ate lunch at The Captain's House, which is a B&B plus a 5 star restaurant. Best seafood chowder I've ever had—the mussels were still in their shells, but cracked open to let the cream sauce in while cooking and it contained Atlantic salmon as well as whitefish, lobster and scallops along with the mussels. We both had the crab cakes on a bed of greens with a superb dressing on the greens and a New England type of Caesar Salad. We ate on the glass window porch overlooking the bay with a beautiful sunshine reflecting off the water where the sailboats were anchored. Go experience if you can.

Next we redid the town of Mahone Bay, which has 3 churches each next to the other with a view of the Bay from each. The bright colors of the houses and the harbor with boats everywhere is scintillating. Pookie had found a needlework shop there when we stopped before and wanted to go back. Duke and I walked around the churches and the waterfront while Pookie shopped. She has been working on a Christmas stocking for Rachel since Rachel was born and Rachel is now 6. Maybe Rachel will have a child named Rachel who can use it when Pookie finishes. A lady came out of a gift shop and told me to make sure Duke didn't pee on the scarecrows she had decorated for the scarecrow festival.

Our next stop was Lunenburg, the city settled by Germans on the coast that turned out not to be Germanic. All the settlers were Protestants from a principality northwest of Switzerland that spoke a Germanic dialect, but is now a part of France and they were all Francophobes, but the locals called them German. It too is very picturesque with an Academy on a hill outside of town that looks like a German castle from a distance. It was the beginning of Octoberfest and the locals were dressed up in period costumes from 18th century Germany. In the harbor there is a Maritime Fisheries Museum, which is excellent. It details all the history and methods of fishing in the Maritime Provinces. Guides give narratives about different subjects all thru the museum during Octoberfest. We listened to a narrative about whales, which was extremely good by a local lady who was also a honey. The Blue Whale is the largest animal ever to inhabit the earth and has a heart the size of a Volkswagen Beetle and a tongue that weighs more than an African elephant—it's the size of 2 18 wheelers parked nose to tail, only with more volume, and a 13 year old child could swim thru its vascular system. The calf weighs 5500 pounds and the father whale pushes it to the surface so it can take its first breath of air. She covered all the whale species and their peculiarities—quite well done. Whale watching is a big deal here for tourists, but we did that in Alaska and of course it's out of season here now. The museum includes 2 fishing trawlers floating on the bay that are from the days of wooden and steel ships. I was amazed at the size and comforts they offered to the crew.

Went back to the campground after Lunenburg and spent the next day traveling to Baddeck on Cape Breton Island in a constant rain. Cape Breton is the northern 1/3 of Nova Scotia and is actually a lot of islands together. It's very Celtic and has nearly a pure Britannic population. We actually got there a little early in the p.m. and I had time to get a haircut. Pookie took a picture of the barbershop, which was a shack in the front yard of the barber's house with a hand painted barber pole. A young Mikmaq Indian was in the barber chair when I went in. He was getting his semi-annual haircut and there was enough jet-black hair on the floor to stuff 2 pillows. Mine was kind of long too and I noticed as it hit the floor that it is turning blonde again. I was a cotton-top blonde as a child and it's getting that way again, or at least that's my opinion. The barber had been in the Korean War and that's all he could talk about. That's where he met a lot of Americans and his memory of the US is stuck in that time period. Reminded me of those people who are forever locked in their college experience—sort of like UT fanatics.

We're now in P.E.I. or Prince Edward Island, but I'm gonna finish the Nova Scotia epistles before I talk about P.E.I. Heard from sister-in-law Sara Smart Ass, who said she is still receiving the stories of a man, his idiot dog and his long suffering wife, but she still has to hit the reply button before the stories come up. As long as she doesn't actually reply, I'm happy and still convinced she is doing something wrong. Several people have said they are receiving a lot of gobbledegook along with the messages. I sent the last message to myself along with yall and it is clear as a bell (not my relatives the Bells) after traveling over the void of cyberspace. Who's wrong?
Evan

Sent: Thursday, October 07, 1999 7:33 AM
Subject: Cape Breton

Our 1st day on Cape Breton we went to the Cape Breton National Park which is in the highlands in the north and along both the Gulf of St. Lawrence and the Atlantic in the east. It's called the Cabot Trail and is absolutely superb. A pretty autumn day with heavy cloud cover in the a.m., giving way to total sunshine later in the day. We started at the large Visitor Center in Cheticamp on the west coast and after spending a little time with the exhibits and video went back into Cheticamp for lunch at another seafood restaurant. Tried the chowder and Caesar salad again, but not even close to Chester. The road is 105 kilometers thru the Park and we stopped at a lot of the look-offs, which is what they call the overlooks. The road climbs to 455 meters, or around 1500 feet when it isn't along the coast and the variety of the scenery is amazing. We did 3 short trails with Duke thru a bog on boardwalks, a 350 year old maple tree forest and along the Atlantic coast over the rocks to give you an idea of the diversity of the scenery. The west or Gulf of St. Lawrence coast is very severe like Scotland while the east or Atlantic coast is more mellow and soft like England. Near the end of the day I took a side road about 7 kilometers long to St. Mary's Falls, some picturesque waterfalls in a conifer and hardwood forest and gravel. Duke got to tour the waterfalls too and on the way back to the main road, at a speed of about 15 mph, I saw a large mouse crossing the road in front of us. I told Duke to look at the mouse in the road. Big mistake as the next thing I heard was the sound of his dog tags hitting the glass on the rear window as he exited the Durango to go hunt the mouse. We leave the right rear window down for Duke to hang out and smell the air when we are going slow, but the problem is that he can get thru any opening he can get his head thru. He's never leaped from the Durango before while it is moving, although he once left thru the rear window of the Blazer at 20 mph when he spotted a squirrel. I stopped and jumped out and started calling him, but was totally ignored as he was hunting live prey. After running 75 yards behind the Durango in the ditch the mouse had entered, he came back and ignored me as he charged 75 yards ahead in the ditch looking for the mouse. I got back in the Durango, cranked it up and blew the horn. He came running back to get in and Pookie was laughing so hard she didn't open her door soon enough. He came around to my side and jumped in looking at me like I was a traitor for trying to leave him behind. We finished the Park tour and went back to Baddeck by way of St. Ann's which has the only Gaelic College in the western hemisphere and actually teaches Gaelic. Nova Scotia is the most Celtic of all the Maritime Provinces, after the expulsion of the Acadians, and is nearly 100% English, Welsh, Scottish and Irish in its population.

The next day we went to Louisbourg to begin the day. That's the French fort, harbor and village on the east coast of Cape Breton that was the site of French power and influence in North America, prior to the final defeat of the French by the British in 1758. Actually, the Fort was captured by yankee colonials from New England in 1745 after a short siege, but was given back to France by the British in the Treaty that ended that war. In 1758, it was captured again by British troops after a long siege and this time the British did to it what the Romans did to Carthage. They dismantled all the fortifications and carried off the building materials so that nothing was left except the foundations of the previous buildings. After WWII, the Canadian government began a project to reconstruct 1/5 of the original site in stone buildings like the original, in order to give employment to unemployed coal miners. A wall surrounded the original site 2 1/2 miles in length, so the reconstruction of only 1/5 is still a huge project and the largest historical reconstruction in North America and another National Park. It's manned by people dressed in period costumes who do drill, fire flintlock muskets and provide tours and oral history. Again it was a beautiful day with a lot of sun as we walked around the park. We ate lunch in a reconstructed stone building, with wenches serving us 18th century food at common benches, with a couple from New Zealand and a couple from New Orleans. I had pea soup, brown bread and trout with carrots and turnips. Pookie had the same except with meat pie. All you get to eat with is a large spoon and a cloth napkin. Ever tried to eat a not de-boned trout with the head still on and nothing but a spoon? Yep, I used my fingers, but it was good. I even ate the eye of the trout to see what it tasted like. Skip it if you get the chance.

After the fort, we did the Marconi Trail along the Atlantic coast where Marconi first sent a wireless message to Europe. Skip that too if you can. Not much scenery and no exhibits on Marconi. We did stop in North Sydney on the way back to Baddeck to check out the ferry schedules to Newfoundland for our next trip. They don't have next year's prices yet, but this year it cost about $600 Canadian for a round trip ticket from Nova Scotia with the trailer taking the short ferry to western Newfoundland and the long ferry from eastern Newfoundland back to Nova Scotia. Since Newfoundland is over 500 kilometers from west to east, I don't want to take the short route both times. The good news is the ferries are not catamarans and there were a lot of 18 wheelers lined up to get on, so maybe I don't have to back on. The ferries are the size of cruise ships and much slower, as the long ferry is 14 hours, but they have kennels for Duke. I also want to take a ferry from Newfoundland to Goose Bay in Labrador, but would leave the trailer and maybe the Durango in Newfoundland. Actually, Labrador is a part of Newfoundland, but is called Labrador for identification purposes.

The next morning we did the Alexander Graham Bell Museum in Baddeck. It's very well done and worth a trip by itself. I never knew that his father and grandfather were both professors of speech and elocution and he was a teacher of language to the deaf. Born and educated in Scotland, he immigrated to Ontario with his parents after the family developed health problems in Scotland. His father developed a visible speech language for deaf students and Alexander taught Helen Keller, among others. His Mother went deaf at an early age and he dedicated his life to teaching the deaf to communicate long before his invention of the telephone. His wife was a deaf student of his. He actually knew a lot about speech and sound, and only a little about electricity when he invented the telephone, modeling it on the physical characteristics of the human ear, which he discovered by dissecting ears from cadavers. The museum is terrific and well designed. He was a prolific inventor who discovered things about genetics, construction, aviation, hydrofoil boats, and a lot of other subjects, but is only remembered for the telephone. He gave all his stock in the Bell Telephone Co. to his wife as a wedding gift, except for 10 shares he kept for himself. Three years later, the stock was selling for $1000 per share. He spent the last 20 years of his life in Baddeck, Nova Scotia, which he adopted and loved, as it reminded him of Scotland. He was an amateur inventor, unlike Edison and quickly lost interest in a project after he figured it out. His wife managed the family finances and made them both rich, although she started out rich and her father backed his invention of the phone. On reflection, maybe he overdid the communication bit with women like my wife, who loves to stay on the phone with other women.

I forgot to mention that on our last morning in the Baddeck campground before we went to the Bell museum, Pookie had the TV on a Canadian talk show as we got dressed. They were interviewing a Canadian author who had just written a new book on dogs. When asked about the worst dogs for family pets, he listed the Border Collie because it had overdeveloped herding and guarding instincts, the Irish Setter because it is so inbred that nearly all are neurotic, the Rottweiler because it is too aggressive and the Jack Russell Terrier. When asked why the Jack Russell, he said it was the Cuisinart of dog problems. After the laughter, he said its worst fault was its overdeveloped hunting instincts and then commented that a Jack Russell hasn't had a really good day unless it's killed something. When the interviewer asked about a Dalmatian, the author said that was another bad choice. He said the only thing dumber than a Dalmatian is 2 Dalmatians. My conclusion is that a J.R. may not be a good family pet, but is great for an older couple that needs exercise and a personal vs. family pet. Pookie remains silent.

After we left Baddeck, we drove all the way to Borden, P.E.I. at the foot of Confederation Bridge, across from New Brunswick, Canada. Until 1997, P.E.I. was a true island and the only access was by air or ferry. Now there is a 9- mile multi span bridge over ice-infested waters, which we took. It rained all the way from Baddeck, and when I stopped for gas at a service station I asked the attendant how long the rain was forecast to continue. His reply was, a day and 1/2, but based on their track record, the sun could come out that night. I assume they have the same forecasters we have in the South. Adios Evan

Sent: Thursday, October 07, 1999 3:42 PM
Subject: P.E.I.

I really like the guidebook we are using—we've never used one traveling in the trailer in the States, but I bought one in a Mall in D.C. titled Eastern Canada—Travel Smart. It's by John Muir Publications and is written by a Felicity Munn. It covers everything in Canada from Toronto to the east and the feature I like the most is that it doesn't try to list all the attractions, museums, restaurants, hotels, shopping etc. in an area. Instead it lists only the best ones and limits itself to a few in each category. The author prefers natural attractions to man-made and her taste is quite good, meaning it agrees with mine. She's especially good on restaurants and shops and attractions and we ignore her suggestions on campgrounds as we pick our own from the Trailer Life Campground guide that covers all of North America.

Our first morning in P.E.I. we went to the Acadian Museum west of Summerside. Really enjoyed the video on the history of the Acadians from the 1700s to today and the exhibits were quite well done. I didn't realize that the ones in Louisiana were sent from Nova Scotia and New Brunswick back to France and were then kicked out of France and sent to Louisiana from France. A lot of them resettled in P.E.I., when they were permitted to do so from other places. Their culture is gradually being absorbed into the majority Anglo community and very few even speak French at home anymore. Next we went up the west coast to see the bottle houses, a chapel, house and tavern made from 25,000 bottles cemented together by a retired fisherman. We knew it was closed for the season and we couldn't go inside them, but thought it might be worth a look anyway. Bad guess although we did see the corners of 2 of them, the view is blocked by hedges and shrubs. After finding a place to eat and buy gas in a tiny town, we drove up to North Cape, the northwest tip of the island where the Northumberland Strait meets the Gulf of St. Lawrence. Nice views looking out to sea where currents from both waters meet on an offshore reef, but the coastline all around P.E.I. is low and not dramatic like Nova Scotia. There is a wind research center at the Cape and a number of windmills. We did the small Visitor Center and the movie on the wind research and the wind was blowing about 40 mph while we were there.

The next morning we went to Woodleigh, a collection of large-scale models of historic buildings in Great Britain created by an eccentric retired Canadian Army Officer. We laughed at the idea, but it was surprisingly interesting. The model of York Minister Cathedral is one of the first you see and the detail and exactness is impressive. We've been in the original in England and even the stained glass windows are an exact copy on a small scale. The largest model is the Tower of London and is big enough to walk in and climb upstairs in the Tower where there are even exact copies of the Crown Jewels. St. Paul's Cathedral, St. Giles Church, Anne Hathaway's Cottage, Shakespeare's Birthplace. Robbie Burns Cottage, and Dunvegan Castle are among about 25 models depicted in a large and well-maintained English Garden. We had never been to anything quite like it. We drove to New London for lunch and I picked out a restaurant that had a tour bus and local cars parked out front. After ordering, I went in the restroom and discovered 2 old geezers from the tour bus stumbling around inside while they loudly badmouthed another old geezer on the tour. It turns out the subject of their ire had accidentally dropped his wallet in the toilet on the tour bus and then raised hell with the driver until he stopped and somehow fished the wallet out. When I got back to the table and told Pookie, she grinned and asked if the driver of the bus had a blue arm. I said I didn't know, but I was pretty sure that the driver now fully understood all the implications of the term "dirty money".

The most famous person from P.E.I. is Lucy Maud Montgomery, the author of Anne of Green Gables and about 20 other books and hundreds of poems and short stories. There are at least 5 sites honoring her, but we only went to the Green Gables site that is part of the National Parks System in the P.E.I. National Park on the North Shore in Cavendish. It is the site of the farm of her cousins and the house that inspired Green Gables and contains Lovers Lane and the Haunted Woods depicted in the book. There are 2 videos that compliment each other and tell about Green Gables and Montgomery's life and several exhibits. We toured the actual house that has been restored and preserved and then did the Lovers Lane walk among the woods by a small creek. I enjoyed it even though I didn't expect to. When the bridge to New Brunswick was being built there was a public contest to select the name for it and the most popular suggestion was Span of Green Gables. The politicians in their wisdom ignored the public and named it Confederation Bridge instead.

Next we drove the 40 km trail along the shore that is a National Park. There are dunes and small cliffs and surf, but not anything spectacular. The entire island is red dirt and the small cliffs are red too from the iron oxide in the soil. Even the surf and sea where it is very shallow and where the sun is in your eyes looks like it has a reddish tint. The island is almost flat with a few gentle hills and valleys and is covered by bike trails on abandoned railroad tracks. Agriculture is a big deal here and the scenery is bucolic (that means pastoral Pamela Sue). It's pretty but not what I expected. P.E.I. potatoes are the biggest deal and are grown everywhere on the island and advertised in all the restaurants in the Maritime Provinces. Big potato trucks are everywhere on the highways. Grains, blueberries, turnips and beef and dairy farming are present also and there is some 2nd growth timber. Fall colors are just now getting pretty and we've been disappointed in the color in all of Canada so far. All the local TV stations have a color person and report on the color each Fall and the consensus is that Fall is going to be late this year or disappointing and only the White Mountains in NH are pretty so far.

Today, our last day in P.E.I., we went to Charlottetown, the capital. Last nite it rained a drizzle all nite and turned cold with terrific winds all nite and today. I even abandoned my uniform and wore socks and shoes and an undershirt and sweater today. Province House is the seat of the Provincial government and was the site of the meeting in 1864 that led to the Confederation of Canada and is still in use today. Tour guides gave us a very good tour of the building and explained the form of government, which is parliamentary. The upper house was abolished in 1891, so it's unicameral. The good news is that in P.E.I. the Conservatives hold 18 of the 27 seats and the liberals only 8 with 1 minority party member (who is called a democrat—poor slob). At the time of Confederation, Canada was only a very loose affiliation between Quebec and Ontario and the Maritime Provinces actually came to Charlottetown to discuss a Maritime Union—not Confederation with Canada. In fact, the Canadian delegates were not even invited to the meeting, but showed up on their own. There was a week of meetings, parties, balls, and speeches and political discussions, with no written agreement, but in the tradition of England, they emerged with an oral agreement to join together. It's ironic that P.E.I., the smallest Province and the site of the meeting didn't join the Confederation at first and joined a few years after the other original members. They have an excellent movie recreating the events and the audience of mostly Canadian tour bus members applauded at the end of the movie. We ate lunch in a pub downtown and walked to Peake's Wharf, which is closed for the season and then drove to Victoria-by-the-Sea, a small village on the southern coast that is quaint. I walked Duke while Pookie went in a shop and then we came home early as it is still windy and cold, but supposed to warm up tomorrow. Fate made it cold, windy and wet on the day I had reserved for Pookie to shop. I've been living right.

We're off to New Brunswick tomorrow and then we start the trip home. I'm saving the Bay of Fundy side of New Brunswick for the next trip, so we won't stay long there this time. Not much more to report on this trip, but maybe another epistle later. I'm finally caught up.
Scribe

Sent: Wednesday, October 13, 1999 3:59 PM
Subject: Trip Home

We left P.E.I. on Oct. 8 and finally found some pretty colors in New Brunswick, Maine and later in NH, VT and N.Y. We stopped in Fredericton, the capital of New Brunswick and toured the Provincial Government House, which is like a state capitol, but this one wasn't too pretty. No tour guides on hand that day, so we did it by ourselves in a short time. Across the street is the Beaverbrook Art Museum, so we did it too. It's named for Lord Beaverbrook, the captain of industry in wartime Britain who promised Churchill that Britain would out produce Germany in airplanes and ships and kept his word. His family donated most of the works of art in the museum. The centerpieces of the museum are 3 works by Salvador Dali with a bench in front of them for contemplation. Didn't take me too long. One gallery was what people call "modern art" and I call junk. "Half a Man" is the title of an oil on canvass of a man in trousers from the waist down. Reminded me of the controversy in NYC between Guiliani and the Brooklyn Museum of Art, except there were no paintings of the genre being debated in Brooklyn. The Mayor is going to lose his fight with the Brooklyn idiots because he's letting it get characterized as censorship. The real debate ought to be over whether or not public funds should be used to subsidize the arts at all. I think conservatives could win that argument, but not one about censorship. Personally, I think the crap put out by immature morons who are tortured by their inner selves and have to express themselves by displaying to the entire world that they never accepted potty training and must throw tantrums like 2 year olds by defecating on religious objects, shouldn't be called art. Duke's poop shows all the artistic merit that elephant dung does. Besides, the last thing of cultural interest that was exhibited in Brooklyn was the last game the Dodgers played at Ebbetts Field and that was at least 35 years ago. We were going to spend a nite in Fredericton and go to an attraction called Kings Landing, which is a recreation of a settlement by loyalists from the States during the Revolutionary War, but changed our minds and drove on to northern Maine for the nite. Beautiful drive down the valley of the St. John's River with full fall colors and a gorgeous sunshine day. Changed my money back to American and got charged $1.48 Canadian for $1 American. Restored my faith in the international brotherhood and fraternity of moneychangers that I got screwed.

The next day was pretty again and more color all along the interstate. We stopped in Augusta and toured the state capitol, which is self guided with some exhibits. They have a plaque commemorating all their Medal of Honor winners and there are 53 during the War of Northern Aggression and only 23 in all the conflicts since then. About 1/3 of the 53 were at Little Roundtop at Gettysburg when they stopped Longstreet's men from winning the battle at a cost of 80% casualties suffered to Alabama and Mississippi troops. Next to the state capitol is the state museum and we spent a few hours there. It's free and quite well done with exhibits that go on forever depicting the history and industry, fishing, agriculture, mining, quarrying, logging and manufacturing in Maine. Then when you think you're finished, it starts the people of Maine, beginning 10,000 years ago. Finally gave up and walked thru the last part and drove on to Hampton, NH where we spent the nite at a campground run by a female Nazi. It was dark when we got there and the sign said no dogs. Pookie told me to go in and ask if Duke could stay anyway. I asked if she wanted me to start the conversation by saying I couldn't read, and suggested that Pookie might be less confrontational than me. She agreed and went in and sweet-talked the bitch into letting us sneak Duke in after being told no and waiting till everyone else left the office and then asking again. Gates with cards to get in and out and speed bumps every few feet and signs everywhere saying don't do this or that. Never been in a campground where the owner treats you like dumb scum. The showers took quarters and then didn't work, so I spilled all my gray water on the ground as we left the next morning to get even. I never did take commands too well.

The next day it started raining as we drove west across NH and VT toward Albany, NY. Rained all day as we went thru the prettiest colors yet, but in drizzle and rain. Saw 1 guy standing out in the rain taking a video. It was Sunday and when we finally got to Albany, the state capitol was closed according to Pookie's book, so we went directly to a campground. The next day was gorgeous again so we hooked up and drove into Albany to tour the capitol and found 2 empty parking spaces a block away that I could get the trailer in and loaded the meters with about $3 in coins. Met a nice lady from NC who asked us if the guided tour had already left and why were the doors to the capitol locked. That's when I figured out it was Columbus Day and the building was closed and that's why we had found a parking space so close to the capitol. It is an impressive building on the Empire Plaza done in Italianate, French and Romanesque styles of architecture. Maybe some other time.

Drove on down the interstate and stopped and called the dealership in Adamstown, PA where I had bought the trailer, to see about some minor repairs being done the next day. They said they were booked up with work till Nov., but referred me to the Sunline factory 1 mile away which does repair work as well. I called them and was told they were booked too, but when I told them I was from TN and there were no dealers within 250 miles of me, they agreed to take us at 8 a.m. the next day. Spent the nite at a campground 1/2 mile from the factory and got there the next morning on time. They couldn't have been any nicer and said to leave the trailer and pick it up after lunch. We went to a laundromat and Pookie did laundry while Duke and I read the paper and walked around. Went back after lunch and the guy had found a few other problems and offered to fix them too. Gave us a new CD player for the trailer free, as the old one didn't work. Found a worn tire with steel belts visible and replaced it too and Pookie talked me into buying a spare, as we've never had one. Don't know why I gave in, except to shut her up, as I'm not going to change any flats on it if we have any and will call a repair truck. I don't even have a jack that can lift it up. Left about 3 p.m. and drove to Coatsville, PA to the first campground that would let us download e-mail in 3 days. Called cousin Larry who has moved to Exton, PA, a few miles away. This cousin is on my side of the family, so he's quasi normal. He said he and Dale would treat us to dinner, but I said no, we'd treat them. Larry said O.K., then we'll go someplace nicer. He gave me directions and we met them for dinner a few miles away at Ludwig's Grill and Oyster Bar. Excellent food and we talked so much; we forgot to show them pictures of the grandkids, Duke and Cousin Paul. Larry wanted to know if I was going to write about him like I did cousin Paul, and I said of course and I'll tell everything. Larry said I couldn't say anything bad about him that hadn't already been said by some one else, but please send him an unexpurgated copy of any comments. We did have a very nice visit and Larry showed us a shortcut to DC taking back roads in PA.

We're now back in Bull Run Regional Park and Duke is having a fit over the squirrels and deer. We'll visit with the grandkids for a couple of days and then go home. No more tomes from this trip. Sortie

Chapter 6. Key West Trip—2000

Sent: Wednesday, January 26, 2000 6:20 PM
Subject: Suwannee River Campground

Yep, we're on the road again. Left Pulaski Jan. 24 with 24 degree temperature and headed South to sunny FL. where the temperature hasn't gone above 52 degrees since we got here and the first nite it was 30 degrees. We spent the first nite in my brother's driveway in Gulf Breeze. I shrewdly had decided to wait till we got to FL to check the propane tanks, as it was too cold at home to bother with checking them. We slept in the trailer with Duke in Will & Sara's driveway and ran out of propane. The furnace tends to put out cold air when it runs out of gas and the next morning the toothpaste was hard as a rock in the tube and the Right Guard was so cold, it didn't want to spray from the can—good thing we didn't sweat, huh!

George & Betty came over for dinner at Will & Sara's and we had a nice visit. Duke came in the house once and terrified both cats who arched their backs, hissed like crazy and departed from sight. Duke never got over it and kept trying to get back in the house for more fun & games. Filled the propane tanks at Navarre Beach Campground and it sure is nice to have heat and hot water. Also flushed the anti-freeze out of the fresh water system so we can drink and shower as well as use the john.

We're now at the Original Suwannee River Campground on the north bank of the river about 140 miles north of St. Petersburg. When we checked in the guy in the office invited us to a free Pig Roast with all the fixins Fri. nite & Sat. nite. Said he had kilt 2 pigs and was providing Live Blue Grass Music for the best dern time this side of the Suwannee River. "Yall Come" was the invite and I'm not making this up. He had on jeans and a Red Man baseball cap. Sorry my Miss. State friends aren't here. Wish we could be here for that, but we have a reservation at Boyd's Campground & Resort in Key West for Jan. 30 to watch the Super Bowl.

Today we went to Cedar Key and our sense of timing remains impeccable. It was low tide, the State Museum is closed on Wednesdays and the high temperature was 41 with a cold wind blowing. Ate lunch at the Brown Pelican and had oyster stew and a fried oyster sandwich, although the restaurant never warmed up. Pookie did a few of the antique and gift shops while Duke and I made every pelican on the city wharf take flight—at least the sun was out. Allen had told us there wasn't much to do in Cedar Key and she was right. We did do a small historical society museum and it took 10 minutes if you read everything there. We did come back to the campground through the Lower Suwannee River National Wildlife Refuge and took a short hike on a loop trail through an archaeological site. It is a midden, or garbage dump where Indians discarded shells, bones and other refuse for more than 1,000 years. It is over 28 feet high and covers about 5 acres. Duke showed no respect for the site and marked the territory anyway.

Tomorrow we go to Sarasota and park in Steve and Allen's driveway for a few days. They are having David & Mary Wade over for dinner Thurs. nite and that should be fun, although the forecast is for freezing weather as far south as Tampa—our luck is holding. We plan to do Dry Tortugas Nat. Park and Key Biscayne & Everglades on this trip, but I've decided to skip the Virgin Islands Nat. Park. We'll also visit more relatives on the east coast of FL and come home thru GA. Only plan to be gone about 3 weeks or so as we have season tickets to Vandy basketball at home and need to get ready for the SEC Tournament in Atlanta in early March. Discovered this afternoon that the phone line for modems at this campground is out—even though they advertise modem accessibility. Will send this when we get to Sarasota.
Scribe

Sent: Monday, January 31, 2000 8:14 PM
Subject: Small World

Here we are in Key West parked next to a bunch of guys from Fayetteville, TN who are down here fishing. One of them roomed with Joe Fowlkes, my state representative, in college—if you can call U.T. college. I bought Duke from Joe's wife and this guy sent Stephanie Fowlkes an e-mail saying she should refund my money as Duke is raising hell with their fish camp. Actually they gave us some fresh fish they caught today so Pookie gave them some pickles and then one of them said it was his idea to give us the fish and he didn't get any pickles, so we gave him another quart and then the 3rd guy said it was really his idea to give us the fish and I told him and the 4th guy no. Larry Craig is the guy who roomed with Joe and he said he sat with Joe at the 1st Titans game this year and with another crazy Giles Countian at the last Titans game, as we watched them go down in flames last nite. We wore our Titans shirts & waved our Titans flag and out-cheered the few Rams fans.

After Suwannee River we spent 2 nites in Steve & Allen's driveway in Sarasota. They invited David & Mary Wade over for dinner Thurs. nite and we ate lunch with David & Mary Wade as their guests the next day as they wanted to repay Steve & Allen. I thought I had managed to get 2 free meals, but I had to pick up the check Fri. nite at the Summer House in Sarasota for Steve & Allen & T.P. & Lynne who live in Palmetto and came over Fri. nite for drinks & dinner. All of us except Lynne are from the Delta and grew up together, so we had to relive a lot of past history and listen to a lot of BS. Fri. we did do the Selby Gardens botanical gardens in Sarasota, which cover 7 acres and are open to the public. Very interesting and well done. Selby had a small oil company that ended up being called Texaco, so he had a few chips to leave to the Foundation that keeps up the gardens.

I was reading the Sarasota paper and commented to Allen that they sure did have a lot of news about the local funeral homes. She replied that Sarasota-Tampa is known as "God's Waiting Room" and funerals are a big business with the airlines making out well too as the deceased is usually flown nawth to be planted and has several services with only the 1st in FL. This is the height of the season here as everybody who can afford to come south has done so by the end of Jan.

We drove down I-75 to Naples and then did the old Hi-way 41 to Miami, as I expected it to have more scenery than Alligator Alley, the 4-lane interstate toll road across the Everglades to Miami. It was scenic, but we passed an accident scene where a 5 or 6-year-old boy fishing from a bridge had darted in front of a car and the paramedics were working on him as we passed and the life flight helicopter came. The little boy was still in the opposite lane lying on the asphalt, as I guess they were afraid to move him, and were waiting on the board from the helicopter to put him on, so as not to move him twice. Makes you think about what is really important.

We did stop at Big Cypress Nat. Preserve and saw the exhibits and the movie about the Preserve, which is very much like the Everglades. This is the dry season and the water is very much reduced. Spent Sat. nite at the Gold Coaster RV Resort in FL. City and skipped the party that they had that included a country & western female entertainer and sloppy Joe's. I think we'll stop here for 2 or 3 nites going back and do the Everglades Nat. Park & Key Biscayne Nat. Park from here before we head north to terrify some more relatives.

Saw a new vanity tag on a customized van camper from New Jersey, which held a middle-aged couple and said CRAMPER. Reminded me of the vanity plate we saw on the Washington, DC Beltway last fall on an SUV with crash bars on the front and middle-aged female driving, which said
X. P. T. P.M.S.

Today we did the trolley tour of Key West where you can get on & off and get a narrated tour of the city, so you can go back and see what you want later. Had lunch at the Raw Bar on the waterfront and did the Flagler railroad museum, the Truman Little White House and the Shipwreck

Museum. Will go back and do more museums and the Hemingway House with the 6-toed cats later. All the cats used to be named for famous actors, but they've broken tradition by naming one Bill Clinton. On the other hand, he may be the greatest actor of them all. The good news is that the Bill Clinton cat has been fixed and the Monica cat has been spayed.

Tomorrow we board the Yankee Clipper II at 8 a.m. for a trip to the Dry Tortugas Nat. Park. It's a 2 hour boat ride, but they have a full bar. The seaplane is quicker, but what would you do with a few more hours at Fort Jefferson? I figure we may get bored with 4 hours there anyway, although snorkeling gear is included in the ferry price. Duke is not happy getting locked up in the trailer everyday while we sightsee, but it's too hot to leave him in the Durango, got up to 80 today—he'll get over it. Superman

Sent: Thursday, February 03, 2000 9:01 PM
Subject: Key West & Dry Tortugas

Pookie finally read my last epistle and said she was disappointed that there wasn't more Duke news about his stay in Sarasota. He made so much noise when we chained him up in Steve & Allen's front yard, that he got put in Driftwood Kennel & Pet Cemetery for 2 days. We didn't let him see the sign that said they had a cemetery when we dropped him off. I did sign him up for a personal playtime each day for $3 extra per playtime. They asked if he liked Frisbee, fetch, ball chasing or what and I told them all of the above. They have a fenced acre for the dogs to run and I would like to have seen them when they tossed the Frisbee and Duke looked at them like they were stupid. I declined the offer of a video of Duke's playtime for an extra $3 and also the offer to let him have a swim in the heated pool for another $3, but did say he would like the nature walk. Wonder if he got the playtime.

The ferry to Dry Tortugas was another catamaran, but not too fast as it took us 2 1/2 hours each way and it's only 70 miles from Key West. The day started sunny, but changed to cloudy and windy as the day progressed. Saw no marine life on the trip, but it did get rough as the day progressed and Pookie took a Dramamine for the return trip as the cat bounced around a good bit. She rode on the stern going out with a barf bag in her hand. Out of sympathy for her, I stood beside her and drank beer as she grimaced—no sacrifice is too great for my baby. The barfers did run off the smokers.

The Dry Tortugas are actually the last of the Keys and there are 7 of them. Tortugas means turtle and dry means there is no fresh water for ships to take aboard. All 7 Tortugas can be seen at the same time and none are very big. Ft. Jefferson sits on the 3rd largest and has 12 acres inside the walls of the fort and there are only 4 acres outside it. We had a really good tour guide named Steve who came with the boat ride and gave us a 1 1/2 hour tour of the fort with all the history and background. The boat ride included breakfast and lunch and after lunch, Steve gave another 1-hour tour of different parts of the fort for about 1/3 of us who asked for more. The boat ride included snorkeling gear also, but by noon it was getting chilly with the wind, so we skipped that part. We got back to Key West just as the sun came back out and saw the daily Sunset Festival from the water. It's a collection of artists, trinket sellers, entertainers and tourists that takes place every night, 365 days a year, on the waterfront and includes palm readers, dog trick acts, escape artists doing Houdini type stuff, fire breathers and other carnival type acts. We went back tonite with Duke and stood around for a couple of hours and watched the entertainment. I asked a dog trainer, who had an act, if he ever tried to train Jack Russells. He laughed and said life was too short.

When we did the Hemingway house yesterday we got the real skinny on the 6- toed cats. There are 62 cats living at the house now and all are descendants of Papa's cats. About 1/2 have extra toes, and a few have 7 or 8 toes. All are named for famous people and the staff is embarrassed at naming one for Bill Clinton, so now they just call it Bill the cat. Hillary the cat is there too, but they swear there is no Monica. Our guide did say that Bill spent too much time at the cathouse and that's why he lost his equipment. The house has a tin roof and I asked if this is where "Cat on A Hot Tin Roof" came from. The answer was no, but they did have a cat named Elizabeth Taylor.

Pookie did the Audubon House while Duke and I sat on a nice cool balcony across the road and watched the tourists and the parking meter police. Saw about 6 $50 tickets given out. The guidebook material says Key West gets over $1million per year in traffic fines. We ate lunch in the restaurant owned by Kelly McGillis of "Top Gun" and "Witness" and it was quite good. Conch fritters and clam bisque for appetizers with Caesar salads. Key West is 2 miles by 4 miles and a lot of people on rented scooters like mine. We actually saw a guy riding a scooter down the street and talking on a cell phone at the same time. The island is 2/3 bigger than it used to be as the Navy dredged out really deep shipping lanes for the old submarine base and enlarged the island with the spoil. We also did the Museum of Fine Art and History today and listened to a docent tell us that the building was the work of the architect Henry Richardson who was famous for Romanesque buildings in Boston and New York. When he finished, Pookie told him that Union Station in Nashville was also the Richardson Romanesque architecture. A few minutes later, while we were in the 1st gallery, we overheard him telling the next folks in line that Richardson did famous buildings in New York, Boston and a railroad station in Nashville. Pookie already wants to come back as the ambiance of the island intrigues her. Why is it that the places on our comeback list, Nova Scotia, San Diego and Key West are all at the extreme ends of this continent?

We now have neighbors that Pookie calls Click & Clack. Two retired men who have given up sailing and bought a motorhome and are trying it out before they bring their wives. They are first timers and keep asking questions about how this or that works on the RV. I told them about the directions Ken & Faye got when they borrowed the motorhome named Beulah from a friend. They got printed instructions on how to light the hot water heater, cut off the propane, hook up to electricity, etc. Instruction # 23 was about what to do when an 18-wheeler passed them going way over the speed limit and nearly blew them off the road—it said to grasp the steering wheel tightly with both hands and yell, "Aww Shit". Instruction # 24 was to wait till the heart slowed down from racing and the adrenaline slowed down, which was usually about 400 yards further down the road and then to say softly under your breath to the 18-wheeler driver, "Asshole"! Back to the Mainland tomorrow. Errett

Sent: Sunday, February 06, 2000 8:39 PM
Subject: Florida City

We're back in The Gold Coaster RV Resort in Florida City, which is adjacent to and directly south of Homestead, FL and the last town before the Everglades and the Keys. There's no way hurricane Andrew could have caused all that monetary damage in Homestead, as there's nothing here to damage. No SunTrust banks in this area, as the locals don't have enough money to attract STI, which only preys on the wealthy, for the most part. The last 2 nites have been very cool, down to 46 one night and 49 the next, but warms up into the 70's during the day as the sun is always out in the daytime.

Yesterday we did the Everglades from the main visitor center down to Flamingo on FL Bay. Left here about 8:30 and got back after dark around 6:30. Did the movie & exhibits at the visitor center and then did a nature walk at Royal Palm visitor center with ranger Bob along a manmade slough or borrow pit where rock had been excavated for a road in the 30's which now contains deep water, over 10 feet deep, plus a boardwalk over a part of the Everglades. It's called the Anhinga Trail and if you come here, it's a must see. Anhinga is a water bird akin to a cormorant, which swims underwater and spears fish with its bill, which it then swallows whole. We got to see that act plus lots of wildlife including alligators up close and personal. Ranger Bob was quite good and pointed out lots of stuff we would have missed on our own. He also gave a talk before the walk on the history and evolution of the Everglades with handout exhibits and maps including satellite photos of changes in the Everglades.

Next, we went down to Flamingo, which is 38 miles further south and on the coast at Florida Bay. Ate lunch at the restaurant there and then did a cruise on FL Bay on a boat that advertised seeing a lot of bottle-nosed dolphin as well as a lot of other wildlife. We did see an osprey catch a fish and then get attacked by a bald eagle trying to steal the fish, which in turn was attacked by 5 or 6 additional ospreys. The bald eagle ignored the other ospreys but did let the one with the fish get away, as the other ospreys distracted the eagle. The tour guide said the eagle would even take on a pelican, which is larger than the eagle. Of course, Duke even bit a pelican that was slow taking off from our Key West campground and it was much larger than Duke. Duke's pelican cratered into the ground when Duke grabbed the wing on takeoff. I must advise that Pookie's dolphin call is every bit as effective as her moose call, and we never saw one. Coming home, we did a few short trails with one to a mahogany hammock and another to an overlook tower looking over the river of grass.

This morning we went to Biscayne Bay Nat. Park, which is east of us a few miles like Everglades is west a few miles. Got up early in order to get a ticket on the glass bottom boat tour as 95% of the Park is water and most of the land part is on Keys accessible only by a boat. Our luck is still holding, as it was too cold and windy today and the boat tours were canceled. Did the Visitor Center and a short walk along the Bay, but we sailed through the Park a few years ago with Linda & Gordon on our way down to the Keys where I lost—or pirates stole—our dinghy and we snorkeled in John Pennecamp State Park and spent a nite in No Name Harbor on Key Biscayne, which is just north of the Park. Did Everglades Alligator Farm and Airboat Ride to finish up the morning. The alligator farm is not necessary, but the airboat ride is super. It was a big airboat carrying 25 people, but at a speed of maybe 40mph. They don't permit airboats in the Park, but the Park only covers 1.5 million acres of the Everglades, which now cover about 10 million acres, down from 50 million originally. Take an airboat ride if you come, and this one is only a few miles from the Park entrance and ecologically done on existing trails, with no new ones added.

Went back to the Everglades Nat. Park at the northern visitor center at Shark Valley this afternoon. Took the narrated tram tour, which I would also recommend to everyone. Saw tons of wildlife and maybe 50 alligators, including an alligator about 15 feet long. Lots of bird life and a lot of Kennys toting tripods, but I never saw a single one who had a cute female gun bearer carrying the tripod, like Faye does—although a lot of the camera freaks were a lot cuter then Ken. Maybe they don't give out mink coats as gun bearer prizes.

Trip Potpourri:

1. 1.Going out to Dry Tortugas the catamaran dodged lobster pots for at least 40 miles. Reminded me of the Gulf of Maine which is also covered with lobster pots. I don't see how any lobsters survive in either place to breed and reproduce.

2. For about 50 years, Key West was the largest and richest city in Florida and for a short time had more millionaires per capita than any city in America—population at the highest was 27,000, which it approximates today if you don't count tourists. The wealth came from ship wrecking which was legal salvaging of wrecked ships under the supervision of a federal court in Key West. The shipwreck museum gave a really good interpretative history of shipwrecking and said there was no truth to the rumors that Key Westers lured ships onto the Florida reef, which follows the Keys south. Right!

3. One night in Key West we heard jets for 2 hours close by. The only jets at Key West airport are private jets and small commuters. Had to be a wing flying in from a carrier to the Key West Naval air station, or flying out to practice night landings on a carrier.

4. At Hemingway House there is a 1935-penny corroded and stuck in the cement by the salt-water swimming pool. Story is that Hemingway spent $8,000 buying the entire house and while he was on a trip to Spain, his 2nd wife, Pauline added the pool at a cost of $20,000. Hemingway got home while the cement was still wet and was not too happy. Story is he told her to take his last penny and bent down and stuck the penny in the wet cement. He had 4 wives and maybe that's why he committed suicide.

5. Henry Flagler built the railroad that went to sea from Miami to Key West, finished in 1912. Flagler was the partner of John D. Rockefeller who sold out to John D. and then spent 35 years building railroads and hotels in FL. The railroad was destroyed in a 1935 hurricane, but on land, not at sea, and the railroad bridges are still here. It would be the equivalent of 1 man building the Alaska pipeline today. Flagler had a few bucks.

6. There are truck farms everywhere here that make California look puny. Every kind of vegetable, flower, and fruit that you can think of, except for pineapple, which is produced cheaper in Hawaii now. Most of them have U-Pick operations too, and for the most part, they are not irrigated. Lots of coconut and date palm groves too. Sandy soil and flat as a board.

7. Prisons are a big business in the Everglades. Federal and state prisons all over the Everglades, kind of like northern Michigan where prisons are a big business as for 9 months in northern Michigan, nobody wants to escape. Here nobody wants to escape year round as the mosquitoes would kill in every season except now, not to mention snakes and alligators. My favorite is one called Everglades Academy for Juveniles. "Political Correctness" at its height. On the other hand, we saw a video of tourists doing the Swamp Stomp where they dress up in

shoulder length wading boots and wade through the muck and slop seeking orchids, snakes and stuff, and pay money to do it. Skipped that. Evan

Sent: Saturday, February 12, 2000 7:00 PM
Subject: Cordele, GA

Yep, that's where we are now, the watermelon capital of the world, watching UT play FL in basketball. Can't decide which I want to lose the most—wish both would. I guess UT is a little more detestable as they have more orange on their uniforms.

We knew it all along guys, but I've discovered 1 more piece of evidence that females are the colder sex. When the female alligator builds her nest for egg laying, she uses mud and organic matter that decays and adds heat to the nest just like a compost pile. The eggs are fertilized internally before they are laid, but all the hatchlings turn out male if the temperature of the nest is 88 degrees or higher. If it is less than 88 degrees all the hatchlings are female. I rest my case.

We spent a nite in Delray Beach, FL visiting Jim & Laura. Laura is Pookie's 1st cousin once removed and also Pookie's Godchild. She just got her own Harley so she can ride with Jim without riding behind him. Duke didn't get along with Tooney the cat, so Duke spent the nite in a kennel where they said it was mandatory that the dog get bathed on discharge. I think they just wanted the extra money, but said O.K. if Duke got to bathe with at least 2 poodles. We spent the nite in the house for the 1st time out on this trailer trip. Had lunch on the upper deck of Boston's, a restaurant on the beach watching the yankees freeze their butts off on the beach. Laura's Dad, Bruce, came over for dinner and we enjoyed seeing him for the first time in years. Bruce creates surfaces for and installs swimming pools and recently got back from Saudi Arabia where he put in a pool for some rich sheik—said he was never going back.

We next spent 2 nites near Cape Canaveral and a whole day from 9 till 6 touring the Kennedy Space Center. It's really well done and a lot better than Houston or Huntsville. Saw 2 IMAX movies, about 4 other movies or videos including a replay of Neil Armstrong landing and taking off and were bused all over the complex to an observation tower near the shuttle Endeavor, which went up Fri., and was on the launch pad when we were there. We also did the Apollo complex and the International Space Station. There is a special display on Robot Scouts, the probes we send out into space and to the moon and Mars, which is really designed for kids and is cute as it can be. The narrator for the Robot Scouts says she is a programmer for the robots, but she doesn't look like a rocket scientist to me—more like Miss July. Rachel would love it, but I wouldn't want to be the one to tell her she couldn't go back through it over and over. The crawler transporter that carries the fully assembled shuttle and external tanks to the launch pad at 1 mph travels over crushed rock as it would break up any pavement. The vehicle assembly building is bigger than the Pentagon and Empire State buildings combined and has it's own huge ventilation system to prevent it from raining inside the building. Go see the Space Center if you are in the area, and we saw alligators and eagles on the premises since most of the Space Center is a game refuge.

Went to Jacksonville next to take my niece Ginny & nephew Will to dinner Sat. nite. Brother Will & Sara came over from Gulf Breeze to see Ginny and to get a free meal off of me. Ginny works at Steinmart, created and run by Jay Stein from Greenville, MS who graduated from high school with brother Will, although she got the job without Jay's knowledge or help. Will called Jay and asked him and his wife to join us for dinner, but Jay declined this time, although he did have Will & Sara stop by his office and visit for about 20 minutes. Pookie, Duke and I went down to Mantanzas Inlet north of Daytona Beach Fri. and pulled into a restaurant on the inlet just as the staff came out to watch the shuttle launch. It had just lifted off on TV and we were 40 miles up the coast with low clouds up to about 35 degrees between us and Canaveral, but it broke out of the clouds after maybe 1 1/2 minutes and we could see it for maybe 10 seconds before it was out of sight and probably going 3000 mph when we first saw it—puts out a very bright flame and accelerates very rapidly. Nephew Will brought a girl he is dating to dinner with us, and we had a nice family visit. Poor girl must have thought she was being inspected for approval.

Pookie bought a Jacksonville Times Union which led to 2 revelations:

1. 1.Jacksonville may be the only city of any size in America that has as bad a newspaper as the Nashville Tennessean, and
2. Tipper Gore will be in Jacksonville Sunday for a fundraiser hosted by Jay Stein at his house for Al Gore. Jay refused comment to the newspaper that speculated the fund raiser would raise more than $200,000 for Al. Maybe brother Will wants to add his check to Al. I'm gonna send a check to Guiliani.

Tomorrow we do Andersonville Nat. Historic site where 13,000 yankees died in the last year of the War of Northern Aggression at the Andersonville Prison. The poor Confederates couldn't feed themselves, much less all 45,000 yankee prisoners housed here, although most died of disease. We'll also do Plains, GA and see the Carter Museum there, although Carter's Library is in Atlanta. Jimmy may be in Plains tomorrow and welcomes visitors to his Sunday School class when he's here, but I don't plan to go.

Brother Will drove up from Gulf Breeze a few years ago and went to Jimma's Sunday School class. He said Jimma asked how many of the visitors were Republicans and nobody raised their hand or answered affirmatively so Jimma reminded them they were in the house of the Lord and should tell the truth. All laughed, but nobody admitted it still, including my brother. Home on Monday nite if all goes as expected. Time for my nightly toddy or two. Have limited my drinking to only those days that end in y since Pookie developed a liver problem, out of sympathy for her.

Chronicler

Sent: Sunday, February 13, 2000 10:20 PM
Subject: Plains, GA

Plains may not be the end of the earth, but it has to be close by. Reminded me of that old Trust Company of Georgia (predecessor of SunTrust) saying that if you took Atlanta out of Georgia, what would you have left? The answer is Mississippi. Nothing but pecan tree orchards, cotton farms, peanut farms and Billy Carter's gas station within miles of Plains. Jimma actually grew up in Archery, GA, about 2 miles from Plains and home to 2 white families and 25 black families. Did his museum, which was his high school till 79 when it was consolidated into Americus about 10 miles away and a few light years ahead of Plains. Jimma is here now and the secret service won't let us stop at his house or take pictures. He did teach Sunday School today at the Baptist Church—another Southern Baptist like Bill Clinton, except that Jimma only lusted in his heart while Bill does it everywhere. Rosalyn is also from Plains and 3 years behind Jimma in the history of Plains, GA. Jimma is a really nice and good man, but was a very weak President. Gerald Ford's pardon of Nixon elected Jimma, just like Ross Perot elected Bill Clinton twice. Funny how politics is a slave to current events. Pookie discovered after we left the museum that she was wearing her shirt from the Ronald Reagan Library with the Ronnie patch on the pocket—I had nothing to do with it—and the attendants in Jimma's museum had too much class to mention it.

Andersonville Nat. Historic site is a MUST SEE. It's a site dedicated to all American Prisoners of War from the Revolutionary War thru the Gulf War and is very well done. I was surprised to learn that we had 12,000 Americans die on British prisoner of war ships during the Revolutionary War, as well as to learn that the War of Northern Aggression prison in Elmira, NY had as high a death rate as Andersonville, even though the yankees had enough food to prevent it if they had wanted. It's really a site dedicated to man's inhumanity to man but called a prisoner of war site. The Confederate commander of Andersonville was executed by the yankees after the war, after a mock trial, which tried to indict and execute Jeff Davis and Robert E. Lee as well, but the yanks had to settle for the prison commander. He went to his grave saying that he understood orders, as he was being killed for following them—sound like WWII? The citizens of Americus, GA, 10 miles away complained of the smell from Andersonville, and we wonder why the Germans didn't stop the Holocaust. In fact, the Andersonville Museum reminds me of the Holocaust Museum in Washington, DC. There are a lot of interactive exhibits where you can get the words of the average prisoner in any of our wars, including Revolutionary, 1812, War of Northern Aggression, WWI, WWII and Korea as well as Vietnam and the Gulf. One of my favorite pictures was the one of the sailors from the USS Pueblo captured off the North Korean coast by the North Koreans and released to the American Press to show that the sailors were being treated well. In it, every American has his index finger extended and the others on that hand retracted—the Koreans thought it was a signal that meant, "I am well", and I think it really was, but they punished the crew when they found out what it really meant. One of the most memorable Nat Historic Parks we have ever visited. Go see and spend some time. Going home tomorrow if not blown away by the tornado forecast for our area tonite. Pookie thinks we should go hide under the Durango if the wind gets loud. Raining kind of hard now and I think we should take the scotch under the Durango too. Bon Voyage

Chapter 7. Pacific Northwest Trip—2000

Sent: Wednesday, May 10, 2000 8:09 PM
Subject: On The Road Again

We're back in WaKeeney, Kansas in the same campground we used last year, 1001 miles from home, and on our way to the Pacific Northwest, including parts of Canada. (Give you 10 to 1 that I get back a few replies asking where are we going this time.) We're still working on seeing all the Nat. Parks and we had to come back this way because Congress in all their wisdom created a new Nat. Park in south central Colorado. It's Black Canyon of the Gunnison, which was a Nat. Monument last year when we got stuck in CO for an extra week and could have come to see it while the Blazer was failing to get fixed—our amazing string of luck and impeccable sense of timing continues. We left home the 8th of May and drove to St. Louis to meet Mel & Elaine again at a campground on I-44 in southwest St. Louis. Naturally, they had a flood in west St. Louis the day before we left with over a foot of rain. It was 89 degrees and humid as could be when we got there, with the ground steaming and giving off humidity. We broke the drought that had existed for nearly a year in that area. Really enjoyed seeing Mel & Elaine, who fed us steaks for supper, but would you believe your scribe fell victim to that demon rum! I really feel sorry for those of you who don't imbibe, as when you get up in the morning, you feel as good as you're going to feel all day, while my day keeps improving as it goes along. We did have to call Betty Jo from the road to put down the garage door after we left home, and Pookie said to tell everyone that she has been right 5 times so far—she doesn't count the wrong times, but I did stop for her to buy $10 worth of Big Game Lottery tickets and I bought $5, but we're still poor. Naturally, there was another thunderstorm in St. Louis that nite, but the big limb that I heard hit the ground missed us by 2 feet.

We drove to Independence, MO the next day in almost constant thunderstorms with the clouds down to the road at times and black storm heads all around us. A guy passed us during one of the rare periods when it wasn't raining and made all kinds of negative gestures while pointing toward the trailer. Being alert and terrified, I pulled over on the side of the Interstate to examine the trailer. The bedroom window which doubles as an escape hatch from the trailer had come open and was flapping in the breeze. After listening to Pookie diagnose the problem incorrectly as usual, I fixed the window, which had suffered no damage and secured it by weighting down the latch release handle with my sandals. During this period, after I had sweetly suggested that Pookie get out of the way and leave me alone with the problem, I heard her talking to someone outside the trailer while the 18-wheelers roared by about 1 foot away. Yep, a highway patrolman had stopped to see if we needed help, so I said as I exited the trailer that I didn't want to stop there, but had to fix a problem. Pookie had already conned him into leaving us alone.

We stayed in Independence in a really nice campground in a city park with cable, concrete pads and super clean restrooms. We were too late to see the Truman Library, so we went downtown to the Visitor Center and saw a short movie on Truman and got the skinny for today. This morning we got up early and made the Visitor Center before it opened and got tickets to tour the Truman home, which is a Nat. Park Historic Site at 9 a.m. Had an excellent Park Ranger named Keith give us a tour with only 1 other couple. This guy was so good and thorough; I couldn't even ask many questions as he anticipated nearly everything. Actually, the home was Bess Wallace's home and Truman moved in after he married her—along with her mother, grandmother, and 1 of her brothers and his wife. I'm not sure I could have done that—in fact, I'm sure I couldn't have. In addition, her other 2 brothers and spouses had homes on the same property and everybody had Sunday dinner together. I would have killed someone. As you can guess, Bess had money and Harry did not. I never liked money that much. Harry courted her for 9 years and was turned down before she finally agreed to marry him. They met when he was 6 and she was 5 in a Presbyterian Sunday School class. I'm not sure if that's predestination or perseverance.

We did the Truman Library 25 years ago with the kids when we went to Yellowstone and Grand Teton, but I didn't remember much about it. I'm sure the kids were pestering me to leave the whole time we were there and begging to stop at the next teepee along the side of the road so they could get fake tomahawks made in China. (Take that kids!) Our luck is still working, and they began a complete restoration of the Library on May 1st this year and have removed some of the exhibits and have construction going on all around the Library. We stayed several hours anyway, and thoroughly enjoyed it. There is a 45 minute narrated slide show about Truman's life that is really well done and impressive. It's not nearly as fancy as the Bush or Reagan or Johnson Libraries, but he was arguably a greater president and made more difficult decisions—even if he was a democrat—but back then there were conservative democrats still in existence. He and Bess are buried on the grounds and Bess has on her tombstone that she was first lady for 7 years—Pookie asked if Hillary would put that on hers? The only reason we stopped in Independence was to see this Library again and I would fully recommend it. "The buck stops here" sign is on display as is the oval office reproduction, as it existed then. I couldn't help thinking that there was no oral sex in it back then, or even the thought of it. When they finish the restoration of the Library in a year, it will have all the fancy interactive computer stuff added, but I'm not sure Harry would approve—he took pride in being an ordinary man. Harry lived to be 88 and Bess to 97, so they must have done something right. Recovering Alcoholic

Sent: Saturday, May 13, 2000 8:11 PM
Subject: Colorado Again

Drove from WaKeeney, KA to Manitou Springs, CO which is a suburb of Colorado Springs and a nice community. Got there in time to drive up to Pike's Peak, but when we got to the Pike's Peak toll road, they told us it was open for 16 miles and the summit was 19 miles, so we demurred and went to The Garden of the Gods instead. That's a city park in Colorado Springs with a lot of red rock formations in unique shapes and very attractive and only 1 mile from our campground. I felt very comfortable and content in The Garden of the Gods—-almost like it was made for me. Super campground named Pike's Peak Campground on Manitou Ave. and we were parked next to a mountain stream that flowed down from Pike's Peak and was 8 feet from our door with the bubbling brook sound all nite. The only defect was a lot of squirrels and Duke couldn't eat for hunting all the time. There was a walking path along the stream and a city park adjacent to the campground, and the Rocky Mountain News from Denver was delivered free to our campsite every morning. Pookie said it still wasn't The Ritz Carlton, but I had room service, even if she didn't.

The next morning, Pookie called the Pike's Peak Toll road and they said the road was now open to 18 miles and might be open by noon as the snowplows were running. I said did she really want to test our luck and she said no, so we went to the Pike's Peak Cog Railroad and bought tickets to the summit. It's 8 1/2 miles up to the summit at 14,110 feet and grades of 25 % at about 7 miles per hour. Our female conductor said to drink a lot of water to combat altitude sickness, but there was no restroom for 1 1/2 hours. Sounded like conflicting advice to me, so I chose to take a chance on the altitude sickness. Good choice. A pretty ride up and gorgeous views from the top, but the temperature outside at the summit was zero degrees and a 30-mile per hour wind, so we didn't stay outside too long. We talked about our boys going to Pike's Peak on a road trip and Pookie decided to send them a postcard reminder. Doyle worked for Southwestern one summer selling bibles and religious books in OK and KA. When it was time for him to come home, we sent Will in Pookie's car to get him. Will was 16 and just started driving, so we sent Rod, a friend of Doyle's with Will. I gave Will a $100 bill and several gasoline credit cards and sent them off. When they got Doyle, they called and asked if they could take an extra day or 2 coming home and I said yes. Two days later Doyle called and asked if I would wire them money. I asked where they were and he said he didn't know so I told him to look out a window and read a sign. He said the only sign he could see said Big Horn Motel. I told him to put Will on the phone and Will immediately said, "I didn't want to do it, but they took my money and made me"! I said where the hell are you and he said Pike's Peak, but we're out of money and hungry. I told them they were going the wrong way and to come home. They said I needed to send money for them to get home and I said NO, as they would go to California if I sent money. They made it home in less than 24 hours driving constantly and eating junk food at service stations that would let them charge it on the gasoline credit cards. Looking at Pike's Peak road in the snow and with hairpin turns for at least the last mile, I decided I made the right choice in the railroad. Every July 4 there is a road race up to the summit with all kinds of vehicles from souped up go-karts to dragsters. The record speed around a hairpin curve is 79 mph. and there are no guardrails.

After eating lunch and going back to the campground to get Duke, we drove to Florissant Fossil Beds Nat. Monument north & west of Manitou Springs. Crossed the continental divide at a town named Divide—clever name. The fossil beds are where a fresh water lake was 35 million years ago. Volcanoes that erupted constantly surrounded it and the ash settled in the lake and created shale, which preserved the fossils. Quite interesting and over 1400 fossils of insects and 140 of plants. You can view them under a microscope or magnifying glass at the Visitor Center and they are very detailed, including worms, fish, birds and small mammals. There is one of a tsetse fly that causes sleeping sickness and today is found only in sub-Saharan Africa, in a belt across the continent. We took a short walk along a trail past petrified stumps of giant sequoia trees as large as those in CA today. After that we drove back to Manitou Springs thru the Cripple Creek mining district that covers about 16 square miles and still has gold mining. Over 21 million ounces of gold so far from this small area, which is more than from Alaska and California combined. Today, about every 4th building in Cripple Creek is a casino and they mine plastic and paper as well as gold. Reminded me of Deadwood, SD.

We were going to tour the Air Force Academy in Colorado Springs, but got some info on it and it is a self guided auto tour with access to a few buildings if you want. After reading the brochure, we decided to skip it. At West Point and Annapolis, they give you escorted and guided tours, walking and in buses and do a class act. The Air Force has more money and gives you crap. Thoeny taught at the Air Force Academy for several years, so I'm not totally surprised that it's cheap.

Driving here today I was thinking about the Los Alamos fire. Pookie and I have walked across the Bandelier Nat. Monument where the fire was set. It has cliff dwellings and earlier Anasazi Indian Kivas, but is not heavily forested. The paper says the Nat. Monument Superintendent has been put on paid leave while the investigation goes on. Boy, that's a helluva sanction. Give him a paid vacation as temporary punishment. I would suggest he NOT use the Pookie Defense. I discovered the Pookie Defense about 10 days before we left on this trip. Pookie got up early to take her car to Nashville to be serviced and called me at 6:30 a.m. to tell me she had hit a culvert and torn up a tire and would I come change it. As I was getting dressed she called back and said she had torn up 2 tires. When I asked for about the 3rd time how she hit a concrete abutment over a culvert without hitting the hazard sign that was 6 feet in front of it, she responded by saying—"Shit Happens"—my first clue that she wasn't gonna tell me—and her defense position. When we were driving into St. Louis, her cell phone rang and it was the Mercedes dealer asking if she was satisfied with her repair work—$600 to realign her car—not to mention 2 $100 tires. They didn't ask me. The Pookie Defense worked for her, but this guy had better take a different approach. When Congress starts investigating and using weather forecasts as justification for action—this guy is in deep doo doo. When did a government weather forecast become anywhere related to a fact? Those guys have never achieved a success rate above a coin toss, and now we're gonna use a weather forecast to hang this guy? Half the time they can't tell if it's raining by walking outside. My suggestion is that he says he's from the government and was there to help. Then I would throw myself on the mercy of the court and the jury and say that I worked for the government and am not supposed to be smart. There's not a jury in the US that wouldn't buy that argument. Even Snake Henry could get him off on those grounds. On to our first Nat. Park of this trip tomorrow.

Garden of The Gods Denizen

Sent: Tuesday, May 16, 2000 5:10 PM
Subject: Vernal City, Utah

Well, we've escaped from Colorado again with less expense than last time. Last year I had to buy the Durango cause the Blazer died in CO. This year, the hair dryer went first, followed by the TV-VCR blowing the picture tube, and then Pookie managed to fall down while walking on a trail in Black Canyon of the Gunnison Nat. Park. She's O.K., but cut her hands and elbow on some rocks. We carry a first aid kit in the Durango and she's still able to function—she's doing laundry right now. Pookie was about 75 yards in front of me when she fell, so no, I didn't push her. I did have to help her up. There are very steep drop-offs along the trails and Pookie commented that I could easily have become a widower if she had gone over the edge. I told her that then Duke and I could become full-time RVers—she laughed, but it wasn't a funny laugh. The Super Wal-Mart in Montrose, CO was glad to see us coming, so I left the old TV-VCR by a dumpster behind their store. I was terrified that I'd have to buy a new trailer before we got out of CO. I did take Pookie to see "Where the Heart Is" at the local movie and took her to eat at the Golden Trough, which is what "the girls" call the Golden Corral, to assuage her discomfort. I'm proud of myself for not calling her a klutz—yet—although she has let Duke get loose twice and I've had to go get him back. Wonder if those were mistakes?

Black Canyon of the Gunnison is a very scenic park, and Duke is permitted on the trails, so he loved it. There are deeper canyons, and bigger ones and all that, but none are as steep as this one. It averages 2,000 feet deep and ranges from 2700 feet to 1750 feet. There are 3 dams up stream from it and a diversion tunnel for irrigation to a nearby valley, but it still has 2/3 of it's original water flow, although maybe 1/2 of the sediment and silt that cuts through the rock is stopped by the dams. It's called black because the sides are so steep that sunlight doesn't get in very much and it's dark. The rock it cuts through is over a billion years old and extremely hard. The river falls 95 feet per mile, which is a lot, and gives the water the energy to cut the rock, but barely. It now cuts the depth of a human hair each year, or about 1 inch per century. We spent a day taking an auto tour and walking a few trails to overlooks. Many are such sheer drops that Pookie gets vertigo and can't go near the edge, even when it is fenced. Duke, on the other hand, goes up and looks over the edge with interest. It's strange to look down and see hawks and eagles soaring beneath you. Mule deer are everywhere and so tame that they walk in front of the Durango, which makes Duke go crazy, trying to get out and give chase. At one point we drove down to the river on a 16% downgrade slope with switchbacks for about 2 miles. The brakes smelled on the Durango, even though I had it in 2nd gear going down. No vehicles over 22 feet permitted on that road which leads to the last dam before the river flows freely. We ate a picnic lunch at the highest point overlooking the canyon, since the food service in the Park hasn't opened yet.

Vernal City is the nearest burg of any size to Dinosaur Nat. Monument, which we did today. Most of the monument is in CO, but the main entrance is in Utah. The actual site where all the dinosaur bones have been removed is called the quarry site and is now partially under a glass roof, and they don't remove any new fossils from this site, but about 200 have been mined so far. It was a sandbar in an ancient river where dinosaurs that died or were killed in the river floated and then were piled up by the current and then covered with sediment. You can still see lots of bones in the cliff where the others were removed, as the site was tilted up on a steep angle over time. Lots of material and exhibits and a few skeletons on display. The Monument was only 80 acres when it was created by Woodrow Wilson and only covered the quarry site. It now covers 210,000 acres and the Green River flows through it on its way to the CO River. Duke got to do this park too and has behaved really well so far. Did another picnic as no food service here at all, but a really nice site at an old homestead cabin by an artesian well under some shade trees.

Vernal City was called Ashley Center until they applied for a post office and then the postal service said the name was too much like Ashley, Utah and sent back the post office application approved as Vernal City. Another fine example of your federal government helping you more than you asked. Speaking of post offices, we have observed from Maine to California, all across this great land, that in the really small, rural towns—say below 2000 people—that consistently it is the post office that is the newest, grandest and most expensive building in town. It refreshes my faith in my countrymen to see that even without— any legally controlling authority—to use Al Gore's words—it is an American tradition to screw the government with the highest contract price or lease possible. Do to them what they do to us seems to be the idea practiced everywhere. I love it!

On to Salt Lake City and further west tomorrow. Have you ever wondered why the LDS Church, as the locals call it here, shares the same initials and almost the same alliteration as the mind-altering drug, LSD? Philosopher

Sent: Saturday, May 20, 2000 9:50 AM
Subject: Chester, CA

Well, I know all of you are vitally interested in how we are dealing with the weather—I can tell cause nobody has asked. Actually, we missed all the bad storms in CO and UT while driving west. At Dinosaur, our last day there was a dust storm and winds of 50 mph, but no 18-wheelers turned over like there were in UT. On our way to UT, we drove between the bad storms and could see them to the north & south, but we only had a few snow showers and had mostly sunshine. We haven't cut on the AC since leaving MO, and it's been as low as 29 at nite and as high as 82 during the day. We got to Salt Lake City early, around 2 p.m., and dumped the trailer and Duke in a campground in the middle of the city and went downtown to see the state capitol. Had a tour guide born in Sweden whose name I can't pronounce, but she was quite good. The capitol is pretty, but pales in comparison to those in the Midwest, East and South. Utah didn't become a state till 1896 and then only after 6 applications and 6 years after the LDS Church said it gave up polygamy. Utah still has the highest fertility rate in the USA and I suspect that some of that polygamy is still going on, even if not church sanctioned. Learned that Utah gave women the right to vote in 1870 while it was still a territory and long before most states and the US. If I had 3 or 4 wives nagging me, I'd let them vote too. In fact, I've always been an advocate of voting on family matters. Each of my children got a vote as soon as they learned to talk, and Pookie got 3 votes so she could outvote the kids. I got 6 votes in case anything serious came up for a family vote. Democracy in action!

After that, we went to Temple Square and stood in front of the flagpole to get a guided tour of the grounds and buildings, although we knew we couldn't enter the Temple itself since we are gentiles and thereby unclean. We did this 30 years ago with the kids, and the tour hasn't changed. I was shocked when 2 young women aged 21 years each came up to us and offered the tour and one of them had on a nametag that said Sister McClure. My grandmother was a McClure and I have a nephew, a first cousin twice removed, and a second cousin named McClure. My first thought was to ask the question that every pretty girl in the whorehouse gets asked—What is a nice girl like you doing in a place like this? However, since I am a sensitive, discerning and discrete person, I asked when did her family become Mormons. She said that they converted after her father's family moved from Scotland to the USA. I knew it! She came from good Scottish stock, who had to be members of the One True Faith—Presbyterians! According to my Mother, all other faiths are heathen, and we're talking about Baptists, Methodists and other vermin too. How could this have happened? After considering the matter I hoped that it was a case of her father falling in love with a Mormon and making the supreme sacrifice. Hopefully it was for a worthy cause like sexual gratification, and not because he bought that stuff. Then I began to think that this might be an offshoot McClure clan that may have moved down to the lowlands, intermarried with the English and become stupid or Camelites—but I repeat myself. I guess you have noticed that I am an equal opportunity offender and don't give a damn about political correctness—it's a disease.

The other Sister was from Brazil, but spoke perfect English. Once when she was proselytizing us I asked her to repeat the entreaty in Portuguese, but she asked if I spoke Portuguese and I answered no. Big mistake. I started to tell her that I would enjoy it more if I didn't know what she was saying, but Pookie gave me a dirty look. Actually, Pookie complimented me on being much nicer than she expected. I have remembered that I haven't ever had any nooky in Oregon or Montana and we're going to both states, so there is no need to offend the sweet one. We did do the Tabernacle again and witnessed the acoustics demonstration where paper is torn, straight pins are dropped and a penny is dropped on the lectern and all can be heard from 250 feet away. When they were finished with us, they asked for our address and offered to give us a Book of Mormon and to have missionaries call on us at home. Pookie said we were never at home, and I said NO. If I had known what was coming, we would have used the names of Phil & Kathy instead of Evan & Pookie and I would have given them Snake Baddour's address. Any brand or off-brand of religion would improve Snake Baddour's odds for eternity, and I would have loved listening to his recount of his visit. After the tour, we went across the street from Temple Square to a Borders music and bookstore. Pookie bought 5 CDs and Mary Wade would have been inspired—there was a whole room of Opera CDs.

Driving to NV was interesting. We stopped at the Bonneville Salt Flat raceway where all the land speed records have been made. Actually, the course is 10 miles long and you have to run both directions and the curvature of the earth on the flat salt makes the start and finish invisible from each other, but there is black paint put on the salt to tell you where the course is located. Current land speed record is 622+ mph. It rained for 3 hours in Salt Lake that nite and there were puddles and ponds all the way across the salt flats. The Great Salt Lake has been expanding for the last 10 years as there has been more rain than evaporation and there is no river outlet. We drove by a Morton's Salt factory with tons of the stuff piled up on the ground. Pookie talked about me going swimming with the boys in Salt Lake 30 years ago. They were treading water like crazy till I told them they couldn't sink and to stop. After their usual period of doubting their father, they stopped treading and were surprised they couldn't sink. I then offered money, if they could go under and stay under, and they failed.

We spent last nite in Winnemucca, NV. A campground with slots, an open bar and package liquor—my kind of place. Driving across NV is expensive as when we stop for gas, I'm pumping gas while Pookie pumps the slots. Actually, we've found new types of campgrounds this trip. One had bathroom scales—a stupid and discouraging addition to services. Another had a full putt-putt mini golf course and then this one with slots and booze.

Tonite we're on the banks of Lake Almanor near Lassen Volcanic Nat. Park. It's a gorgeous lake with mountain peaks covered with snow reflecting in the water. Still, I prefer Chester, MA to Chester, CA. Really pretty country with Douglas fir and Ponderosa pine down to the waterline, but the road thru the Park is closed till May 31 with snow plows working now and the Visitor Centers don't open till May 31. Pookie can't even buy a patch for her & Ken. We'll stay here 2 nights and figure out where to go next.
Religious Advisor

Sent: Tuesday, May 23, 2000 6:27 PM
Subject: Trinidad, CA

Lassen Volcanic Nat. Park reminds me of the eastern part of Yosemite. Heavily forested, but with a lot of meadows and snow melt streams. It's about 180 miles northwest of Reno and almost due north of Yosemite. Lassen Peak was the last active volcano to erupt in the lower 48 states until Mt. St. Helens. It's over 10,000 feet high, constantly covered with snow at the peak and erupted violently like St. Helens in 1915, and kept erupting less violently till 1922. It's the southernmost active volcano in the Cascade Range and is dormant now, but very much alive. The road thru the Park is open for 7 miles at the southern entrance and for 10 miles at the western entrance, but closed by snow until more melts and is plowed. It gets 40 feet of snow per year at the higher elevations and I'd hate to be driving the plows and trying to find the road in the Spring, as there are no guardrails and steep drop offs. They now use GPS satellite data to find the road, but what did they do before, and what if the GPS data is off by 10 feet?

We drove up the west access road and Pookie gave a park ranger lady at the gated entrance a self addressed envelope with some money to buy her 2 patches and mail them, after the visitor centers open in June. She risked my money, not hers, and then told the lady to put any left over funds into the donations jar—no risk to her. We stopped at the Sulfur Works, but Pookie wouldn't walk around it as the smell bothers her. Mud pots bubbling and fumaroles steaming sulfur gas just like Yellowstone with hot water pools, but no real geysers. The road ended at about 8,000 feet in a parking lot, so we went around to the other entrance in a 60-mile detour. Much less snow on the northwest side, but an area called the devastated area as the eruptions took place on the northwestern slopes. Trees are back in this area, but stunted and yellowed and lots of lava rock and huge boulders thrown 2 or 3 miles by the blast and tons of ash and lava that is still not life bearing. Mount St. Helens is supposedly recovering faster than this area because of a difference in the materials disgorged by the volcano. An interesting Park, but not one of the best. We did meet an interesting couple in the campground at Chester who had a 15-year-old Jack Russell Terrier in a trailer and there were 2 more Jack Russells in other trailers. Pookie has said all along that Duke was the only Jack Russell trailer dog in America— wrong again. Shorty was the name of the 15-year-old terrorist. Duke is normally friendly when he meets another dog with tail wagging & no growling. Shorty took this as a sign of inferiority and tried a free nip. Duke is bigger, younger, and quicker and has sharper teeth and proceeded to work on improving Shorty's manners. The leashes got all tangled up, so I gave Duke a lot of slack and let him administer justice. Shorty's owner dove into the fight and lifted Shorty up out of harm's way with Duke hanging onto Shorty's leg, so I pulled Duke off. Shorty decided it was time to go to his trailer.

From Lassen, we drove to Trinidad at the southern entrance to Redwood Nat. Park on the coast about 300 miles north of San Francisco. It was 99 degrees in the Sacramento Valley and 62 when we got here. Crossed 4 mountains in the trip over the coastal ranges and tough climbs. The secondary roads have much, much steeper grades than the interstates and a lot of switchbacks and hairpin turns. The transmission overheated again on the 3rd mountain, but not till we were 200 yards from the summit, so I ignored it. Duke loves climbing the really tough grades as the Durango will slow down to 15 mph on a really steep one and he can hang out the window. I did pass a Range Rover pulling a pop top camper, like he was standing still on a steep grade, so Ken & Faye can do this without an expensive motorhome.

We're in a campground off US 101, the Redwood Highway, in a grove of 2nd growth redwoods. This is private property, but was logged in the 19th century. Redwoods cling to life tenaciously and can reproduce from burls, which are kind of like bulbs at the base of the tree. There are huge stumps all over this campground with new redwoods over 100 feet high growing from the bottom of the old stumps. They say some redwoods, which live about 2,000 years, have lasted for 7 or 8 generations using the same root systems and are genetically the same tree for 15,000 years. They are not as large as the Giant Sequoia in volume or mass, but grow much taller, up to 365 feet, and both species are redwoods.

We did the southern half of the Park yesterday and the northern half today. Coastal redwoods are over 165 million years old and have outlived the dinosaurs. Over 95% of those in North America have been logged, but there sure are a lot left. California had 3 state parks in this area before the National Park and the Nat. Park incorporates the 3 old state parks plus new lands. Twenty-five years ago, Pookie & I rented a car on a trip to San Francisco and drove up to Muir Wood north of the Golden Gate, but it was not nearly as impressive as this. We watched a 1-hour video at the Visitor Center on the history of the redwoods and their preservation. Fascinating facts and statistics, but the most impressive thing is just walking through a grove, or driving through a redwood forest. You turn off the CD or radio and just feel awed. We did a 1-mile trail thru the Lady Bird Johnson Grove and I congratulated Pookie for not falling a single time. She replied that we weren't thru yet. We passed a much older couple, shuffling and teetering along holding each other up and I commented that there go we in a few years. Pookie said no, there wouldn't be any trails left to do by then.

After lunch yesterday we did a drive through Prairie View State Park, another state redwood park not in the Nat. Park and along Gold Bluff Beach. It was very lightly used and no people for miles. The surf was 200 yards from the bluffs, so I let Duke loose on the beach. He ran wide open for at least 20 minutes burning up energy. Out in the surf, off 1/3 mile and then back, in big circles around us and then he found a solitary girl asleep against a driftwood log and leaped on her at about 20mph and startled her. I called him back and she left the beach with her solitude rudely interrupted. Duke got soaking wet in the surf and when I finally called him & put him back on the leash, he rolled over on his back in the gray & black sand and got happily filthy. Big Day for Duke.

There are a lot of overlooks high above the ocean with majestic views of surf, sand & rocks and the Nat. Park is 50 miles long, but no motorhomes are allowed on the best and most rustic roads. Today we went all the way to Crescent City at the northern end of the park. Last nite a couple in a Hi-Lo metal camper that lifts up parked next to us. They had 3 huge dogs who travel in the van pulling the trailer and sleep in the trailer with them. Two were mastiffs and the 3rd was a cross between a chocolate lab and a mastiff. All weighed over 100 pounds and each had a huge pet taxi that I could have fit into. All 3 stayed outside in a folding metal pen about 3 feet tall and 10 feet long that Duke would have jumped over in a heartbeat. Pookie marveled at the food they must have to carry. I wondered about the poop disposal. Duke was not intimidated and wanted to challenge them as they barked aggressively at him. Of course, Duke thinks he can alter the behavior of an 18-wheeler if he charges it and attacks. I decided not to let Duke get close to their pen.

Saw on the news where William Jefferson Clinton has reproved that old adage that 99% of lawyers make the rest of them look bad. On to Oregon tomorrow. As Bruce Willis would say in a "Die Hard "movie, Yippie Ki Yay.

Sent: Saturday, May 27, 2000 10:08 AM
Subject: Lakeside, OR

We drove from Redwood NP to Crater Lake NP in OR and camped in the Crater Lake Resort campground in Ft. Klamath, OR, population maybe 100. When Resort is added to the name of a campground, it either means they charge more for junk you won't use, or they are lying. This campground was inexpensive, so figure it out. We've also learned that if a campground advertises—away from the noise of the interstate—the odds are 10 to 1 that it's next to a railroad track with trains running all nite, or it's at the end of the local runway with airplanes taking off all nite at full throttle overhead. This was actually a nice campground with an artesian fed stream 6 feet from us.

Crater Lake is impressive and very scenic, but there isn't much to do this time of year. The Park gets over 500 inches of snow yearly and as usual, the roads aren't fully opened yet. Last year they didn't open the rim road that goes around the lake at the top till mid July. It's a 30-mile drive, but only a few miles were open now. The lake surface is at about 6200 feet and it's 6 miles across and a stunning cobalt blue. Of course, water is transparent and doesn't have color, but reflects back the blue light spectrum and absorbs other colors, depending on the depth. Crater is 1932 feet deep at the deepest spot and averages over 1500 feet deep. It's the clearest and deepest lake in North America and about 7700 years old. Formed when the caldera of an ancient volcano collapsed on itself after the magma chamber had emptied itself in an eruption, the lake is a closed ecological system as no streams flow in or out of the lake. The water is totally snowmelt and rain and the lake level varies no more than 3 feet annually. The rim averages about 8000 feet all around the lake and there are 2 small islands in the lake. There were no fish in the lake till man stocked it in the 19th century and only 2 species survived to today. Valleys below the Park contain a lot of springs and artesian wells and it's thought that some water leaves the lake underground and fuels the springs. The Visitor Center is old and dinky, but we ate lunch at the lodge, which is circa 1915 and kind of plush. Temperature at the rim was 47 degrees at 1 p.m. with the sun shining and down to 42 at nite in our campground at a lower elevation.

When we entered the park, the ranger at the gate saw Duke in the back of the Durango and gave us a printed notice about pets that said we couldn't take him anywhere off the pavement and couldn't leave him unattended in the Durango. We carry the pet taxi in the back of the Durango and frequently leave him in it while we eat lunch or do a short trail, go in a store or see a movie, if it's cool enough to leave him. Another stupid federal regulation that I had to break. Probably conjured up by the same type idiot who burned down Los Alamos. The variation in Nat. Park Service employees is enormous. Some are helpful, courteous, friendly, informed and nice and others make you think the Park Service is the employer of last resort and will take anyone with an IQ of 60 or more. Seems the George Washington commercials aren't working, either —NP employees are now issued the new dollar coins and not 1-dollar bills to give as change. Another government success story?

We're now camped in a campground on a lake back on Hi-way 101 that goes north along the beach. We want to do the Oregon Dunes Nat. Seashore and maybe take a dune buggy ride, but it's raining steadily. Can't complain as this is the first daytime rain we've had since MO, and In Redwood NP, we had gorgeous weather which is unusual this time of year.

Trip Potpourri:

1. After reflecting on it, I am more and more convinced that Truman made more difficult decisions in his presidency than anyone else since Abe Lincoln conducted the War of Northern Aggression. Think about it. He first had to decide about using the A bomb that he didn't even know existed till FDR died. Then he put forth the Truman Doctrine that pumped money into Greece & Turkey to defeat communism and created our containment policy. Then he had a domestic railroad strike that threatened to shut down our economy totally. He beat it by threatening to draft all striking railroad workers into the Army and was addressing Congress with his legislation request to achieve this, when an aide interrupted his speech with a note that the railroad unions had capitulated—and this by a pro union president. Next he had the Berlin Airlift crisis, which we beat without using ground troops. The Truman Library even claims that the Marshall Plan was Truman's idea, but he let Marshall be the front man and public author because Marshall was much more popular than Truman and could get it passed by Congress. Even his re-election was an extremely difficult

decision and victory. He also set the framework for NATO and the general rules, although it was a British idea. The same is true of the UN and at least in the case of Korea—another crisis—he made it an effective force. Then he had to fire McArthur, another difficult and unpopular decision. The man was good!

2. While we've been on this trip, the government has announced that saccharin no longer causes cancer, but alcohol does. A totally unacceptable swap. I'll wait on the next revision of government expertise.

3. The Rogue River flows through Grants Pass, OR and highway signs direct you to Rogue C. College. Is that Rogue Christian College or Rogue Community College? In either case, does the name help or hurt in recruiting students?

4. Roosevelt Elk, a subspecies of North American elk roam freely in Redwood NP, but they are solid Republican elk, named for Teddy and not FDR.

5. Speaking of redwoods, they have outlived the dinosaurs by 650,000 centuries. That's the same as 65 million years, but is a more comprehensible time frame description for most people.

6. Pookie says I talk to the Durango. My response is that the Durango is the only thing on this trip that consistently tries to do what I ask. It's my source of positive feedback.

7. There was a pithy little saying tacked on the wall of the men's room at the Ft. Klamath campground. It said it was written by that ancient Greek writer, Anonymous, but it sounded like something Tom would say. I'll repeat it for his benefit: "Man is like a Fine Wine. He comes as raw as grapes, and it is Woman's job to stomp on him and keep him in the dark until he matures into something she would enjoy having dinner with." Underneath the saying someone had written in a clear, legible hand, "Let's hang this in the women's restroom".

Dynamic Durango Duo and Duke Da Dog——Kimmie gave us that moniker.

Sent: Wednesday, May 31, 2000 7:03 PM
Subject: Castle Rock, WA

Well, we didn't get to take a dune buggy ride. It rained for both days we were at Oregon Dunes Nat. Seashore and we didn't feel like doing it in the rain. We did do the Visitor Center and see the video and such. The dunes are 56 miles long on the coast and in the middle of a rain forest, which they choke out and kill as they move around. It's the only place along the Oregon coast that doesn't have steep bluffs or rock cliffs for most of the shoreline. The sand comes from the Umpqua River, which reaches the ocean in the middle of the dune area and deposits sand from the Cascades in a huge bar across the mouth of the river. The wind and ocean push the sand up on the beach and the winds take over and move it wherever they want. We drove down to Coos Bay where the dunes begin, but gave up the first day, as visibility was no more than 100 yards thru the mist and rain. The next day we did get to some overlooks and short trails thru the dunes. There are a lot of freshwater lakes created by a dune damming up a creek and we camped on 10 Mile Lake about 2 miles from the beach. The third day it was raining again, but stopped as we left, so we drove to one of the beach access points and there were no dogs on the beach—I later learned there is a local leash law—so I turned Duke loose again on the beach. He had a good time running again, but wasn't as wound up as he was the first time I let him loose on the beach at Gold Bluff. He did terrify some kids with his exuberance by jumping on them at full speed, so I called him back and put him back on the leash. There are areas where ATVs and dune buggies have free rein and other areas where no vehicles are permitted. I did watch 1 dune buggy stand up on its rear wheels for about a quarter mile as the guy accelerated from a stop to maybe 80 mph. The Dunes may not be there in 100 years as European beach grass was introduced in the 1930s and is stabilizing the dunes which native grasses could not and causing them to be replaced by vegetation. They can't figure out how to kill the foreign beach grass.

We also toured a lighthouse at a state park in the dune area that was the best lighthouse tour we've ever had and we've done a lot all over the country, as Pookie likes them—I may be correct about a phallic symbol. The tour guide was a retiree, who was really into lighthouses, and let us go up inside the 1st Order Fresnel lens as the light was turning and working. The lens is 9 1/2 feet high and 7 feet across, so there's room for a person to stick the upper half of his body up inside the light. The light is only 1000 watts, but is amplified to 220,000 candlepower by the lens and can be seen 20 miles out at sea—quite interesting.

We drove up the coast to Warrenton, OR on highway 101, which hugs the coast and gives magnificent views of the beach or rocky cliffs and high surf. It's a slow trip due to the road turning and twisting and climbing and descending which limits speed to an average of about 35mph when towing the trailer. The sun was out and a gorgeous day, but it never got over 60 degrees the whole time we were in OR. I could enjoy the cool weather, which doesn't change a lot all year long, but the rain for over 200 days per year and the lack of sunshine are more than I could take. It took a whole day to get to Warrenton, which is on the coast and only a few miles from Astoria and the Columbia River. On Memorial Day, we went to a ceremony at the Ft. Stevens Nat. Cemetery in Warrenton. Ft. Stevens was a military post from the 1860s to recent days and is now in a state park. It is the only part of the lower 48 states of the US that has been attacked by foreign forces since the War of 1812, as a Japanese submarine surfaced offshore from it and lobbed a few shells from its deck gun in 1942.

It was quite a ceremony with bagpipers, buglers and several varieties of military personnel ranging from naval cadets to retired military in uniform to Civil War Re-enactors dressed in Union clothing and carrying black powder rifles and muskets. All the graves had American flags flying on them and again it was a beautiful day, but cool with a strong breeze. Duke went with us and stood in the cemetery till the 1860s cannon was fired 3 times which caused him to crawl between my legs and lay down there. We had 3 volleys of 7 black powder rifles for a 21 gun salute also, so Duke took up permanent residence under me, but he never barked or howled like some other dogs there. After wreath laying, speeches from the local mayor, VFW head and a local pastor we witnessed something I have never seen at such a ceremony. A local man about 50 came to the microphone and told about his protests against the Vietnam War during his student days. He recounted being on Dupont Circle in DC on a Memorial Day then and chanting Ho, Ho, Ho Chi Minh. He got quite emotional and apologized for his behavior in his youth and thanked all the veterans present and deceased for making it possible for him to be able to burn the American flag by their sacrifices in the name of Freedom. Pookie thought his speech was out of place, but I was impressed by his candor and public apology and thought it was not inappropriate.

After lunch we did Fort Clatsop Nat. Memorial, also in Warrenton. It's the reconstructed wooden fort where the Lewis & Clark Expedition spent the winter of 1805-06 after they reached the Pacific Ocean. It's a living history park and we watched and listened to a very vivacious and lively Park Rangerette give a talk on the Corp of Discovery, the 33 people on the trip. She was quite good and involved the audience by asking questions and assigning parts to different people. Pookie was Sgt. Patrick Gass, but wouldn't wear his coonskin cap. Sgt. Gass lived to be 99, so maybe it's a sign. The Visitor Center had a lot of exhibits and 2 movies on the Expedition and we spent a few hours there and then rode over to Astoria, OR a few miles away and viewed the Columbia River as it enters the Pacific. A huge, high bridge reaches across to Washington, maybe 5 miles long including the approaches, and a few ocean freighters were in the harbor.

The next day we crossed the Columbia on that bridge and went to Ft. Canby on the north shore at Cape Disappointment where Lewis & Clark first saw the Pacific. The Union fortified the Cape in 1863 when they feared the Confederate raider, Alabama, might raid shipping on the Columbia. It too is now a state park and we toured the Lewis & Clark Interpretative Center built on the fort site. Fort Clatsop is better, but both are worthwhile seeing. We then drove along the north shore of the Columbia to I-5 and up a few miles near the entrance to Mt. St. Helens Nat. Monument to a campground. We went to a movie at the CineDome, only a mile from our campground, on the

1980 eruption. It's a 70-millimeter IMAX movie and we sat in the eruption seats, which shake, rattle and roll during the eruption. If you're out here, go see the movie.

Today we toured the Monument and it's a lot better than a lot of the Nat. Parks. There are 3 Park Service Visitor Centers and each has different movies, exhibits and facts on the volcano and they are spread over 50 miles. The one near I-5 is the largest and oldest and has the most exhibits, but I found the new ones on Coldwater Lake and Johnston Ridge near the volcano to be more interesting. The new ones were built in 1986 and have a lot of interactive exhibits and touch screen technology. At Johnston Ridge the movie is shown on a screen that lifts up at the end of the movie and curtains behind the screen open and you are looking at the mouth of the crater about 2 miles away—except in our case. The Visitor Center and volcano were invisible from 200 yards away due to fog, mist and rain. We got the exact same view of St. Helens that we got of Mt. McKinley in Alaska in Denali NP—none. Pookie took a picture of me pointing in the direction of the volcano in the fog.

We ate a volcano burger at the Coldwater Lake center. Know why they call it a volcano burger? Insert drum roll here————————it causes an eruption of sorts———— Ta Da.

The mountain erupted 7 weeks after it first started quaking and shaking so there were a lot of observers, movies, pictures, seismograph readings, etc. There were even aircraft circling the mountain and taking videos when it blew up, so the events are recorded in great detail. The statistics are impressive. A 15 mile high plume, the Columbia River filled with sediment from a channel of 40 feet to one of 12 feet, the top 1300 feet of the mountain gone, debris avalanche at a speed of 180 mph and a temperature of 200 degrees F traveling 14 miles and a lateral blast of hot gases at speeds up to 700 mph with a temperature in the blast zone up to 750 degrees F and a blast area of 230 sq. miles—and this was a small volcanic eruption. We were living in Monroe, WI at the time and I remember everything outside being covered with a reddish brown dust for 3 weeks after the eruption. Jimma Carter was president and after flying over the blast zone in a helicopter said the moon was a golf course compared to this. 57 people killed despite evacuations before the blast.

The amazing thing is the speed at which the area has recovered with new life. New plants began to emerge from the ash in 12 days. Aquatic life back at normal levels in Spirit Lake only 5 years after the event. Nobody expected such rapid recolonization by plants, animals, insects and birds. If you get a chance, go see. On to Mt. Rainier NP tomorrow.

My cousin Mary Nelson has been bitten by the genealogy bug and is now doing a lot of research into the family tree. I told her and her brother about the possibility of our great, great, great maternal grandmother being an Indian as she is buried in the old family cemetery north of Columbus, MS as Elizabeth with no last name, next to Taylor Nelson who got the land grant from President Andrew Jackson in the 1830s. Sure enough, she's dug up the fact that Elizabeth was a Chickasaw Indian. That makes me 1/32 Indian and if there are no Indians in Pookie's woodpile, the kids are 1/64 Indian. It's too late to get the kids scholarships, but maybe I can open a Casino in Pulaski. Indian Lover of Nature

Sent: Monday, June 05, 200 12:08 PM
Subject: Port Angeles, WA

Driving into Mt. Rainier NP to the south entrance, we could see Mt. St. Helens to the south and Mt. Rainier to the north at the same time as the skies cleared and we had pretty weather. I think Rainier is more impressive when viewed from Seattle to the north even if it is a long way away. It is one of only a few mountains that rise so steeply from its base that it is clearly visible from a long distance, even though it is only 14,411 feet high. We camped in a Thousand Trails Member Campground at Randle, WA that is a part of NACO, the national association of campground owners. We don't belong and there are only about 50 Thousand Trails campgrounds in the US, but we could stay by paying a little higher than normal price. I made the right decision in not joining NACO, as it seems to be a rip off. That's the first stop on this trip that had no TV reception of any kind—way out in the boonies. We entered the NP that afternoon at the southern entrance, but the Visitor Center there is only open on weekends now, so we went back to Packwood, WA and Donna gave me a haircut—definitely not a showgirl. The lady in the liquor store who recommended Donna said she would cut my hair if she had more time, which caused Pookie to even offer to cut it, but it was too late for her to be considered, besides, I know about Delilah and tricks. Pookie cruised around Packwood while I got my haircut and found a Forest Service road not on the Rand McNally map that was a shortcut to the west entrance of the Park. The next morning, we took it thru the Mt. Rainier Nat. Forest, a pretty drive and a decent road too.

Mt. Rainier is another active, but currently dormant volcano that has erupted countless times in the past, the last being about 100 years ago. It gets an average of 650 inches of snow annually and supports 25 glaciers on its slopes, the most of any single mountain mass in the lower 48 states. Those glaciers retreated steadily in the 20th century till the 1970s when the mountain got a snowfall of 1132 inches, 93 feet, one year and 1000 inches another and the glaciers began to advance. They now are stable again. Driving across the Park from west to east, there are parts of the mountain that look almost exactly like the Tetons when they are viewed from the east—steep granite crags so steep they accumulate very little snow. There are countless streams and waterfalls from the melting snow and glaciers. The name Cascades means falling waters and is very appropriate. We let Duke play in the snow some and were going to take the trail in Paradise Valley thru the wildflower meadow, but the trail was beneath 5 feet of snow and no wildflowers yet. The trail was marked in the snow, but I had on shorts and sandals and the wind was blowing so I treated my girl to lunch in the Paradise Inn instead. Built in 1917, it has a 1st class dining room. The first time on this trip that it cost more to fill us up than it cost to fill up the Durango. We finished the day driving to the eastern access road and then back out the southern entrance. Lots of overlooks and trails, but we didn't do any trails. While we were at Crater Lake NP, a 71-year-old woman fell on a trail at Mill Creek Falls and rolled over the edge and fell 200 feet to her death. She was the 2nd death at that site in 2 years.

The next day we drove back to I-5 and north and then west again back to the coast and Hi-way 101. We stopped at a Wal-Mart in Aberdeen, WA for restocking and to get film developed and spent the nite at Copalis Beach, WA. Took Duke for another walk on the beach at a state park and turned him loose again. He took off like a rocket and made sure that all local sea gulls became airborne. Then he spotted a family having a picnic on a blanket about 500 yards away with 2 small, toy dogs. That required his immediate attention, but the little dogs were no fun and couldn't keep up. Next he saw a big golden lab playing in the surf 500 yards further away and charged over there to seek a suitable play companion. The owner of the lab commented to me that Duke sure did cover a lot of ground in a hurry. The lab was old and tried to play, but quickly got tired so both dogs lay down in the surf and got soaked. I finally put him back on the leash and took him back to the trailer. Pookie and I went to Alec's Seafood Restaurant for dinner.

The next day we drove up 101 around the west side of Olympic NP. We had driven down the east side with Heidi and Bob when they lived in Olympia and we came for a visit. Back then we had gone to Vancouver, Canada with them and then took a ferry to Victoria on Vancouver Island and a ferry back to WA at Port Angeles, WA. I saw a sign for Buchart Gardens yesterday and remembered our visit. I also remember entering Canada and Heidi was driving and was asked some question by the Border Patrol guy. I was sitting in the back seat behind Heidi and after her reply to him in her German accent; I told him she was an East German spy, which drew a swift rebuke from Heidi.

We stopped at the Hoh Rain Forest Visitor Center in Olympic NP on the west side of the Park. There is a Hoh Glacier, a Hoh River and the rain forest, all of which are named for the Hoh Indian tribe which has lived here for 10,000 years. In fact, we drove within a mile of the Hoh Tribal

Headquarters and I asked my traveling companion if she wanted to go visit some of my relatives. Pookie White Roots responded negatively. I've taken her all over the US to visit her weirdo relatives, but she turns up her nose at some of mine, just because they happen to be savages. I consider it narrow minded to look down on them. After all, they can't help it if their mammas are all Hohs. Actually, Pamela Sue gave Pookie the name White Roots in an e-mail, but she probably doesn't know that it is a perfect Indian name for her. If it weren't for the magic of modern day medicine men that create war paint for women, Pookie's hair would be snow white, so she really is a white root.

We ate lunch in the trailer at the Hoh Visitor Center and took a short trail thru the forest. Average of 12 to 14 feet of rain annually and without Roosevelt Elk to browse on the undergrowth, it would be solid greenery. Lots of air plants like Spanish moss clinging to the trees and an old growth forest with huge trees that give it a grotesque look in the shade. A beautiful sunny day—we can bring drought to the rain forest—and the foliage is so thick that no sun reaches the forest floor. It's a temperate zone rain forest at low elevation and if it ever gets a snow, none of that reaches the ground either. We drove on to Port Angeles around Crescent Lake, which is very scenic. We'll do the Hurricane Ridge Drive and Visitor Center later. This Park is extremely varied as it has ocean beaches, rain forests and conifer forests, mountains and glaciers and dry areas on the east side of the Olympic Mountains that are in the footprint of the mountains and get very little rain.

Evan's Keen Observations, but only a few:

1.   1, Pookie normally uses the shower in the trailer and I nearly always use the shower in the men's room in these campgrounds. In the men's room, the toilet paper is almost always the slick, thin stuff you can almost see through, but in about half the restrooms, if you use the handicap stalls you will find a softer, thicker toilet paper. What do these people think is the handicap? I'm not making this up. After all, my ancestors are responsible for the creation of that famous expression, "Honest Injun".

2.   2, My son Will sent an e-mail saying he had received a solicitation from the Committee to Elect Hillary. He wrote "refused" on it and put it back in the mail, hoping that Hillary would have to pay postage on it twice. That is an absolutely superb example of genetics at work.

3.   The blonde honey on Seattle TV that masquerades as a meteorologist was broadcasting a Sunshine Alert the other day. She actually warned people not to drive without their sunglasses or they would risk wrecks in the glare. People

who live out here are used to gloom. When Lewis and Clark were at Ft. Clatsop they recorded 12 days in their 106-day stay that had no rain and only on 6 of those days did they see the sun. Not for me, but this is our 4th visit to the Seattle area and we've had sunshine every time.

4.   The Eugene, OR newspaper is one of the best I've ever read. Reminded me of when I took the Manchester Guardian at Tulane, printed on onionskin paper to reduce weight as it was flown across the big pond every day. In fact, these people are so literate that the road signs would be beyond the comprehension of many Tennesseans, particularly the retards that scream Go Big Orange. I guess that if it rains all the time, you stay in and read a lot. When there is a steep or no shoulder on the road, the sign says Abrupt Lane Edge. One that wouldn't work anywhere in the South—the Bubba's would shoot them all down—says Delay of 5 Vehicles Illegal—Slow Vehicles Use Turnouts.

Chief BS That is an abbreviation for Chief Big Spear. If you thought it had anything to do with bull scat, you have a perverted mind

Sent: Friday, June 09, 2000 7:22 PM
Subject: Adios Washington

Well, our good luck with weather in the Seattle area ran out. We spent 2 days and 3 nights at Port Angeles and the rain began on the 1st morning and never stopped. We took the opportunity to treat the Durango to a Jiffy Lube— 5500 miles on it and maybe 3500 pulling the trailer— and ate at some great crab restaurants, but got depressed by the weather. We rode up to Hurricane Ridge Visitor Center in Olympic Mountains NP, but couldn't see the mountains for the fog and rain and we were at 4500 feet. We couldn't even see the Visitor Center from 100 yards away. The mountains aren't very high, but support about 60 glaciers and a lot of wildlife. We did do the main Visitor Center at the foot of the mountains and rode around the town and out to Dungeness Spit. The blonde honey on Seattle TV was then forecasting a complete week of POSSIBLE sun breaks—a sun break is when the sun pops out at the end of the day of rain for about 5 minutes and then the rain starts again. I talked to the campground owner about taking the ferry from Port Townsend to Whidbey Island, which is connected to the mainland by a bridge north of Seattle. He said it was a gorgeous drive up to North Cascades NP and only a short ferry ride so we got up early and made the 8:30 ferry about 55 miles away. I could drive on and off with no backing either way and the fare was $43 and saved us at least 200 miles driving down to Olympia and back up thru Tacoma and Seattle.

It wasn't raining that morning, but a low ceiling, but the rain started while we were on the ferry. Duke has gotten spoiled rotten out here by the gas stations and national park entrances. A lot of gas stations have female attendants who pump your gas, even at the self serve islands—but at the prices I'm paying they ought to give you something— and they all give Duke dog bones as do the rangers who let you into a park. Whenever I roll down the driver's side window and talk to someone, Duke sticks his head out next to me and whines for a treat. I told the guy at the ferry toll booth that Duke wanted a treat and he told me he hadn't had a raise in 16 years, but he gave Duke a rawhide strip anyway. The drive may have been pretty, but we wouldn't know as the ceiling came down to about 150 feet and we couldn't even see the tops of the tall trees. We drove up into North Cascades Nat. Park and parked in Rockport State Park within the NP. The rain stopped and we unhooked and I paid for 2 nites, as it was one of those parks where you register yourself and they check on you later. It was another rain forest and looked just like Hoh Rain Forest, except this one only got 9 feet of rain per year.

We drove up to the Visitor Center and were impressed with their stuff. They had a lot of modern exhibits and had apparently gotten a special deal on motion detectors. As you walked around the exhibit area you would set off a motion detector unknowingly and a video hidden in the wall would start up roaring like a grizzly bear, or a salmon jumping up a fish ladder or a volcano. When we went in the restrooms later after the movie and slide show, both restrooms were dark and as we felt along the wall for a light switch, lights and a fan came on—more motion detectors. I particularly liked the instructions about what to do if you walked up on a cougar on a trail. The advice was to face the cat, make yourself as big as possible by standing on your toes, waving outstretched arms and make aggressive sounds—no advice on the appropriate sound— and never, ever run away or turn your back. If attacked, fight back aggressively was also suggested. I told Pookie that they left off the part about turning Duke loose so he could attack and serve as an appetizer while we backed up slowly. This is a new park established in 1968, mainly at the behest of Sen. Jackson from WA, and not very highly visited. It was raining again when we came out of the Visitor Center, but very lightly so we went further into the park and saw some of the overlooks and cascades and lakes until the rain got heavier. Back to the trailer to listen to the rain. The canopy of the forest turns the drizzle into a series of random splats by big raindrops if it's not raining very hard.

The next morning, I got up and said let's go make our own sun break by getting out of Dodge and go find the dry side of these mountains. Pookie said she hoped they enjoyed the extra day of rent and gladly agreed. Bill Gates hasn't got enough money to get me to live out here. I hate February where I live because of all the rain and clouds and I just couldn't cope with living under these conditions all the time. Talking about Gates, the Seattle paper had nothing but the Microsoft case in the front section and is pro Microsoft. Personally, I hope they break it up and the more pieces, the better. Gates makes John D. Rockefeller look absolutely humble and contrite and he is not an innovator by any stretch of imagination. If he can't compete fairly, tie his hands and what he did to Netscape is unforgivable.

Speaking of news, Fox TV News did a story on the Nashville Tennessean newspaper the other day. When the story broke about Al Gore being called a slum landlord by his Carthage, TN tenant, the Tennessean refused to assign a reporter to the story or to print any of it for 2 days and then they only printed a small Associated Press blurb, according to Fox TV. I read the story in USA Today, which is owned by Gannett, which owns the Tennessean also, and USA Today gave both sides of the story and had a picture of the female tenant who lives on disability income with a disabled husband and had a month-to-month lease. Gore's rental agent had told her to vacate the premises when she complained and she then went to the media, but the Tennessean ignored her. The house was in terrible shape, particularly the plumbing that was unusable. Gore said he was unaware of the rental agent's actions, and I can easily believe that, but Gore is responsible for the actions of his agent. Gore called the woman, arranged for free temporary housing for her until the plumbing could be fixed and invited her to dinner on his next visit to Carthage. He couldn't have done anymore after the fact and the story was not a total public relations disaster, but Frank Sutherland, the editor of the Tennessean and a Gore friend and advisor refused to carry the story until he was forced by competition to acknowledge it. Gore used to work at the Tennessean and Sutherland has a prior history of lack of editorial ethics and proved again that he has a position and not a job. Yellow rag journalism at its best, and an example of why people don't trust the media.

We drove over the North Cascades, which are called the American Alps, but we don't have a clue, as we never saw the top of any mountain or even the upper slopes in the rain and fog. The literature says a few of the peaks are so steep and snow-covered and inaccessible that they have never been climbed. The rain stopped once we got over Rainy Pass and the visibility cleared up as we drove to Grand Coulee to see the dam on the Columbia River. Found a campground that had a shuttle bus to the laser light show at the dam that runs from May to Sept. every nite. The shuttle didn't leave till 8:15 p.m. and the laser show doesn't start till 10 p.m., as there is a 50-minute film on the construction and use of the dam and some exhibits about it in the Visitor Center where they show the films. The show is interesting and on a big scale, but past my bedtime—Pookie says I slept for 25 minutes of the film. The dam is 5237 feet wide and they show the lasers on about 80 per cent of the dam. At one point they showed the outline of an aircraft carrier and it was 2/3 the size of a real carrier and the airplane they showed bombing it was full size. The spillway is 350 feet high and there is a little water flowing down it during the show. The show is narrated and has music playing in the background—"Chariots of Fire" was one song. The show is about 30 minutes long and is free and was attended very well. It's really a government commercial by the Bureau of Reclamation that operates the dam. The show only cost you, the taxpayer, $800,000 to create.

This morning we went back to the dam and had a guided tour by Craig, who works there and did a mostly good job. It generates 6800 kilowatts at full capacity as opposed to 2800 by Hoover Dam. When built, beginning in 1933 and finishing in 1941, it was the largest concrete structure in the world. Now there are 2 dams in South America that produce more electricity and used more concrete. I was amazed to learn the newest powerhouse is a producer of last resort and only turned on when demand rises above the level of coal fired, gas turbines and nuclear generators. Turns out that they can turn on another generator in 10 seconds and if they ran all of them full time would empty the reservoir in a few months and couldn't reload for a year. A sign at the top of the dam tells how they increased the kilowatt capacity by 3 times in 1964 with a new powerhouse and can double it again, but then a hydrologist told them that generating and continuous generating are different things. A single GE generator can put out 805 kilowatts, but if they ran all 4 at once they would run out of water soon. Government work again. When we were there, only 1 generator in the new powerhouse was running and they soon shut it down. 12 million yards of concrete in the dam, but trust me, Hoover is a better tour. We rode an elevator down one of the concrete penstock tubes to the new powerhouse and stopped at the midlevel to get another view before entering the powerhouse and going inside a turbine housing to watch it turn the shaft for the generator. While outside watching a generator turn on and off and generate huge bubbles in the water below, a swallow cruising overhead dumped a load on me. Reminded me of my visit to Pocatello, Idaho years ago after a week in the poptop with the kids and no shower, when after a 1-hour shower a bird pooped a big purple mess on my head walking back to the poptop. To make matters worse, Craig asked in a loud voice, so everyone could hear, if I had been bombed. Then he said let's go inside so the guy from TN doesn't get hit again. Gives a whole new meaning to the name, Chief BS—where B stands for bird instead of big and S rhymes with it.

Drove on to Spokane where we are now. We're going into Canada Sunday and do Canadian Glacier NP, Revelstoke Mt. NP, Banff NP, Yoho NP and Hootenay NP and then meet Kenny, Faye, Tom & Carole in Waterton/Glacier back in the USA. In Canada we have to use MCI credit card to download and send at 35 cents per minute, so don't send any long files. Chief BS renamed

Sent: Tuesday, June 13, 2000 6:26 PM
Subject: Revelstoke, B.C.

In Spokane, we ate lunch in an old flour mill on the bank of the Spokane River across from Riverfront Park that has been converted to shops and restaurants. Nice view of Spokane Falls from the restaurant tables and the best French onion soup I've ever had. Not quite as good as the 3 egg omelet I had at Grants Pass, OR, which had honey baked ham cubes, Swiss cheese, diced tomatoes and mushrooms inside and the whole thing was covered in hollandaise sauce. Had a really good lunch in a small cafe in Twisp, WA driving to Spokane and sat next to 2 women from Huntsville, AL—small world. We walked around Riverfront Park in Spokane with Duke and walked by the historic marker in front of the local YMCA commemorating the origination of Father's Day by a lady in Spokane many years ago in honor of her father. Since that event is coming up soon, and I have a couple of POTENTIAL heirs on this e-mail distribution list, I thought I'd mention Father's Day. We drove out to Gonzaga College to see the campus, but didn't do much else in Spokane. We wanted to make sure Gonzaga exists as nobody ever heard of it until they started playing basketball and now they upset some high seed every year.

We drove up to British Columbia on Sunday and reentered the rain forest. I am concerned that this trailer is going to turn green with moss and mildew. I did notice that the closer one gets to the Canadian border, the more one sees American flags being flown at ordinary residences along the way. I understand it. The difference in wealth is obvious and material. It is more apparent in the lower income homes and neighborhoods than in the higher income areas. When we were in Sault Ste. Marie a few years ago, where twin cities sit side by side across a river from each other, it was really an even more striking difference, but it shows up everywhere. Socialism, even if limited like in Canada, just doesn't create the wealth that capitalism does and egalitarianism just lowers the standards for everyone.

Revelstoke is a nice little town at the foot of Mt. Revelstoke Nat. Park. It was so wet and miserable yesterday that we just did the Revelstoke Dam tour. We're becoming dam experts and I can now give a dam good tour or a good dam tour, but it had to be better than the railroad museum. The US built 5 or 6 dams on the lower Columbia River in the 30s, 40s and 50s with Grand Coulee as the centerpiece. We then negotiated with Canada to have Canada build a series of dams on the upper Columbia and tributaries, which would increase the hydropower of the lower Columbia as well. That's why Grand Coulee could be expanded and power capacity doubled in 1964. Water in the Columbia usually passes thru at least 5 or 6 dams and turbine generators on its way to the sea, so it really works hard. Hydro-electric power is really solar power created by the sun's energy evaporating seawater and wind, also solar generated, carrying the water vapor to mountains where it condenses and falls as rain or snow and then is converted from mechanical energy of falling water into electric energy by a turbine generator. Revelstoke dam is one of the bigger ones on the upper Columbia and the whole system, which is jointly managed by the US and Canada now generates over 35 million kilowatts. Canada gets to keep all the power they generate and half of the additional power that their dams increase in the US. A different kind of tour, self-guided with wands that you hold in your hand as you move from exhibit to exhibit, that begin speaking as you walk up to an exhibit. The volume is higher or lower as you move nearer the exhibit or further away. Of course, if there is a group of Germans at an exhibit and one German is translating for the others, you can't hear what the wand is saying. We meet a lot of Germans again this year, but not nearly as many as last year in the Southwest. Most of them are in rental RVs-1-800-RVforRent—but some are in rental cars. The other day I met 3 rental RVs on the road and commented to Pookie that here comes a convoy of krauts. She said Heidi wouldn't like that comment, but Heidi's used to me by now.

This morning we drove up Revelstoke Mountain Nat. Park, but the road is closed by snow about half way up—surprise, surprise. The lower part is rain forest that changes to sub-alpine forest and then to tundra and then to glaciers and ice. The weather is much better today and visibility is unlimited with intermittent showers and a ceiling at maybe 5,000 feet so we can see more than yesterday. Can't believe I'm getting where I consider a lack of pouring rain to be good luck. We then drove over to Glacier NP, the Canadian one. We ate lunch in a lodge and did the Visitor Center, which had 2 good movies. It's in Rogers Pass on the trans-Canada highway, which is kind of interesting by itself. The highway goes thru the middle of Glacier Park and they keep the highway open all winter, even though it gets over 9 meters of snow each year. There are snow sheds all along the highway, which are concrete structures kind of like a tunnel with a sloping roof to let avalanches pass over the highway instead of blocking it. One of the movies is called Snow Wars and shows how they keep it open by plowing and intentionally setting off avalanches to remove dangerous snow. They have all kinds of metering equipment on the slopes and take other measurements on ski patrols and then set off avalanches in dangerous spots by firing a 105mm artillery round high up on the slopes to start intentional avalanches in a controlled manner. The Royal Canadian Horse Artillery provides a gun crew all winter, but they use trucks to haul the field piece up and down the Pass, sometimes firing 50 rounds in a day. They close the highway while doing this, but usually have it open again in a day or two. It's very clear where the avalanches occur, as there is no vegetation left after an avalanche for many years. Glacier NP has over 400 glaciers and many steep craggy peaks. Driving back thru Glacier I saw an adult black bear on the side of the road laying in the tall grass. Backed up till we were opposite him on the other side of the highway about 35 feet away and watched him eat dandelions for about 10 minutes. A car pulled in front of me and 2 young men got out and walked back to us and used a camcorder. Reminded me of the idiot woman in Yellowstone years ago when we stopped to watch a female grizzly and her cub eat a dead elk by the side of the road. Back then a man pulled in front of me between the grizzly and us, and his wife got out and walked toward the bear with a camera in her hand. The grizzly charged her and she dropped the camera and barely beat the grizzly back to the car and slammed the door in its face. The grizzly then jumped on the hood of the car and tried to get in thru the windshield. The man began honking the horn and yelling at me to back up so he could get out. Being the caring and concerned type, I gave him a 1-finger salute for cutting off our view, confident that he wasn't going to get out of the car and complain, and he didn't. I was kind of hoping this black bear would charge the 2 young men, but he ignored them.

Heading to Banff Nat. Park tomorrow through Yoho Nat. Park. We'll try and get a campground in Lake Louise, but may have to stay in Banff as all campgrounds in the Nat. Parks are 1st come 1st served with no reservations. We probably won't have e-mail access till we get to another commercial campground near Kootenay Nat. Park after Banff. Looking forward to getting out of the rain, as the forecast is for more sun and warmer the rest of this week. Wet in BC

Sent: Saturday, June 17, 2000 8:23 PM
Subject: Yoho, Banff & Jasper

The campground owners in Revelstoke were a couple of Swiss immigrants from the Canton of Lucerne who were as nice as they could be. The husband asked where we were from and I told him TN and then asked about the rainy weather. He replied that the current weather was not normal as it was unusual to have this much rain and cold in June. I started laughing and he grinned and said in his broken English that whenever you are traveling people always say that the weather is unusual. I replied that we had never been anywhere in season or where the weather was normal. The wife told me as we were leaving that last June there was no rain for the whole month and they had worried about the grass dying. Well, the forecast turned out to be wrong and it rained the whole drive thru Yoho NP to Banff. Yoho is named for the northern branch of the Hoh Tribe who moved to the mountains and learned to yodel making the sound Yoho. If you don't buy that, it's named for the snooty people like Pookie White Roots who used to look down on the mama Hohs and yelled Yoho at them when they walked by. Actually, I don't have a clue as to where the name came from and don't care. We never saw the top of a peak in Yoho through the fog and rain, but did stop and do the Visitor Center. We got there just as 2 tour coaches of Japanese tourists drove up and it wasn't much of a Visitor Center, so we left. There was a mudslide on the trans Canada highway that delayed us about 45 minutes, but we were lucky as the local paper the next day said the highway was closed for 5 hours before it reopened.

When we got to Banff NP we drove right to the campground at Lake Louise and read the sign saying that a male grizzly bear had been seen recently courting a female grizzly in the campground and no tent campers or poptop campers with soft sides were being admitted to the campground, and no food could be left outside a hard sided camper. We entered the campground and paid for 4 nights and I told Pookie she might have to walk Duke after dark if the grizzlies were on the prowl. The campground has electricity and we can camp on our internal water and sewage tanks for a week or longer if we shower in the camp restrooms and the heat is propane, so no problem. I was amazed that we pick up 2 Detroit TV stations on the TV antenna. They must be on a repeater in Calgary or Edmonton or somewhere as we are a long way from Detroit, but the stations are on Eastern Time while we're on mountain in Alberta.

The next morning the skies cleared for a change so we decided to go to the Visitor Center at Lake Louise and then eat lunch at a restaurant next to it. When leaving the campground, we saw a handwritten sign taped to the Stop sign at the campground entrance that said "Message for Evan Davis". I couldn't believe anyone had tracked us down and wondered what family crisis was happening. I drove up to the window and said I'm Evan Davis. The guy grinned and handed me my Visa card I had not received back when I paid for the campground the evening before. He came out to take the sign down and Pookie asked him to wait till she could take a picture of it. I guess she figured nobody would believe I had made a mistake, unless she had photographic proof.

Nice exhibits at the Visitor Center and a couple of good videos. One was on the grizzly bear study and management program in all the Canadian Rocky Mt. NPs. The biggest problem has been having grizzlies lose their natural fear of man and then becoming dangerous to people and having to be destroyed. They tried tranquilizing the offending bears, putting radio collars on them and transporting them under a helicopter as far as 70 air miles away over numerous mountain ranges. The problem is that the bears kept returning to their home ranges, sometimes within a few weeks. After filling up all the available zoos, they had to start killing them again. Then, about 4 years ago they started a program of hazing the bears to restore their fear of man. They now shoot them with rubber bullets that sting but don't kill and then fire a flare from a pistol, which ends with a loud noise like a skyrocket. They've also put up tall wire fences along the highways and built underpasses and overpasses to let the bears cross the highways and they haven't had to destroy a single bear in over 4 years. The video showed a warden shooting the rubber bullets and flares at a bear, which can outrun a racehorse for a short distance, and it really took off when hit. They still have a problem with black bears being killed by trains. The black bears are attracted to the railroad tracks by grain cars that leak grain between the rails and they are now trying to get all the railroads to fix their cars.

After lunch, we drove to the lake at Lake Louise a short distance from the Visitor Center. It's gorgeous with Victoria Glacier and the mountains in the background and the aquamarine green color of the lake. All of these glacier melt lakes and streams have ground up rock debris in them called rock flour or glacial flour. Depending on the type of rock, the depth of the water and the amount of flour, the color can be from milky white to aquamarine to pale blue. It was windy and cold so we skipped the canoe rental but we took Duke with us and drank in the view. Next we drove to Lake Moraine about 5 clicks—kilometers—further and I think it may be even more attractive. We started on the trail around the Lake with Duke but Pookie missed the sign saying that a grizzly had been spotted around this lake too. She thought I was kidding when I told her about it and asked what it said. I told her the instruction in the biggest print said to make plenty of noise as you walked along so as not to surprise the bear and make it charge you. She acted suspicious of my answer till the guy behind us about 60 yards started singing loudly in a terrible off key voice. We didn't complete the trail. Next we drove to Lake Herbert, billed as a photographers dream. It's a freshwater lake from rain and snowmelt with no glacial flour and has no unique color, but reflects the snow covered mountains very clearly when the water is still. Naturally, it started raining and the drops helped the wind ripples destroy any reflection, but we did see and hear a solitary loon and found moose droppings. We almost never see moose. By the way, is the plural of moose mice? Back to the trailer for a drink. This NP has a liquor store, which is a distinct improvement on the American NPs. The name Banff comes from a town in Scotland where they distill the "water of life", so it's appropriate to have liquor here.

The next day we drove down to the town of Banff, which is about 60 clicks from Lake Louise. We took the Bow Valley Parkway, which is billed, as more scenic and slower than the trans Canada highway and stopped and did the Johnston Canyon Falls Trail on the way. The trail is built in a narrow canyon and about half the trail is over the rushing water of Johnston Creek and is on a walkway supported by steel rails driven into the sheer rock cliffs. Very scenic, but the Falls are not spectacular. We ate lunch in a restaurant and I had another omelet, this time crab and asparagus covered in hollandaise sauce, but not nearly as good as the tomato and mushroom job. We walked around town after lunch and found the Visitor Center, but the exhibits and videos are not worth seeing. Then Pookie had me drive by the Banff Springs Hotel so she could see it, but construction is going on and I wasn't impressed. Next, I asked my navi-guesser for directions to Lake Minnewanka, about 5 clicks from Banff as I had seen a promotion for a boat tour of the lake with a tour guide giving the history and geology of the area.

Pookie sent me down Banff Ave., after consulting her map, which was not the way we came into Banff. Just as I left a 50kph speed zone and entered a 30kph zone, which is less than 20mph, I saw a cop standing on the right side of the street and a policewoman in uniform standing on the concrete median between the lanes of traffic. I looked down to make sure I was not speeding and I wasn't. When I looked up, the lady cop stepped in front of me and held up her hand. I stopped and she said I was not wearing a seatbelt and to turn right at the next intersection, about 15 yards in front of me. I did and discovered it was a short dead end street with about 4 cop cars and 2 other civilian vehicles parked there. A cop walked up to me and said I had violated the seat belt law and to produce my driver's license. I told him I was from a state that did not have a mandatory seat belt law and I rarely used one driving around town. Actually, I never use one, but he didn't know that. He rudely informed me that the Province of Alberta had a zero tolerance for seat belt use and I was getting a $57 ticket—that's about $40 US. When I said there were no signs about the law entering Alberta through the NP, he just shrugged his shoulders and asked the model year of the Durango. The Jeep in front of me had Montana plates and was getting a ticket and a car with Massachusetts's plates pulled in behind me to get a ticket. I have to admit, it was a sophisticated ticket trap that put small town speeding traps to shame. Setting up with a dead end street to hide the cop cars and give a safe place to direct traffic, doing it in a 30 click speed zone to make sure the traffic is going slow enough to see into the windshield and look for a seat belt shoulder strap, using the lady cop standing on the median to be sure you went slow and to get the left hand traffic lane with another cop on the right hand side to eyeball the right hand lane. Well designed and productive. I bet they generated 3 or 4 thousand dollars an hour as they did about $300 the few minutes I was there. I didn't see any non-American licensed vehicles get tickets, but surely they didn't gig only the foreign tourists who support their local economy. I started to tell the bozo who was writing my ticket that Sergeant Preston of the Royal Canadian Mounted Police and his loyal Husky police dog, King, would both be embarrassed by this kind of chickenshit police work, but decided that wouldn't be a wise move. I asked where I could pay the ticket and he said a small town about 20 miles from Calgary, where I'm not going, or I could mail a check to the court. I couldn't resist commenting that my check would be in American dollars and not this play money. I must have gotten a little under his skin as he snapped back that I could buy a money order. After we drove off, it became apparent that we were not on the route to Lake Minnewanka, at least not according to Pookie navi-guesser's map. A gentle interrogation of my navi-guesser about whether or not this ticket would have been received if I had been given the correct directions got her ticked off. I could tell this when she said she was glad I got the damn ticket, but at least now I wasn't the only one in a foul mood.

Lake Minnewanka turned out to be a tourist trap. We could see the whole lake from the top of the dam that created it and the tour boats were dinky and the mountains not snow covered around the lake, so we decided to skip it. The road back to Banff went across the dam and half way across we drove up to a herd of about 10 Rocky Mountain goats walking across the dam. Duke had a conniption fit and his noise made the goats accelerate their pace. At the end of the dam a tour bus had pulled off to the side of the road and began to unload its passengers to stretch their legs and look at the view. As they got off, it became clear that all were dressed alike in a gray material that looked like terry cloth and was shaped kind of like pajamas. All were Asian and had shaven heads. We were viewing a busload of Buddhist monks & I wondered instantly if the democrats were having a fundraiser here in Canada to avoid the press. The windows of the bus were dark and I couldn't see inside, but could Al Gore be hiding on the bus? He was in Spokane while we were there and maybe he's still hanging around out here. For that matter, were the people of the Province of Alberta being endangered by a bus driver not wearing his seat belt? The Gore question at least deserved an answer, but I've given up on Janet Reno ever investigating the democrat fund raising techniques. I'm firmly convinced that even if Janet could be compelled to investigate democratic fund raising, she'd appoint an incompetent who would make Inspector Clouseau of "Pink Panther" fame look good. One guy who would probably be near the top of her list would be the Head of Security at Los Alamos.

It started to rain as usual, so we drove back to Lake Louise on the trans Canada highway, which I think is even more scenic than the Parkway. This morning we went to the Gondola at Summit Peak, which is actually a ski lift to ride up the mountain and see the view. It was a bright sunny day and I bought the tickets that included lunch and the ride. When we got to the lift, it was broken down with people suspended in the air all up and down the mountain. I could hear the attendant say he'd already tried that twice and it didn't work. He was talking on the phone to another teen-age wonder at the top of the mountain that worked the apparatus up there. The next thing Pookie heard was our ski lift guru telling the other guy to call somebody who he thought was still at home and he might know the answer. Builds all kinds of confidence to hear this stuff, but it was a pretty day and we were planning on having lunch at the top of the mountain. They finally got it going and we chose an open seat lift instead of the enclosed gondolas to get better views and take pictures. It was a spectacular view and well worth the ride up. At 11:30 I told Pookie we should go inside off the observation deck and get our lunch. All they had was hot dogs and junk food so I asked the teen with the nose ring behind the counter where we got the lunch I had paid for and showed him my ride and lunch ticket. He informed me that the lunch I had bought was at the bottom of the lift in the Lodge dining room. Why hadn't the teen at the ticket booth explained that? The material had suggested that you ate at the top. We went back to the lift and got another open seat chair to ride down. The damn thing stopped 4 times on the down trip and we could hear the guys at the top and bottom blowing horns at each other. I guess the total delay was only 15 minutes or so, but it was cold and now cloudy and a strong wind blowing. I tried to cheer up a couple stuck opposite us on the upride by telling them they had sent for the rescue helicopter. We finally got down and went in the Lodge to get our lunch. We were told there was a group of 90 coming in and we had to sit at the bar on stools.

We went back to the campground and got Duke and decided to ride up to the Columbia Icefields at the north end of Banff in Jasper NP. Huge and impressive, but we had already ridden a helicopter to the top of a glacier in Alaska and walked around the glacier, so we skipped the ride out on the glacier in the snow buggy that carries 56 people at once. Speaking of already having done stuff, Pookie expressed worry and concern on the way back to Lake Louise that she wasn't going to have any new things left to explore with the other widows after I croak. I'm having great difficulty developing any sympathy for her. In fact, she just called me on the cell phone from the laundry at the Lake Louise Inn and said she was delayed by selfish old Inn Guests using the machines ahead of her and would be late getting back to Duke and me. I think we'll survive the delay.

Chief BS where it means Been Screwed—by Alberta's finest of course

Sent: Wednesday, June 21, 2000 5:30 PM
Subject: Big Sky Country

We left Banff on a day forecast for rain, but got a nice clear day for most of the day. Drove through Kootenay NP, the last of Canada's Rocky Mt. Parks. Gorgeous views of the mountains as you drive. We stopped at a trail to the Paint Pots and took Duke with us on the trail. These are ochre pits where the ancestors dug up ochre and vermilion for making paints. The pits were mined commercially until the early 1900s. Spring water flows over parts of the ochre pits and Duke waded out and got his paws colored orange. Spent that nite at Radium Hot Springs, BC and received 72 e-mails when I downloaded. Most of them were junk and we sure do get a lot of spam lately. The mineral baths at Radium Hot Springs weren't much. Banff has much nicer baths for those so inclined. The town of Banff got started as a spa for taking mineral baths, but it's not nearly as fancy as Hot Springs, Arkansas.

We crossed back into the States north of Eureka, MT and stopped at the Duty Free shop on the Canadian side of the border. Glenfiddich scotch at $36 Canadian for a liter. Dewar's for $21 Canadian per liter, but they call the US Customs and tell them how much you bought, give them your license plate # and walk to the border to hand it to you. You then have to stop and declare how much you have and pay $3.50 US for every liter over 2 per couple. Naturally I said there was none in the trailer and these were for gifts in the US and didn't declare the 2 liters in the trailer, but had to pay $3.50 for the 3rd liter I did declare. I have to make back my Alberta losses someway. When I went inside the customs house to pay the duty, the guy put in his machine a duty due of $35 instead of $3.50 and then couldn't figure out how to get it out. An off duty border patrolman told him to put in another $35 and then he could void it, but that didn't work either. I told the guy to just give me the difference since if he kept it up, he'd go broke. The off duty guy is now laughing and telling his buddy that there is no way to void it and to just pony up the $70 out of his pocket. I told the guy struggling with the machine that if I had to work with a big picture of Bill Clinton hanging on the wall over me, I'd screw up too, and they all fell out laughing. Finally, I just gave him the exact change and he said I could go.

We drove to Missoula, MT and spent 2 nights. We drove over the U. of Montana campus, which isn't too big and isn't very attractive, but does have the Clark River flowing down one side of the campus and fly fishermen standing in it casting. The mascot and name of the sports teams is the Grizzlies. After lunch at Cracker Barrel to get a taste of soul food, we did a tour of the Forest Service Smoke Jumper Center where they train all the smoke jumpers in the US. Exhibits, videos and displays and then a guided tour of the campus where they live and train. Very interesting and an excellent tour guide. There are 400 smoke jumpers in the US and 25 are women. Mandatory retirement at 55 and seasonal work only, as they are only needed from April to Oct. All are GS-5 federal employees, but get hazardous duty pay when fighting a fire, which is double pay, so not bad for part time work. Physical requirement is to carry a 120 pound backpack over moderate—read hilly, but open—terrain for 3 miles in 90 minutes and an 85 pound pack for 3 miles over rugged—read mountainous and wooded — terrain in the same timeframe. The main firefighting tool is a thing that looks like an axe with a large grubbing hoe on the back of the axe blade. It's called a pulaski, but what would you expect when you have a Polish name? We went in a large sewing room where they make all their own packs and webbing. There is a parachute loft for hanging and inspecting used chutes before they are repacked and a rigging room for repacking them, where we watched some being packed. The whole campus is on the Missoula airport and their planes are parked out back. They use a DC-3 for big jumps and a smaller plane for smaller jumps and have 2 aerial tankers to drop retardant. The pictures you see on TV of tankers dropping orange colored retardant are misleading. They never drop on active fire as it appears on TV. They drop on unburned areas at the edge of the fire to douse them and keep the fire from spreading through that area. The retardant is fertilizer based and helps new growth after the fire and is rapidly decomposed by sunlight to eliminate the color used in the retardant. The jump suit is Kevlar to prevent cuts or gashes by tree limbs or rocks, but there's no protection from bruises. They live in dormitories on site, if not from Missoula. They only jump on small fires of 1 to 3 acres, which a few people can contain. They've had so much rain in the Northwest this year that about half their resources were sent to Los Alamos and Colorado to fight as regular ground based firefighters. They always have more volunteers than they need and are very selective. There's what looks like a Marine Corps obstacle course out back for training and PT and a track for running. 2 hours daily of physical training is required. Not for me, but worth a tour if you are out here.

We're now in Helena, MT and will do a quick tour of Helena, Great Falls, Butte and Bozeman before heading back to the woods as Pookie calls it and doing Glacier/Waterton. Refilled with propane and washed the Durango and trailer in Missoula. We'll meet Kenny, Faye, Tom and Carole, a.k.a. Bear Bait, in Whitefish on the 30th.

Random Ruminations:

1. George Marshall threatened to resign as Truman's Sec. of State if the US recognized Israel as a state when they declared statehood and were invaded by the Arabs, to begin their first war with the Arabs. Marshall wasn't opposed to Israel, but thought it would ruin any future relationships with Arab states if we didn't wait till the war was over and see what happened. Truman couldn't afford to lose Marshall, who was much more popular than Truman, but he thought about if for a day and then called Marshall back and told him he sure hoped he wouldn't resign, but the US was going to recognize Israel the next day because Truman thought it was the right thing to do. Marshall backed down and the US was the 2nd nation to recognize Israel, which allowed them to buy more arms legitimately and helped win the war.

2. Duke has now been in 32 states, DC and 5 Canadian provinces and will pick up 5 or 6 more states on our way home, depending on how we go. He realizes that he has a very large territory to mark, but he has handled the challenge in an admirable fashion so far. I think he drinks more water when we travel in order to have more marking material available.

3. I decided to try and recoup some of the money wrongly taken from me by the Alberta provincial police. Fortunately, I have a law degree, so I am not totally unequipped to use lying, cheating and stealing to regain lost goods. You are required to pay a $10 daily use fee for 2 people in most of the Canadian NPs. We bought 3 days of passes for $24 at Revelstoke, which only charges $8 per day, but the passes are good in the $10 parks too. The weather was so bad; the lady ranger who sold us the passes left 2 of them blank for us to fill in the dates when we used them. We entered on the 13th which my navi-guesser

/forger changed to the 18th in the same red ink the ranger used. A pass is good till 4p.m on the day after dated, so we didn't use another till the 15th, which my now accomplished forger changed to the 16th the next day. We used it until 4 p.m. on the 17th and then used the forged 13th on the 18th. We still have an unused 1-day blank pass if anyone wants it and saved $30 in fees as we were in the parks for 6 days. Take that Alberta! You now owe me only $27 in play money!

4. The animal warning signs say that playing dead sometimes works in getting a grizzly to break off an attack, but almost never works with a black bear. Since both species may range in color from light brown to black with mixtures of red and silver and a yearling grizzly is about the size of an adult black bear, I have concluded that playing dead is not an acceptable choice unless you are a real whiz and aced the Bear Identification Course. Take note Bear Bait.

5. The Columbia Icefields are huge and cover over 325 square kilometers. Melt water from the Field, which sits on a triple continental divide flows north to the Arctic Ocean, east to the Atlantic thru Hudson Bay and west to the Pacific. It furnishes a significant amount of Canada's river flow.

6. My navi-guesser has materially improved her accuracy ratio on this trip. She accomplished most of this improvement with a simple little rule change that works like a charm. The error tolerance level has been expanded to allow this change. Now, if you are approaching a 4-way intersection and the correct instruction is to turn left and she gives the instruction to turn right—she says later that her instruction was close enough to score as an acceptable solution. Why didn't I think of that? Coup Counter

Sent: Thursday, June 29, 2000 11:27 AM
Subject: Montana Five

The Nashville Tennessean newspaper had a full page article this spring about touring the 5 cities in west central MT. It suggested staying in Helena and making a series of day trips to Missoula, Great Falls, Bozeman and Butte. We spent 2 nights in Missoula and then drove on to Helena to try their recommendation. Duke hated to leave Missoula. The campground there had a petting zoo attached to it and was overrun with squirrels. I'm talking about teasing squirrels that love to torment dogs. A squirrel would get on a limb right outside the window of the trailer and bark at Duke to drive him crazy. When I put him out on his stakeout chain, the squirrels would figure out the length of the chain, and then get maybe a foot further away than the chain length. This nearly cost 2 of them their lives. Duke first broke his collar lunging at one and then after we bought a new collar and a harness, he broke the stakeout chain. A lady we met in the campground said she had lost all contact with her dog in that campground as the dog only hunted squirrels all day long. Had to leave to get some peace and quiet.

Our first day in Helena, we did a tram tour of the city for an hour with a tour guide narration. Then we did the state capitol with another tour guide who really knew his stuff. I was surprised that the capitol was as nice as it is as Montana is such a young state. Then we did the Montana State Museum, which is across the street from the capitol. It reminded me of the state museum in Maine in the way it was laid out and organized. After lunch, we went north of Helena about 10 miles to the Gates of the Mountains National Recreation Area on the Missouri River. Meriwether Lewis gave it the name of Gates of the Mountains when the Lewis and Clark expedition passed through. We took a narrated boat tour with about 35 others for 3 hours and saw some bald eagles, ospreys and bighorn sheep. We stopped at a picnic area where Lewis & Clark camped and passed Mann Gulch where 13 smoke jumpers, including one from Paris, TN died in a 1949 fire fighting disaster. A nice day and very informative.

The next day we drove 90 miles north to Great Falls, MT. None of these cities is very large, and Great Falls at 55,000 is the largest. About 10 miles south of Great Falls, we turned off and drove to Ulm Pishkun State Park. Ulm is the name of the nearest small town, and Pishkun is an Indian word meaning buffalo jump, or a place where Indians ran bison off a cliff to kill them for meat and hides. There is a new Visitor Center that is quite well done with a lot of exhibits and explanations of the site. At the foot of the cliff, bones were 13 feet deep, and carbon dating shows that the Indians quit using it after they acquired horses in the late 1500s. I was walking Duke on a trail outside the center when a lady asked why I didn't turn him loose, so I did. There was nothing there except the prairie and Duke had a good time running around looking for ground squirrels. He saw a stuffed buffalo inside the center and kept trying to get in until I put him back in the Durango. Up at the top of the cliff there was an active prairie dog colony, so I couldn't turn Duke loose there. Prairie dogs make a lot of noise whistling to each other, which Duke didn't appreciate.

In Great Falls, we did the Charles M. Russell Museum, studio and house. Russell produced over 4,000 art works and they have a lot of the original paintings and sculpture here. Most interesting were a lot of his personal letters to friends and his wife. He would insert little drawings and etchings in his letters—most in color—to emphasize his comments. For example, when writing his wife from Chicago, he inserted a skunk to illustrate his distaste for cities, which he said, stank. Quite interesting and I was shocked at how much he resembled Will Rogers in appearance. I commented to a docent that he sure did look like Will Rogers and she just smiled and said yes. Later while going through his house, I saw a picture of him sitting on a curb with Will Rogers sitting next to him and both laughing. Russell was a lot older, but they could have passed for twins otherwise.

After lunch, we toured the Lewis & Clark Interpretive Center on the banks of the Missouri. It's a US Forest Service Center and was having its grand opening that day. I'm damn near an expert on Lewis & Clark now. Then we drove downstream about 15 miles to see the great falls of the Missouri that it took Lewis & Clark about 3 weeks to portage around. There were 5 falls originally, but dams and lakes drowned 3 and the Great Fall isn't worth seeing. There is a dam 100 feet above it and only 1% of the water now goes over the falls. The upper Missouri is as used and abused as much as the Colorado River. We ate dinner in a local subway shop and finished the day by seeing the movie "Chicken Run" on its opening day before driving back to Helena. I think we were the oldest people in the movie—in chronological age anyway.

Bozeman was next on the list so we drove there the next morning. The Museum of the Rockies with Planetarium is on the campus of Montana State University, the home of the Bobcats. They had a traveling exhibit of giant insect robots that move and make sounds—a tarantula 12 feet long and beetles 15 feet long fighting each other. They had a huge caterpillar, but no snakes for Alicia. They are best known for the dinosaur exhibits which came for the most part from Montana. We saw a 50-minute film on the sun in the planetarium, but Pookie said that it was over her head—Ta Da! She also said she had seen enough crap about tectonic plate movements and volcanoes. Need to move this girl to the Great Plains and some more museums about my relatives. Speaking of them, the Yoho tribe in Canada finally admitted their lifestyle, moved back to the States and later had a territory and State named for them. It's called I—da—ho. The American Computer Museum was next in Bozeman. It starts out with the Babylonians and claims that computers went from sand to sand—silicon. The Museum gives Samuel Morse credit for inventing the first Internet when he invented the telegraph and sent the first message—"What hath God wrought?" I'm sure Mr. Morse unintentionally overlooked the still unborn, future theology student, Al Gore, when he was giving out credits. Pookie suggested that we donate the laptop to them as an example of prehistoric computing. She wants a new one that isn't so slow. Her name is not Patience. I did enjoy seeing an IBM 360 that I remember installing in my bank in Jackson, TN when it was state-of-the-art. The laptop is more powerful than it now. On the way back to Helena, we stopped at Headwaters of the Missouri State Park where the Gallatin, Jefferson and Madison rivers all meet to form the Missouri River. Called Three Forks, it was a historic crossing area where tribes met and traded goods. All 3 rivers are first class trout streams and Lewis & Clark followed the Jefferson to where they met the Shoshone Indians and acquired horses to cross the Rockies. The Shoshone Chief turned out to be the older brother of Sacajawea, who had been kidnapped as a teenager by a tribe from the eastern prairies.

Butte, current population about 30,000 was last on our list, but one of the most interesting. Historic Butte looks like a war zone with a lot of old dilapidated buildings scattered around. When copper was king, the mining companies bought up a lot of properties and demolished them to mine under them. The shrewd people who held out for more money got screwed and still have worthless old buildings. We took another narrated tour around the historic district for 90 minutes. It was 52 degrees with the wind blowing and overcast and cold. Our tour guide said Montana has 4 seasons—early winter, winter, end of winter and construction. I asked when did construction start and he said we were in the middle of it. Four people from Georgia were on the tour and they said they liked Tennesseans, except on Saturday afternoons. I told them we were Vandy fans and no threat. We stopped at the Berkley open pit mine, which has 900 feet deep of water in it and is filling from ground water and is an ecological disaster. Everybody is arguing over who should reclaim it and how. They still do some open pit mining nearby and we watched a huge dump truck carry 170 tons at once to an ore concentrator, but now the mining companies have laws forcing them to reclaim the modern mines. Silver, gold and other metals were produced in small amounts and during WWII, a single mine in Butte produced 90 per cent of the manganese we used in our war production efforts. The copper area only covers 3 square miles and is very small in size, but the old underground mines go a mile deep. Another tour guide remark is that Butte is a mile high and a mile deep, but its inhabitants are all on the level. Speaking of residents being horizontal, we took a guided tour of a 100-year-old brothel, the Dumas Brothel that was built as a brothel with what are called cribs for the girls to work. Eighty per cent of Butte's population of over 100,000 were single males during the mining heyday and sadly, they only have mannequins in the brothel today. We also toured the mansion of William Clark, one of the Copper Kings who was among the world's most wealthy people. Of course, he was of good Presbyterian stock and probably never visited a brothel.

We're now in a campground outside Columbia Falls, MT, near Waterton/Glacier NP, waiting for Bear Bait, Tom, Kenny & Faye to get here tonight. Two hikers were attacked by black bears in Glacier day before yesterday, but managed to limp out of the Park and trails in that area are now closed. We've already toured Waterton/Glacier, but I'll describe that later. I heard on the news this a.m. that some group is trying to get Congress to declare 15 more Nat. Parks. When I told Pookie, her comment was not publishable. Chief BS—Brave Spirit

Sent: Sunday, July 02, 2000 7:17 PM
Subject: Waterton/Glacier NP

Yeah, I'd put it in the top 5 National Parks. Our first day, we drove up the "Going to the Sun Road", considered an engineering marvel by itself, past Lake McDonald. The first 15 miles or so is beside the Lake and by McDonald Creek, which empties into the Lake. We stopped several times and did a trail at Avalanche Creek and went into Lake McDonald Lodge. The Lodge has a huge oversized fireplace with pictographs chiseled into the stone that are possibly the work of Charles Russell, but nobody knows for sure. The road begins to climb after that for another 15 miles to Logan Pass, which is also the Continental Divide. The road is very narrow and unlike most mountain highways, has only 1 switchback. It's blasted out of the side of mountains with sheer drop-offs on the side away from the mountain. There are only 2 short tunnels and the views are spectacular and include a number of glaciers, hanging valleys, streams, waterfalls and avalanche paths. It's rated as the most scenic drive in America, but I think there are too many to give a single one the top rating. There are three Visitor Centers in the Park, but none of them are very good, compared to most Parks. It takes about 2 or 3 hours to drive all the 50 mile length of the road across the Park, if you're lucky and don't get stopped for construction work at the one lane part for very long. We stopped at Rising Sun on the east side of the Park and ate lunch in a nice restaurant operated by a concessionaire. At St. Mary, the eastern entrance, we went north to Many Glacier, a separate drive and area with a Lodge. It too is pretty and has a view across a lake like Lake Louise in Canada. We drove back through the Park driving west and the views are just as good as driving east. Got back to our campground around 7:30, but it doesn't get dark until 10 this far north.

The next day we drove over the Going to the Sun Road again, but left earlier and had no delays and got across the Park in 1 1/2 hours. The road is named for the Going to the Sun Mountain which Blackfoot legend says was climbed by a Sun God Spirit on his way back to the Sun after he had helped the Blackfeet overcome an earthly problem. This time we drove much farther north into Canada to see the Waterton part of the Park that is all in Canada. Waterton/Glacier is managed jointly by the Canadians and Americans and is an International Peace Park as well as a World Biosphere site. Two Rotary Clubs, one in Alberta and one in the USA are responsible for having the Parks declared Peace Parks by both nations and jointly administered by both nations. Glacier is much larger than Waterton and the Parks are very different. Waterton has 3 large lakes, but all 3 combined are smaller than McDonald Lake or Saint Mary Lake in Glacier and all 3 are depressions carved out by glaciers. The prairie comes right up to the edge of Waterton, unlike Glacier, which is bounded by other, smaller mountains. If you go, be sure and see both parks, as they are quite distinct. We ate lunch in the Prince Of Wales Hotel dining room with a gorgeous view over 1 of the lakes to the mountains beyond. The hotel itself is beautiful, sitting up on top of a hill overlooking the lake. The outside grounds host a whole colony of Columbian ground squirrels and after walking Duke around the grounds, straining on his leash to escape and hunt squirrels; he exited the Durango through a rear window at about 15 mph as we drove down the hill. A whole lot of people were walking around the grounds taking photos and all started laughing at Duke and at us trying to recapture him. Every squirrel escaped, but Duke kept running from one burrow entrance to another as the squirrels kept coming up to see where he was. Finally, I caught him as he dug into a burrow and put him back on the leash. Only twice has he leaped out of the Durango while it's moving and both times have been in Canada. We walked around the town of Waterton Lakes, which is small, but cute. I let Duke go in the lake as I thought he wanted a drink, but he walked out in the water like he was going to drink, and then laid down and rolled over to get soaking wet. Must have been hot.

We drove up to Lake Cameron for a short walk along the lake and then drove to Red Rock Canyon to do the trail along the canyon. The parking lot at Red Rock Canyon had a small herd of mountain goats walking around the parking lot and crawling up under cars to lick salt off the undersides. There were both sexes of goats and kids as well as adults, but they ignored the people in the parking lot. Duke they didn't ignore. Dogs can go on the trails in most Canadian Parks, but Duke wanted some of the goats and the mother goats wanted some of Duke. Duke didn't back down, but I did, as I was attached to his leash and the mother goats were big. I drug him away and the goats didn't follow very far. The canyon rock is extremely red and flaky and is in layers separated by gray and white sedimentary rock. It is quite striking and very pretty and the creek continues to erode the rock at the width of a nickel per year. Driving back to the Park entrance, we passed a black bear cruising along a hillside about 200 yards from the road and digging up something to eat in the meadow. Since we were going to exit Glacier on the south side and drive that way later, we re-crossed the Park on the Going to the Sun road for the 4th time and got back late again.

We took the next day off and did no touring. Slept late, and then put Duke in a kennel to be free of him while we met the Webbs and Stevens. Did our Wal- Mart run to refurbish supplies, did a grocery store, ran the Durango through a wash and wax and vacuumed out most of the Duke hair, ate lunch and then went to see the movie, "The Patriot", playing in Kalispell, MT a few miles from our campground. I enjoyed the movie, which reinforced my opinion that Tom Brokaw is wrong. The greatest generation is not the generation that endured the depression and then won WWII. They may have preserved freedom, but to me the greatest generation is the one in colonial times that created freedom by declaring war on the world's most powerful nation, the Evil Empire of that time and winning. Not only did they win, they organized an entirely new form of government and structured it for success.

Pookie went to the airport to meet the Stevens and Webbs at 10p.m., but I sacked out. The next morning we went to the Grouse Mountain Lodge where they were staying and joined them for breakfast. Kenny had continuing education courses that morning, so Tom, Carole, Faye, Pookie & I took off in the Durango. We rented a pontoon boat on Whitefish Lake and cruised around the lake for 2 hours on an absolutely perfect day. Lots of nice lake houses on one side of the lake and a state park on the other. Faye's cell phone has nationwide access at no extra cost, so the women called a bunch of people from the boat. The weather was so nice that Faye took off her long pants and wore one of Pookie's long shirts. Tom & I decided that Faye didn't have to pay for the boat and would get a free ride.

We picked Kenny up at noon and drove to Big Mountain to take the ski lift up to the top and eat lunch there. We split up, 3 & 3 and rode chair lifts up instead of the gondolas. About 1/4 of the way up, I dropped my jacket by accident and watched it sink into the brush below us. We took some pictures, ate and walked around a little and then went back down in the chair lifts. My jacket was between the 5th and 6th poles of the ski lift. When we got to the bottom, I decided to climb up and retrieve my jacket. Faye said she'd go with me, so we set off. Definitely not a good idea. Damn near straight up and a helluva climb. At the 3rd pole, Faye asked if I really, really wanted that jacket. It was sunny and hot and by now I'm sweating and getting light headed, but now I'm determined to get the damn thing. We start zigzagging up, as we're too tired to keep up the direct ascent. Finally Faye says let's try going through that brush as it's a shorter way, and I'm ready to get bloody from thorns, as I'm wearing shorts, if it'll make it shorter. My sandals are not the best hiking boots either. We finally get the jacket and head down a different way and make it back to the rest of the group after an hour plus of hiking up and down a mountain. That jacket is now invaluable. We met a retired dentist from Columbia, TN and his wife for dinner at a really nice restaurant in Whitefish. Before dinner and while we're drinking wine, I make a presentation to Kenny of the book Pookie bought him in Revelstoke NP in Canada. Kenny, Faye and Tom say they are going on an 11-mile hike up to Grinnell Glacier in Glacier Park, so Pookie bought Kenny a book entitled "How to Shit in the Woods". Everybody loves the book, which Pookie has wrapped in brown paper tied with string. The first chapter is titled "Anatomy of a Crap", the 2nd chapter is "Digging the Hole" and there are separate chapters of instructions for men and women.

The next morning, we met the group again for breakfast, but then we went to spring Duke from the kennel, hooked up the trailer and headed east around the south side of Glacier NP. We stopped at the Museum of the Plains Indian in Browning, MT for an hour or so and drove east to Havre, MT for the night. This morning, we decided to go south again and do the Little Bighorn Battlefield east of Billings and then go south into Wyoming and see Devil's Tower Nat. Monument on the way to Wind Cave NP in South Dakota. We're now in the first ever KOA in Billings, MT on the bank of the Yellowstone River, but we've got to move tomorrow as it's booked for the 4th for the 10,000 Gold Wing Riders Convention in Billings this week. Yep, lots of big and fancy motorcycles. Pookie just set off the alarm on the Durango and let Duke get loose when she went out to cut off the alarm. Took me 15 minutes to chase him down and get him back. Chief BS—Been Screwed—again

Sent: Thursday, July 06, 2000 5:42 PM
Subject: Sundance, WY

We didn't have to leave the campground in Billings, MT after all. By moving to another, more expensive site, we were able to stay another 2 days. Funny how money works isn't it. I forgot to mention that the drive from Havre to Billings was through several Indian reservations on state roads with almost no traffic. I stopped at the Belknap Indian Agency to get some gas as it looked like 200 miles without another gas pump. When I went in to pay, there was a big hand written sign over the beer cooler stating that absolutely no alcohol would be sold before 8 a.m. Sounds like discrimination against my blood brothers to withhold alcohol early in the morning. A cold beer tastes better early on Sunday morning than at any other time. We saw very little traffic, but did see our first pronghorn antelope of this trip. I startled a big buck coming over a hill and he was maybe 30 yards from the Durango. They sure are fast when they want to move. We later saw several herds near the highway, grazing and ignoring us.

Our first morning in Billings, we drove about an hour southeast to the Little Bighorn Battlefield Nat. Monument. The Visitor Center is small, but fairly well done, but there were a ton of people there. We must finally be in season, so it's nearly time to go home. The battlefield is on a Crow Indian reservation and the rangers are mostly Crow Indians. A Crow rangerette gave a very interesting lecture about the battle before we took a narrated bus tour of the battlefield. Our tour guide was a young Crow student at a nearby Indian college who did an excellent job of explaining what happened. Custer had about 30 Crow and Arapaho Scouts, who were traditional enemies of the Sioux, with him in the battle, and they fought against the Sioux too, so it wasn't totally a red vs. white fight. Custer had to be dumb as a post. The Scouts told him they were facing maybe 2000 to 2500 Indian warriors, but he ordered an attack by Major Reno, who had only 3 companies of the 7th Cavalry, or about 150 men. The entire 7th Cavalry was only about 600 men, including the Indian Scouts, and not all were wiped out. The 5 companies under Custer's direct command were annihilated, but

Major Reno and Major Benteen, who joined forces and fought a separate battle from Custer, survived with their combined 7 companies and lost only about 40 men. A total of 263 troopers and scouts were killed and the Indians lost from 40 to 100 warriors. Custer's 2 brothers and a nephew were killed with him, so the Indians helped clean up the gene pool that day. A white tombstone marks where each dead trooper was found, and you can trace the battle disintegration by seeing where they died. The burial party had only 8 shovels and 263 corpses; so all the graves were very shallow. They were later reburied in a mass grave on the hill where it ended with a common Memorial engraved with their names, except for some of the officers whose remains were shipped home. Custer's remains are now at West Point. The battle stretched over about 4 miles and Benteen received his orders to come to Custer's aid, but he and Reno said it was impossible and the one attempt was driven back. It seems that they didn't like Custer anyway and they probably would have died too if they had marched away from their high ground position. Of course, it was a phyrric victory for the Indians as within 2 years they were all back on the reservations or in Canada.

We drove back to Billings after lunch at the Purple Cow in Hardin, MT and went downtown to see where the streets were blocked off for the Honda Gold Wing Convention. Nearly 14,000 Wing Dingers in Billings from all over. I told Pookie I could upgrade the scooter to a Harley and she could be a Biker Babe. She said we might fit better with the Wing Dingers, as they don't seem to have tattoos or attitudes. Of course, we'd have to get a sidecar for Duke to ride in and a trailer to haul stuff. I guess Duke could wear goggles like Snoopy and we could tie him in with a harness. There are lots of gray haired Wing Dingers and Pookie said she'd try it if I would. I won't. We did go see the movie "The Perfect Storm" before going back to the campground. Pookie asked what I thought and I told her I had seen 2 George's in one day who had more balls than brains. George Custer and George Clooney. The storm is the star of the movie.

We slept late on the 4th and then drove to Laurel, MT, a small town of 5600 about 10 miles from Billings. According to the newspaper, they had a lot more going on for the 4th than did Billings. We ate hotdogs and cheeseburgers at a local park with the locals and then watched the parade for an hour or so. Lots of antique cars, antique tractors, local floats, politicians, and some music groups, but no local marching band. The pet parade had llamas and a lot of parrots and a few dogs. Everybody was throwing candy to the crowd. Duke got frightened by the black powder musket fire from the Lewis & Clark float and hid under my legs for a while. A thunderstorm blew up and we left right before the rain and hail and went back to the campground and watched the local weather on TV as a tornado had been sighted about 15 miles away. Duke's spending some time in the pet taxi with the AC on in the trailer as it's too hot to leave him in the Durango, even with the windows down.

We drove to Sundance, WY yesterday and did Devil's Tower Nat. Monument today. It's a cone of an ancient volcano that sticks up abruptly from the plain as the surrounding area has eroded down and left it exposed. It's all magma and very hard rock and erodes much slower. It's 867 feet high with sheer rock walls and there are a lot of rock climbers who scale it every year. We watched several climbers make it to the top and we walked a trail all around the Tower. Legend says that 7 Indian maidens were being chased by a bear and jumped on a rock about 3 feet high and the Great Spirit made the rock grow up with them and kept them from the bear. The bears claws scraped furrows in the rock, which can still be seen today, and the maidens went on up to become the seven stars of the Big Dipper. Now you know the rest of the story—as Paul Harvey would say. Lots of prairie dog colonies near the entrance to the Monument and we saw all the deer and antelope playing—I almost broke out in song. We also went to Aladdin to see an old coal mine tipple and to the Cook County Museum to see where the Sundance Kid was jailed for 18 months. He left here after serving his term for grand larceny and joined up with Butch Cassidy and the Hole in the Wall Gang nearby. Tomorrow it's on to Wind Cave NP and then to Theodore Roosevelt NP in ND. We did Badlands NP in SD and Mt. Rushmore and the Crazy Horse Monument years ago and these 2 Parks we have left are the only 2 in the contiguous 48 states we haven't done yet. There is a NP in the Virgin Islands on St. John that we haven't done yet, although we've been in the American and British Virgin Islands before on a cruise ship. There are 2 NPs in Hawaii that we have left and 1 in American Samoa and 6 in Alaska that we haven't seen yet. I think we'll take the trailer to Alaska next year, but we'll have to charter a floatplane to get to 4 of the remaining NPs in Alaska. Pookie wants to go to Hawaii and American Samoa——no trailer.

Scribe

Sent: Tuesday, July 11, 2000 7:56 PM
Subject: Buffalo Dog

We drove to Hill City, SD about 10 miles from Mt. Rushmore, and left Duke in the trailer while we toured Jewel Cave Nat. Monument a few miles west of Hill City. It's an interesting cave, but not nearly as impressive as Carlsbad Caverns or Lehman Cave in Great Basin NP. Jewel is a wet cave and has all the stalactites and stalagmites, but they are small and not impressive. The difference is that when the mites go up, the tites come down, in case you didn't know. The tour involves climbing about 700 steps, but a lot more are down than up. An elevator takes you down to one level and you come back up by the elevator from a deeper level. Temperature is a constant 53 degrees, so you wear a jacket and the humidity is high. The flowstone and soda straws and calcite crystals are not impressive either when compared to other caves. Tour guide and ranger Ken was quite good and answered a lot of questions from everybody.

The next day, we toured Wind Cave NP, and it made Jewel Cave look better as Wind Cave is mostly a dry cave, like Mammoth Cave in KY and has very little in the way of impressive formations, except for boxwork, formed millions of years ago when it was a wet cave. Boxwork looks like what you would have left if a massive brick wall eroded all the brick away and left just the mortar all connected together. It's mostly a red color but varies. Wind Cave has about 90% of the world's known boxwork and is a very large cave with 122 miles of known passageways and is still being explored, as is Jewel Cave at 91 miles of known passageways. It is not believed that the 2 caves are connected even though they are only a few miles apart as they have different water tables and Wind Cave has a slightly lower constant temperature, but nobody knows for sure. Mammoth Cave is bigger than both combined and it too is still being explored. The world's 2nd largest cave is in the Ukraine, but I digress. Wind Cave is named for the wind sound that led to its discovery at the small natural entrance. All large caves have wind blowing in or out nearly all the time as the atmospheric pressure changes. High pressure makes air flow into the cave and when the atmospheric pressure falls, the air flows out. Very large caves take a long time for the air pressure to empty or fill the cave, so at the entrances, air is always flowing one way or another. Ranger Don wasn't quite as good as ranger Ken, but did an acceptable job on the tour. Wind Cave has a large surface area in the Park and a lot of wildlife visible on the driving tour. We saw bison, or buffalo, pronghorns and deer playing together as we drove to Hot Springs, SD south of Wind Cave to eat lunch.

After lunch we went back to Hill City to pick up Duke and then took the driving tour of Custer State Park in the Black Hills. We had done this in 91 when we were here before, but it's a very scenic drive and has a lot of wildlife and ends up at Mt. Rushmore, which we decided to see again. We saw Big Horn sheep up close and personal, from about 12 feet away, whitetail and mule deer and pronghorns and the begging burros that in 91 stuck their heads into the car, but this time we knew better. We were disappointed that we hadn't seen any buffalo except at a distance of a half mile and in spite of all the warning signs that buffalo are dangerous, some people in a motorhome with NY plates had walked out on the prairie to see them up close and were standing maybe 50 feet from the herd. We saw several prairie dog colonies and they were so tame that they would come right up to the roadside to beg. About 3 miles from the end of the park, we came over a hill on the prairie and the road was covered with a huge herd of buffalo, with buffalo on both the right and left sides of the road and maybe 500 total. We stopped and the right hand herd decided to cross from the right side of the road to the left and were walking so close to the Durango that they were brushing up against it on the right side and in front. Duke decided to sound the alarm to warn us and shifted into his "Let's Kick Ass" mode. We travel with the back seats folded down for Duke to walk around in the back and he was leaping from side to side and emitting barks and whines and growls and all kinds of high pitched noise. He ignored me and went berserk and I couldn't get hold of him to throttle him. Buffalo can't see very well and some began to move their heads from side to side to try and see what was the commotion and they speeded up a little. I looked in the rear view mirror and a poor couple on a Gold Wing had pulled it up to the rear bumper of the Durango to at least get some protection from the front. The guy was grimacing and it was obvious he wanted Duke to shut up. I was concerned that the Durango might get gored and then it occurred to me that one of them passing in front might charge the Durango and set off the airbags. Pookie had her ears covered as Duke was at a high decibel level and I had all the windows closed to try and muffle the sound from the buffalo. After what seemed like 5 minutes, but was probably only 2 or 3, they finished crossing the road and I could ease ahead through the newly deposited buffalo chips. Duke shut up and when I turned around to look at him, he was panting with his tongue hanging out and I would swear he was grinning and his expression was like he was saying—see how I took care of that problem for you.

We stopped at Mt. Rushmore about 7 p.m. and they have really changed the place, except for the rock carvings. Now, in addition to the flat surface parking they have a 3 deck parking garage for $8 per car, a marble terrace of the states that you walk through to see the monument, a visitor center and an amphitheater at the base of the monument. In 91 there was a small gift shop and an observation deck and that's all. I let Duke go with us, but he wasn't impressed. Earlier in the day we had ridden by the Crazy Horse carving near Hill City and it hasn't progressed a whole lot in the last 10 years, so we didn't go again.

We drove to Theodore Roosevelt NP in ND the next day in constant rain and now it's getting hot up here, in the 80s and 90s and they are having their annual 2 weeks of high humidity up nawth. We saw 4 roadkill pronghorns on the trip up. They are the fastest land mammal in the Americas and have been clocked at 60mph, but aren't fast enough to cut in front of an 18-wheeler. I-94 runs through Teddy Roosevelt NP and we saw wild horses and more buffalo from the interstate when we got there. We camped at Medora, ND, which is in the Park and did the Visitor Center after we dropped off the trailer and Duke. It's well done with a lot of good exhibits, but the movie is circa 1940s. The Park was created during Truman's administration and includes TR's old ranch site and the area where he did his hunting. Teddy was our first conservationist president and oversaw the creation of 18 national monuments, 5 national parks, the Antiquities Act of 1906, which lets the president create national monuments on federally owned properties, and the US Forest Service and the national forest program. In all, he protected 244 million acres and did more for the national parks program than anyone before or since. We ate an excellent dinner at the Iron Horse Saloon in Medora, which is a cute little tourist town.

The next day we drove to the North Unit of the Park, which is 60 miles from the South Unit to begin the day. I let Duke go since it was going to be too hot for us to do many trails anyway. The North Unit Visitor Center had a good modern video on the Park and was surprisingly full of people. There is a 14-mile scenic drive with pullouts and overlooks. Both units of the Park are in the Badlands of ND, but they are very scenic and beautiful, unlike the Badlands in SD, which are grotesque and have very little vegetation. Erosion has revealed all kinds of colorful strata and formations and the Little Missouri River flows through the Park. It would be a photographers dream with all the weird colors and 4 levels of ecosystem. There is a lot of lignite, or coal exposed and the prairie dogs that have been burrowing in the lignite come out looking black instead of brown. We took a picnic lunch, as there is no food service or even a town near the North Unit. There is a small herd of longhorns to commemorate the days when they were driven from Texas to ND to fatten on the ND prairie. The drive ends at Oxbow Overlook, a cliff above the Little Missouri River. When we got there, the entire overlook was occupied by a herd of about 60 buffalo with calves and cows, with a couple of yearling bulls butting heads in the parking lot. No cars were in the parking lot, but a few were stopped on the road a little before the overlook. I pulled into the parking lot to turn around and Duke decided that was the absolutely perfect moment to convert the overlook into a buffalo jump. He went into his "I can herd your ass routine" like he does with the cows in the pasture behind the house at home. The noise was dreadful again and I put up the windows, but the yearling bulls quit their head butting and began to move back to the rest of the herd. Pookie suggested we leave immediately which we did. Duke has learned by experience that the best way to get his way with a herd is to chase the calves which will run away much more quickly than the adult cows, but make the cows run after them. I swear he would have driven them off the overlook if I had let him out.

We drove back and did the South Unit Scenic Loop Drive, which is a little different, but I don't think quite as impressive. This morning we drove to Bismarck to get closer to Gene & Paula in MN as we're going to spend a couple of days with them. This will be my last travelogue on this trip as we're through touring and will drive home from here with a stop in Terre Haute to see brother-in-law Louis at his new job at Rose-Hulman Institute of Technology. A few final observations follow:

1. The loss of the 7th Cavalry wasn't really a big deal anyway. They were nearly all damn yankees, but the loss of my blood brothers was sad.
2. Wyoming has the 1st NP, Yellowstone and the 1st Nat. Monument, Devil's Tower. The difference is that only Congress can create a NP, but a Nat. Monument can be created by a president without Congress. Incidentally, there are nearly 400 properties administered by the National Park Service including national historic sites like the Truman Home, national historic

parks like Appomattox Court House, national memorials like Mt. Rushmore and the monuments and parks. We only plan to see all 55 parks and not all the properties, but we tour them when they are close to the Parks and appear interesting.

3. Pygmy rattlesnakes inhabit the top of Devil's Tower, which is about the size of a football field, even though it has nearly sheer walls on all sides. It's assumed that they climbed up like the chipmunks, mice and squirrels that are there also.

4. A study of bones from the buffalo jump sites has led scientists to conclude that the bison species is in the process of dwarfing itself to a much smaller size. Nobody knows why.

5. USA Today had an article the other day on a new professional career. It's called a Professional Organizer, who helps people organize their lives. I married one 36 years ago, so it wasn't news to me.

6. In my last episode I misspelled Pyrrhic victory. It's named for a Greek general, Pyrrhus, who defeated the Romans in a battle in 279 BC. It was such a costly victory that the Greeks were soon after defeated and conquered.

Homer on the Range

Chapter 8. Carlisle, PA Trip—2000

Sent: Saturday, November 04, 2000 7:47 AM
Subject: Carlisle, PA

We're on a short Fall road trip to see the grandkids in Carlisle, PA and for me to get a botox shot in NYC on Nov. 6th. We decided to bring the trailer and sight-see a little going up & coming back and take up to 2 weeks. I actually miss not being on the road since late July. We left home Tuesday morning and drove to Frankfort, KY the first day. We had never been to Frankfort and decided to tour the state capitol there. The next morning we toured the capitol and had an ex-marine tour guide who was VERY positive about everything, but did a nice job. He said KY was the only state to have its Supreme Court in the state capitol, and I know that's not true, as we've toured some others that do. He also said the Justices carry a .357 magnum under his or her robes as anyone can carry a concealed weapon in KY. Smoking is permitted anywhere in the capitol and I was surprised to read that KY refused to ratify the War of Northern Aggression human rights amendments for years. The KY capitol is not in the same category as the gorgeous mid-western capitols, but is still much more impressive than Tennessee's. They have statues of Jeff Davis and Lincoln and were neutral in the War of Northern Aggression with troops fighting on both sides. My friend Doug Henry of Nashville, a state senator, says that when it came time to fish or cut bait, Arkansas fished and KY cut bait. Frankfort is a very nice small city of about 30,000 and unlike Jefferson City, MO has a lot more going for it than just State business. It's in the heart of Bluegrass Country and has a lot of horse stuff. We stayed in a campground on the bank of Elkhorn Creek, which flows into the KY River a few miles from where we were. The campground bathhouses are closed for the winter, so we had to use the trailer shower but it was still a nice campground, except for the false advertising. Pookie picked it because they advertised a modem hookup, so we never asked as we were checking in—only to discover when I went up to download e-mail that the ad had been placed in the wrong campground and belonged in the one below it on the Trailer Life Directory page. Not a good sign to begin a trip. We drove on to Charleston, West Virginia after our tour and couldn't find a single campground in Charleston, the largest city in WVA. Pookie commented that West Virginia is not a destination point for most people, but I was tired of riding up the Shenandoah Valley in VA and wanted to see some different country. It is different! In eastern KY and WVA, when they cut through the tops of hills to lower the grade on the interstate, they expose coal seams instead of rock.

Pookie finally found a campground operated by the Church of God (I'm not making that up!), about 20 miles north of Charleston on I-77. Being my trusty naviguesser, she also found a shortcut across to I-77 from I-64 to get to it without going into Charleston. We called several times on the cell phone, but God was out and didn't have an answering machine. Finally, we got an answer and yes they did have a space and yes we could download e-mail if we got there before Church started. I was afraid to ask if we had to go to Church, or listen to an offer to be saved. The trusty shortcut only delayed us about 30 minutes. I had forgotten how twisting, curvy, up and down hill the state roads are in WVA, but shall remember from now on. With the trailer trying to pop the whip, max speed is about 30 mph. if you're lucky, and all the curves are blind. At last we arrived at Rippling Waters Church of God Campground after dark, about 3 miles off the interstate back in the woods near where Deliverance was probably filmed. There is a small white frame chapel like a rural church with a huge steeple located across a small lake that is spotlighted after dark and absolutely breath taking. The lady who checked us in was as nice as she could be and did invite us to Church, but no hard sell. She let me crawl under a desk and plug into her phone line to download e-mail and I just got through in time for her to leave for Wed. nite services. That's the first non-smoking campground I've ever seen. I considered the church offer for about a nano second, but fortunately I'm predestined and therefore have no need for it. Another way to put it follows: Proper Presbyterian pre-destination prevailed, punishing pitiful, pathetic pariah priests preaching poor protestant philistine philosophy. Pretty powerful production, huh? I decided not to walk Duke while drinking my scotch. It was a very nice campground and one of the cleanest bathhouses we've seen.

The next morning we drove into Charleston to tour the WVA state capitol. WVA was created by presidential proclamation in 1863 by Lincoln, as the 39 counties of northwestern VA did not wish to secede from the Union. I guess secession is O.K. to leave a state, but not the Union, or maybe might makes right—I'm not sure. Anyway, the best thing that ever happened to VA was WVA leaving as it's been a ward of the federal government ever since. There is a statue of Robert Byrd in the rotunda. It's highly unusual to see a statue of a politician who's still living, but I guess if you bring home enough pork, the rules change. The capitol building is beautiful, and I would put it in the top 10. The dome is covered in gold leaf and it was a bright sunny day and it shines for miles. There are no paintings or murals hanging from the walls, unlike most capitols, and the stark simplicity of the white marble is striking with crystal chandeliers everywhere. We had an excellent lady tour guide and met a couple from Blaine, WA.

Pookie commented that we had already voted for Bush, and it was like opening a floodgate. The guy from WA said this was the most important election of this century—not even I believe that—and he had his absentee ballot sent to him by FedEx to vote for Bush. The lady tour guide said she wasn't supposed to talk politics, but she was for Bush too. There was even graffiti in the men's room saying Gore was an idiot—in WVA—which never votes Republican—those polls are wrong!

I walked Duke on the capitol grounds after our tour and he caught a squirrel while on his leash! His first success that I know of, but he hunts them all day in the woods behind our house. It turned out to be a baby squirrel about half grown, so I made him let it go and it climbed gingerly and slowly up a tree, with only a few teeth wounds. It must have been very slow, or stupid to let him catch it. Of course, since it was a WVA squirrel, it might be a mongoloid or something—there's a lot of inbreeding in Appalachia.

We drove from Charleston to Hagerstown, MD for the night and another campground on a creek, but this time a KOA, but off the interstate a few miles. Lots of ducks swimming in the creek to entertain Duke. The next morning we went to Antietam Nat. Battlefield, a few miles away and spent the whole morning touring it. The best battlefield tour I've ever had and an outstanding talk by Ranger Brian about the bloodiest day ever in the War of Northern Aggression. We rented the driving tape and drove around the park listening to the battle description. They give you a tape player to use rather than the one in your car as the tapes are played over and over and might damage your car player. You can also get out and walk and take the tape player with you. We let Duke go with us and he loved running up and down the Sunken Road, or Bloody Lane as it was called. 23,000 casualties and actually 3 separate battles, but a tactical draw while a strategic victory for the bad guys. 87,000 federals vs. 40,000 good guys and more dead feds than rebels, but the battle was probably the true high point for the South. In the actual fight, McClellan did everything wrong and Marse Robert everything right except for one thing. Lee's only error was to under-rate the willingness of yankee troops to keep fighting even as they were getting slaughtered and keep their morale in spite of bad leadership and punishing losses. It was actually a fight of 23,000 rebels vs. 57,000 federals as part of Lee's forces were at Harper's Ferry and McClellan was too stupid to commit 30,000 of his troops. The thin gray lines broke 3 times, but always rallied to continue the battle. 450 Georgians held off 12,000 yankees for 3 hours at one point. You can see nearly the whole battlefield from the Visitor Center and there is a really good 30-minute film shown through Lincoln's eyes as he visited the battlefield a few days after the fight with flashbacks giving the preparation for and actual fighting. Go see it if you are in the vicinity.

After Antietam, which is a Delaware Indian word meaning swift flowing water, we drove on to Carlisle, PA where Will is on staff at the Army War College and we're in a huge campground with over 250 sites. We spent last evening with Will & the grandkids as Alicia went to some Catholic fundraiser. We went to Cracker Barrel for dinner as Rachel wanted pancakes, but she was politically smart enough to tell Pookie that they weren't as good as Pookie's pancakes. Connor had the best time and was happy and laughing and playing the whole time. The kids took turns getting in Duke's pet taxi and Duke met the next- door pair of Jack Russells. Will even admitted that Duke is a well-behaved Jack Russell by comparison. Too bad Alicia wasn't there, as she'll never believe it.

Pookie, Perfect & Puppy

Sent: Saturday, November 11, 2000 10:15 PM
Subject: Carlisle, PA II

Well, I pulled a klutz act and yanked the data port connector out of the laptop by trying to move the laptop without disconnecting the telephone line first, so I cut off my modem access to the outside world on the way home from PA. We're back now, but I'll pick up where I left off.

On Saturday, we went with Will, Alicia & the kids to Gettysburg to tour the battlefield. Pookie & I had been there 11 years ago on a July 4th when Civil War Re-enactors staged Pickett's Charge all over again, but we didn't tour the battlefield because of the crowd, and Will & Alicia had been earlier this year on a short visit, but didn't get to see the electric map display or tour the battlefield. This time it was cold and windy and Will & I were the only 2 people wearing shorts at the battlefield and I was the only one wearing sandals with no socks. The electric map display takes about 25 minutes and uses little lights on a topographic map of the entire area to show what action occurred on each day of the 3 day battle with a narrator explaining the actions while the lights are going on & off. Gettysburg was the single bloodiest battle of the war, but took 3 days while Antietam was a single day. 51,000 casualties on both sides with a few more rebels than yankees killed. It also saw the largest artillery barrages of the entire war, with the Confederates actually having more cannon than the yankees. Unfortunately, most of the Confederate barrage preceding Pickett's Charge, was fired too high due to being long distance—1 mile—away and the smoke of the shells hitting and the smoke of the Union batteries" return fire obscured the scene and most rebel artillery went over the Union lines rather than into the lines. It killed a lot of yankee horses behind the lines, but not many yankees. I think it was the yankee general, Sheridan, who once said that if he was given enough Confederate infantry and enough yankee artillery, he could conquer the world.

We bought a tape of the battlefield tour and rode around the battlefield listening to the narrator describe the events. The battlefield is much larger than Antietam and cannot all be seen from a single point. The most visited points are "Little Roundtop" across from the "Devil's Den" at the southern end of the battlefield where the Confederates almost won on the 2nd day and the "High Water Mark" of Pickett's charge where the rebels actually pierced the yankee lines after a 1 mile advance into point blank artillery and musket fire from behind stone walls, on the 3rd and final day. Although one of the commercial observation towers has been torn down as detracting from the battlefield, one is still left at the southern end of the Confederate lines, but is obscured by trees and not as big an eyesore. If you haven't been, go sometime.

Alicia fed us Sat. nite, and Sunday afternoon Pookie & I baby-sat so they could go to a movie. We played at the playground on the post until Duke & I had to go back and watch the Titan's win their game. Alicia actually walked Duke and acted like he is now acceptable! I think it's cause the kids like him and Connor was smitten. Connor ran around the house yelling Duke, Duke Duke! Will rode us around the post and showed us the various sites. It's small and compact and he can walk to work and the facilities are very attractive. Will said he had even thought about doing a hardship tour to Korea or somewhere just so he could pick his next assignment and come back to Carlisle. We took them all to dinner Sun. nite and Pookie, Duke & I drove into NYC the next day. It's about 200 miles, but takes 4 1/2 hours to get to Mt. Sinai Hospital due to all the traffic. They are working on the 42nd street entrance way and exit from the Lincoln Tunnel and I got forced by traffic to take a tour through the bus depot. My naviguesser loved the detour! My doctor informed me that he is leaving academia (he's in research) in January and moving to Irvine, CA to go to work for the drug company that makes the botulism toxin that I get. He'll no longer have private patients and I've never had much success at Vanderbilt, so I guess I'll go back to Dr. Blitzer at Roosevelt Hospital in NYC. Blitzer actually taught my doctor how to do the injections and I've used him before when Brin has been unavailable and got good results. We were after dark getting back to Carlisle Mon. nite, so we just went to the campground and let Duke walk some and watched TV. We had called from the road Mon. and got an appointment Tues. afternoon at the Sunline dealer in Carlisle to repair the damage to the trailer that I did in West VA. Yep, I pulled a Bush, and didn't announce that I clipped a guy's bumper with the rear of the trailer in a gas station in WVA while his car was parked at the pump. It only rubbed off some of the rubber trim on his bumper and actually hurt the trailer more. I got the trailer fixed for $47, but the guy in WVA turned down my offer of $100 cash, so I turned him over to my insurance agent. The poor guy was only semi- literate and didn't even know his own zip code and couldn't communicate with my agent, but his wife was able to understand. The guy insisted on calling the state patrol and I waited till they came and told him that they didn't file accident reports for accidents on private property. I would have paid him $150 to forget the whole thing, but I learned a long time ago that you can't win by negotiating with yourself and the poor guy was afraid to make any decision. He was as nice as he could be and I listened to him tell me over and over how much he loved Dollywood and his vacations in TN. I was a little rough on my property on this trip.

Tues. nite we watched the election returns till after midnight at Will & Alicia's, when I finally got Pookie to leave and go back to the trailer. We got all the networks at the trailer, but no cable. Pookie stayed up till 2:45 when the networks gave FL to Bush and then the next a.m., I discovered that they had taken it back again and it was too close to call. Wed. we drove to Staunton, VA and to a very nice campground with a phone line at every site. That's where I screwed up the laptop after downloading e-mail. We did have time to tour the Woodrow Wilson birth site and museum in Staunton that afternoon. It's on the edge of Mary Baldwin College, the first ever college solely for Presbyterian women, and we drove around the college also. Wilson was born in 1856 and was the son, grandson and nephew of ordained Presbyterian ministers who were well educated with extensive personal libraries. The family didn't own slaves, but had 3 slaves in Staunton provided to them gratis by a wealthy church member. Wilson's first name is Thomas and he went by Tommy until he became president of Princeton College in NJ. Woodrow was his mother's maiden name and his middle name. He actually vetoed the congressional resolution that became the Prohibition Amendment, but Congress in all their wisdom over-rode his veto. As a good Scotsman from Ulster, his father enjoyed the "water of life". His career is very interesting and the father was paid the very generous sum of $1000 per year in Staunton, but moved to GA a year after Woodrow's birth, for the princely sum of $3000 annually from a Presbyterian Church in GA. Notice the Presbyterian affection for money and Scotch that is nearly universal! My Guys! We were late getting to the museum and had to leave before finishing it as it closed early.

The next day we drove to a campground at Baileytown, TN near Greeneville, TN. We did the Andrew Johnson National Historic site the next morning after all the storms, high winds and rain during the night. Poor Johnson, even the local phone book has a picture of his statue on the cover, but it is mislabeled as Andrew Jackson. Johnson was from a dirt poor family and uneducated, but he taught himself to read and write with his wife's help. He was a run-away apprentice from a tailor in NC who moved his whole family, mother and sisters, from NC to TN at age 16 and took on a wife at 18. His father died when he was 4. His tailor shop is preserved inside a brick building and you hear the sound of scissors when looking inside it. He was a democrat, but Lincoln picked him as his VP in 1864 to attract votes from the border states, and because Johnson was clearly a Unionist who totally opposed secession. He remained a Senator from TN in Washington until Lincoln made him military governor of TN in 1862. He absolutely venerated the Constitution and most of his actions as President were strict interpretations of the Constitution. He even vetoed the Civil Rights Act of 1866, not because he didn't agree with it, but because he thought it infringed on the rights of States who should pass their own civil rights legislation. He was a slaveholder who freed his own slaves before the Emancipation Proclamation, but objected to federal emancipation. An extremely interesting man who was re-elected to the Senate by TN in 1875, after his presidency and in spite of his impeachment and Union sympathy. A true man of principle, who could convince people of his beliefs. They say he was a master debater, even if self-taught. He fully understood the founding father's fear of the "tyranny of the majority" that led them to construct so many checks and balances in the Constitution to preserve the rights of the minority. They had learned well from the weakness of the parliamentary system that England employs. Worth a visit, but it's off the beaten path. There is a well-done video about him narrated by Fred Thompson. Pookie says Fred is in all the good movies.

Trip Potpourri:

1. The tour guide at the Capitol in WVA observed that WVA had never produced a US President. However, she added that if Arkansas could get by with Clinton, there was lots of room for WVA.
2. VA has produced 8 US Presidents.
3. The democrats in FL are actually getting their own voters to sign affidavits that they are too stupid to vote! I always knew that it wasn't an absolute requirement to be brain dead to be a democrat, but it sure makes it appear that way!
4. Jeannie Moos, the CNN reporter who does the lifestyle and human interest reporting from NYC, took to the streets of Manhattan with a stack of Palm Beach County ballots on Friday. She stopped about 15 people of all ages on the sidewalks and showed them the ballot on camera. Every single person commented that the ballot looked confusing with comments like, "My mother would never get that right" or "old people would be totally confused" or "my eyes aren't what they used to be" etc. Then she asked each person to punch out the hole to vote for Al Gore. 100% of the people, including a majority who were elderly, got the vote correct, even though all had said it was confusing to begin with and they were on a busy NYC sidewalk! The last person she interviewed was a little old lady very smartly dressed in a suit and hat who appeared to be about 5 feet tall, in her 80's and Jewish, as she spoke with a Yiddish accent. After she voted correctly Jeannie told her that everyone said the ballot was confusing, but everybody got it right and what did that mean about the people in Palm Beach County? The little old lady thought for a second or two and then said, "I think it means that they need to get out of the sunshine"!
5. The election in NY of the First Witch to the Senate guarantees full employment for Rush Limbaugh for the next 6 years. He'd be miserable without a Clinton to mock. Thanks NY!

Any bets on how long before Bill is caught chasing a new skirt?

Democratic Dementia Demographer

Chapter 9. Newfoundland Trip—2001

Sent: Thursday, May 31, 2001 5:49 PM
Subject: Rockport/Camden Maine

Not a lot to write about on this trip until now. I figured yall didn't want to hear about our visit in Carlisle, PA with our grandkids, so I'll only comment that they are close to perfect and that Rachel spent one night with us in the trailer at the Western Village Campground. It was packed with people and had a constant venue of entertainment. We skipped most of it, but I did get to dance with Rachel to the Sunrise Band in the pavilion one night and we played on the playground for a while. The campground has horses as well as all the amenities, but they can't spell yall. Damnyankees spelled it "Pardners, Ya'All Come Back" on the sign as you drive out.

We drove up I-81 to I-84 and across New York and Connecticut to Massachusetts after leaving Carlisle and spent a night at Sturdivant, Mass. Gasoline costs $1.83 for regular in NY and $1.84 in Mass. and 20 cents cheaper everywhere else—I love it when the democrats have to pay more for their stupidity—couldn't happen to more deserving folks. Won't it be sad if they run out of electricity too! Stopped at the New Hampshire State liquor store on I-95 and loaded up on the cheap booze and drove to Bath, Maine. We also stopped in Freeport, Maine to let Pookie go to L.L. Bean, both the factory store and the retail store. I bought a pair of moccasins at the factory store that had been returned and were reduced in price by 1/2. Poor Pookie didn't buy anything. This is an event similar to a major earthquake or realignment of the stars. Finally we began our tour the next day by touring the Percy & Small Shipyard in Bath, which is also the Maine Maritime Museum. It's quite unique in that it is an actual shipyard where they built wooden ships, rather than a typical maritime museum. It has a gallery of art about ships, but also gives walking tours of the shipyard by volunteer guides who explain all about the process of building ships from wood. Until last year, it was still a working yard, and small boats were built by students, but now it's just for tourists. Eighty ships were built there over the years and it operated commercially till 1920. All the original buildings are intact and the ways where the ships were built and launched are still visible. The pitch used to caulk the ships came from the South and most of the wood for the ships came from Georgia and Alabama, as all the Maine appropriate wood was gone by the mid 19th century. In fact, during The War of Northern Aggression, output of the Maine shipyards declined sharply due to lack of appropriate wood. At one time there were 40 shipyards near Bath along the Kennebec River, which is ideal for shipbuilding due to the depth and width of the river, and the gently sloping banks, which make for ideal launching ways.

The Museum also provides a tour boat up and down the Kennebec River for an additional fee. It's the only way you can see the Bath Iron Works, which builds Aegis class destroyers for the Navy, as the Iron Works is closed to visitors for security reasons. The War College in Carlisle now has some security at the gates too due to the threat of terrorist attacks by Osama Bin Laudin or other terrorists, and Will tells me that all US bases will soon have more security for the same reasons. The Bath Iron Works has 3 destroyers under construction now and is the largest private employer in Maine. On June 23, the last destroyer to be built on ways and launched in the traditional fashion will be christened and slide down the ways. All future ships built in Bath will be built on a huge floating pier and built on the level and then rolled into a huge dry-dock and launched by submerging the dry-dock. The dry-dock has only been there for a few weeks and was built in China (low bidder) and towed to Bath. General Dynamics owns the Bath Iron Works and also the Electric Boat Works in New Groton, CT, which builds nuclear subs. A few miles down the Kennebec River near its mouth was the site of the 3rd English colony in America, the Popham colony, founded in 1607, 3 months after Jamestown. You probably never heard of it because after 1 winter in Maine, all the colonists went back to England. The 1st colony, Roanoke, disappeared without a trace except the word Croatan found on a tree in North Carolina.

Yesterday we drove up to a campground on the ocean a mile or so south of Rockport, Maine. Pretty view of the ocean and all the lobster pots near the shore. We walked around the port at Rockport and at Camden, Maine and both towns are picturesque. We drove up to the top of Mt. Battie in Camden Hills State Park a few miles north of Camden late in the day for a spectacular view of the Maine coastline, mountains and lakes and the city of Camden. Maine is larger physically than all the rest of New England combined, and is my favorite New England state. It has more islands and islets off its coast than the rest of the contiguous US combined, including the Great Lake states. The people are also very friendly and nice—hard to believe they are yankees.

Today we went back south to Thomaston and spent a bunch of money in the Maine State Prison Shop. Made up for Pookie's lapse at L.L.Bean. I couldn't believe how cheap the stuff was. I got a beautiful wooden model of a Maine schooner with sails for $60—feel like I stole from the inmates, but I'll survive. Got Betty a present reduced from $42 to $6 and it was not over priced to begin with—$6 is about right for her too. Then we stopped at the Henry Knox Museum right north of Thomaston. It's a Georgian Colonial mansion similar to the White House, although the original was destroyed and the replica was built in 1929/30. Knox was George Washington's artillery commander and captured the British cannon at Fort Ticonderoga, which we went to in the early 70's with the boys. We didn't notice that the sign said closed for the season, but when we went to the entrance, 4 volunteer guides were there getting ready to open it the next day. They took pity on us and we got our own private tour for about an hour and the old gentleman sure knew his history about Knox.

This afternoon, we went to see "Pearl Harbor" and Duke is mad about spending so much time in his crate today. It's in the high 40's at nite and low 60's in the day with a constant breeze, so we can leave him in the Durango even in the sunshine and he doesn't get too hot. "Pearl Harbor" is less than I expected and the critics were correct. Not very good romance or history and they could have left the Doolittle raid for another day. After the movie, Pookie went to the Shore Museum in Rockland, but Duke & I stayed outside. It's a lighthouse museum and built by the Grand Army of the USA Lodge and has a monument to the Grand Army outside on the lawn. I let Duke pee on it to show the proper respect for damnyankees. The last surviving War of Northern Aggression soldier was a Confederate, so we won in the end. Fortunately the Museum closed right after Pookie went in—I've seen enough lighthouses and Fresnel lenses to last a lifetime.

On to northern Maine or New Brunswick, Canada tomorrow. The tour guide at the Knox House told me there would still be snow in Labrador, but he thought we would really enjoy Newfoundland. If I find time, I'll do a tome on Fiji next.
Your Reporter

Sent: Monday, June 04, 2001 5:42 PM
Subject: Lubec, Maine/St. John, New Brunswick

Pookie got to go to the easternmost gift shoppe in the USA in Lubec, Maine, population 800. Of course, it was required that she purchase a few items. Her acquisitive instincts have returned, and are completely intact! Lubec is across a strait from Campobello Island, the site of FDR's summer cottage where he spent all his summers before he became president and is the primary reason we came here. We stayed in a campground where we were the only guests and right beside a bay with water a few feet from the trailer—at high tide. At low tide, there was an enormous mud flat as there are 20+ foot tides this far up the Gulf of Maine. I turned Duke loose as we were a mile from the highway and no one was around. He loved it and got to run for the first time since we left home. Pookie was afraid he would go down in the mud flat and come back filthy, but he didn't, and I let him run at high and low tides and each time he came back to the trailer after about 20 minutes. Our first afternoon we went over to Campobello, but the Visitor Center and Cottage were closed, so we toured the island which is about 10 miles long and connected by a bridge to the USA. The post office and customs office share the same building at the foot of the bridge on the American side. I refuse to believe the government is ever that efficient on its own merits, and suspect it was the Maine instinct for frugality that caused this efficiency to occur. Duke had to show his passport—vaccination certificate—to go into Canada. We rode all over the island which has a provincial park also and some gorgeous views of Lubec, Eastport, Maine and out over the Gulf, including some very pretty lighthouses.

We went back to the trailer at dark and I offered to take Pookie to dinner in Lubec, but it didn't happen. She had been complaining all day that one of her bridges on the upper left side of her mouth felt loose. It came out and she forgot about food and went into a stage 3 panic. Not only did the bridge come loose, but it was over an implant and covered 2 teeth, a false tooth and the implant. She announced in a shaky voice that the implant had come out too, and sure enough, a piece of metal that looked like a bullet tip and was 1/4 inch long was still attached to the bridge and she had a huge hole in her jaw where the implant was located. We went back to Lubec to call some of her dentists (she has a dentist, periodontist, endodontist and a prosthodontist that I know of). Our first discovery was that my cheap rate Voice Net phone credit card didn't work, even though it worked last year in Canada. I couldn't remember the pin # for the AT&T Universal card, so Pookie asked some teenagers hanging out at the store where the pay phone was if there was anyplace in town where she could get her cell phone to work, as it showed no service available. They told us to go to the top of the tallest hill in town and it would usually work there or down on the waterfront. We went to the top of the hill and parked next to a church (might as well try everything) and it worked! She couldn't get any of her dentists on the phone on Fri. nite, even though she has some home phone numbers. She couldn't even get Tom, a retired dentist friend who has never worked on her. Panic increased.

The next a.m., after very little sleep, we went back to the top of the hill & no service. Down on the waterfront the thing worked and she got P.D., the periodontist in Memphis at home. This is the guy whose children I have sent to college and for whom I have built a few offices and who she has seen for 30+ years. He once told me to bring my 2nd wife to him for him to check out her teeth before I married her. P.D. convinced her that the implant had NOT come out and the prosthetic device had just failed and the implant is still there. Panic subsided and she grinned, showing her lovely missing teeth for the first time. She looks like she's from Arkansas or Alabama when she grins. No dentists within 75 miles, so we went back to Campobello to do the Visitor Center and Cottage.

FDR first came to Campobello as a 1 year old child and returned every year till he was 39. Both his parents were rich with the father having railroad money and the mother even more shipping money. I always thought he was an only child, but he had a 26-year-older half brother from his father's first marriage. The film at the Visitor Center is introduced by FDR Jr., who was born on the island and is the 2nd child by that name. The first Jr. died as an infant and Eleanor and FDR named the 2nd Jr. exactly the same. Very interesting film about FDR & family with very little political info and mainly personal stuff. The parents built a 34 room "cottage" where FDR spent nearly all summer each year as a child and learned to sail, hike, swim etc. all over the area. Other rich families from NYC and Boston also had summer homes and spent the summers, so he had a lot of friends to run with. After he married Eleanor and they had the five surviving children, his mother bought him the adjoining "cottage" which only had 18 bedrooms and they only employed about 5 servants for the summers. The parent's cottage has been destroyed, but FDR's is in mint condition and has about 5 tour guides stationed throughout it to explain the stuff. Everything is from the period when FDR used the cottage and I noticed a huge map of the Canadian Maritime Provinces. Of course it doesn't include Newfoundland since Newfoundland was an independent self-governing British colony and member of the Commonwealth until 1949 when it joined the Canadian Federation. Very pretty views of the Bay of Fundy, which is the upper part of the Gulf of Maine. The FDR Park is 10.5 acres and contains the Cottage and 2 adjoining cottages and is owned jointly by the USA & Canada and is operated jointly and is the only one managed like that in the world. It was here that FDR came down with polio at age 39 and had to be evacuated from the island on a stretcher. The local tour guides say he already had the virus in his body when he came to the island, but he had been there about 2 weeks before he became paralyzed, so who knows. He only came back 3 more times after that, but that was probably because he no longer could spare the time, as he became president shortly after he recovered his health and was too involved in politics. Once he came back as president on a US cruiser, but the fog moved in and the cruiser was stuck there for a week and Eleanor got tired of entertaining the ship's officers. FDR had a kind of rough time with vacations. He developed polio on one and died on his last one in Warm Springs, GA.

We moved on to St. John and got the names and phone #'s of an oral surgeon, a periodontist and an emergency weekend dental clinic from the phone book, but Pookie wanted to try gluing the bridge back in herself first. We travel with dental glue and antibiotics for emergencies. She failed and I convinced her to go to the emergency clinic. We drove by there Sun. a.m. and the doors were locked and they didn't return her phone calls to the cell phone from the voice mail she left, so she gave up till Mon. We're staying in a huge city-owned campground in a huge city park in downtown St. John. It rained steadily Sat. nite in New Brunswick and drizzled all day Sun. We drove part of the walking tours in the rain Sun. and then went to the new Market Square which is a huge downtown multi-story office and restaurant and shopping area built where 7 warehouses previously stood. We found the seafood restaurant recommended in our tour guide to eastern Canada and went there for lunch. Delicious seafood chowder and a Caesar salad. Pookie managed to gum down the chowder, which was her first meal other than ice cream and pudding since the teeth came out.

The New Brunswick Museum is in Market Square and we spent about 3 hours there. They had an excellent hour-long movie on New Brunswick and exhibits on the history and culture and economic development of New Brunswick and very well done. There is also an art gallery and exhibits on other subjects too. I found out that a lot of the yankee warships that Maine couldn't build for lack of wood, were built in New Brunswick as the yankees lost 1/3 of their ships during the War of Northern Aggression. As usual in museums, Pookie goes faster than me as I read more of the material about the exhibits. She usually sits down and waits for me to catch up or goes to the gift shoppe till I finish. I caught up in one place and she led the way to the next gallery, which had material on the earth's natural history. We started off with the end of the last ice age and it soon became apparent we were going backward and back in time in the wrong direction thru the exhibit. Luckily for me, I have followed Pookie's navigational directions for enough years to recognize when she has it ass backwards. I told her we were going to end up with the big bang, when the universe started expanding, and we did end up with the formation of the earth.

It had stopped raining temporarily so we drove to the "reversing falls" in the middle of the city, which is about 75,000 in population. This is where the St. John River empties into the harbor and the Bay of Fundy. The tides here are maybe 30 feet and high tide was coming in when we got there. The tides move billions of cubic feet of water each cycle and are so strong that the St. John River runs backwards at high tide and runs forwards into the Bay at low tide. The mouth of the river is shallow, about 16 meters deep at high tide, and the power of the tide creates huge whirlpools and a lot of foam when the river runs backwards. Instead of falls, it really is a series of rapids running in 2 directions and quite spectacular. There is a 17-minute film that explains the whole thing and how tides are created by the rotation of the earth and the gravity of the moon and sun. There is also a restaurant there and the usual gift shoppe. I let Duke watch the falls, but he wasn't impressed and wanted to chase squirrels instead.

Today, Mon., Pookie got serious about finding someone to fix her problem. The oral surgeon said he only did extractions, the periodontist doesn't do bridges and the referral to a prosthodontist in Fredericton, about 70 miles away hasn't worked as the calls were never returned and she could only get voice mail. The emergency service now says the phone book is wrong and they only work Wed. and Fri., but she's found a dentist who will see her at noon and we're waiting for her appointment time. I did finally remember the pin # for the AT&T card and called them and set up an international rate from Canada so we can use payphones now. Saga to be continued! Scribe

Postscript: The dentist she saw was as nice as he could be, but didn't know anything about implants and couldn't get the bridge back in. He did an x-ray and yes, the implant is still there, but he thought tissue had grown over the implant and didn't know what to do. He offered to call the prosthodontist in Fredericton, and make us an appointment for this afternoon, but no one was there so he asked us to call back at 2:30 this afternoon. We went back to the seafood restaurant in Market Square and I had seafood—lobster, shrimp, scallops, mussels and white fish—cooked in a white wine sauce over rice with cheese melted on top and oysters on the half shell. Hope I don't have to stay here till I've done the whole menu. Pookie gummed seafood manicotti and it was superb. Pookie called back at 2:30 and the dentist couldn't reach the prosthodontist in Fredericton either—there is only one, and she must be out of town. He did make Pookie an appointment here for tomorrow at 10:45 a.m. with dentist #2 who he says has had some experience with implants. #2 is the same guy Pookie called this a.m. and was told she could see him on June 12, but with the local dentist paving the way, she can now get in to see him. If that doesn't work, we may have to go to Halifax, Nova Scotia (we were there 2 years ago and didn't plan to go back on this trip) to the dental school to see someone who knows something. This socialized medicine system ain't all it's cracked up to be. The good practioners leave Canada and the quality of healthcare here is much lower than ours. Today's papers report a strike in Nova Scotia of all x-ray technicians and all physical therapists over wages and a strike in Alberta by all medical emergency response teams over the same thing. A baby died in Alberta and the strike is being blamed for contributing to the death. We never read about that in our media, which keeps suggesting that we emulate Canada's healthcare system. If we ever do, we'll rue that day.

Pookie got Melendy, the Memphis prosthodontist's girl Friday, on the phone a little while ago and she's going to have Bill, the prosthodontist, call this guy and tell him what to do. Bill is a former football player at Mississippi State—I call him the redneck dentist—who has been on the payroll for about 25 years. I've only educated 2 of his kids. I remember the first time Pookie used him and he did 16 crowns, all gold, in the mid 70's. It was $400 per crown and I wasn't making much money then so I asked if I could pay him a few hundred a month. He said no, he didn't have any accounts receivable—he spent most of his time teaching at the U.T. dental school and had a small outside practice—but he would do 4 at a time and after I paid him he would do 4 more. I commented that he must save a lot in postage and asked if he wanted it in small, unmarked bills. He said no, he would take checks.

We booked another nite in this campground and will find out what's next tomorrow. Still drizzling and cloudy. I may work on my liquor supply tonite! Duke makes an excellent smokescreen when passing through customs and lying about my quantity of liquor. He sticks his head out the window looking for a dog biscuit and they always ask if he's a Jack Russell or ooh and ahh over how cute he is while I lie about how much booze I have hidden in the trailer. Of course, as a professional banker, I'm a pretty good liar without Duke, but the extra cover never hurts! Serial to be continued later!

Last P.S. 7:30 p.m. We're on Atlantic time, an hour ahead of eastern US. The prosthodontist from Fredericton just called on the cell phone and we have an appointment with her at 11:30 tomorrow morning in Fredericton, the capitol of New Brunswick, which we toured 2 years ago. She's going to call Bill, the Memphis guy after she sees Pookie's mouth & bridge. Pookie has alerted Bill and canceled the appointment in St. John & we'll leave in the a.m. The prosthodontist was in Moncton, New Brunswick, the 3rd largest town in New Brunswick, all day. St. John is only 73,000, Fredericton 59,000 and she's the only prosthodontist in all of New Brunswick, which must have a total population of less than 300,000. Hope is rising and maybe we won't have to go back to Halifax after all. This lady dentist also said she was trained in the States, so she should know what she is doing! Fog may be lifting!

Sent: Tuesday, June 05, 2001 4:47 PM
Subject: Teeth

Pookie is no longer the Queen of Snaggletooth. Dentist #3 is young, blonde, cute, unmarried and was able to put the bridge back in and discussed it all with Bill in Memphis and was apparently able to handle him too. And yes, Virginia, money can buy happiness, or at least a smile! Later!

Sent: Thursday, June 07, 2001 5:36 PM
Subject: North Sydney, Nova Scotia

We're booked on a ferry in the a.m., June 8th, about 10 minutes from this campground, for Newfoundland. Duke has to ride in the trailer or in a kennel on the ferry, and I think I'll leave him in the trailer. We go to Port aux Basque on the southwestern tip of Newfoundland and come back from Argentia, Newfoundland on the east south central coast on June 23. Some of the campgrounds in NF advertise modems, so maybe Hershel's watt line will work from there. It'll have to travel on an undersea cable if it does.

We spent a day & 1/2 fooling with dentists, so we haven't done a lot of touring, but we did go back to the Bay of Fundy coast and tour Fundy Nat. Park south of Moncton, NB. The season doesn't start here till the 3rd or 4th week in June, so not everything is open yet, but all the natives say the weather is abnormally cold and wet for this time of year. Of course, we've never been anywhere where the weather was normal and I can think of damn few places we've been where we were in season. Even in the Outback of Australia it was abnormal this year. The Outback has had more rain in the last 2 years than in the previous 9 and is green, and it's supposed to be the most arid place on the most arid continent. I could see lakes from the air when we landed at Ayres Rock and asked about them. They were saltpans that had filled with rainwater and hadn't held water in the last 20 years.

Fundy NP has the worst roads I've ever seen in a Nat. Park in Canada or the US, but there are some pretty views of the Bay of Fundy and some spectacular views of the mud flats when the tide is out. At Hopewell Rocks, about 35 kilometers north of Fundy NP, we walked on the bottom of the ocean at low tide. It's a rock and sand bottom there. The rocks themselves look like giant flower pots at low tide with green growth on the top few feet where the tides don't cover the rocks and seaweed at the very bottom which is out of the water the shortest period of time. They have been eroded from the shore and are eroding away fairly fast. New rocks are being created by the tides at the shoreline and there are a lot of caves and overhangs where erosion has eaten away the rock, but they are very unstable and only Duke walked into a few caves on his leash. He didn't read the signs that warn you to stay away. The rocks are about 50 feet high and the tides nearly reach the top of them and must be at least 40 feet. The highest repeating tides in the world are here and the highest consistent tide is about 16 meters in the northern part of the Bay. That's over 50 feet! The fishing boats rest on steel cradles on the ocean floor at low tide and are floating a lot higher at high tide. Alma is a quaint little village adjacent to the Park and we ate some more good seafood at a local restaurant. Red-throated hummingbirds, just like we have outside our windows at home were feeding at feeders outside the restaurant windows. They winter in Central and South America and it's hard to believe they can fly this far north. We stayed 2 nights in a campground near Hopewell Rocks. I thought it was on an isthmus between two fresh water lakes since the water level didn't change, but Duke and I walked way down to the end toward the Bay of Fundy and it's 2 man-made brackish water wetlands covering at least 65 acres. The guy has damned up two salt- water inlets and put in some overflow pipes and let the tides fill up the wetlands, which no longer rise and fall more than a few inches. He's created a large wetland marsh area and we never think of wetlands being created, only destroyed. It's like touring the rain forest near Cairns, Australia and stopping at the information center in the middle of the 8-kilometer ride in a gondola over the rain forest and using the touch screen computers in the information center. I was shocked to learn that 40,000 years ago, there were no rainforests near Cairns, which now is surrounded by rain forest. Back then it was a very lightly forested area of eucalyptus trees like a lot of Australia south of Cairns now. You can make the computers draw maps going backward in time, of the rainforests in Australia and they were tiny back then and are quite large today. As Australia moves farther north toward the equator, they continue to expand; yet we never hear about it.

Trip Potpourri:

1. We buy and read the local newspapers wherever we travel and you learn a lot of stuff. In New Brunswick for example, there is a touring museum exhibit on the history of the toilet, loo, john, water closet, commode or whatever you call it. It's traveling around to different locations on an 18- wheeler for public viewing. If you can prove your name is John, or Lou, you get in free. Tenhula thinks I make this stuff up, but I'm not that inventive. Attendance has been high as it's just been on the road a few weeks and New Brunswick is small with maybe 300,000 people total. At the end of your visit to the exhibit, you get to vote on whether or not the toilet paper should be mounted so it unrolls over the top, or from the bottom. So far there are over 8500 votes for under and only 4200+ for over—not even close. It means my Mother was right and Pookie is wrong! Speaking of that, to describe my Mother as strong willed would be charitable. She didn't much care for anyone's opinion, other than her own and let you know it. Whenever we would visit her and stay in her apartment, it would normally only take 20 to 30 minutes for her to hack off Pookie. Of course, Pookie is too sweet and nice to ever argue with her, that job was assigned to me and there are some who say I may be a little like Obie and some even say I relished the assignment. Anyway, if Pookie got peeved enough, she would wait till Obie wasn't around and then go in the bathrooms and turn the toilet paper rolls around the other way to get even and vent her frustration. How's that for payback!
2. One of the local papers we bought had a weekly column by a reporter who went to all the local barbershops and beauty shops and reported what the locals were telling their hair stylists to REALLY get the skinny on what was going on. It was cute and reported something different from each shop, although for all I know they all told the same thing and the reporter only just reported one item from each shop. A cute idea. Maybe Hershel will try that at home.
3. Pookie read me out of one paper a quote of the day from George Bernard Shaw. It was "It is dangerous to be sincere, unless you are also stupid". Shaw was a world-renowned cynic as well as an intellectual, but he had a bad habit of picking on some people who disagreed with him politically, but were NOT his inferiors intellectually. He once challenged G.K. Chesterton,

the poet, author, playwright, essayists, theologian and social commentator, who converted to Catholicism late in life and who was perhaps even better known than Shaw in the early part of the 20th century, to a series of public debates. They held 3 debates and the public who attended overwhelmingly voted Chesterton the winner of all 3, so Shaw quit the debates. Shaw was not a political supporter of Winston Churchill either and once when Shaw had a play opening in London and Churchill was prime minister, Shaw sent a messenger to 10 Downing Street with an envelope containing 2 tickets to his opening night play on the morning of the opening. He enclosed a note that said, "Bring a friend, if you have one." The story is that Churchill told the messenger to wait, opened the envelope, read the note, grunted and sent back the tickets with his own note that said, "I have a conflict this evening. Send tickets to the 2nd night performance, if there is one".

4. The cute little dentist #3 who is the only prosthodontist in all of New Brunswick now has a small dowry. If any of you know a late 20's, early 30's male who wants to be kept in style by a woman who appears to have good prospects for an above average income, I can give you the name and address in Fredericton.

5. I was wrong about the emergency response team strike in Alberta. The newspaper said only the name of the town, which is Edmundston. I misread and didn't see the s and thought it was Edmonton, a large city in Alberta, but it's New Brunswick. The infant who died was 5 months old and had respiratory failure and the emergency room was closed because there are only 7 physicians in Edmundston plus the emergency room physician and to give him some time off, the other 7 had to help staff the emergency room in addition to their practices. This had gone on for a long time and they finally refused to staff the emergency room and the hospital closed its emergency room so the child had to be transported 35 miles away to an emergency room. Today they announced that another emergency room in another hospital has been closed for 5 months for the same reason. Also, on national TV today there was an obviously poor man on crutches who grimaced when he moved and said he had been waiting for over a year for orthopedic surgery to replace his knee and he was in constant pain and couldn't work and was fed up with the wait. That was in Nova Scotia where the x-ray technicians are going on strike over wages and the nurses union in New Brunswick says they may strike because there are 400 fewer nurses than 2 years ago and they can't schedule any vacations or time off and are all working overtime. The health minister for Nova Scotia was on TV too and said

yes, they were short of orthopedic surgeons, but they were better off than some other jurisdictions in Canada—what a response! It appears to me that socialized medicine has managed to successfully reduce the supply of healthcare in Canada, but hasn't done a thing to reduce demand. Why don't we ever hear that side of it in our media? Here the wealthy appear to be able to get adequate care, just like in the States, but the less affluent are even worse off than ours.

6.   Speaking of toilet matters, the Ponderosa Pines Campground at Hopewell Rocks, NB is the reigning world champion at providing the slickest, thinnest toilet paper in existence. You can fold that stuff 4 times and still see through it. It's hard to fold it anymore, as it's too slick to stick together. Prior to now, I thought the Lawrenceburg branch of my old bank provided the thinnest and slickest toilet paper. My wizard of procurement in Lawrenceburg, Buddy Parker, got that stuff somewhere very cheaply. I never said anything since I rarely had need of the toilet there and if it was cheap the bank made more money and I got more incentive pay. Now that I travel in the trailer and sample this sort of stuff, I am more conscious of the need to upgrade toilet paper standards. I do not expect Ponderosa Pines to relinquish its title anytime soon. Social Commentator

Sent: Tuesday, June 12, 2001 7:20 PM
Subject: St. Anthony, Newfoundland

When we got our boarding passes for the ferry, they gave us a pamphlet on the dangers of driving in Nfld. from moose on the highways. Pookie didn't believe it one bit and scoffed at the notion that we might actually see a moose. We never saw one in Alaska that wasn't stuffed or from a train or airplane and a long way away. I was going to get a copy for Paula & Sue, but we started loading on the ferry before I could walk back to the ticket booth. It was a 5 1/2 hour ferry ride and Duke rode in the trailer on the vehicle deck. If he cried and complained down there, nobody would hear him over all the engine noise. Coming back on the ferry from 400 miles further west, the ride is 14 hours, and I may put him in a kennel then. We're on Nfld. time, which is 30 minutes ahead of Atlantic Time, which is an hour ahead of Eastern Time and it gets light at 3:30 in the morning and dark around 9:30. I just changed the time on this computer to local time. When we got to Channel—Port aux Basque I was outside on deck #5 way up high taking some pictures, and kept wondering how the spray could get up that high before I figured out it was snow, not salt spray, and the wind was at least 40mph.

We drove to a Visitor Center about 2 miles from the ferry and after quizzing the staff and loading up on visitor info, I left the trailer in their parking lot and we drove east about 45 kilometers to the end of the highway at Rose Blanche. Very severe scenery with a lot of rock, bogs and quaint little fishing villages along the way. It looked a lot like Peggy's Cove, Nova Scotia, but Peggy's is an isolated fishing village in terrain unlike the surrounding area. We toured the lighthouse in Rose Blanche which is probably Pookie's 45th lighthouse tour, but Duke couldn't go in, so Duke and I stayed outside shivering in the wind for a few minutes and Pookie didn't stay long. It's a granite block lighthouse and looks more like a church than a lighthouse. Went back to get the trailer and started up the west coast of Nfld. through a very high wind and signs warning about high wind conditions. I later read in a guidebook that when Nfld. had a railroad, the wind blew over a rail car where the highway is now located. I wondered why they don't put up windmill turbines to generate electricity, but later figured out that there aren't enough people around to use it and you can't bottle that stuff. We found a campground about 40 miles up the Trans Canada Highway, or TCH as they call it on the highway signs and it started to rain just as I got the trailer set up. Went down to 40 that night with high winds and rain. We haven't cut on the AC yet on this trip.

Newfoundland, which includes Labrador, as a 2nd state of Nfld. is a lot bigger than I thought. Just the island part, which is Newfoundland, is larger than Nova Scotia, Prince Edward Island and New Brunswick combined and with Labrador included is larger than the landmass of Japan and over 3 times the physical size of the other Maritime Provinces. It only has about 550,000 in population and only 50,000 in Labrador. I had thought it was 560 kilometers from Channel—Port aux Basque to St. Johns on the island, but it's 560 miles, not clicks. We may change the date we come back to a later date. We decided to go up the west coast all the way to the top of the island and do a side trip to Labrador if it could be worked out, and then drive 3/4 of the way back to the TCH and across to St. Johns on the east coast.

We drove to Rocky Harbor in Gros Morne Nat. Park the next day and had lousy weather all the way up and the coastal highway once the TCH turns east is rough surface about half the time and limits speed to 45 mph pulling the trailer where it's rough. Ate dinner that nite in a seafood restaurant after the obligatory tour of the Rocky Harbor lighthouse where the lady let Duke come in and me hold him while we watched the video on Gros Morne NP. I had pan-fried cod tongues. Quite good! They aren't really tongues and are muscles at the back of the cod's mouth, but Pookie wouldn't eat more than a taste. She remembers me eating the oxen tongue in Germany and seeing it shiver and shake when it's cut. In Australia, she got braver and sampled kangaroo, wallaby, possum, crocodile and emu. Gros Morne is a World Heritage NP and very diverse with a lot of seacoast, inland mountains and lakes and bogs as well as forest. The sun came out the next day and the park is gorgeous and it warmed up to about 60 in the sun, but still windy. We drove to Woody Point on the south side of the coast and then to the tablelands, which are devoid of vegetation and very red in color. There are so many heavy metals in the soil like iron, nickel etc. that vegetation can't grow, but across the highway where the soil is different there are forests and greenery. Newfoundland contains 80% of Canada's iron ore and huge nickel deposits too. We went to Trout River, a very attractive fishing village past the tablelands, and then back toward Rocky Harbor. There are cute highway signs in the Park that show pictures of moose butting cars with their antlers and a sign with changeable number slots saying that there have been 6 moose/car collisions this year and 5 caribou/car collisions and to keep a sharp lookout. We were joking about it and I said that I bet each moose had a puffin riding on it's back (we've never been able to see a wild puffin either) when Pookie started yelling moose and we saw a huge bull, with no antlers standing beside the highway chewing on some bushes. I was going too fast and went past him before I could stop, so we turned around and came back and stopped about 40 feet away. He ignored us and even when I told Pookie to blow the horn so he would look at us, while I got a photo, he ignored us. He even ignored Duke who went into his "let me at him" routine with barks and whines. The moose was as big as a Clydesdale horse and oblivious to anything but his meal. About 3 miles further down the road, Pookie starts yelling again and a yearling moose crashes out of the woods on her side of the road and runs across the road right behind us. Glad I was going fast that time as it too thought the Durango was no problem and would have hit us if I was going slower. They have terrible eyesight and depend mainly on hearing.

Gros Morne, which means large mountain standing by itself and can also be translated as gloomy mountain is a relatively recent addition to the Canada Parks system and has a lot of villages and towns inside its boundaries. We went north along the coast to Broom Point where park interpreters explain the fishing life at the site of an actual 3 family fishing site where 3 brothers and their families lived and fished for 50 years—in one small house. All their fishing gear, and boats, which are motored and oar powered dories is in a shed on site. Duke couldn't go in, so Pookie held him outside while I talked to the guy. In Nfld., fish means cod and if you get fish chowder or fish & chips, it will always be cod. All other fish species are called by their names and are not called fish. The cod stocks collapsed in the early 90's and nobody fishes for cod anymore, but they catch enough cod while fishing for other species to supply the restaurants and for food for the locals.

Yesterday we drove up the rest of the coast on another glorious day and whenever the sea is in sight, you always see a dory every half-mile or so working lobster pots or nets or hand fishing. It's a hard life and they are not overly prosperous, but the people are friendly everywhere and very independent. Nearly all the houses are small and heated with firewood and everybody has a huge stack of next winter's firewood drying outside. There are a lot of vegetable gardens along the highway right of way, with people planting vegetables where the highway construction uncovered good soil as most of Nfld. is rock, and the telephone poles are held up by a box of timber around the base of the pole filled with stones and anchored against the wind by cables, as the soil is too rocky to get the pole in the ground. (That was a Faulkner length sentence!) In the good weather, sunshine and around 50 degrees and a mild wind, the locals are all walking along the highway for exercise and to bag rays—even pushing baby carriages and wearing shorts as they think it's warm. Reminds me of coming home for lunch in Wisconsin one day in the spring after a long winter, and finding Pookie sunbathing on our little patio in a bathing suit at 50 degrees. You get used to it.

We stopped at some natural arches eroded by the tides and again at Port aux Choix where we toured a really good Parks Canada historic site where they have uncovered 4500 years of constant human habitation and have good exhibits and a video explaining everything. The lady asked if I had any questions and I couldn't resist telling her we had just been in Australia where they have documented 40,000 years of constant aborigine habitation. She grinned and commented that maybe the Nfld. people were newcomers. We stopped in St. Barbe where there is a ferry over to Quebec and then a coastal road to Red Bay, Labrador and I booked the Durango and us for tomorrow. Also paid a local guy $10 for the right to leave the trailer overnight in St. Barbe at the local volunteer fire dept., so we don't have to take it to Labrador and I booked a room at a motel that will admit dogs in Labrador. Went first class and got the works, cable TV, telephone, private bath, ground floor with outside entrance and a balcony. Pookie will stay up all nite watching TV. We only get 1 channel in Nfld. and its CBC and plays cartoons most of the day and hockey at nite.

We began to see icebergs along the coast and could see Labrador from there on till we turned inland. Just think, in April Pookie was sitting in a deck chair on a sailing schooner cruising past the islands off Fiji where "Castaway" was filmed, on the way to 2 islands where we went snorkeling over the coral and beautiful fish and stayed in a 5 star resort. Last nite she could see icebergs in the harbor at St. Anthony where we ate dinner and we're staying in a campground with moose poop all over the place. What I won't do to please this woman!

We did L'Anse aux Meadows Nat. Historic Site this morning, the only documented site of Norse settlement in North America and the Wilfred Grenfell Historic site in St. Anthony this afternoon, but I'll talk about them tomorrow and send everyone their first and probably only e-mail ever from Labrador. Pookie has been buying jams made from the local berries and we learned today that there is a local berry called Clintonia, also called Blue Bead, but my favorite local name for it is Poison Berry, just like Bill!
Scrivener

Sent: Wednesday, June 13, 2001 6:24 PM
Subject: Red Bay, Labrador

Yep, we're here, but it was very entertaining to get here. The Northern Penn, the local paper for the northern peninsula of Newfoundland had a hilarious letter to the editor by a guy who took the ferry last Thursday that we took today. He commented on the total incompetence of the crew of the Apollo, the ferry, and how it took them an extra 30 minutes to unload the ferry and an extra hour to load it and they were very late. Well, they haven't gotten any better. I'll be discrete for me and call it a Chinese fire drill, but there is a better term, starting with cluster, if you know what I mean. The loadmaster or whatever he is called couldn't decide what to do, so he and his trusty crew of 7 helpers would meet for five minutes and then rush out in all directions and give contradicting instructions to everyone about what to do. We were all lined up in lanes as instructed by the ticket seller, but they had people backing up instead of going forward, going away from the boat, blocking each other and they damn near jack-knifed an 18-wheeler. They even plucked an 18-wheeler out of the back of the pack and had him navigate to the front of the line. A new meeting was held every time total chaos was in place, and then it would start over. The Moscow State Circus was trying to get across the strait of Belle Isle to perform in Labrador this afternoon and had 17 vehicles ranging from 18-wheelers to campers and they spoke Russian and thought they all had to be consecutive in getting on the ferry, but were lined up in different lanes, at least initially. We finally got on and left 45 minutes late, but I thought Pookie was going to die laughing before we got on. Then we went to the cafeteria on the ferry and met the kitchen staff. They ain't gonna build any rockets either. In fact, if they combined all their talents together—there were 4 of them—, I don't think they could launch a skyrocket from a Coke bottle. If they replaced the guy serving bacon & eggs with Duke, the average IQ of the group would expand exponentially. After so much exposure to the crew, I began to worry about crossing an iceberg- infested strait with this bunch. The fog rolled in after we were gone 30 minutes and they started the foghorn and I had visions of living out the "Titanic" movie. It's a 90-minute crossing and visibility got down to maybe 1/4 mile. Traveling with a social registry of circus freaks and "carnies" wasn't too reassuring either. We did pass an iceberg damn near as large as the ferry, but the fog finally lifted and we saw 2 small Minke whales in the harbor on the other side. The circus is going to go back with us tomorrow and I can't wait.

The Parks Canada Visitor Center and exhibits at L'Anse aux Meadows, the Norse site, are exceptionally well done. We got a guided tour from Stephen, a ranger who really knew his history and facts and knew when to say he didn't know. The actual site is a few hundred yards from the Center and we walked all over it with him explaining everything and answering questions. There were 8 buildings constructed by the Vikings and he explained all of them in detail. The Norse were here in 1000 A.D. and stayed for a few years and then left. There were about 75 of them altogether and only a few women, and most of the men spent the summers exploring further to the west. They had a smithy and smelted iron for nails to repair their boats. The bog near the settlement contains iron ore that chemically matches the nails found and all kinds of implements and artifacts are on display in the Visitor Center. There are reconstructed sod huts built by Parks Canada adjacent to the site, modeled on ones uncovered in Iceland that were covered by volcanic ash in 1100. The whole thing was made possible by a couple from Norway who explored from Rhode Island to Baffin Island looking for the site as described in the Norse Sagas. Back then, the sea level was a meter higher and the temperature was 3 or 4 degrees Celsius higher (they had global warming without carbon dioxide greenhouse gas— why can't we?), so the topography of the bay was a little different than now. The Norwegian couple were an archeologist and her husband, a history professor who theorized differently than everyone else and figured the Vineland terminology was hype to attract new settlers, just like naming Greenland green was hype. We stayed about 3 hours and really enjoyed it.

The Grenfell Center in St. Anthony is also quite good. Grenfell was a young doctor in England who became a missionary and was also an adventurer. He came to Labrador in 1892 and over the years created a medical service that grew to 6 hospitals, 5 nursing centers, 5 orphanages, 3 agricultural stations and numerous craft centers that made and sold crafts to help support the medical work. He had a fleet of hospital ships and ultimately created an air ambulance service and personally would create a new project and then get others to implement it while he went on to the next idea. He did house calls by dog sled and took a lot of risks. One time he was dog sledding across pack ice too late in the season and broke through and went into the sea along with his dogs. He was alone, but got out of the water and onto an ice floe. He saved all the dogs and killed 3 to "borrow their coats" and survived for 36 hours till he was rescued. Grenfell taught nutrition and disease prevention to an illiterate population and lectured and toured around the world to get donations to support his work. He was knighted and lived until 1940. A truly energetic and amazing man.

Pookie took a picture of a restaurant sign that advertised "Northern Fried Chicken" on the way to L'Anse aux Meadows and she asked the ranger there what kind of vegetables people planted in the roadside gardens. He said mainly potatoes, so I asked—drum roll here—if they planted any iceberg lettuce. We could see icebergs from the Norse site. He said yes and also spinach and carrots. The local McDonald's advertise McLobster, but we haven't tried that. I may get a caribou steak tonite to add that to my list. I forgot to mention that on Fitzroy Island on the way to the Great Barrier Reef we took a tour in the Rainforest with a naturalist and he showed us a green ant nest and mentioned that the aborigines ate them as a delicacy. He asked for any volunteers and I raised my hand. You hold the front of the ant and eat the green bulge toward the back. Tastes like lemon/lime. In New Zealand and Australia, a lot of things are named Fitzroy, lakes, islands, mountains, botanic gardens, public parks, etc. My theory was that Fitzroy was a half brother to Kilroy, but it turned out that he was a prime minister of Great Britain. In Newfoundland, a lot of stuff is named Codroy and I suspect he's a cousin to Kilroy, but haven't asked—don't want my theory upset.

It's raining again and we are in our motel room now. Two queen sized beds, one for Duke & one for us if I can keep him out of our bed. Nice tours today of the Red Bank Basque Whaling Exhibits. Travel day tomorrow to central Newfoundland. I had thought I would take a ferry from here to Goose Bay, Labrador as we're a lot closer to it than the ferry from Lewisporte, Nfld., but the ferry to Goose Bay from here doesn't start until July 1st and I learned that the ferry back to Nfld. from Goose Bay is a 35 hour trip and I'm not going to do that even though it would save me a lot of driving.
Onward!

Sent: Sunday, June 17, 2001 7:51 PM
Subject: St. Johns, Newfoundland

To finish the Labrador story, Red Bay has about 300 people and is a typical fishing village like all those up and down the Newfoundland coast, except it has an excellent harbor and is a stop for all the supply boats and ferries that go up and down the coast of Labrador in the good weather months. It was established as a European settlement by Basque fishermen from what was then the Basque nation in the Pyrenees between Spain and France. Now 95% of the Basque country is in Spain and 5% is in France. This happened in the last half of the 16th century, yep, around 1550. The Basques had learned how to hunt whales in the 11th century and came to Labrador to hunt whales and fish for cod. They usually only stayed for the good weather months and went back to Basque for the winter, except sometimes a few would wait too late to leave and get trapped by pack ice and have to over winter in Red Bay. Most of them died and a large burial ground has been found full of them. Parks Canada has 2 Interpretive Centers in Red Bay with exhibits and videos about the history and natural history of the area. By researching the libraries in universities back in Spain, they found old records of ships sailing to Labrador and one detailed record of a ship named the San Juan that was sunk in the Grand Bay port in 1565 during a gale. A similar gale hit in 1966 and sank a modern steel ship off Saddle Island, which protects the entrance to the Bay from the ocean. Underwater archeologists went looking at the site of the modern wreck and found the San Juan, remarkably well preserved. All kinds of artifacts have been brought up and preserved and are on display including navigation instruments, clothing, tools, barrels, whaling gear etc. They also found 3 smaller dinghies or boats and have a lot of articles from the cemeteries, including shoes and hats and personal effects. The center also gives a brief history of the Basque mariners and explains how they lost their monopoly on whaling and the sale of whale oil when other Europeans copied their methods. It's estimated that the Basques harvested over 25,000 whales from Newfoundland waters over 2 centuries before they depleted the whale population.

We actually stayed in a motel in Ste. Modeste, Labrador since it is closer to the ferry and we had to re-board at 7 a.m. the next day. The circus beat us to the ferry, but there was no repeat of the previous day's foul up and we boarded and got off on time, of course they didn't have to unload first. The guy serving bacon and eggs was gone too, and the cafeteria line even went at an acceptable speed. Some guy had left a 5th wheel trailer next to mine when we got back, so maybe I helped somebody figure out how to leave his rig. We drove over 600 kilometers after the ferry and spent the nite at Gander, Newfoundland, but the sun came out and it got up to 76 degrees in the interior of Newfoundland. Had to cut on the AC for the first time in the Durango since we left PA, but I stopped and refilled one of the propane bottles anyway as we've been running the furnace every nite. The problem is the roads. About half the distance, the road surface is so rough that I had to go below 50mph. The Durango isn't the smoothest riding vehicle I've owned, but when you hang 5,500 lbs. of trailer off the rear end, with around 700 lb. of hitch weight, you really need a decent road. When Pookie got up after our trip across Newfoundland, she said she felt like she had Shaken Baby Syndrome.

We did stop to tour the Museum of Flight in Gander. It's kind of small and not very well done, but is in honor of all the aviation history of Gander. Gander is far enough away from the coast to miss most of the fog and coastal rain, but still close in relative terms to Europe. There is a huge freshwater lake at the airport also and it was a base for the early flying boats and Clipper flights to Europe. WW II was the heyday and the museum is mostly about the Royal Air Force Ferry Command that was based here. In 1940 when Britain was fighting alone and desperately needed airplanes they set up Ferry Command to fly US made bombers to England. The first flight was 7 Lockheed Hudson medium range bombers outfitted with extra fuel tanks in the bomb bays. The Atlantic crossing by air was a rare thing back then and navigation instruments and engine reliability were crude. The Brits were so desperate that they figured if they got 4 of the 7 across, it would be worth the loss of 3 plus their crews. They only sent 1 navigator as they were short of them too, and told the other pilots to follow the leader and if he went down to go by compass and dead reckoning. All 7 made it, so Ferry Command was greatly expanded and by war's end over 10,000 American made planes got to Europe through Gander. The Hudsons turned out to be so reliable that the Brits modified them to be long-range anti-submarine patrollers. One of the original Hudsons became the first ever airplane to bomb a U-boat and then hover over it until a surface ship arrived and be officially recognized as "capturing" a sub. The first few flight crews had to return by ship, but after that the RAF flew crews back on B-24 bombers converted to carry airmen. By war's end, women pilots were ferry pilots also and the technology for airplanes and navigation had improved so much that the crossing was routine. Of course, after we got in the war, it was mostly a US operation rather than British. Actually, our first troops were deployed to Newfoundland in January 1941, or within a month of Pearl Harbor. That's how much emphasis we placed on the strategic role of Newfoundland in the air and naval war. There is only one small exhibit about the crash of the chartered Arrow Aviation jet that crashed in 1985 with 266 of the 101st Airborne killed on a trip home from Germany.

We're in Pippy Park, a 1300-acre city-owned park in the middle of St. Johns with nice campgrounds and all the hook-ups. Memorial University is in the park also along with Botanical Gardens, The Fluvarium, a water research facility, golf courses, The Newfoundland/Labrador Art Gallery, hiking trails, etc. We've toured some things here already, but it's time for Random Ruminations:

1.   In New Brunswick, there was a mass die-off of frogs this year. They tested everything they could think of to try and find out the cause including excessive ultraviolet light from ozone loss in the atmosphere, pollution, bacteria or fungi, frog disease, and so forth. The final conclusion was the damn things froze to death, as the winter was longer and harder than it had been in many years.

2.   We saw a PEI potato truck on the road in Nova Scotia with a potato caricature on the side saying "This Spud's for You!" I guess Budweiser doesn't mind as it just supports their advertising.

3.   Whales from the northern hemisphere don't cross into the southern hemisphere and vice versa. Nobody knows why. Maybe it's because the water goes down the drain in the reverse direction in the southern hemisphere. Sounds as good as anybody else's guess.

4.   They think most of the Vikings at L'Anse aux Meadows were Christians. The King of Norway forcibly converted his subjects to Christianity in 950 A.D. and Iceland soon followed and Greenland after that and the Vikings in Newfoundland came from Greenland. They did, however, find a soapstone ornament that had Thor's Hammer, a pagan symbol, on one side and a Christian cross on the other. Sounds like somebody was hedging his bets. Probably a Viking lawyer.

5. The only 2 Norse Sagas that mention Vineland or Vinland are the Saga of Eric the Red and the Saga of Greenland. Eric was expelled from Iceland for murder and a few other indiscretions and was the father of Leif Ericsson, who is thought to have captained the settlement at L'Anse aux Meadows. Anyway, the Saga says that Eric the Red's wife converted to Christianity first and then refused to let Eric sleep with her due to his paganism. Eric was mightily upset according to the Saga, but shortly thereafter he found salvation. Sometimes the Lord works in mysterious ways and sometimes it's fairly obvious.

6. Atlantic salmon are plentiful and avidly fished in Newfoundland. The sign on the Fluvarium says they are back now in the rivers which flow through St. Johns. In New Brunswick they were eliminated by the lumber industry silting up all the streams and building dams to float logs. Recent attempts to restock in New Brunswick where the rivers are now clear and not dammed have been failures. 40,000 releases of fry in a single river resulted in the return of less than 200 fish. They can't figure out why they can't be reintroduced.

7. Canadians have always looked down their noses at Americans with regard to the environment and consider themselves good stewards and us bad. A recent government report however says that Canadians use about 500 kilowatts per capita more then do Americans and are the world's top energy hogs. They claim the difference is due to the need to heat more in winter. Sounds like hogwash to me. I bet we use a lot more energy for AC in the Sunbelt than they do for heat in the ice belt—I know I do. Besides, most people in the Maritime Provinces use firewood for heat, not man-made energy and I bet a lot outside the cities do everywhere in Canada.

8. The ace loadmaster at the St. Barbe ferry walked up to each vehicle and used a common hole punch to punch a hole in your ferry ticket so it couldn't be reused. Pookie observed with glee that he left a hanging chad in our ticket both times. Of course, the circus is based in Sarasota, Florida, while they are in the States, so they probably thought nothing of it.

We're going puffin hunting tomorrow and not taking Duke. He might scare off puffins with his "let me out and I'll kick butt" routine. He met an older Airedale terrier today and the Airedale's owner told his dog, which was twice Duke's size, to stay calm or he'd get whipped. Puffin Guide

Sent: Thursday, June 21, 2001 8:36 PM
Subject: Puffins Galore!

Not only did the Great White Hunter find a puffin, he found 500,000, give or take a few. We drove down to Bulls Bay, about 35 miles south of St. Johns and took a boat tour in Witless Bay, an ecological preserve and seabird sanctuary. A glorious sunny day with temperature around 65 when we left at 10 a.m. for a 2 1/2 hour boat ride. Only 7 tourists on the boat, which would have held maybe 65. A really cute and energetic Newfie college student to give us the skinny and serve as our naturalist. She was a biology major at Memorial University in St. Johns and planning on med school. Witless Bay is the bay directly south of Bulls Bay and has 4 uninhabited islands, all removed from the coastline and from each other by a few miles where all the seabirds nest and raise their young. Puffins are small birds, maybe 8 or 10 inches long at most and in Newfoundland are called PPF birds. That means piss poor flyers. They are absolutely comical to watch as they eat more than they can handle and then can't fly at all till they digest the excess. When overloaded with food and the boat is approaching, they try to fly and just can't get up. They make like a duck trying to take off, but the wings and feet strike the water and it's like watching a kid splash in the ocean. They crash headlong into a swell or wave and finally dive under the water to get away. They can dive down 200 feet to eat and feed on capelin, small smelt like fish extremely rich in protein and fat. From up on the flying bridge you can see them underwater and they fly in the water too, with fast wing movements, just like in the air. Wings are short and the red and orange markings on the bill are just there during breeding season and are shed like a snake sheds its skin after the season and the bill is then black. We got up close to the island they breed on and they were standing at the mouth of their burrows watching us. They dig burrows up to six feet into the soil and kill all the trees by destroying roots where they burrow. They mate for life and can live 20 years. They do a puffin kiss with their mate which is a bill clicking where each clicks the others bill. The reason they are so rarely seen is that they are a true water bird and never come ashore except to breed and raise a single chick. They spend the entire winter out on the Gulf Stream and have totally waterproof feathers. Maybe 10,000 tried to get up at the same time and the water looked like it was being hit with a rainstorm as they splashed away from us. When they can fly, they are so fast that it's impossible to get a decent picture. We also saw a number of other species of seabirds and maybe 2,000,000 Common Murre, which are larger than puffins and without the bill markings, but behave the same way. They can dive to 400 feet and you can smell their island before you get close enough to see them. Guano everywhere. No whales were seen although the skipper reported seeing a humpback the previous day. He also reported that they had 27 feet of snow last winter as opposed to 7 or 8 feet in a normal year. A really nice boat tour and 3 co-passengers paid $6 each to become honorary Newfoundlanders at a screech-in ceremony. That involves sticking your shoe in a pail of seawater, repeating a long phrase in Newfie dialect and swallowing neat an ounce of screech, which is cheap Jamaican rum. I could have handled the last part.

We ate lunch with the boat tour people who also run a restaurant and a B & B and then drove down to Ferryland, another seacoast fishing village, but one with a unique history. That's where George Calvert a.k.a. Lord Baltimore established his colony called Avalon in the New World in 1621. His wife couldn't stand the weather, so he relocated most of the colony to Maryland after she spent 1 winter in Newfoundland. Sounds like wives had a lot of influence in the past as well as now. The really unique thing about Ferryland is that it has been inhabited continuously since 1621 and now is the site of a major archaeology project to uncover the Avalon colony. We got an excellent tour guide with a great Newfie accent and toured the site. Digging was going on at the time and we got to watch and see them sifting the dirt through a strainer with water to make sure nothing is missed. They use trowels and hands to dig up the site and it is a painstaking process. They have uncovered the site of a forge, houses and the seawall and dock and storage sheds. They even found a stone privy that was flushed twice a day by the tide from inside the dock storage shed. Called it the first flushing toilet in North America. Unlike Jamestown or Plymouth, Avalon was settled by an upper class as they have uncovered a lot of gold and silver items and other items that only the wealthy could have owned. It's a 4-acre site and only a small bit has been unearthed so far. Sea level was higher then than now at Avalon also. A very different kind of tourist attraction, but the tour ends up in the gift shop like most do. All the artifacts are on display in an interpretative center with the usual video on the background.

On the way to St. Johns, we stopped briefly at Terra Nova Nat. Park west of St. Johns. It's a park for hikers with no amenities except a serviced campground and a marine center. The marine center has exhibits and a recreated tide pool with all the sea creatures found there. I tried to get Pookie to pick up the large crab, but she didn't. I picked up several starfish and the water is really cold. We only stayed about an hour.

In St. Johns, we went to Signal Hill first. That's a tall hill overlooking the harbor where they used to fly signal flags announcing the arrival of ships and what kind and from what fleet, etc. It's where John Cabot first saw Newfoundland in 1497. The hill was fortified and changed hands 4 times in the British and French wars and even had naval cannon put there in WW II. The young girl selling tickets at the Visitor Center said she really liked my accent, so I gave her my most exaggerated "Sho nuff, honey chile" till Pookie told me to stop. I told the girl that in Greenville, Mississippi where I grew up we had a large Chinese population and how would she like to hear a Chinese with a Southern accent. She said that would seem totally out of place. Nice exhibits on the history of St. Johns and its occupation over the years. Outside, the Tattoo was practicing for their daily performances, which begin in July. We got to watch them march, play the bagpipes and drums and fire off their black powder cannons. When we got back to the Durango, Duke was cowering on the floor on the driver's side. He hates black powder shots, either rifle or cannon and is terrified of them. The only creatures he is afraid of that I can tell are humans. Smart dog! They sell a lot of crystal radio sets in the gift shop here as several exhibits are about Marconi flying a kite with a 400 foot aerial attached—there's plenty of wind— and receiving the first transatlantic wireless signal here from a station he built in England. The signal was S for success.

We did the Newfoundland Museum after Signal Hill for an hour or so. It opened in 1907 and Pookie thinks it has the same exhibits it had then. It's the only museum I can remember without a gift shop, so maybe that's why she was uncharitable about the museum. On Sunday, we went to Cape Spear, the most eastern point in North America. When you are standing there, you are closer to Ireland than to Manitoba, and Manitoba is in central Canada. You can see Signal Hill from Cape Spear and the Cabot Tower on the crest of Signal Hill. You can also see the Narrows, which is the entrance to St. John's harbor. Duke left a few deposits on Cape Spear to remember him by. There is a unique lighthouse on the crest of the hill at Cape Spear. The tower is surrounded by the house which is built around the tower so that the inside walls of the house are circular. We got another very informative Parks Canada ranger who gave tours of the house. One family kept the light keeper job for 6 generations and the last light keeper is still on the public payroll, even though the light is automated now. Government jobs last forever. This place did have a gift shop and that's why Pookie climbed all the stairs to get there.

Church was over by now, so we went to the Anglican Cathedral in St. Johns. A young priest gave us and another couple a tour of the Cathedral, which is quite impressive. I put $10 in the donation box and the priest got very friendly. The Canadian dollar costs 65 cents American, or I wouldn't be so generous. With gasoline at 90 cents per liter or about $3.60 per gallon and the Durango taking $60+ to fill up, I couldn't afford it if we weren't using play money. They have a small museum in the Cathedral, which was totally destroyed by fire in 1892 and rebuilt. The pictures after the fire looked like Berlin after our air campaign in WW II. The Cathedral seats 1700 and the priest said maybe 200 were there for Sunday a.m. services, so I bet it looked empty. A very pretty church with all the stained glass windows you see in European cathedrals.

We've also done the Fluvarium where you look through glass into the brook or stream that flows by the Fluvarium and see the trout and salmon underwater in their natural habitat and the waterfront, which is full of ships from everywhere. We also did the Botanical Gardens, which aren't too impressive. I was tired at the Gardens and on the way out told Pookie to come sit in the shade with me on a bench and we would commune with nature. I had pushed back the greenery before I sat down, but Pookie just sat down on nature rather than communing with it. Squashed that bit of nature flat as a pancake.

Driving in St. Johns has been quite an experience. I don't think the old part of town has any square intersections where 4 streets meet at right angles. Most intersections have 3 to 6 streets meeting at all kinds of crazy angles and some streets may be one way and others 2-way. There are no lines dividing the pavement into lanes and they don't put up any yield or stop signs, so it's kind of every man for himself. The only helpful hint you get by way of signage is a big yellow sign at nearly every intersection that says "Dangerous Intersection". Wonder what genius thought of that. Of course, it's also quite helpful for my naviguesser to be yelling out "watch out" or "stop" or "NO" or my personal favorite, "They ought to take your driver's license away!" This from the expert professional driver who when I let her drive in Labrador, with no other vehicles in sight to distract her, drove into the exit from a Visitor Center rather than the entrance while ignoring the "Do not enter" sign. She's already told me that if I get sick she's selling the Durango and trailer and we're flying home, as she can't pull the trailer. She also told me not to croak till we can get home and I write down what she needs to do when I go. Crazy about me!

We're moving to a campground about 10 minutes from the ferry in Argentia tomorrow and take the ferry back to Nova Scotia Saturday at 8 a.m. Now I'm told the ferry ride is 15 to 16 hours rather than 14, but they have a bar on board and a movie theater. Sage

Sent: Wednesday, June 27, 2001 5:48 PM
Subject: Gaspe' Peninsula

My beautiful, sweet, kind, generous, witty, wise and on rare but delightful occasions, horny wife has changed her mind and now says I do not have to bring her home around July 1 so she can attend her high school reunion. This is in marked contrast to her previous hard-headed, obstreperous, non-negotiable and patently wrong position, especially when you learn that the Class of 1961 has these damn reunions every 5 years at a minimum and sometimes every year so Andy can relive his high school glory years and it's always the same and always boring. They will survive, even without the class valedictorian (that's why she chose me—extra smart even though the class only had 50 members). In view of this brilliant change of strategy, we have returned to the mainland and turned north again and are now on the easternmost point of the Gaspe peninsula camped on the bank of the Gulf of St. Lawrence in Quebec. Pretty view, and the campground owner is from Pearl, Mississippi and spends the winters in Jackson, MS. He was originally from Iowa, but saw the light and is trying to hide his innate yankeeness.

We drove from St. Johns, Nfld. to the information center a mile from the ferry terminal in Argentia, Nfld. Found out the campground near the ferry had lost it's license, so we decided to spend the nite in the departure lane of the ferry terminal along with about 15 other RVs and a bunch of cars with people sleeping in them. Everything but the micro-wave and AC and TV works off the trailer battery or propane, so it was OK since the temperature got down to 50 at nite. The Visitor Center had a number of exhibits on the meeting of Churchill and FDR in Argentia harbor in August 1941. They met on the water with Churchill arriving on HMS Prince of Wales and FDR on USS Augusta and hammered out the Atlantic Charter which became the foundation for the United Nations, before the Charter got perverted by too many members and too many changes. It's an impressive document and composed of only 8 short paragraphs, some only one sentence long. Russia was already fighting the Nazis and Churchill even then was talking about total victory. We were already flying anti-sub patrols from Nfld., even though not a combatant, and here we formalized lend-lease with us leasing British bases in Gibraltar, Nfld., Bermuda and the Caribbean and paying $1 rent plus 50 old WW I destroyers. The US Navy base at Argentia was built quickly thereafter and became the primary support base for all North Atlantic navy activity during WW II, including ours, Canada's and Britain's. We left the trailer there at the Visitor Center and went to Castle Hill, the old fort dating to the 1600's that overlooks the former French town of Placentia, a few miles from Argentia. Duke got to tour the old fort with the great view over the harbor. Nice exhibits and a short video and then lunch in Placentia. After lunch we drove down to Cape St. Mary at the tip of the peninsula about 45 miles south of Argentia to the seabird sanctuary. Audubon spent a good bit of time there as you can get to within a few feet of a colony of gannets, kittiwakes and common muerre at Bird Rock. It's about a 1-mile walk from the Visitor Center to Bird Rock, but well worth it. The gannets are at the top of the pecking order and nest on top of the rock with the kittiwakes and common muerre nesting on narrow rock ledges below them. Gannets have a 2-meter wingspread and are graceful and beautiful flyers that can soar like an albatross for hours. They have white wings with black wing tips and yellow heads. They mate for life and whenever one of a pair returns to the nest, they go through elaborate greetings with their bills, necks and wings as if to say, "Hi Honey, I'm Home". Bird Rock has been separated from the cliff by erosion and no predators other than gulls can get to it and the gulls are driven off by the gannets. The female of the common muerre lays a triangular egg—ouch—but there is a purpose for it. They nest on very narrow rock ledges and if the egg is accidentally kicked or moved, it rolls in a short circle no bigger than the axis of the egg so it won't fall off the ledge. The good news for the female is that after the chick hatches, she is off duty till the next year and the father feeds and raises the chick and teaches it to fly by pushing it off the ledge when it's ready. There are about 50,000 gannets there and a slightly lesser number of the other species. No puffins as they need soil for their burrows instead of rock. A nice ride down and back and very interesting to watch the birds.

The ferry ride back was 15 hours and the movie theatre was broken and the big screen video played cartoons all the way. We did see at least 2 and maybe more large whales from about 1/2 mile away who kept displaying their flukes and broaching for 15 minutes, but we don't know what kind. I went down on the vehicle deck to let Duke out of his cage and offered him the chance to relieve himself, but he's too well trained and refused to go on the metal deck or even on the tires of other cars. Finished a paperback and most of another. Camped a few miles from the ferry and drove the next day to St. Louis, New Brunswick. Flash report from a NB newspaper—the premier of New Brunswick gave the commencement speech to the 52 graduates of the Jan Raymond School of Beauty and Aesthetics. It was the typical "follow your dream" commencement speech. This guy must be desperate for publicity. Why didn't he lose the invitation?

The girl at the NB Welcome Center told me to be sure and go swimming on the beaches of northern NB as they have the warmest water north of Virginia. Hell, there is no warm water north of Virginia other than in a shower or bathtub or geothermal pool. We spent a half-day at Kouchibougac Nat. Park (bet there is not a single one of you who knows if I spelled that correctly and none of you who can pronounce it either—even the spellchecker I married can't do it!). Duke was prohibited from the beaches, but he and I tested the waters anyway and the lady is nuts if she thinks it's warm. The salt-water marsh mosquitoes are horrible and similar to the human species; it's only the females who suck your blood. Of course, the mosquito females, unlike the human variety, have the good taste not to attack their own kind! We were in Acadian NB, so we drove to Calquet to Acadian Village where there is a reconstructed Acadian village with actual buildings moved from elsewhere in NB and costumed interpreters acting out the parts of farmer, fisherman, tinsmith, blacksmith, hotelier etc. It covers about 70 acres and you walk from location to location and go in the buildings and talk to the people, all of whom are present day Acadians. French is the first or only language for all of them, although the girl at this campground (who is one of a small number of English extraction in Quebec) says they don't speak English or French either and Acadian is a separate, bastardized version of French. It's all frog to me anyway. My brother likes to go to France and visit the frogs, but not me. The place was not overloaded with tourists and I commented to Pookie that I couldn't understand how they could keep expanding it with new buildings costing up to $2 million until I was walking Duke after the tour and saw the plaque where it is a make-work project of the NB government to provide employment for the Acadians. And these are the descendants of the quick-witted Acadians who managed to escape the British deportation. The slow-witted ones got shipped to Louisiana and I went to Tulane with some of their descendants. Boudreaux and Thibodeaux were OK, but Charbonnet was a 4th year pledge in my fraternity my freshman year who never made his grades and managed to stay at Tulane 9 years without graduating—or maybe he was smarter than us. We finally broke the rules and initiated him secretly anyway. My senior year when I was president of the fraternity, he got us put on social probation by standing on the frat house porch and shooting out all the streetlights on Broadway with a Thompson submachine gun, which I had to explain to the authorities. I explained that he was a coon ass and didn't know any better. I thought that might work, but we were put on social pro anyway.

This morning, we did another boat ride around Isle Bonaventure at Perce', Quebec. It's another seabird sanctuary and the island is about 2 miles from Perce' Rock which is a striking rock formation with a hole worn all the way through it at sea level. More gannets, common muerre and kittiwakes but this time we saw 10 or 12 seals swimming close to the tour boat plus another Minke whale. A full tour boat and a gorgeous day, so the season must be here. The Minke is the smallest whale, usually travels alone and has a dorsal fin with a sharp hook and is easy to identify. Counting all the ferries and boat rides, I bet I've spent $1500 on boat rides, but I ain't gonna add it up. Keep no receipts and avoid the pain of knowledge. Perce' is a neat little tourist town and has a big winter snowmobile crowd too. There is a snowmobile track all the way around the Gaspe' and a lot of B&Bs and motels if anyone is interested and can put up with frogs. Duke is still interested in French squirrels, but he doesn't know any better.

It appears to me that Canada is on the threshold of a major healthcare crisis. Both British Columbia and Nova Scotia have threatened healthcare worker strikes and it's all over the TV and newspapers. Both provincial governments have or are passing legislation to prohibit healthcare workers from striking and imposing $2,000 per day fines on strikebreakers in Nova Scotia. BC just passed a 60-day cooling off law prohibiting strikes, with similar dire threats if they are ignored. Saskatchewan just got over a similar crisis by caving in to the strikers, but these 2 provinces on both coasts say never. I think everybody in Canada belongs to some type of union. Some cancer patient awaiting surgery flew to Germany yesterday as they can't do surgeries without people to do x-rays, blood tests, nursing, etc. Even the cleaning staffs and people who sterilize surgery equipment are walking out and thousands of surgeries have been put off. Even Jean Chretien, the premier of the federal government has appointed a commission to investigate what to do and is now speaking, after campaigning against it, about imposing user fees—believe it or not, there are none now—or, horrors, turning some healthcare management over to private companies— heresy in Canada. Sweden has done both and has a lower expense healthcare system as a percentage of GDP than Canada with a similar ethnic population who go to Drs. half as much as Canadians. Help me out here; is any of this making the national news in the USA? Give me some feedback. If it's not being reported, it's a total disservice to the American people not to let them know about the mess in Canada. Hope I don't get sick. I shall drink some wine or other form of alcohol to protect my heart!

Self-Medicater

Sent: Monday, July 02, 2001 7:59 PM
Subject: Quebec City

We love Keebeck—that's how they pronounce it. It's like taking a trip to Europe with no jet lag. Unlike Paris however, the locals are friendly, delighted you came to their city and desirous of showing it off and happy to speak English if you ask for it. They don't display any of the arrogance that the Parisians use to cover up their insecurity. I'd recommend Quebec to anyone, but first the rest of our trip here.

We did Forillon Nat. Park north of Gaspe' after Perce'. It's about the most easterly part of the Gaspe Peninsula with some gorgeous views up and down the coast. There is a northern and southern part of the park with an interpretive center in both. The northern part is opposite the port of Gaspe' to the east of the port and has a fort opposite the town. I assumed it was a 17th century fort, but it is a WW II fortification to protect the port and is entirely underground. I was just going to walk Duke when I discovered what it was, so Duke and I toured the fort underground. There are two 5-inch naval guns still in bunkers and since they are protected from the elements, they are in remarkably good condition. Exhibits explain that over 20 merchant and naval ships were sunk by U-boats off the Gaspe' coast in sight of land in 1942. The fort was also intended in 1940 to protect Gaspe' port which the British and Canadians had picked as a port to house the British Fleet in case Britain was successfully invaded by Germany, and had to carry on the fight from North America. The British had absolutely no intention of ever giving up. Cape Bon Ami is one of the most photogenic sights we have seen on this trip. Back in Gaspe' city, we did a museum on Jacques Cartier, who discovered Canada in 1534 and claimed it for France. He might be called the First Frog. Actually, they think he was on the ship that Verrazano captained that sailed from Florida to Newfoundland some years earlier for the French King, but made no claims. Verrazano was an Italian hired by the French to search for a passage to India. The French were the last continental power to explore the New World and behind the Spanish, Portuguese, English and Dutch. John Cabot who claimed Newfoundland for the English in 1497 was also an Italian employed by the English, but he at least made claims for England. His real name was Giovanni something, but it got Anglicized to John Cabot.

It was only after we got through touring Gaspe' that we realized we were on the wrong time. Gaspe' is much further east than New Brunswick which is on Atlantic time so we assumed it was on Atlantic time also. Not true. All of Quebec is on Eastern Time. Pookie figured it out by seeing a clock in the campground laundry. It only took us 2 full days to figure it out. Pookie said it felt like living in the Twilight Zone. We had actually refused to eat in some restaurants because they had no customers for lunch at 11:30 (real time 10:30). Pookie was really horrified to learn she had been getting up at 6:30 a.m. instead of 7:30. Ruined her whole day when she figured it out. It gets light at 4 in the a.m. and dark at 10 p.m. so it's hard to tell by light.

I shrewdly picked a shortcut across the interior of the peninsula instead of going all the way around on the coast. Heard about it for days. Terrible road through the only mountains in Gaspe' at a max speed of 40 mph. We had already done some hills around Perce' with 17% grades pulling the trailer. Steep grades bother me a lot more than they bother the Durango. Going up is a piece of cake, but going down makes me nervous as I never fully trust the trailer brakes and I couldn't stop it if they failed on a really steep downhill grade. Driving along the north coast is prettier than the south coast.

We did stop at Cape Chat and toured the world's largest wind tower. It's in the middle of a wind power farm with about 50 huge 3-propeller wind turbines that generate electricity. The wind tower is a tall tower that an aerodynamic wind foil rotates around. It was quite interesting and the thing is huge. It works, but no longer generates power as its original contract with Quebec Hydro expired and the company can't agree with Quebec Hydro on the terms of a renewal. Wind power is much more expensive than coal or gas or hydro or nuclear generated electricity. The whole wind farm is non economic, but is pumping out power steadily from the operating propeller windmills as their contracts are not expired yet. The web site is http://retscreen.gc.ca if anyone wants more information about it. We also stopped briefly where an artist has created outdoor art from concrete alongside the road and rafts with wooden art figures on them anchored close to shore. The tide was out, so the rafts were high and dry when we got there. Duke christened one of the concrete art objects that looked like a penis to me, and a female tourist exclaimed to me that Duke had expressed his opinion about the art. I had the same opinion, but kept my fly zipped.

Our first full day in Quebec City we did a 9 1/2 hour tour with a local tour guide on a small tour bus. They came to the campground and picked up about 15 of us and we had a really good French tour guide named Elaine. She was so obviously proud and enthusiastic about her hometown and had so much energy that she rarely shut up. I feel sorry for her husband, but she really knew her stuff. We're parked next to a coon ass from Houma, Louisiana named Hebert (pronounced A bear) and enjoyed being with him and his wife, also a Cajun, on the tour bus. I saw a vanity nametag with his name on his trailer and asked him if he was a coon ass and got a big grin in reply. He's pleased that he met someone who knows how to pronounce his name and doesn't call him Herbert. I asked him if he was here visiting his relatives, but he said no. Elaine drove us all around the city and explained what everything was. We got 2 hours off for lunch downtown and had a few stops where we got off the bus for 30 minutes or so. Quebec is a fortified city and still has intact the city wall that surrounded the old city, which is 4.7 kilometers in total length. You can walk all around the old city on top of the wall, just like in York, England. Quebec is an Indian word that means, "Where it narrows" and describes the St. Lawrence River. At Quebec, the river is less than a kilometer wide and cannon could control the river passage here, but nowhere further east. Modern Quebec is 183,000 population and is surrounded by 13 other municipalities that adjoin it which will be annexed into Quebec this year and jump the population to 600,000, but it's still less than half the size of Montreal, but is the provincial capitol. Samuel de Champlain in 1608 founded Quebec and it still has the cobblestone streets and old Norman style buildings with no skyscrapers in the old city. It really looks like a European city with the narrow streets and medieval appearance. Chateau Frontenac dominates the skyline and is surrounded by churches and sidewalk cafes and city parks. Like London, it has a few modern buildings scattered here and there, but they don't really detract from the appearance.

The plains of Abraham where Wolfe defeated Montcalm in 1759 and sealed the fate of New France are named for a man named Abraham Minter, who owned the flat level land west of the city. The city is protected by steep cliffs that the British scaled at night, and the battle that won Canada for the British only lasted 20 minutes. The British added the Citadel as a huge fort attached to the city walls and it has cannon facing both the river and the city. It was built to protect Quebec from the Americans who attempted to conquer the city during both the Revolutionary War and the War of 1812 and cannon were aimed at the city just in case the French population rebelled against the British. Our tour was on July 1st, Canada Day, the equivalent of our July 4th and we got to see the Royal Regiment Band parade past our sidewalk cafe during lunch with their tall bearskin caps and red tunics and bagpipes and drums. We also saw a small, less than 40 people, demonstration by Students for Quebec Separation parade by also. Separation referendums have failed 3 times since 1980 and would probably fail even worse today.

After lunch, we toured the Isle of Orleans just east of Quebec, which is full of summer homes and farms and is beautiful. All up and down the St. Lawrence there are Catholic churches built near to the river at 13.5 kilometers distance from each other. The steeples were navigation markers for the French back when all traffic was by canoe. We stopped for about 45 minutes at Montmorency Falls about 15 minutes east of Quebec, where a river pours off the cliffs into the St. Lawrence and makes a waterfall 84 meters high, 30 meters higher than Niagara. We also stopped at a bakery, selling hot fresh bread covered in maple butter—superb. Perhaps the highlight of the tour was the Shrine of Ste. Anne de Beapre' Basilica. The modern church is the fifth on the site and was built from 1922 to 1976 to replace the previous one destroyed by fire. It is relatively new and doesn't have the age of the European Cathedrals, but is to me more ornate and beautifully decorated than the ones I have seen. I haven't been to Rome yet, but I have seen the cathedrals in Chartres, Cologne, Paris and Westminster Abbey in London and none of them are as impressive on the inside. Saint Anne, the mother of Mary, is known for miracles and the two huge pillars inside the front door are wrapped in canes, crutches and prosthetic devices that people left when they were healed at the church. The chapel in the basement is impressive also. We also did a quick visit to the Cyclorama near the church, which presents the Crucifixion of Christ with a mural of the city of Jerusalem, and the countryside around it as painted by a German painter with an English narration.

Today we went back to the Old City by ourselves and walked the city wall and the boardwalk along the river, got an excellent tour of the Parliament building by a multilingual guide, walked around the Chateau Frontenac, ate lunch again across the street from the Chateau and went to a museum where the 1759 battle was depicted on a model with narration and video. An absolutely perfect day, with sunshine and a cool breeze. Last nite the furnace cut on and this morning it was 46 at 7:30 and a high today of 75. Too bad for those of you suffering down south.
Frog Friend

Sent: Sunday, July 08, 2001 8:07 PM
Subject: Ottawa & Gananoque

We decided to skip Montreal as we spent nearly a week there with the kids in the poptop in 1975 when I was a delegate to the Kiwanis International Convention in Montreal. Pookie says we stayed in Henri's Campground and Will was our interpreter with the French, as he seemed able to get them to understand him. This time, as we drove through Montreal, Pookie's bridge came out again. Yep, the girl in New Brunswick couldn't fix it properly as she used a different type of prosthesis and had no parts for Pookie's so she had just glued it back in with temporary glue. I stopped at the Ontario Info Center and got an Ottawa phone book and looked up both prosthodontists in Ottawa. Pookie called one and made an appointment for the next day. This guy couldn't fix it either, but he got it back in and used a stronger glue which he says will last till her appointment in Memphis on July 23. Bill, the Memphis prosthodontist, told Pookie not to forget that she belonged to him when she called him again. He's afraid he'll lose the gravy train. I feel like I'm driving around Canada dropping little piles of money here and there, but the guy in Ottawa was only 40% of the fee charged by the girl in New Brunswick. I'm sure Bill in Memphis will figure out a way to cost me a lot more.

Ottawa was fun. After our (I get to pay and this guy didn't take credit cards—just cash) dentist appointment, we went to Parliament Hill and took a tour of the federal parliament building in English. Toured the House of Commons and the Senate, which is the upper house. The Senate has been abolished in several of the provincial parliaments like Quebec and Nova Scotia, but not at the federal level. It is appointed by the Queen or her representative, the Governor General, who is a woman at the present. We also visited the Library of Parliament, which is, sort of like our Library of Congress, but not nearly as extensive in works. All 3 Parliament buildings are massive Gothic architecture and very impressive sitting on a hill overlooking the city with copper green roofs and next door to a hotel chateau that also is Gothic style.

The next day we went back to Parliament Hill to watch the changing of the guard at 10 a.m. The Regimental band followed by the Grenadier Guards came marching up the street to the Hill with bagpipes and drums and their red tunics and tall bearskin hats, except for the bagpipers who wear kilts and green plaids. The ceremony is longer than at Buckingham Palace and took over 30 minutes, but then we hit the jackpot. The Royal Canadian Mounted Police Equestrian Team showed up after the Guard marched off and did their Musical Ride on the lawn of Parliament Hill. They travel around the world and spend the summers traveling across Canada as a good will gesture from the Mounties. 32 black horses and riders, both male and female who perform to loudspeakers playing different musical themes like "This Land is My Land" and "The Magnificent Seven". The horses all have the same trappings and bridles and the riders are wearing their red coats, Mountie hats, navy blue breeches with yellow stripes and brown gloves and boots and pistol holders and each rider carrying a lance with pennants attached below the blade. They opened the show with a local singer performing in French and closed with a young boy singing in English, but the horses and riders did various maneuvers for over 30 minutes without ever repeating the same maneuver twice. They did circles, squares, lines, crossing patterns and in groups of 4, 8, 16 or 32 and demonstrated a charge and lance defense and attacks. It was a super presentation and ended with the riders and horses spreading out about 15 yards apart and doing a meet and greet with the audience at the rope line to let people, mostly kids, plus Pookie, pet the horses. I even found MY Mountie! The previous day a single female Mountie dressed in the full regalia was on the sidewalk in front of Parliament when we left and I had surrendered to her and told her she could take me into custody. Pookie took my picture while I tried to surrender, but she wasn't interested. Too bad, as she was almost old enough for me.

We went to the Museum of Contemporary Photography after the horse show only to discover that the Union of National Gallery Workers was on strike and had a picket line set up across the entrance made of their shoes, a warm day. I took great delight in crossing the picket line and Pookie followed me across. A female striker ran up and asked me if I wanted some material on why they were striking and I politely said no thanks and walked in the entrance. Only guards were there and the museum shop was closed and we could only tour 2 exhibits. One was a female photographer's explanation of her tortured soul as expressed by her self-photos of her in various masks engaged in various perverted sexual poses and activities. Spent about 20 seconds on that crap and skipped the self interview of her on video which explained her innermost feelings and other garbage. The other exhibit was by a Canadian male photographer, who explained in writing at the entrance that he was apolitical and never took sides, and then showed a lot of black and white photos of the guerillas who fought against the government in El Salvador with lots of shots of government atrocities and none of guerilla atrocities. Another section (also deemed by the artist to be apolitical) showed the poor Palestinians being mistreated by the awful Israelis in the last 8 months. No shots of bad guy Palestinian terrorists, just bad guy Israeli army troops. I was sort of glad the damn strike was on when I left. Got the web site for Kenny as surely they have some other stuff on the web.

We then did lunch at Le Cafe, outdoors on the bank of the Rideau Canal that connects the Ottawa River with the St Lawrence Seaway. Pookie likes this type of restaurant and describes the type as one that doesn't offer you a toothpick when you leave. Translation of Pookie code by Evan—lunch for 2 costs a minimum of $50. Pookie says her next husband is going to like traveling by airplane and staying in hotels—how soon she forgot Fiji, Australia and New Zealand! The Rideau Canal is about 5 miles long and is known as the world's longest outdoor skating rink in winter. Lots of pleasure boats were locking through the locks from the Ottawa River during lunch and they have people on the locks to do the work for you. Bob & I used Heidi and Pookie for that part in England as we drove the boat, but it didn't work again when we did a canal boat in Ireland. After lunch we did the Museum of Civilization (modest title) in Ottawa for several hours.

We stopped next in Gananoque; about 30 clicks east of Kingston, mainly to take the boat cruise through the 1000 Islands in the St. Lawrence, which the coon ass had recommended. Actually, there are 1865 islands and islets rather than 1000, with half of the landmass in the USA and half in Canada and the boundary drawn so that no island is split in half. To be designated an island, rather than an islet, it has to be six square feet and have two trees. It was a 4-hour cruise with narration in French and English and an hour stop at Boldt Castle. George Boldt was an immigrant from Prussia who came to the USA at age 13 alone. He got his first job in a hotel kitchen in NYC and ended up a famous hotelier in Philadelphia and later in New York where he operated and co-owned the Waldorf Astoria. His steward invented a new salad dressing on a visit to the 1000 Islands that George liked so much that he put it on the menu of the Waldorf Astoria and it became known as Thousand Island salad dressing. The steward ended up chef at the Waldorf. George built the castle, which was modeled on the Rhine castles in Germany, for his wife as they summered in the 1000 Islands along with the rich and famous, like John Jacob Astor, who owned summer homes there. The castle has 127 rooms, an elevator, indoor swimming pool, a bowling alley in the playhouse which is a separate building, a separate power house, a free standing tower for his birds and a huge boathouse for his 3 yachts and 50 odd other boats. It was a present for his wife and he had told the architect and builder that money was only a minor consideration. After 4 years of construction and $2.5 million expense with it about 80% complete, his wife died suddenly at age 42 in 1904. He sent a telegram to the builder and stopped construction forever and never came back to the island, which he had named Heart Island. He died with an estate of $22 million in 1916, so the refusal to finish the castle had nothing to do with money. His kids sold it to a rich neighbor but it deteriorated until 1987 when the neighbor gave it to the 1000 Island Bridge Authority, which has stabilized the castle and outbuildings and is restoring it to the condition at the time of the wife's death, but has a long way to go. Tourist fees are the source of revenue and they should get a lot of money from that, as it was covered up with tourists from Canada and the US. It's in the States and marked our first return to the States in over a month, if you count New York. We did cruise past a summer home for Irving Berlin where he composed several of his hit songs. Out by the wharf at Berlin's home, there is an oversized sculpture of Nipper, the RCA dog with her head cocked as she listens to her master's voice coming from a gramophone. For those of you who haven't met Duke, he's a double for Nipper, except for sex, even the black spot on one eye and no brown, just black & white.

The next day we went into Kingston to get the Durango a quick lube and did another restaurant with no toothpicks, Chez Piggy, for lunch. It's in an old courtyard with an outdoor patio and Pookie observed that it was the type of place her niece, Holly, would like. Holly is going to need a rich husband. We also did the Museum of Correctional Services, yep, that's a museum of prisons. Some of you have asked how I find these places and it's a talent. Kingston has the most prisons in Canada. We walked around the downtown and lakefront and remembered the last time we were here when we were stopped by the Mounties on the highway outside Kingston for 2 hours by a roadblock because the Queen was in Kingston. When you are traveling with 2 small children in the hot summer and have to sit on the roadside for 2 hours, you remember.

Canadian Trivia:

1. Until 1947, Canadians who traveled abroad carried British passports.
2. Queen Victoria selected Ottawa as the Canadian capitol to resolve the dispute between Montreal and Toronto over the capitol designation. She did the same thing in Australia, picking Canberra, between Sydney and Melbourne. Too bad Prince Charles didn't inherit some of Victoria's diplomatic skills.
3. About 2/3 of Canadians live in Quebec and Ontario and the rest are scattered over 8 other provinces and 3 territories.
4. About 75% of Canadians live within 40 miles of the USA border.
5. A recent poll discovered that very few Canadians knew much about their own history, compared to the USA. 85% of US citizens could name our 1st president, but only 7% of Canadians could name their 1st Prime Minister.
6. Canada lost 60,000 soldiers in WWI, a higher proportion than England.
7. Ottawa is the coldest capitol city in the Western World.
8. Quebec City has tides of 3 to 5 meters, but no salt or brackish water. The volume of fresh water from the St. Lawrence overcomes the tides so you have to go 20 miles east of Quebec City to find salt water.
9. Canada is the 2nd largest country in the world, after Russia, but only has 31 million inhabitants, which makes it the country with the fewest inhabitants per square mile in the world.

Finis

Sent: Saturday, July 14, 2001 11:37 AM
Subject: Toronto & Niagara Falls

Toronto has traffic worse than L.A. and nearly as bad as Washington, DC. They've got an interstate system that is a total loser. Going through town there are 3 or 4 express lanes on the inside and divided by concrete, 3 or 4 "collector" lanes going the same direction on the outside. About every 3 miles there are crossovers from express to collector and vice versa, but on the same level. This means that anyone getting on a collector who wants to get on the express has to cross about 6 lanes minimum to get there and the same is true for people leaving express to exit the whole system who have to cross a bunch of lanes to exit. The result is a huge slowdown or stops every few miles and traffic just crawls along since the volume is so high that all 6 or 7 or even occasionally 8 lanes are full. Everyone told us to take the subway downtown and after driving through the city to our campground, we did. Toronto is Canada's largest city and really spread out. There are clusters of high-rise buildings scattered all over town and not just downtown on the lake. Our first day, we parked at a huge mall that had a subway stop adjacent to it and accessible from the mall, but it took 30 minutes to get to the mall.

The CN Tower (CN stands for Canada National) is worth seeing, but the crowds were so large that it took us 2 hours, mostly standing in lines, to tour it. It's the world's tallest freestanding structure and has 2 observation decks with the tallest at 1465 feet, the highest observation deck in the world. Spectacular views all around from the top deck and you can see New York State from there. A beautiful sunshine day, but it got hot for the first time in a month—up to 91. The tower is right on the lake with a small airport adjacent to it and airplanes are landing far below the tower. The lower observation deck has a revolving restaurant and 2 levels of deck with the lower deck floor made of Plexiglas in places so you can look down under your feet for 15 stories. I had to shame Pookie into standing on that part, but she finally did. There is a movie at street level about the construction of the tower in 1976 that is a lot scarier than the tower. Watching construction guys standing on the very top, 1833 feet up and about 2 feet wide while they unfurl a Canadian flag in a strong wind and totally ignore the ground. The antennas on top were lowered into place by a sky crane helicopter, but guys were hanging on the sides of the receiving sections to guide the antenna sections into place and bolt them on. Those guys ought to get paid more than NFL quarterbacks.

We rode the subway back to the Mall after lunch to see "Cats and Dogs" and the electricity went out in the whole mall 15 minutes into the movie. Emergency lighting came on and we were all escorted out before it got hot and told to come back the next day and keep our ticket stubs as they couldn't open the cash registers to give refunds. It was still early, but we went back to the campground as we had left Duke in the trailer with the AC on and were concerned he might get too hot with no AC. Electricity was still on at the campground, but it stayed off for 2 hours at the mall.

The next day we went by subway to the Bata Shoe Museum. Yep, the history, and examples of all kinds of footwear. Pookie is an Imelda Marcos type who owns as many shoes as Imelda and just HAD to see this museum. She said she was really sorry that her shoe shopping buddy, Sally, never got to see it. She and Sally used to drive 150 miles one way to go shoe shopping in Humboldt, TN at a Simmons Shoe Store. Sally once gave Pookie a pin that said, "If the shoe fits, buy it". The first thing in the museum is a copy of fossilized footprints of a male, female and child of Homo erectus carbon dated to 3.7 million years ago. Pookie said they were probably going shoe shopping, as the prints were bare footed. The museum was on 4 floors and was surprisingly interesting. One floor was all about the Chinese custom of foot binding with examples and the types of shoes the women wore with bound feet. Kind of revolting. The exhibits of Native American and Eskimo footwear were really interesting. One half of one floor was an exhibit of all the types of athletic shoes made worldwide. I never knew Nike even made that many.

After lunch, we did the Royal Ontario Museum, known locally as the ROM. A really excellent museum and the 4th most visited in North America. It's huge and is sort of like visiting 3 or 4 Smithsonian Museums at the same time as it combines archaeology with history and minerals and culture and natural science. They do their own archaeology projects worldwide and have special exhibits on them along with the dinosaurs, Egyptian mummies, Etruscan artifacts and other things you expect. For the first time I can remember, we did a guided tour of the Museum, which takes you to all levels and highlights a few galleries on all floors with a tour guide, before you begin to explore on your own. After the guided tour, we did another detailed guided tour of a single special exhibit on Dionysus, the Greek God of Wines and Revelry, a.k.a. Bacchus to the Romans. Pookie got her shoes, so I got the booze exhibit. Fascinating! The average Roman drank a liter of wine per day. No wonder they conquered the world! They thought they were sword proof! I too become more powerful when I drink. Dionysus had a mortal mother, but Zeus was his father, so he really was a god, and kind of complex too. He was not only the god of wine and revelry; he was also the god of fertility for crops and of the netherworld and of theatre. Dionysus led a band of cult followers comprised of satyrs (male) and maenads (female). Satyrs were lusty forest creatures who spent their lives drinking wine and chasing women. Need I say more? We went back to the movie and saw "Cats and Dogs" completely this time. O.K., but not really good. Dionysus was better.

We moved to Niagara Falls, NY the next day, which we had done in 1975 with the kids also. Back then we did the Canadian side or Horshoe Falls, which is much larger than the American side. This time we did the American Falls and took the Maid of the Mist boat ride up to the edge of the Falls. Before we had done the tour under the falls where you walk through a tunnel wearing a heavy yellow oilcloth slicker back then and got all wet from the spray. Now you get a lightweight blue disposable plastic poncho to wear on the boat, but you still get wet. I suggested to Pookie that we were just a couple of honeymooners doing Niagara Falls, but not much response. Bridal Veil Falls, the small fall on the American side has tours under the fall, but we skipped that. On the Canadian side, the eco friendly, ultra green Canadians have permitted some high rise hotels to be built overlooking the Falls and messing up the view, but on the American side it is all a state park and much prettier without development. There is now also a hot air balloon ride on the American side attached to a steel cable tether that takes tourists up to overlook the Falls from outside the state park, but isn't as offensive as the hotels. Another gorgeous day and the State Park had beautiful grounds with a lot of flowers in bloom. At night, the flow of the Falls is greatly reduced and more hydropower is produced and used to fill a pump storage facility nearby that releases the water in the daytime to generate power. In the 1960's the American Falls flow was totally diverted to the Canadian side by a dam so scientists could study a huge rockslide that collapsed on the American side. They decided to leave it in its natural state as it is slowing down the erosion of the Falls and propping up the ledges and will eventually erode anyway. Pookie treated me to a virtual reality ride in a helicopter over the Falls done with a video mask and sitting in chairs that move up and down and sideways. She's still a little kid at heart.

We're now in New Milford, PA on the way to Carlisle, PA to pick up our son Will and take him to Nashville where his family has been visiting his in-laws for 4 weeks. No more tours on this trip. Got to go take Pookie to Cracker Barrel for lunch. No soul food in 6 weeks.
South Bound and Down

Chapter 10. Florida Tour #2—2002

Sent: Saturday, January 26, 2002 12:14 PM
Subject: Florida Tour #2

Hi Gang! We're in Miami, or rather 10 miles west of Miami in the fruit, flower and vegetable fields surrounded by migrant farm workers and in a campground with maybe 40 loose cats to keep Duke active. No travelogue on this trip yet because the laptop died a few days ago. It can be repaired, but only by Toshiba, so I bought a used laptop yesterday. It has all the functions of mine, and I think it's stolen. 450-megahertz processor, 64 meg memory, 6-gigabyte hard drive, Windows 98 SE and CD Rom and floppy disk with 56k modem. Paid about 1/3 what mine cost 18 months ago. Got the e-mail addresses from several of you, as the old laptop can't be turned on to access the address book. No user manual for the used laptop and no software either, so I had them copy a Windows 98SE CD Rom to the hard drive in case I need it. I don't have a spellchecker program and won't till I can add a word processing program, so bear with me.

We're doing a repeat of our trip to Florida 2 years ago, except no trip to Key West this time and touring different things while visiting friends and relatives—two distinctly different groups which sometimes are similar. We spent 2 nites at Will & Sara's in their driveway and won't make that mistake again. They have 2 cats and Duke isn't welcome in the house and makes us acutely aware of his displeasure. Will says Duke becomes manic—depressive when he loses eye contact with me. I call it separation anxiety, but Will thinks Duke may be emotionally scarred for life when he can't be with me, although Pookie is a satisfactory temporary substitute. She sat out in Will's front yard with Duke on a stakeout chain and he was quiet. Will asked how often she had to baby sit. Of course, one of Will's cats he calls Norman Bates, from the "Psycho" movie, as the cat is totally psychotic, so he doesn't have a lot of room to talk.

Pookie has tried to punish me for not giving her more than 2 days to load all her nesting materials into the trailer before we left. For example, the laptop was working fine when I shut it down the last time and Pookie tried to turn it on and the on/off switch is now broken. Guess who gets credit for that? It was near freezing when we left home and got up to 78 on the trip down, so the next day I put on my sandals & shorts. Discovered that Pookie had picked up a left sandal from one pair and a right from another. They look similar, but the right one is about 1/2 inch higher due to a thicker sole. Wearing them makes you limp, or you tend to walk in a circle. It was only after we couldn't find a new pair that she admitted that my cheap plastic sandals were in the trailer—she hates them and wanted me to buy a new pair of Birkenstock sandals. Next, I asked if she had brought the remote for the Dish satellite receiver—the answer is not printable. You can't use the satellite without the remote. I told her I would buy another remote, so we began calling dealers. Couldn't find one who had extra remotes to sell, but finally found one in the old downtown part of Pensacola who said he'd sell me a remote for $45 (Pookie had called our dealer and he said he'd give us another one free, but he's in Tennessee). Will & Sara rode with us to show us where the dealer was located. The building was in a slum area with a concrete block in front of the door and a hand painted sign that said to come around to the side door. Only one guy wearing a dirty t-shirt there and the place was filthy and junked up. The guy said he ran 15 trucks from that location. Will & I think he never saw a truck except the high jacked ones he bought from. The price was now $48 plus as he added on state sales tax. I'm convinced Jeb Bush will never see that tax. As we drove away, Will said he wasn't coming back to that neighborhood and if the remote didn't work I'd have to come back by myself. I told him the guy would be gone forever before we got 5 blocks away. When we were about 6 blocks away, Pookie turned the remote over and on the back was tape with "Master Bedroom" printed on it.

We spent the next 2 nites in Tallahassee in the "Big Oak" campground right north of I-10 under huge live oak trees with Spanish moss. I was walking Duke and met a couple walking a black dachshund and a yellow parakeet. Yep, "Ole Yeller" was the name of the bird perched on the guy's shoulder and "Blackie" was the dog. They were from Houston and the guy had never seen such big live oaks. He got a tape measure and measured the crown of one tree at 150 feet, but I told him there were a lot of bigger ones in MS and LA. There was a private cemetery across the street where we walked Duke and we discovered walking around it that it had a crematorium, funeral home and florist shop also located on the cemetery grounds. That guy has a better and more certain monopoly than Bill Gates. I guess he hasn't thought to add a nursing home yet.

We toured the old State Capitol building and caught a private tour for a group of Boy Scouts. I told them I used to be a scout and they let us tag along. It's a pretty old building and about half of it is a state museum and the rest still has state offices. The Senate and House chambers are done in red, white and blue with period furniture from the time when the capitol was opened in the 1840's. It was quite interesting as FL is unique in a lot of ways. For one, the governor is a particularly weak executive, by design and can't even choose his own cabinet. Six cabinet officers are elected by statewide vote including the attorney general, secretary of state, comptroller, treasurer, etc. Isn't it funny that during all the hoopla about Katherine Harris and certifying of the FL vote, we were never told she was elected by the voters, and not an appointee? We were there on a Sunday and all the material, including the internet report that the new Capitol, which is a modern skyscraper adjacent to the old Capitol, has tours on weekends and holidays, but it was closed. Pookie asked in the old Capitol and was told that it has been closed on weekends and holidays since 9-11 for security reasons. We couldn't park anywhere near the Capitol and there were armed guards and concrete barriers at all driving entrances to the Capitol complex. I guess with a Bush as governor they are at heightened risk of a terrorist attack. Florida was the 3rd state to secede from the Union after SC and MS and had the smallest population of any Southern state during the War of Northern Aggression.

We also toured the Mission San Louis in Tallahassee for an hour or so. It housed about 1500 Apalachee Indians and Franciscan monks and Spanish soldiers in the 17th century. It has been excavated by archaeologists and reconstructed except for the fort, which is now being excavated. There is the customary video and a walking tour around the complex, which includes a church compound of 3 buildings, a Spanish house and 2 huge Indian thatched roof council houses and the chief's house. They even have interpretative guides in period costumes. The Spanish themselves burned and abandoned the Mission in 1704 two days before a British raiding party from Charleston would have done it for them. It's worth a visit if you get to Tallahassee.

We drove to Homosassa Springs the next day, Confederate Flag Day as Emmett calls it, in a carwash rainstorm for all of the morning. Ate lunch at Barbeque Bill's restaurant in Chiefland and if any of you are constipated, go there for rapid relief. We stayed at Turtle Creek RV Resort and Campground in Homosassa Springs. While we were checking in the phone rang and some guy asked the lady if they had a heated pool. She said yes, how many in your party. Then I heard her say that they wouldn't accept 6 children and the campground was really for old folks and adults. When she hung up, I told her I had a Jack Russell Terrier, which was kind of like having 2 children and would he be O.K? She said they had 4 Jack Russells as permanent tenants and that would only be $1 extra per nite. The office building had a wide porch around both sides and the front and in front were several old geezers sitting in chairs watching the activity going on. There was a campground blackboard on the front porch between two of the lounge chairs and I asked Pookie if she had read what it said. She said no, so I told her to read it. Written in white chalk in a beautiful cursive handwriting was, "Roy Edwards died last nite". Immediately following that sentence was written, "Bingo on Wed. at 7". Pookie fell out laughing and wanted to take a picture of the blackboard, but was too embarrassed to do it with the old geezers watching. I'm sure old Roy is pleased that he got top billing, but I bet he gets erased before the Bingo schedule does as there was an eraser on the ledge below the blackboard.

That afternoon we toured the Homosassa Springs State Wildlife Park. It is very well done and houses nearly all the bird and animal species native to FL. We started with the manatee feeding and a talk by a park ranger. There are 9 female manatees in the Springs, which put out 2 million gallons per hour of water at 72 degrees. They can't have males in the same area as the offspring wouldn't survive in the wild without training by their mothers and the area where the females are kept is too small for additional manatees. A fascinating lecture about manatees and we watched the feeding from only a few feet away. The largest manatee is 3,000 lb. and there is an underwater observation area also. They were feeding carrots and lettuce and vitamin pills by hand while we were there. The lettuce was Romaine and better than what we buy. Manatees live 50-70 years and nurse their young with a nipple under each flipper. The Springs are full of salt-water fish also, including red snapper, yellow fins, etc. and nobody knows how long they can stay in freshwater. We walked all over the Park which has deer, black bear, Florida panthers, bobcats, foxes, squirrels and a lot of native birds including pelicans, flamingos, herons, ibis, ducks, etc. and of course the alligators, turtles and reptiles. Pookie noticed a lot of mirrors in the bird area and asked about it. It turns out that the mirrors are a failed experiment. Flamingos will not mate or breed unless they are in a large flock and the Park only had about 25 so they added mirrors to try and fool the flamingos. Now they've added more flamingos to try and get them to breed. A very well run State Park with a boat ride down the Homosassa River to get to the Park and a tram ride back.

Duke pulled a new one that nite. There were squirrels all over the campground, but he usually stops hunting at nite. That nite, a cat kept hanging around the trailer to keep Duke stirred up after dark, but we thought nothing of it. In the bedroom of the trailer there is a window designed as an escape hatch if the door gets stuck. It's a large window that opens from the bottom and pushes out with a removable screen and is labeled as an escape hatch. We noticed Duke was missing and looked in the bedroom and the escape hatch window was open with the screen gone. Duke had launched himself at it from the bed and gone out cat hunting as I had left it open for a breeze. He had been gone maybe 20 minutes before I noticed, but I found him under a tree where the cat had taken refuge. Now we keep the window shut. I wonder if he read the label.

We left the next morning for Sarasota to see Steve & Allen and I'll pick up here on the next episode.
Pookie's Perfection

Sent: Wednesday, January 30, 2002 9:04 AM
Subject: Heading South

We stopped on the way to Sarasota at Weeki Wachee Springs, a few miles south of Homosassa Springs. Pookie asked why and I told her we had stopped there on our honeymoon and I wanted to see how it had changed. She had no recollection, so I told her they had mermaids performing underwater and breathing from air hoses. Still no recollection, but she recovered well by telling me she was so intensely in love that she couldn't remember anything else—obviously she wants something. I don't think they have even painted the place since 1963, and some of the mermaids may be the same, but they've added a water park, which was closed for the season. After buying tickets, we were directed to the Wags & Whiskers Pet show where dogs & cats performed tricks, yep, even cats. An Australian Shepherd did about 5 tricks and then they brought out a Jack Russell. Pookie said, "See, they can be trained"! The Jack Russell did only one trick, walking on his hind legs across the room while trying to eat a treat. Duke does that routinely without any training by anyone, which Pookie had to admit, under duress. A bus tour came in and then we went to the underwater observatory to see the mermaid show. After a short delay, they announced that the mermaids had the flu and the show had been canceled—after selling us the tickets 45 minutes before. Instead, we got to see a mermaid demonstration by Geena and Holly, a redhead and brunette. It was like I remembered with underwater ballet and deep dives down to 117 feet and a narrator telling us how they breathed through the hoses, kept their vertical distance stable underwater and how long they could hold their breath. We should have skipped it.

We got to Sarasota about 3:30 and went directly to the kennel where we had left Duke 2 years before. Pookie had called from the road and they had his records out on the counter. We presented his passport, his rabies vaccination record, and were informed that under FL law, he couldn't be boarded because he had no kennel cough shot. The kennel called a vet about 2 miles away and we raced over there and got him a kennel cough inoculation by fluid in the nose, which takes effect immediately instead of after a few days like a shot. Raced back to the kennel, which closed at 4:30 and made it with 5 minutes to spare. A different person was at the desk and she informed us that he still couldn't stay, as he had no distemper shot on his record. I got a little mad at not being told before about the distemper, but the lady called our vet in Pulaski and got the blue haired little old lady receptionist on the phone to see if the distemper shot had just been left off of the certification, as it is usually combined with the rabies shot. Pookie said blue hair was sweet and would never let Pookie pay for anything, which she charged to me, but I said she was barely competent and we rarely got charged. Blue hair proceeded to tell the Sarasota kennel that they hadn't seen Duke in Pulaski since 2000. The Sarasota lady said she was holding a certificate dated in March 2001 and signed by our vet. Blue hair said she couldn't work the computer very well. After coaching by the Sarasota lady, Blue hair decided Duke had received all his shots in 2001, but she had left them off his record. We paid for extra playtime for Duke and escaped without him.

Went to Steve & Allen's house and set up in the driveway and then I began to sample his scotch inventory. Allen fed us a great meal. The next day we went out in a rented boat into the Gulf and Intracoastal canal and the bays and inlets around Sarasota. I offered to split the cost of the boat, but Allen wouldn't agree, so I told them we would return in a few years after they had replenished their bank accounts. Ate a picnic lunch on some key near Midnight Pass where 2 big houses are sliding into the surf and have been condemned. A gorgeous day with sun and clouds and about 82 for a high. The weather here has been about 10 or 11 degrees above normal the whole time we've been here with a high of 89 and usually in the mi 80s. Greenie (My name for Allen) fed us again that nite and the last nite we ate at their Country Club with Mike (retired CIA agent) and Cristina—a really good leech job, even if I do say so myself. We met David & Mary Wade from Pulaski the last day at Mote Marine, a Sarasota aquarium and afterward ate lunch at the Salty Dog. A superb grouper sandwich and friends of Mary Wade & David from Tunica, MS joined us for lunch. Brad & Brenda and he farms 9,000 acres of cotton. He knew my ex brother-in-law and I knew Roy Flowers and his nephew David Flowers who was a good friend of his. I managed to out fumble David who picked up the check for everyone while I talked on Pookie's phone to Betty. If anyone needs lessons, I can be persuaded to provide leech training for a small fee, or you can go see my brother Will, the master leech.

When we went back to the kennel on our way to Miami, I walked in and met a 3rd person on the desk. When I told her we were there to pick up Duke, she started laughing. I asked if Duke had been entertaining them and she said they all had played with Duke as he was so much fun. She said all the other dogs slept on their beds, but Duke jumped up on a small wall in the kennel and slept there where he could see up and down the row of dog runs and keep everything in view. We took Alligator Alley, the toll road across the Everglades, which was open to the east, but closed going west due to a huge wreck that morning in the fog. Sixteen 18-wheelers had collided in the fog headed west and their loads were all over the hi-way. Three people had been killed and the hi-way had re-opened to the east a few minutes before we got there. One flat bed truck had carried a load of telephone poles, which had ended up in the eastbound lanes and killed 1 person. All the trucks were still in the west bound lanes and torn open with cargos everywhere and heavy equipment was trying to separate them and clear the hi-way. Two loads of Canada Dry were all over the place. Checked into the KOA campground west of Miami and discovered they had a 9/10-

mile asphalt, walking track around the exterior of the campground, so I took Duke around a few times.

Saturday afternoon we went to Biscayne Nat. Park and booked the 3-hour boat tour in a glass bottom boat over the coral reefs for Sunday morning. When we were here 2 years ago, it was in the 40s and windy and all boat tours had been canceled. Biscayne is mostly water and covers 285 square miles and can only be seen from a boat. We had sailed through it in a rented sailboat with Linda & Gordon about 15 years ago on the way down to the Keys. Biscayne is the only Nat. Park I know about that has no admission fee and the grounds around the Visitor Center were covered up with picnickers, kayakers, fishermen, etc. on a warm day with a lot of young people in bathing suits. More later. King Leech

Sent: Friday, February 01, 2002 4:12 PM
Subject: Key Biscayne & North

Sunday we did the glass bottom boat ride in Biscayne Nat. Park with about 35 others. A beautiful day with a nice breeze and about 82 when we left and about 86 when the ride ended 3 hours later. Had a young male Park Ranger on the boat describing the coral and the few fish we saw. He did explain how the mango trees and sponges keep the water so clear. The boat engines made enough noise to scare away most of the fish. We rode through a channel between the islands out to the coral reef, the 3rd largest in the world that goes from Biscayne Bay down to the Dry Tortugas. Viewing through a glass bottom is not nearly as striking as snorkeling and leaves a lot to be desired. We did pass over a 15th century shipwreck, but all that remains are the ballast stones as everything else has been removed or rotted away. About 15 years ago we snorkeled over this same reef in Pennecamp State Marine Park off Key Largo when we were on the sailboat trip with Linda & Gordon. The best sight I saw this time was a guy rubbing sun tan lotion on his blonde honey while she wore a thong bikini—a lot better than the fish & birds. Saw one boat that had tried to leave the channel stuck on a mud flat and about 1 mile further our captain radioed a red towboat that was anchored, waiting for the business. The captain warned us about hanging our arms and legs out of the boat as we left or returned to the dock. He suggested that we did not want to experience Biscayne Nat. Park—are you ready for this? —Pier pressure. A nice excursion, but no dolphins or other marine life spotted. I was amazed at the number of private pleasure boats in the Park and the crab and lobster pots that the Park Service permits to be used in the Park.

After the ride, we drove to the condo of our friends Rudy & Yolanda on the very tip end of Key Biscayne. They are Cuban and came to the USA in the 60s and speak Spanish fluently. We met them on the trip to Australia, Fiji & New Zealand last year. Their condo is on the 15th floor of a 27-story building and they have balconies overlooking the Atlantic to the east and Biscayne Bay to the west with breathtaking views. Later that evening we watched the sun set to the west and then went to the east balcony and watched a full moon rise in the east, casting shadows from clouds on the dark waters as cruise ships sailed past on the horizon bound for the Caribbean. A large sailing schooner was anchored about 1/2 mile off the beach with red & white anchor lights outlining the shape of its masts. From both balconies we could see No Name Harbor at the tip of the key where we had anchored one night in the sailboat. Views to kill for if you don't have vertigo.

Rudy & Yolanda took us to a Cuban restaurant in Little Havana for a traditional Cuban meal. The menus were in Spanish and English, but the waiters were old men and spoke no English. I had a very thin steak with onions and fried plantains with white rice and black bean sauce and Pookie ate a chicken and yellow rice meal with fried sweet potatoes—delicious. I tried to pick up the check and almost got it until Yolanda said something to the waiter in Spanish and he snatched the check back. I asked and she laughed and said she had told him my credit card was stolen. Out fumbled them again! They gave us a riding tour of Little Havana and Pookie asked what a sign on a storefront in Spanish meant. Rudy laughed and said it meant Jewelry and commented that women didn't need to know the language to smell them out. We also rode around Coconut Grove where the houses start in the millions. Our hosts were delightful and we had a very nice day.

Drove up I-95 the next day to Delray Beach to see Jim & Laura. We parked in a campground in Delray and left Duke in the trailer and drove to their house. They have a 17-year-old cat and Duke was specifically uninvited. Laura fixed Omaha steaks that someone had given them for Xmas and made a salad and a potato dish (eat your heart out Dan Quale). Best of all, she had out some of her Granddad's scotch, and he died 15 years ago. I got one drink of the good stuff and then was switched to Clan McGregor. Laura must know me fairly well. I think she was trying for the Betty Crocker Award, as I sure didn't know she was that domestic. She rides a Harley sometimes and I didn't know she could cook like that. Nice visit with them that we enjoyed a lot. Laura is Pookie's 1st cousin once removed, but is more like a niece than a cousin.

The next morning we drove to Lake Okeechobee as I had never been in that part of FL and wanted to see it. It's the 2nd largest fresh water lake wholly in the USA in area and there is a dike around all of it for water flow control with a 110-mile hiking/bicycling trail on the top of the dike. You actually can't see the lake for the dike except where canals lead out of the lake and the highway is elevated over them. About 30 miles before you get to the lake from the east you enter a rich black dirt agricultural area that is about 90% sugar cane. They grow it constantly and some fields are being burned while others are freshly planted and others are half mature or awaiting harvest. It's all drained swampland and extremely fertile. The lake is only about 10/12 feet deep on average and is noted for bass fishing and fish camps are all around the eastern side, although I don't know about the rest of it. We stayed in a public campground at Pahokee right on the shore of the lake with electric & water hookups. The lady at the campground was funny and Pookie had called for a reservation from the road and was told she got one even before she gave out any name. The lady did say that they might not have a shore front space left when we got there. When we arrived we discovered that ALL the spaces were shorefront. We got site #24 and I asked where that was as most campgrounds give out site maps or lead you to your site. The lady told me that #24 was 6 before I got to 30. I knew we were on a roll when we pulled up at our site and parked next door was a car from TN with a "Gore in 2004" bumper sticker. It turned out that the guy was the democratic party chairman for Knox county or Knoxville. I cheerfully told him that I didn't vote for Gore, as I knew Gore personally. Pookie told me to quit being ugly. We did watch a gorgeous sunset over the lake, which the locals call The Big Lake. Met a nice couple from New Jersey who drove a converted Greyhound bus and had been to Alaska in it the year before. They had taken a bus trip with a group above the Arctic Circle and really enjoyed Alaska. Like us, they said they saw a lot more wildlife in British Columbia than Alaska and they too had spent 3 days in Denali Nat. Park and never saw Mt. McKinley.

We left the next day for Vero Beach to visit Samantha & Chris, another 1st cousin once removed of Pookie's. Again we left Duke in the trailer and went to their house, as they have 3 cats and a black Labrador. It was Abbey's 3rd birthday and I had offered to take them to dinner, so we ended up at the Ocean Grill, about 20 feet from the surf. It was a superb seafood restaurant, but we had to wait about 30 minutes to get a table. I headed for the bar with Chris and we both ordered a double scotch. Chris insisted on picking up the bar tab which was $24 plus without tip and I went into deep depression anticipating the dinner check. I did get our waitress to bring Abbey some ice cream in a small bowl with a candle and get other waitresses to join in singing Happy Birthday. Abbey was a little shy about it but seemed very pleased. An excellent dinner and the bill was less than I expected. It was our first visit to Chris & Sam's house and after dinner Chris' Mom & Dad came over for a short visit before we left. Another enjoyable evening with Pookie's relatives. Pookie committed us to come to Greenville, MS next Thanksgiving to see them again with Laura & Jim at Pookie's cousin's house. On to Jacksonville to see Ginny, and check out her new boyfriend. Ginny is my real niece. I'm sure brother Will has told Ginny to select a 5 star restaurant. The good news is that Will thinks Chili's is a 5 star restaurant, according to Ginny. Ex Leech

Evan Davis

Sent: Tuesday, February 05, 2002 8:33 PM
Subject: Gini, Ginny, Okefenokee & Warm Springs

O.K. Gang, we're home now and it's COLD. Got tired of the 89 degree and 90% humidity in Miami, but could get used to it again. Currently about 30 degrees and humidity still around 90%. I finally added the Norton Symantec anti-virus software to the laptop and discovered 18 infected files, 17 of which I could repair and 1 of which I had to delete. Had the party virus and another that I didn't know called majistry or something like that? I warned yall that I thought I was infected.

Being partially brain dead (that means OLD) I completely forgot to mention that we visited Gini & Alberta after Laura & Jim (also forgot to give Jim credit for the cooking of the Omaha steaks—but Laura got credit for the marinating that made them great). Gini has a condo on Springer Island in Palm Beach County where we had lunch before we drove to the Big Lake. Met Gini in a parking lot of a Mall and left Duke in the trailer while we went to Gini's condo for lunch. Alberta has a condo nearby and met us at Gini's. I BOUGHT (read that Charlie!) salads and a bottle of wine at a fancy delicatessen at Singer Island for lunch and we ate on Gini's balcony on the 11th or 12th floor of the condo overlooking the Atlantic and Palm Beach Bay. Nice view, but Gini is scared of heights, so I had to give her the inside of the table. Really enjoyed seeing Gini & Alberta and catching up on Nashville dirt.

In Jacksonville, we went to Fernandina Beach the first day. We had almost moved there after I retired and really like the town. Went to the real estate homes we looked at, and the one we liked at $190,000 is now on sale for $419,000. I have good taste! Spent the morning at the Beach and it was about 95. Sorry Duke couldn't go, as it was too hot to leave him in the Durango.

Met Ginny for dinner at her apt., and liked it better than her old one. Off Marco Blvd., and only a few blocks from the old one. Went out to the beach at Jacksonville to meet David, the new boyfriend that brother Will told me not to run off. During the dinner conversation, Ginny managed to mention that he was an Eagle Scout! He was much more subtle & just mentioned the Boy Scouts and asked me about Arizona & New Mexico. I asked if he had ever been to Philmont and opened the floodgates. Ginny found a 5 star restaurant—happy Will? —for dinner and it was great! Best dinner I had in FL this trip! I like FL weddings if Ginny can keep him that interested. May offer to subsidize the honeymoon if I get a good trip out of it!

Left for Okefonokee Swamp in GA the next day. A really nice state park, Stephen S. Foster State Park, in the middle of the swamp, if any of you want to go. It's leased from the Nat. Park Service by GA and really well done. I was amazed at the campground. Cable TV, and electric & water hookups in the middle of the swamp, about 18 miles from anywhere, and the cell phone worked too. We took the guided tour boat trip by a female ranger and if you go, do that. It's about a 2 hour tour, but she makes it interesting and well worth the cost which is $10 per head. Lots of alligators and turtles, and a lot of interesting bird life too. The swamp is fed only by rainwater and is in the middle of a 3-year drought. You can see the normal water level by looking at the cypress knees. I wished we had enough time to go to the east entrance (we did the west) as the east is totally different and has open grassland prairies and marsh instead of cypress swamps. I may go back sometime when Pookie isn't in a hurry to get to a Vandy game.

Drove to Forsyth the next day to get cable TV for the Super Bowl. I'm really proud of myself for staying up to the end and seeing the Patriots win. Good thing I went double or nothing with Mel on the outcome. Now I don't have to buy him a dinner. I'm sure he'll be magnanimous about it! Did Warm Springs, GA on the way home, and don't bother. FDR owned his only house here, but it's not impressive. I don't know how he found the damn place as we had a Rand McNally Road Atlas, and it was damn near impossible for us. Took us about 1 1/2 hours to do the Museum, Little White House, and we skipped the warm springs which were a 1 mile drive away. Do Tara instead!

Finis Chronicler

Sent: Thursday, February 07, 2002 7:26 PM
Subject: Random Ruminations from Florida Tour #2

1. North Florida & South Georgia must have the highest percentage of rednecks in the entire world. You would think that Arkansas would have the lead, but Arkansas is so thinly populated that when "White Trash Clinton" moved to New York, Arkansas dropped in the rankings.
2. Why do the automobile makers put the fake rear view mirror on the outside right of autos with the words "Objects are much closer than they appear" written on the mirror? It can't save that much money, can it? Is it to cause wrecks so they can sell more cars? Write your local car dealer and let's get real mirrors put there.
3. Florida was the only Confederate state east of the Mississippi River that did NOT have it's state capitol taken by Union troops during the War of Northern Aggression. The Yankees tried, but were defeated by a Confederate force east of Tallahassee and only entered the capitol after the Confederate surrender.
4. Okefenokee is a Creek Indian word meaning "trembling earth" or something like that. There are 17 islands in the Okefenokee

Swamp ranging from 5,000 to 2 acres (the Park is 396,000 acres) and the rest is peat bogs, floating on water or methane gas that "trembles" or moves when you walk on it. The state park rents canoes and small flat bottom boats with 7 horsepower motors as well as offering guided ranger tours. We surprised and motored past a young couple in a rented canoe in the cypress swamp who were "making out" on a peat bog. Must be sort of like a waterbed.

5. When we got to the Visitor Center we found there is a boat harbor next to it where they rent the canoes and small boats. An alligator about 7 feet long was lounging in the middle of the boat harbor. I heard a couple renting a canoe ask, "What do we do if the canoe turns over?" The ranger said to not make any splashing sounds or churn the water and just upright the canoe and climb back into it quietly and the alligators will ignore you. RIGHT! Sounds like good advice to me. We took the pontoon boat.

6. Listened on the radio to a lot of economic statistics. Why do they always say, "The core rate of inflation—-excluding the volatile energy and food components—-is x%. When prices vary a lot, do you quit using food or energy? If food or energy prices go up or down a lot, do you quit consuming them? I don't. Why in the hell would we exclude these components, like we quit using them when we don't? Another example of your government trying to mislead you? A plot to think the government is doing better than they are? What am I missing here?

7. I finally cut Duke's dewclaw toenails a few days before we came home. Pookie said he looked like Howard Hughes with the curved and long toenails and shamed me into it.

8. This second hand laptop computer is called a "Power Note", but has no name of a manufacturer on it and I can't find a new battery for it and Battery Plus can't either, but offered to remake my battery for $179, but we passed. Anyone heard of the maker? I only paid $500 for it and I ain't gonna pay $179 for a battery.

Poor Leech

Chapter 11. Alaska & White House Trip—2002

Sent: Wednesday, July 03, 2002 12:39 PM
Subject: North to Alaska (Maybe) By Circuitous Route.

Well, we're off to Alaska by the most indirect route anyone ever took, if we make it. We're currently in Carlisle, PA visiting the grandkids and got here by way of Terre Haute, Indiana where we visited with Evelyn & Louis for 2 days. Not too many things working as planned yet, but we are hard headed and will keep trying for a while. We stopped at a convenience market in Henderson, KY to get some gas and the 2 redneck cashiers were most entertaining. The one waiting on me looked out the window and saw the trailer and Durango and asked, "Are you coming or going?" I answered that I was going and she asked where. I said Alaska and she said, "Can I go, I've always wanted to go". The other one piped up and said, "Me too, and we won't eat much". She couldn't see the trailer and asked if we were coming back on one of them boat things. The other one said, "Naw, he's taking his house with him, but we could ride in the trailer and not bother them at all". Actually, we could take the ferry back down the Inside Passage with the trailer, but we've already done that on a cruise ship and the ferries don't have decent accommodations for pets and Duke would be miserable, so we'll drive both ways. I really want to do the Alaska Highway and we've been to Fairbanks, Anchorage, Seward, Juneau, Ketchikan, Sitka and Glacier Bay on the cruise a few years ago. We've never been to Manitoba, Saskatchewan or the Yukon Territory and want to see parts of them.

We had a nice visit with Ena & Louis and stayed in the Terre Haute KOA as they have 5 cats and it doesn't work to stay in someone's driveway if they have cats and Duke can't go in the house. Actually, Ena & Louis have a huge new (to them) old house on 1.6 acres with a lot of trees and shrubs. I called it a money pit and they didn't object. It was built in 1920 and Louis has been slowly rewiring the whole house. It's in an exclusive section of town (actually in the county and not the city) known as Allendale. Louis says he doesn't often tell new people he meets that he lives in Allendale as they then assume you are wealthy. I told him not to worry, since as long as he drives that 12-year-old Toyota hatchback, they'll figure out he isn't rich. We watched a mother raccoon and her 2 babies eat out of his bird feeder and he says deer eat out of it every night too. Ena made Pookie feel good as they still have moving boxes unpacked from 2 years ago, so the ones we have from 12 years ago may soon have company. We drove past a "Christian Tattoo Parlor" in the old part of Terre Haute. Yep, the guy will only do tattoos of Jesus, angels, the Cross, or other Christian symbols or figures. We ate shish kebob from their grill one nite and it was delicious. We also did Sunday brunch at the main dining room of St. Mary's-in-the Woods College in west Terre Haute and overate again. St. Mary's is a small liberal arts women's Catholic college with about 400 students and I think there are several of them in different states.

We drove across Ohio to Wheeling, West VA and I must admit that Ohio has vastly improved their interstate system since 30 years ago when it was rough as a cob. The next day I took a shortcut thru a rural part of West VA that only cost us about 1 & 1/2 hours, including the detour. Needless to say, my naviguesser was not impressed. Of course, I didn't look at the map like she does, so it wasn't my fault. After a liberal application of wifely advice, I have decided to go back to Ohio through Pennsylvania on the Turnpike. We also enjoyed a 2 hour visit at the friendly Dodge dealer in Morgantown, West VA as the ABS brake system light came on and so did a brake light on the dashboard of the Durango. Seems that an ABS brake sensor on the rear differential that monitors vehicle speed for the braking system had a failure and had to be replaced. We've also had tons of problems with the trailer electrical system and keep blowing the main circuit breakers over and over, in campgrounds and in Will's driveway although it never acted up for the 2 weeks we had it parked in our yard before we left home. I talked to the manufacturer in Denver, PA this a.m. and he can't see us until the 12th of July as he's backlogged, so I'm taking it to the dealer here in Carlisle this afternoon as he can get to it on the 9th, he thinks. The weather has been miserably hot and we can't leave Duke in the trailer if the AC won't work, and I am not staying there either. We're moving to base housing here in Carlisle this afternoon and we put Duke in a kennel here until we can get it fixed.

Now for the real reason we went east to Alaska. Some of you already know, but Pookie's cousin is getting the Congressional Medal of Honor posthumously at a White House ceremony on July 8 and we made the guest list. The way our luck is running, we'll get Cheney instead of Bush. There is also the dedication of a Vietnam Memorial Plaza in Alexandria, VA on July 6 for the same cousin who is the first Army Viet Nam POW to be awarded the MOH. He was Captain Humbert Roque Versace, called Rocky by his friends, and was executed by the Viet Cong. He was a 1959 West Point graduate and Green Beret advisor who was captured by the Viet Cong after a firefight when he accompanied a South Vietnamese patrol that was ambushed. He was severely wounded in the leg, but tried numerous escapes. Since he spoke fluent Vietnamese and French, he understood everything the Viet Cong were saying and absolutely refused all cooperation with them. He insisted on giving only his name, rank and serial # and led the other prisoners in defying his captors. He caused the Viet Cong innumerable problems and was the reason for resistance by his co-prisoners. One of them, a Major James N. Rowe, who escaped after 5 years of captivity, wrote a book, "Five Years to Freedom" in which he describes all Rocky's efforts and activity. When the Vietnamese finally decided to get rid of their problem, they marched Rocky off into the jungle and killed him. He was singing "God Bless America" as they marched him out of sight. He lived in Alexandria, VA when a child and when in the service and the Plaza also honors all other Alexandria residents killed in Viet Nam.

On July 8, the NBC "Today Show" will have a bit about Rocky, but it's a 3 hour show and we don't know how much or when he'll be on. The NBC News Hour at 5:30 or 6:30 that nite will also have a bit about Rocky, if you want to watch. We actually have an old home movie showing Rocky at about age 4 or 5 when he had a head of curly black hair and Pookie sent a copy to his brother, which is probably why we made the White House guest list. Assuming we can get the trailer fixed, we'll head toward Alaska after the ceremonies in DC, which end on July 9. Onward!

Sent: Monday, July 08, 2002 7:40 PM
Subject: Carlisle and DC

Well, we enjoyed the grandchildren in Carlisle, but I discovered that being around Connor (age 3) is sort of like having a Duke that can talk, but doesn't wear a leash, and both have their own agendas, that may or may not coincide with mine. Once when I was walking Duke, Connor insisted on coming along. Duke dived in the creek that goes through the Army base and swam across, so Connor & I walked back on the other side of the creek where no one could see us. When we got back to Will's house, Alicia, Pookie and Rachel were all running around like chickens with heads cut off screaming for Connor to come home. Will had figured he was with me, so he stayed home with Ryan. I promptly received quite specific instructions, from three different generations of females in my family, to advise all when Connor went with me, and he tried to go everywhere I went. He even tried to get in the kennel with Duke when I left Duke at the kennel. It was brutally hot in Carlisle, so we didn't go out too much, but Will did a chicken and shrimp shish kebob on the grill one nite that was great.

We drove down to DC on Fri., following Will and family who lived in DC for a year. We did lunch in Alicia's favorite DC restaurant and checked into the Radisson hotel in Old Town Alexandria, VA with adjoining rooms— Pookie's idea. The kids were really well behaved, except that Ryan (almost age 1) also has his own agenda and tunes up if his Mom gets out of sight. We met Gene & Barbara in the hotel lobby and Tony & Pat Dowd also and retired to the hotel bar in the late afternoon, where Barbara & Pookie were on the alert to meet new family members if they dared to show up. Steve Versace was in the lobby and we did meet quite a few unknown relatives, theirs not mine. I didn't see a single Indian. Will & family joined us in the bar later and all visited for quite a while.

On Sat. morning we all went by car to the Mt. Vernon Community Center and city park in Alexandria, which is about 100 yards from the house on Forest Street where Rocky Versace spent his Jr. High and High School years. That's where the Rocky Versace Vietnam Memorial Plaza has been built directly outside the entrance to the community center and adjacent to the ball fields where he played as a kid. Chairs for maybe 350 had been set up and a tent was there to house the cookies & punch for the reception after the dedication of the Plaza. It had cooled off and there was a nice breeze on a beautiful sunny day. I was genuinely impressed with the ceremony and the Plaza. An assistant Sec. of the Army was present and the Pershing Army Military Band in full dress uniform played before the ceremony. All the local politicians were present and quite a few made comments. There was 1 other MOH winner from Rocky's 1959 West Point Class and 89 members of his class were present, coming from as far away as Europe, Hawaii and even Australia. Retired Brig. Gen. Pete Dawkins was the keynote speaker and I understand why. He was President of the West Point 1959 class, the Heisman Trophy winner in 1958 and captain of the last West Point football team to go undefeated. He also had addressed the West Point cadets last year for the bicentennial celebration of West Point, and is a dynamic speaker and currently a vice-chairman of Citicorp. I was impressed, even if I am a recovering banker.

The crowd was an overflow and maybe 5-600 were present with many standing the whole time. There was even a group of Vietnam Vet Bikers present from "Rolling Thunder", a DC Harley Davidson Bikers Club. I loved reading the patches on their leather jackets. My 2 favorites were, "I'll forgive Jane Fonda when the Jews forgive Hitler" and "Jane Fonda, Communist by Nature, Traitor by Choice". The Plaza is a circle with a concrete bench around the inside and the names of all 65 Alexandria residents who died in Vietnam are carved in the wall above the seat of the bench with a gold star by each name. Twenty-five were officers and 40 enlisted men in all the service branches. In the center of the circle is a bronze statue of Rocky with his hands on 2 Vietnamese children, as he planned to become a priest and serve as a missionary to Vietnamese children who called him Captain Candy. The statues were draped until the end of the ceremony and then unveiled. The artist who created the concept, a young man who lives near Harper's Ferry, made a brief talk and became all emotional and broke down at the end of his remarks. He said his commission became conviction. The black woman who manages the community center sang God Bless America and a bagpiper played "Amazing Grace" at the end of the ceremony followed by the Army bugler playing "Taps". It really was quite moving and I'm glad we and Will & family got to view it.

After the ceremony and the punch and cookies, we all adjourned to the Birchmere Club, about 1/2 mile away, where we had a buffet lunch and a female entertainer/country singer on tour from Branson, MO who entertained us, after an 8 minute video on the creation of the memorial and the work that went into the memorial. We all came back to the hotel and later walked down to the waterfront about 1 block from the hotel where the Alexandria City Symphony was set up in a band shell in a City Park, right on the Potomac, and played a concert for several hours. We ate from the food vendors in the Park—sweet potato French fries and shrimp for me—and around 9:30 p.m. a barge pulled up behind the band shell and the 4th of July fireworks began, 2 days late. The Park was full of people and the fireworks were spectacular. Will's kids were mesmerized and of course, the event ended with the William Tell Overture accompanied by 4 howitzers from the Old Guard at Ft. Meyer, VA that fired off rounds as fast as if there were 12 cannon. I got my hopes up that maybe they were really shelling the Democratic Republic of Maryland across the river, but Will said they were firing blanks. The commercial airliners kept coming down the Potomac on their approach to Reagan Nat. Airport during the fireworks and cannon fire and were about 600 feet above the river and the fireworks were going up several hundred feet. I wonder if any of the pilots needed diapers. More later on the White House ceremony and the stuff we got to attend at Ft. Meyer. Diligent Scribe

Sent: Thursday, July 11, 2002 7:23 PM
Subject: White House

On Sunday, after Will, Alicia & kids left and after Gene & Barbara left along with Tony & Pat, we went to a reception and dinner at the hotel sponsored by the Army. We received nametags there plus our personal hand written, using a flowing calligraphy, invitations to attend the White House ceremony on July 8. We sat at a reserved table for family members, and they had more tables reserved than family present by far. After dinner we viewed a tape of the NBC "Today Show" that was aired on Memorial Day, 2000, more than 2 years ago, about Rocky and another video detailing the efforts to have a local school named for him in Alexandria that was unsuccessful, but led to the successful effort to get the MOH. We also had a short presentation by a General from the Special Forces Command who explained the special ceremony they performed in Sarasota, FL at the nursing home where Rocky's mother lived, shortly before she died in 1999. The nexus of the efforts to honor Rocky came from a very eclectic group called "The Friends of Rocky Versace" started by a group of old friends from Alexandria, but encompassing people from all walks of life as well as his West Point classmates. They raised over $450,000 and the Plaza and

Memorial did not cost a single cent of public funds. We met Duane Frederic, the official Historian of the Rocky Versace Friends, a postal worker from Cleveland, Ohio who never knew Rocky but had put in thousands of hours researching the Army Archives to document Rocky's Vietnam experiences and corroborated all that Nick Rowe had written in the book, "Five Years to Freedom" from other sources and old Army intelligence reports. This was crucial in the award being made, as all the fellow prisoners were dead before the award was approved. Pookie had corresponded with Duane by e-mail, which led to the contact with Steve Versace and our invitation to the White House.

On Monday there was an Army sponsored breakfast where we viewed live the Today Show on NBC. The clip on Rocky came on about 24 minutes into the third hour of the show. NBC had told the Friends it would be on at 9:09 DC time, but it was about 15 minutes late. It was quite well done and lasted about 7 or 8 minutes. We then viewed a 22-minute videotape created by the Special Forces Command titled "A Soldier's Story" which documented the Rocky Story visually and was used to help convince the Army bureaucracy, which has a tradition of not recognizing any POWs for high medals because they got captured in the 1st place, to approve the MOH. After it was over, I asked John Gurr, the chief PR guy for the Friends, how I could get a copy of the tape and about 10 minutes later he brought me a copy containing both the 22 minute "Soldier's Story" and the 2000 "Today Show" clip and wouldn't accept any payment.

At 12:45 we boarded the buses for the White House. Pookie & I got to ride on the 1st bus, a full size 48-passenger Air Force blue motorcoach that was reserved for the family and led the motorcade of 6 buses. We had a motorcycle escort of 7 motorcycle DC cops with red lights flashing who would drive ahead and block off all side streets all the way into the White House. Pookie grinned at me as we drove along and said, "Aren't you glad you married me?" I replied that yes I was, but not for this special treatment. I told her that this was a partial payback for all the first class travel she got free going to banker's conventions in NYC, Chicago, San Francisco, New Orleans, Palm Beach, Bermuda, etc. when she rode on the coattails of her own personal banker. She said that this was more important. When we got to Constitution Ave. the escort turned on sirens and blocked off all traffic until we turned into the approach to the east portico of the White House. I could get used to the big shot treatment. There are concrete barriers and a hydraulically operated steel gate that allows access for vehicles. The Air Force Sergeant driver had to park at the steel gate, turn off the engine and let a bomb sniffing dog sniff all around and under the bus before we were admitted. When we got off the bus, we had to present a government issued ID and get checked off the guest list and then go through metal detectors and purse x-ray machines, just like an airport, and finally were admitted. I heard the rotors of a heavy helicopter and just as we entered the porch,

240

Marine 1 sat down on the south lawn. I told Pookie it was probably bringing Bush back from Kennebunkport where he spent the July 4th weekend. I found a gap in the shrubbery where I could get a very narrow view of the helicopter and got the camera ready. A Marine guard told me I could get a much better view if I went up the marble stairs quickly and looked out the window of the Blue Room. I raced up the stairs and across the large reception hall and got a great shot of W., Laura and the dogs leaving Marine 1 and walking to the White House. The White House has original leaded windowpanes that look wavy if you look directly through them, but I had the camera at an angle and the flash off, so I hope it turns out.

There were 244 of us on the guest list and we had access to the large reception hall, the Blue, Green and Red rooms and a large dining room where large tables laden with heavy hors d'oeuvres awaited us and side tables had soft drinks, coffee, tea and ice tea and tons of waiters hung around picking up any plate you laid down. There were portraits of some of the presidents hanging in no particular order in all of the rooms. I had Pookie take a picture of me standing in front of Reagan's portrait while I stretched out my hand toward him and said, "That's my Man"! Reagan was by far the president of choice and more than half our group followed my lead. Bush Sr. was around the corner from Reagan, but no one stood in front of him. Kennedy was on one end of the hall, and no one stood there either, or in front of FDR who was across the hall from Reagan. I never saw any portrait of Clinton, but maybe his is in the Map Room where he gave the famous deposition that got him fined $50,000 by a federal judge for perjury and obstruction of justice, and which holding was never appealed by him, and caused him to be disbarred by the Arkansas Bar Association. To be fair, I never saw a portrait of Nixon either, that other modern day sleazebag president.

The reception lasted about 1 hour and then the door was opened at the east end of the reception hall and we all filed into the East Room where chairs were set up for all of us with the first row reserved for the immediate Versace family. The East Room is where the presidential press conferences are held and has the dais, podium with the presidential seal and flags. Pookie and I sat on the 3rd row at an aisle. Having watched a lot of press conferences on TV, I almost felt an urge to ask a stupid question like the press does. Of course, I could have done like Helen Thomas, the so called dean of the White House Press, and made a political speech based solely on faulty logic and incorrect facts and then asked a REALLY stupid question based on the assumption that my speech was correct! The media filed in after us and set up their klieg lights and packed the room behind us. On my left was a guy who I think was a friend of Steve Versace, who had told me he was a federal administrative judge of some type, maybe a magistrate. Pookie had said the guy, whose wife was from New Jersey, looked young enough to be a Clinton appointee, so I commented to him that I had carefully observed all the carpets in the various rooms and had found no stains from the former occupant, so I guessed they had brought in Stanley Steamer. He didn't crack a smile and responded that I had a weird sense of humor, so I felt the warm glow of satisfaction from scoring a direct hit. Yes, dear reader, when applied with skill, a sense of timing and just the right portion of chutzpah, anal-retentive behavior can bring self-gratification.

Bush was right on time and sent an aide in ahead of him and had the immediate family come out and meet privately with him for 2 minutes before he sent them back in. Then, with a flourish of "Hail to the Chief" from a few trombones and trumpets Bush entered and strode to the podium. A Brigadier General in the Chaplin Corps that Pookie & I had visited with during the reception gave an invocation. W recognized all the dignitaries present, which included Senator Allen from VA, several Army Generals, the Alexandria congressman and others. Bush was about 15 feet from us and spoke in very measured and deliberate speech about Rocky, his activities and conduct in Vietnam and gave a short synopsis of the reasons for the Medal of Honor. He asked Steve Versace to join him on the dais and then asked a Major to read the specific citation that awarded the Medal to Rocky. Afterwards, Bush presented the MOH in a wooden box with a glass front to Steve who promptly raised it over his head for all to view. After the applause, the Priest/Chaplin gave a benediction and the President left, shaking hands with people along the aisle. The ceremony was carried live by CNN and Fox News Channel and Tom Brokaw had about a 5 or 6-minute clip on the NBC Evening News that nite at the end of the program. My brother watched it live and sent me an e-mail with the endearing comment that he didn't recognize my bald spot from behind in the crowd. The Washington Post and USA TODAY both carried stories with the same photo of Bush and Steve Versace holding up the medal over his head.

The ride back to the hotel without a police escort was not nearly as quick. An hour after our return, we boarded the buses again and went to Ft. Meyer by the back entrance through Arlington Cemetery, where the Army hosted yet another reception at the Officer's Club with heavy hors d'oeuvres, beer and wine. I wish the Army had started feeding us before Will left with his tribe. The vice chairman of the Joint Chiefs, a General Keane (sp) made a short talk about Rocky and the official Army photographer, who had been with us all weekend, took pictures of everyone who wanted with them holding the Medal of Honor. Pookie had hers made, but I declined as I am no kin and didn't do anything to help get it for Rocky. We finally went back to the hotel and the next morning had another free breakfast on the Army before we left. All military personnel and the immediate family had a Wednesday morning ceremony at the Pentagon where Rocky was inducted into the Hall of Heroes at the Pentagon, but we were not invited to that.

Now for Alaska!

Sent: Saturday, July 13, 2002 9:17 PM
Subject: Wawa, Ontario—Virgin Territory for Us

We're finally in Canada on the northeast shore of Lake Superior on our way around the north side of Superior. We did the south side a few years ago on our Midwestern trip. Temperature around 68 and 2 nites on the way here, it went down to 50 in Ohio and Michigan. Feels great!

On our way back to Carlisle, PA from DC, we stopped at Camp Dowd, Tony & Pat's retirement home on a lake near Gettysburg. Pat fed us lunch and we watched Tony's tape of the White House Ceremony taken from NBC and showed him our tape of "A Soldier's Story". Will, Alicia & kids had stopped there for a few hours on their way back on Sun. and Tony had baited 2 fishing rods with worms and Connor and Rachel both caught their first fish, small perch too small to keep. I got to join Tony in his "medicine" before lunch—2 martinis each. In Carlisle, we got the trailer back from the dealer who had tested the electrical system and found nothing wrong. It must have been the campgrounds we stayed in that had inadequate electrical systems, especially in 100-degree heat with everyone running AC, as we have had no repeat problems anywhere else we've stayed. I did get the dealer to bolt a dolly wheel about 6 inches in diameter in a swiveling caster to the rear frame of each side of the trailer. The original angle iron steel skids that drug on the pavement if the frame went too low in a pothole or entering some place with a steep grade had worn off and no longer protected the rear stabilizer jacks. The trailer rides much closer to the ground than the Durango, which saves gas, but makes it hit bottom some and I'm told the Alaska Highway has some severe undulations in spots where the permafrost has thawed and re-frozen. In theory, this should work and I've already used the new wheels on low spots and they worked. When we picked Duke up at the kennel, he had a cut under one eye with a scab on it. I had paid extra for Duke to get treats, walks, play time and play with other dog's time. I think the play with other dogs probably didn't work out too well.

We left Carlisle on Wed and drove across PA on the Turnpike to Canton, Ohio. Cousin Larry, who lived in PA for a few years, said that PA had Philadelphia in the east and Pittsburgh in the West and Alabama in-between. He was right! For those of you who don't know Cousin Larry, you can't imagine how rare it is for him to be right about anything. The Turnpike Authority has infrequent but funny billboards along the way that are very bright colors, flowers and have cute sayings. "All you need is Peace and Love, and Smoother Lanes" was my favorite. "Rome Wasn't Built in A Day, Either" was another.

Thurs. we went to the NFL Hall of Fame in Canton, but only stayed an hour or so. It's well done, but unless you are a dyed-in-the-wool NFL football fan, it's too many statistics and stuff. They have re-plays of all the close finishes and all the Super Bowl winning plays, but there haven't been too many good Super Bowls. I did notice the Chicago Bears had 26 people in the Hall of Fame while the New Orleans Saints only had 1, the founder/owner of the Saints. Pookie says it was payback to her for making me go to the Bata Shoe Museum in Toronto last year. The Hall is in Canton cause it was where the first professional league was founded and organized. Back then, the Canton Bulldogs were the world champs and their star, Jim Thorpe, is still considered by many to be the greatest player ever. He played at the Indian School in Carlisle, PA before joining Canton. In the early years, there were more small town teams than big city teams, but only the Green Bay Packers are still in a small town today. The first record of players getting paid is in 1892 in western PA.

We drove to Cleveland and spent nearly 4 hours in the Rock & Roll Hall of Fame on the lakefront in a brand new building. Doyle would have spent all day. We really enjoyed it and particularly the movies called "The Mystery Train" which showed all the musical background of rock & roll with old films of Blues, Bluegrass, Gospel, Soul, Jazz and the other influences on Rock & Roll. There is also a 42-minute video of all of the inductees into the Hall from 1986 forward to 2002. The psychedelic and punk rock turns me off, but the rest is great. Memphis is given credit for the birth of Rock & Roll and the first record in the genre is said to be "Rocket 88" recorded there in 1951. The Delta greats like John Lee Hooker, Howling Wolf and Lead Belly were very influential in the style also. Of course, the King, Elvis, is the one who really made it popular. There are also big billboards containing all the quotes from congressmen, senators, The John Birch Society and others who said that Rock & Roll was evil and sinful and would be the downfall of America. Tipper Gore got her own billboard for her efforts to censor lyrics a few years ago. There was a traveling exhibit on display about John Lennon and all the clothes worn by all the entertainers are on display. Touch screen kiosks let you play tapes and videos of every performer you can imagine and there are a lot of exhibits on 5 floors. We ate lunch on the third floor balcony overlooking Lake Erie and the harbor, which has been cleaned up, is full of ore boats and other Great Lakes boats to tour if you want. Music is always playing in the background while you are in the Hall, if not blaring out at you. I recommend it highly. Can you believe that you exit through the gift shop?

I have tried once or twice to let Pookie read these e-mails before they are sent out, but it doesn't work, so now she reads them after-the-fact. I have a real problem accepting editorial alterations and suggestions prior to publication since I usually prefer my opinion to anyone else's. Besides, how can I be wrong, before I do anything, other than by reason of my sex. Also, as a veteran of 38+ years of marriage to Her Sweetness, I am superbly conditioned to hearing criticism after-the-fact and can handle that type much better. It just sort of ricochets off most of the time.

It took over an hour to cross the International Bridge into Canada at Sault Ste. Marie due to the traffic this afternoon and the delays at Customs and Immigration where they only operated 2 of 5 lanes. I wonder if it's payback by Canada for the delays getting into the States now due to terrorism concerns. I'm glad we toured all that area and the Soo Locks a few years ago when we did Mackinac Island. The ride up this side of the Lake has some gorgeous scenery, especially where they cut through the ridges to lower the grade on the highway and exposed all the red, pink, green, charcoal and brown marble along the road. Have 2500 miles on this trip so far on the Durango and we aren't even close to Alaska after all our detours. Hell, we're still EAST of Pulaski! We've managed to get a little ways north, but not far west. Pookie asked if we needed to go home due to the market decline. I told her not yet, but I know my buddy Tom, the retired dentist, will wire me some money, if he has any left.

Newly Poor Retiree With No Govt. Check!

Sent: Wednesday, July 17, 2002 9:59 PM
Subject: More Dental Problems?

I forgot to mention that when we entered Canada, the female customs/immigration officer asked a question we have never had before. After the usual questions about alcohol, tobacco and firearms she asked if we were bringing in anything that we intended to leave in Canada. I said no and Pookie volunteered, "Maybe a husband". I assume that Pookie was just tired and a little grumpy. There was a guy in the Wawa campground that had lost the transmission in his truck and had to borrow the campground truck to back his trailer into a site. The guy was on his way to Alaska, but I bet it takes forever to get a repair in Wawa and will cost a bundle.

There are moose warning signs all along the highways in Ontario and we passed a dead moose on the shoulder of the highway. It was as big as a mature good-sized horse and I hope it was a big truck or something big & heavy that hit it, as it would destroy a car or pickup.

We stopped for lunch at Pukaskwa Nat. Park on the Superior coastline. I think we spent less time in that Park than any other we have ever visited. The black flies and mosquitoes are so bad that there was no way we were going to walk any of the trails through the boreal forest and on the shoreline trails it was too cold and windy. We did watch a video about the Park, which is really for backwoods enthusiasts and hikers. The video started with the last Ice Age and said that the glaciers moved all the topsoil to the States, but Canada got the scenery. Even the original discoverers of that part of the Superior coast never ventured inland due to the insects and who can watch the scenery while being eaten alive. They were bad at Wawa too, but not that bad. Duke began to act sickly at Wawa and got worse all the next day and at Thunder Bay where we spent the night and the day after while we traveled. He quit eating much at all, was lethargic, which never happens with a Jack Russell, and started keeping his mouth open all the time. He slept all day in the back of the Durango and didn't bug us and even kept his mouth open while drinking so that the water drooled back out, mixed with a lot of saliva. His stool was normal, but less frequent as he wouldn't eat much. He even quit eating the hard cracker treats I give him every morning and acted like he couldn't crush them with his teeth anymore. When I walked him, he just trotted by my side instead of trying to drag me wherever he wanted to go. We stopped at a vet in Kenora, Ont., but the vet was out and we left after waiting a short time and we drove on to Winnipeg and got in late. Pookie got the name of a Winnipeg vet near the campground where we were going to stay from a girl at the Visitor Center when we entered Manitoba. It was 97 when we arrived and after unhooking the trailer and getting it all set up, the AC circuit started to trip. I walked back up to the campground office and told the lady that my circuits kept tripping. She said everyone on the 30amp wiring had the same problem and all had been complaining. She admitted the campground wasn't wired for such a heavy load on 30amp, but said it would handle 50amp with no problem if I wanted to pay $6 more and move the trailer to a 50amp site and she would loan me a 30/50amp adaptor if I put up a $50 deposit on it. I stood there speechless for a few seconds and decided not to blow up, as I had a sick dog and needed to have AC if I left him in the trailer. I paid for 2 nites and went back and moved the trailer.

Pookie had diagnosed Duke as having an abscessed tooth, based on all her dental problems. She said he looked just like she does when her teeth hurt. Of course, this was after she had offered to clean out the freezer so we could put Duke in it and take him home if he expired before I got him to a vet. The next morning we drove Duke to see Dr. Mould. Pookie loved the name. He was very friendly and seemed concerned and caring. We described all Duke's abnormal behavior and gave Pookie's diagnosis. Duke's temperature was normal, so we left him to be anesthetized so the vet could examine all his teeth, gums, tongue, cheeks and the back of his throat and I asked that he clean Duke's teeth while he was doing his exam and the vet wanted to do some blood tests also. We traded cell phone #s and he told us to check back about 3:30 p.m.

We drove downtown in Winnipeg to The Forks. That's where the Assiniboine River joins the Red River. It has been developed into an urban center and was formerly the marshaling yards of the Canadian Pacific RR, and originally an Indian trading site dating back to antiquity. They have discovered Indian artifacts from tribes as far south as Florida and Los Angeles and as far west as Vancouver and east as far as Maine. Maybe that's where I get my wanderlust, the Indian blood. The old horse stables that held hundreds of horses have been converted into a market with all types of food shops, vegetable and fruit stands and restaurants on the bottom floors and upstairs specialty retail shops. The old train station has also been converted to retail space and there are parks, a children's museum, playgrounds, amphitheatre, outdoor cafes, and docks on the rivers and a lighted river walk. Of course, since we've never been anywhere that the weather was "normal"; the Red River was at flood stage and the water buses that run from the Forks all up and down the rivers to downtown Winnipeg were not running, as the concrete docks they use are all under at least 6 feet of water, and the street lights on the river walk are covered except for the round fixtures at the top of the metal poles.

We did get tickets on a tour boat that was really just a large pontoon float boat with an awning covering the entire top. All the large tour boats had been taken downriver, as they could not get under the city bridges now. I commented to the captain/tour guide that there sure wasn't much current in the river for it to be so high. He replied that we got on the boat on the Assiniboine River and it had no current because it was backed up for miles by the Red River, which was in flood and just wait until we got into the Red River. It was a gorgeous sunny day with the heat and humidity gone for the day. We went up the Assiniboine to the Manitoba Legislative Buildings built in 1920 on one bank of the river. The guide commented that they had a replacement value of $600 million today, or about the same as $100 American. All Canadians complain that they can't leave Canada because their money isn't worth anything anywhere else. Even now, with the US dollar falling against all major currencies, it continues to go up against the Canadian dollar, which is worth a little less than 65 cents US.

When we went back down, into the Red River, the current pushed the boat around and was very strong. We stopped at several sites, one of which was where the largest Catholic Basilica west of Quebec had burned years ago and the rebuilt church is much smaller and inside the old walls of the destroyed church, which surrounds it, but has no roof. It was a nice tour, even with the flood. We ate lunch in one of the restaurants and went up the 6-story observation tower to view the downtown skyline. On the way downtown, we had stopped at ATMs for 3 different banks and could not get any cash as all 3 rejected our withdrawal requests as refused or canceled or not authorized. I watched other people get cash from machines that had refused us and told Pookie that I would bet that SunTrust was having computer problems. Having worked there and seen them overdraw the Fed by several billion dollars, due to wire transfer problems and computer screw-ups; I had every confidence that they could screw up operations even if Bob Whitehead has taken early retirement. After lunch we were able to get cash from a bank ATM that had turned us down earlier that morning, so I guess SunTrust got their interface to the Cirrus switch working again.

We went downtown to a huge mall and saw "Horses" at the Imax Theatre. It's filmed in Australia and is about 3 horses it follows from birth. One becomes a racehorse, one flunks out of dressage, but becomes a stunt horse in the movies and one escapes and joins a herd of wild horses in the Blue Mountains. It's quite entertaining and the scenery is beautiful. After the movie, we called Dr. Mould who gave me a verbal report that Duke was fine, but he was unable to find anything wrong with Duke's teeth, mouth or throat. He told us to come get Duke and we would have a long talk. Using wisdom gained by experience, I refrained from criticizing Pookie's mis-diagnosis. After stopping for me to get a quick haircut from Ultra Cuts, we met Dr. Mould who brought Duke in with us. Duke's blood tests were all normal and indicated no internal problems and physical examination had turned up no other problems. He did however still seem hesitant to close his mouth or to eat a dog treat that was hard. The vet said that maybe Duke had picked up something at the kennel in PA that was not showing up on any tests or maybe he had Lyme disease from ticks, even though he's on flea and tick protection pills. Pookie called it TMJ, which is a joint soreness in his jaw. Lyme disease in dogs can also affect joints and settle in a joint that becomes unusable. Anyway, we now have Duke on aspirin as an anti-inflammatory and on anti-biotic to kill any bacteria if it is Lyme disease. If that doesn't work, the next step is x-rays to see if there is any physical problem in his jaw.

Duke already seems better. He's on soft canned dog food and eating like he used to. He's perked up some and is taking more interest in the outside world, but is still not normal. If he's no better in a week or so, we may try another vet, but this one saw me coming. $432.05 which is more than Duke cost when he was new, even when the cost is converted to US dollars. Last year we went around eastern Canada leaving little piles of money with dentists for Pookie. This year it's Duke. Why am I blessed with dependents that have dental problems? We're in Regina, Saskatchewan now and will spend a few days here. Met some full-timers who just left Alaska yesterday and they told me to go slow on the Alaska Highway where it's marked slow.
Duke's Benefactor

Sent: Monday, July 22, 2002 7:13 PM
Subject: Edmonton, Alberta

We're in the home town of that great American hero, Bernie Ebbers, former CEO of World Com, who the local papers say may have to take personal bankruptcy. What a shame! The local papers also say Canada has nothing to crow about over the Americans on accounting fraud and not even Congress can match the accounting scandals that Ottawa (read Parliament) is guilty of creating. Somehow, that doesn't make me feel any better. I did read an article last week by Peter Drucker, the management guru, who says the current corporate scandals are nothing new and he (age 91 and still consulting) has lived through 4 cycles of corporate fraud.

We really enjoyed Regina, Saskatchewan which was originally named "pile of bones" for the buffalo bones piled up there by the Indians who had a buffalo jump. The city has planted 350,000 trees where originally there were none. Maybe that's part of the reason scientists say that North America now has 20% more forest coverage than it did when the Europeans first came here. We spent an enjoyable morning touring the Royal Canadian Mounted Police Academy where all the Mounties receive basic training. It's a free tour, which starts at the RCMP Museum, and we had a delightful young woman as a tour guide. She wasn't a Mountie but took us on a walking tour of the campus, which covers maybe 200 acres. They have 4 criteria for admission and turn down thousands of applicants each year. To get admitted one has to have a high school degree, have a driver's license, pass a physical exam and score in the top 1,000 on a written admissions test. There are no quotas, ethnic, racial, sex, or other political preferences and yet 20% of trainees are women and ethnic minorities accepted exceed the percentages of the population of Canada. That's the way it ought to be for everything. Years ago there were height and weight qualifications, but they were eliminated 25 years back. A troop of 32 trains together and even sleep jointly in dormitories all packed into 1 room with cots for each and a sink shared by each 2 cadets. It's a 22-week basic course of physical and classroom work covering a lot of subjects. They are issued new articles of uniform clothing according to the stages of training completed and you see troops marching around the campus dressed differently. Some troops are reduced to 25 or so members due to dropouts, but the troops stay together until they graduate. We stopped at a building that had garage doors on each end and she explained that all recruits are sprayed in the face with pepper spray as part of their training so they will understand how it feels to someone they have to subdue with pepper spray, and the garage doors are to help ventilate the building after a spraying. Another building contains a mockup of a commercial Mall and holdups and bank robberies are staged in the Mall to give them actual experience in confronting those types of crimes. The old stables have been converted to a huge drill room the size of several basketball courts with hardwood floors and the regimental flags of all the Mountie regiments. None of the trainees receive equestrian training as basic training and the only ones who get that are based in Ottawa and perform the Musical Ride spectacle that we saw last year. Today all Mounties are mounted on cars, motorcycles, airplanes, helicopters etc. instead of horses. We ended the tour with a visit to the chapel, a non-denominational old church and the oldest building in Regina constructed entirely of wood with stained glass windows where weddings are performed, but only if one of the betrothed is a Mountie.

After the tour, we spent an hour or so in the Museum, which chronicles the history of the force, which originally was named the Northwest Mounted Police. When it was created in 1873, all of Canada west of Ontario, except for British Columbia, was the Northwest Territory and the other western provinces didn't exist. There are some old movie posters of mostly American movies that popularized the Mounties and are largely fiction, but no mention is made in the Museum of any fictional characters like my childhood hero of the comic books and movie serials, Sgt. Preston and his Husky dog, King, of the Yukon Territory. The seal of the Mounties has the French words for "Maintain the Right" and has a bison or buffalo in the center. Our tour guide pointed out that some of the buffalo, when contractors from the east who had never seen a buffalo created the seals, look more like pigs or dogs than buffalo and some have horns while others don't.

After the tour we went to the local Imax Theatre and saw "Shackleton's Antarctica Adventure" which recreates the amazing story of survival by Sir Edward Shackleton and his party of 27 explorers who were trapped in the Antarctic icepack for over a year in 1915 and then, when their ship was finally crushed to pieces, lived on the ice pack for months before making their way to uninhabited Elephant Island off the coast of Antarctica in the salvaged lifeboats when the icepack finally broke up. From there, Shackleton and his captain and 3 others made an 800 mile sail in one lifeboat to South Georgia where they landed on the wrong shore and then trekked 32 miles over the snow covered mountains to a whaling station, where they then led a rescue ship back to the men on Elephant Island. All 28 survived an ordeal that lasted 22 months without contact with the outside world, but they had a photographer who took pictures and movies of the events. An amazing film, with breathtaking scenery.

We drove to Battleford, Saskatchewan the next day and were going to tour an old fort there, but the trailer AC electricity finally died completely in a city park campground. We still had DC, which works all the lights and water pump and the refrigerator works on propane as well as electricity, and we were finally far enough north to get by with no AC as it cooled off and rained all night. We did have an electric cord and hooked up to 15 amp power and used the cord to run the toaster, hair dryer, water pick, fan etc. but only one at a time which is a nuisance. The next day we drove straight to Edmonton and stopped at the first campground I have picked out on this trip. They said they were completely full as Klondike Days is going on for 10 days. I asked if anything was available and the girl said only overflow parking which has no hookups, but then her coworker said what about site 59? The first girl said she forgot, it was open, but nobody ever wanted it as it was small and very hard to get into, but it had all the hookups. I said let me see it and we got in a golf cart and drove to it. She asked if I had 4-wheel drive and I said yes and it looked like a piece of cake to me. I signed up and paid for 3 nights and backed the trailer uphill at an angle on loose gravel into site 59 which is definitely not level, on the first try. We carry 3 boards to put under the wheels to level the trailer and it is now perfectly level. Would you believe the campground has 2 RV technicians and a young guy came to our site in a few minutes and took off the panel on the front of our power distribution panel, which holds all the circuit breakers, and revealed that the 30-amp cord had come loose from the panel. That's why we've been tripping the circuits all the time and finally the last few strands of the copper cable had come undone. He reconnected it and charged me $10 Canadian. I gave him $15. Pookie told him that now she had to go to Alaska and did he really have to fix it.

Yesterday we went to the West Edmonton Mall, the largest in North America and bigger than the Mall of America in Bloomington, MN. We parked at one end and walked to the other. On the way we passed a full size ice rink, a wave pool as big as 4 or 5 ice rinks and a lake with a full size pirate ship and 3 submarines for kids to go underwater in groups of about 30 per sub. We ate Chinese in one of 2 huge food courts and then saw "The Bourne Identity" at one of the 2 Cinemax multi screen theatres in the Mall. Pookie called it a good "dick flick" as opposed to a "chick flick". Lots of action, a good suspenseful plot and a really great car chase through the streets of Paris and a surprise ending. I read the book so long ago that I didn't remember the entire plot until half way through.

Today we backtracked a few miles and toured Elk Island, a Nat. Park and the first wildlife preserve created in Canada in the early 1900s. It's the only scenic Nat. Park in North America totally enclosed by a fence. The ranger exclaimed that they shipped elk to Tennessee somewhere and I told him it was Land Between the Lakes where I have seen the herd. We only saw some bird life and one Buddy Bison grazing along the shoulder of the road. Duke went into his "let me at him" routine. He doesn't do that with cattle or horses, but does with moose or bison. We watched a video of the annual roundups of elk and bison that take place in the winter to reduce the stress on the animals from heat the rest of the year. Not much to do here, but Duke & I did take a walk of maybe a mile on one trail. Pookie wouldn't go and stayed with the "rice brothers and sisters" in a parking lot. There was a plaque at the start of the trail about the Pope being here in 1984. That guy gets around.

Duke Report: Duke is much better. He still keeps his mouth open most of the time, but has started closing it some and is eating well, but still avoiding the hard food and drooling when he drinks. His energy level is back and he tugs us on the leash and bugs us to pay attention to him and tries to get in Pookie's lap in the Durango. Pookie said she liked it better when he laid in the corner. He even went back to leaping up in the air and doing somersaults on his stakeout chain, but now acts like he has a pinched nerve or something in his left rear leg and cries when he lands on it. That has stopped the somersaults for the time being, but he has no trouble jumping up on the couch when he wants to take a walk or jumping into the Durango. He's still ambidextrous when peeing and lifts both rear legs about equally. His continuous interest in hunting is back and the pet walk here is a 40-acre field full of gophers and ground squirrels and he wants to go all day. I'm not going back to another vet till we finish all the anti-biotics and see if he's well.

Random Ruminations:

1. The next time we have to go see a vet or a dentist, Pookie's going to take off those diamond rings and put them in her purse and we're going to be the poor Southerners who saved up for the trip of a lifetime and have suffered a catastrophe.
2. Winnipeg means, "muddy waters", but nobody in Manitoba could tell me what Manitoba means. The best answer I got from maybe 10 inquiries was "they didn't teach us that in school". Saskatchewan means "swift flowing river".
3. There is a highway marker about 30 miles into Manitoba from Ontario that says you are at the longitudinal center of Canada.
4. Winnipeg has over 700,000 people and holds more than half the population of Manitoba.
5. The British Columbia police have started posing as homeless "squeegee men" (who wash your windshield at busy intersections for tips). They have a spotter beside the road watching and they signal the spotter if the driver isn't wearing a seatbelt and the spotter radios a description of the car ahead to a catcher patrol car who pulls them over and issues a ticket. It wouldn't work in Pulaski, Art, as there are no squeegee guys in Pulaski. The public is up in arms about it as the police used to give the real squeegee guys tickets for not using a crosswalk or for blocking traffic. The cops are getting about half the tips that the real guys get and say they are donating them to a food bank. Alberta may be jealous of this scam.
6. We were listening to a "golden oldies" radio station last week when "Heat Wave" by Martha and the Vandellas was played. Pookie commented that we had seen them perform a live show on our honeymoon in Nassau in 1963. I told her I was too focused on other things at the time to remember. About 3 days later I commented that when we saw Martha and the Vandellas they asked for volunteers from the audience and the band played the limbo song and a young Bahamian guy, who I think was a waiter, won the contest by getting under the bar about 18 inches off the floor. Pookie broke out in a big grin and said, "I remembered first". I replied that I had remembered the whole show and not just the lead act.

Off for Dawson Creek, BC tomorrow. It's only 1853 miles to Fairbanks from here. Pookie White Roots just finished re-dying her hair. A redhead again! Elephant Memory

Sent: Monday, July 29, 2002 10:07 PM
Subject: Duke Is Healed!

Yep, the Duker is well again. He got better the day before we ran out of anti-biotics and now closes his mouth, even when drinking and no longer drools everywhere. We have the old Duke back, but aren't sure that is good news. He still won't do leaps and somersaults on his stakeout chain as he remembers the pain of landing on a sore hip, but is normal, or abnormal, in all other respects. We still don't know what was wrong with him, but Dr. Mould said Lyme disease in dogs usually settles in joints and makes them lame, but he had never seen it settle in jaw joints, but he supposed it was possible. We had a contest of wills about getting off of the canned dog food that gives him bad breath, but I won. This was not a certain outcome, since he wins at least as often as I do, if not more. Compared to Pookie, I am a tough taskmaster. I told her that he was back manipulating her again, but the response I got was, "So what, everybody else does too!" Since there are only 3 of us on this trip, and using my immense powers of deductive reasoning, I concluded that there was a remote possibility that she was referring to me as a manipulator also. Naaah, there's no way she could have meant that!

We drove from Edmonton to Dawson Creek, BC, the official beginning of the Alaska Highway. We did the Visitor Center and did the hour long video of the actual building of the Alaska Highway in 1942. It is considered one of the most amazing engineering feats of the 20th century. They built a road through absolute wilderness for 1567 miles to Delta Junction, AK, about 200 miles below Fairbanks, in 8 months. The Corps of Engineers had 11,000 troops working on it and ended up with 7,500 civilian workers too using 42 Canadian and US contractors, after the Japs bombed Dutch Harbor, AK and invaded Attu and Kiska in the Aleutians during the building. They had to build over 130 bridges and used 8,000 wooden culverts. We actually sent troops and surveyors a month before Canada agreed to the highway, as we were subtle as usual. Canada provided the right-of-way and the local materials like gravel, sand and timber and waived the import duties, while we did the rest. As our troops described it, Canada provided the soil and we provided the toil, although Canada paid us for about half the cost of construction in 1946, after the war when we formally deeded the Highway to them. It is amazing to watch the old movies of a guy walking through the forest with an axe blazing a trail and barely keeping ahead of the bulldozers knocking down trees behind him. We're 900 miles down the Alaska Highway and I now understand the quote from the American GI who was asked to describe this country. He said, "This country is nothing but miles and miles of nothing but miles and miles". We did the mandatory pictures in front of mile Zero after the film and ate lunch in the Alaska Cafe before driving to Grande Prairie, BC, the last town of substantial size before Fairbanks. I offered to take Pookie to a nice restaurant in Grande Prairie, but she turned me down. I suspect that she is sneaking onto the bathroom scales that she keeps hidden in the trailer while I take a shower in the campground showers in the mornings and doesn't like the results she gets. I have suggested that she could get more exercise by walking Duke more, but she says, "That ain't walking". Now that he has recovered, she thinks walking him is more like combat than walking.

We parked next to a nice couple from MI in the Grande Prairie campground. He was a retired pipe fitter and his wife was funny. They had been stuck there for 7 days since he lost the transmission in his Dodge pickup and were waiting on spare parts from the states. We offered to take them to the grocery, but they would rather have some of Pookie's movie videotapes, so she loaned them 2. I told the guy that I pulled in 3rd gear at 2400rpm at 60mph instead of 4th gear to protect my transmission and I had the same transmission and engine as he did with 71,000 miles on the Durango and maybe 60,000 on the trailer. He replied that he pulled in 4th gear at 1750 rpm at 55mph and had 21,000 miles on his truck and had had no problems. He was waiting on a transmission and I wasn't, so I quit arguing with him. They were on their way back home from AK.

We played leapfrog with 3 RVs full of FIPs for about a day. FIP is a term of endearment that Wisconsinites use for their friendly neighbors to the south from Chicago who flood into Wisconsin on weekends and during the summers. In fact, there used to be a highway billboard near Lake Geneva, WI stating in big letters, "FIPs GO Home!" At Illinois State University in Bloomington, IL they used to sell sweat shirts with "University of FIP" emblazoned on the front and Illinois State U on the back. If you haven't already figured it out, the IP in FIP stands for Illinois Person and the F word rhymes with trucking. We stayed in a campground at Lake Muncho, YK where there were 3 separate caravans of 3 different RV clubs with about 10 or 12 RVs in each caravan, where they all travel together and stay in campgrounds together. Pookie was talking to some lady from one of the caravans who asked if we were in one of the caravans. Pookie said, "No, my husband doesn't play well with others"! My girl is really proud of me.

At Lake Watson, YT we stopped for lunch and toured the "Sign Forest". It's by the side of the highway and consists of 43,000 different signs, at last count, covering several acres and left by all kinds of travelers. It started in 1942 when a GI from Danville, IL, a FIP of course, left a crude wooden sign pointing to his hometown. Pookie was upset that we didn't bring a "Pulaski, All American City" sign to leave, or at least an old TN license plate. Then she cheered up and announced that if we ever ran into anyone else dumb enough to make this trip, we could give them a sign to take and leave for us. Reinforcement of my ego is not her strong suit.

We made it all the way to Whitehorse in one day and moved to a campground with cable TV and 81 channels whereas we got no TV, radio or even phone service in Lake Muncho, out in the boondocks. Whitehorse was named for the rapids in the Yukon River that the namer thought looked like the mane of a white horse. It's 23,000 in population and contains more than half the population of the Yukon Territory. We stayed 3 nights and liked the place. The first day we went downtown and replenished supplies at Wal-Mart. Over half the parking lot was full of RVers who spend the night at Wal-Mart to avoid paying for a campground site. We also toured the Beringia Interpretive Center, which is a very well done and interesting sort of Museum. We haven't been to the web site, but it is www.beringia.com if anyone wants to look. Beringia was the name for the land mass, the size of the continental US, that existed on both sides of the Bering Strait and in Alaska, Yukon and Siberia when the glaciers had all the water locked up and the sea level was 100 meters lower than today. Back then there were huge mammals inhabiting Beringia, including wooly mammoths, huge bears and beaver, steppe horses and even huge sloths along with extinct lions and tigers. They have actually found fossils of all these animals in modern day Yukon and even some fleshy whole animals frozen in the permafrost and discovered by gold mining. Some animals were perfectly preserved from 30,000 years ago.

That night we went to the "Frantic Follies", a vaudeville show that lasted an hour and a half. It is darling and has the cutest dialogue, again, like a Neil Simon play. It has can-can girls, skits, magic, music and stand up comedy. I wish I had videotape, as it was hilarious. They got people up out of the audience for various scenes and the lead female can-can girl drug up a bald headed old guy that she named Pookie. I started to offer the real thing but got a dirty look when I suggested it. My favorite skit was the "Cremation of Sam McGhee", from the poetry of Robert W. Service, the famous Yukon poet. If you remember the poem, Sam was from Plum Tree, down in Tennessee, and had never been warm since he went north. A delightful evening show.

The next day we drove down to Skagway, AK on the Klondike Highway. I told Pookie we might enjoy Skagway, but I wasn't going to drive anywhere for another day, so she offered to drive if I would go—my ploy worked like a charm! See, I'm no manipulator! We left early and went to the Fish Ladder in Whitehorse first. It's the longest wooden fish ladder in the world, 366 meters, and lets the salmon get around the hydroelectric dam that now floods the rapids at Whitehorse. The salmon have traveled 1800 miles upriver by the time they get to Whitehorse and only have 50 more miles to go to their spawning grounds. As usual, our timing was off and the fish were scheduled to arrive on Aug. 1st, according to the downstream reports, so we were 3 days early. They probably got there the next day. They weigh up to 100 pounds and have turned all red and grown the hooked beak on their upper jaw by the time they get there and have not eaten since they left the ocean. They actually count each fish and keep a record of all that pass. The high count in the last 20 years has been over 2900 and the low, about 5 years ago was 679. They have spent 3 to 6 years in the ocean before they migrate home and spawn and die. Each female lays 5,000 eggs and about 6 survive to return home and propagate the species. They actually capture a few and artificially mix sperm and eggs and hatch young ones who have an 80% chance of reaching the ocean instead of the 20% who survive to that stage naturally. They clip the back fins of the hatchlings so they can tell which returnees are natural and which are artificial. A fascinating story.

On the way to Skagway, we stopped at the world's smallest desert in CarCross, YT. It's about 4 or 5 square kilometers and is the remains of an old glacial lake that the high winds have kept moving around, and where very few plants can live in the barren sand. Duke added a little moisture to help the plants survive. Skagway is the home of the White Pass and Yukon RR that climbs the route to Whitehorse, but doesn't go all the way anymore. It's a cute little place with one main street filled with shops for the tourists off the cruise ships. We ate lunch in a restaurant I picked out and Pookie loved. Crab cakes and a seafood bisque that is to die for. Crab, shrimp, fish and scallops in a white cream sauce with shallots, herbs and spices. After we toured the National Klondike Historic Park (sorry Kenny, no patches again) and saw the video, I went back and got Duke out of the Durango, Pookie did a few of the shops while Duke and I walked up and down the main street. Some lady from a cruise ship came up and asked if she could pet my Jack Russell and said she had left her 3 at home and missed them badly. I said sure, but if she had 3, was she a glutton for punishment? Her husband managed to refrain from petting Duke and said he was almost free from dog hair and would not join in. The Ryndam, the cruise ship we took from AK 5 years ago was in the harbor, along with 2 others and an Alaska Ferry. The cruise ships have stopped going to Sitka where we went because of the lack of docks there and the need to ferry passengers ashore in a tender and have added Skagway as a replacement. Skagway means fierce winds and it was blowing about 35 mph and 50 degrees. I was the only person in town in shorts and sandals, but Pookie says I am impervious to cold, rain, sleet or other conditions. I love it and am no longer hot. Pookie went back to the restaurant and bought 2 of their cookbooks for her and Sue, to get the recipe for the bisque.

We're now in AK again about 250 miles from Fairbanks and almost at the end of this damn highway. The Durango has over 6,000 miles on this trip so far and we're almost at the furtherest point. We won't be home until sometime in Sept. if the money holds out. Traveler

Sent: Thursday, August 01, 2002 6:30 PM
Subject: The Alaska Highway

Pookie says she knew there was a reason we flew and cruised our last trip to Alaska and this road is why. Actually, it's not too bad, but it is very, very long. The whole road is hard surface asphalt, except for the "gravel patches" and the dirt where it is undergoing new construction. The longest gravel patch is about 10 miles as is the longest dirt part. The first few hundred miles—what we call the "suck you in" part is as good as any 2-lane asphalt anywhere and the whole road has wide shoulders. The gravel patches are for the most part very short, from 20 yards to 300 yards long. We had to follow a pilot car several times through construction areas and a very few of the gravel patches are rough as a cob where even the potholes have potholes in them. On the asphalt after the first few hundred miles, they take a can of yellow or gold paint and spray a circle around the pothole so you can dodge it if you stay alert. I don't know why they don't fix it instead of painting around it. The real pain in the ass part is what they call "frost heaves" where the permafrost under the highway has warmed enough to thaw and then refreeze in the winter and the roadbed then may still have a smooth surface, but riding on it is sort of like riding on a small roller coaster. There is a 300+ mile stretch between Whitehorse and the Alaska border that combines the worst features of the entire highway and took us an entire, long day as you can rarely go over 40mph pulling a trailer. The trailer weighs a few thousand pounds more than the Durango and on the frost heaves, the Durango and the trailer take turns trying to launch the other into the air with the trailer hitch as the fulcrum point. Everything in the trailer gets thrown around inside it if it isn't tied down. I was afraid I would break a spring on the trailer or the Durango. They are trying all kinds of experiments to avoid frost heaves, from putting Styrofoam pads under the pavement to venting the culverts so they won't hold water and melt the permafrost, but nothing has worked yet.

There are motels or campgrounds with gas pumps every 50 miles or so and the price gets higher the further north you get, topping out at 90 cents Canadian for 1 liter or about $3.30 per Canadian dollar per US gallon. Converted by the credit card to US dollars, the cost is about $2.20 per gallon US dollar and the Durango gets around 10 miles per gallon dragging the trailer. Once you get to Alaska, the price falls to $1.60. Most of the distance there are no telephone or power lines to get in the way of the scenery or your camera viewfinder, but it takes several minutes to get a credit card approval as the card is swiped and then sent by satellite modem to a computer somewhere which then sends back approval. Most satellite modems operate at a max speed of 14.4k. I found this out by asking one guy who spoke very poor English if his electricity was slow. He grinned and pointed at the credit card terminal and said "satellite" and I watched the small screen as it dialed, transmitted and received the reply. The machines are battery operated and I guess are recharged by solar panels or a generator. I think some of the phones along the route are satellite also as several times the laptop, which has a 56k modem, has connected at 12 or 14k whereas at home I routinely get 48k out of it. About 80% of the vehicles you see are RVs or heavy trucks and very few cars or pickups that are not pulling trailers.

We bought a "Milepost" which covers about 10 or 12 major highways in the Northwest including the Alaska Highway. It describes everything along the road, both commercial enterprises and scenic points, giving the milepost location of each item. The trouble is that there are no actual mileposts until you get to Alaska, so you have to find a landmark like a motel or a river or a campground and get it's milepost # from the book and then figure out where you are and what is coming up next. To make it more confusing, the highway has been shortened by nearly 100 miles since it was built by cutting out a lot of curves and changing the route and some items are listed by the historical milepost # and some by the current milepost # and a few by both and the advertisements are also listed differently. The good news is that all this activity requires some concentration and kept Pookie occupied for hours each day. The bad news is that she decided the best way to figure all this out was to read from the "Milepost'" out loud and ask me my opinion, which occasionally led to some verbal disagreements. I could tell when I needed to defer to her opinion by the little clues like, "You only have one clean shirt left and it would be best for you to adjust your attitude!" Another subtle hint might be, "Do you REALLY, REALLY wish to argue with the sex slave?"

The thing that bothered me the most was following some other vehicle into a long gravel patch. If it was dry, the dust is so thick that you can't see more than 30 yards in front of you and the trailer brakes tend to grab on loose gravel and then the trailer just slides along while you are trying to stop, pushing the Durango to make me apply more pressure to it's brakes which then makes both units start to slide and lengthens the normal stopping distance to double or triple what you are used to. I thought I was going to run over some lady once who began stopping in front of me, probably because she couldn't see. It can get scary on a long downhill gravel patch with someone in front of you. On our long day, it rained all day and the dust turned to mud. That day we traveled alongside the Kluane Nat. Park for over 100 miles, but the ceiling was so low we couldn't see the mountains at all. That gives us something to see on the way back as it's supposed to be the most scenic part of the whole trip. We also skipped some other stuff so we could do it on the return trip. We did stop at the Tetlin Wildlife Refuge in Alaska and pick up an audiotape that describes all the things in the Refuge, which you drive through for about 70 miles in Alaska, and you return the tape to the Visitor Center on the other side of the Refuge. We stayed at Border City campground inside the Alaska state line that night and the RV Park had a place to wash your vehicle on a concrete pad. Neither the Durango nor the trailer has ever been that filthy before and both have been all over North America, north of Mexico. You couldn't see in or out of the trailer windows for the mud. We got the trailer quasi-clean using my telescoping brush which connects to a hose and the water flows up to the brush pad through the handle while you are using the brush. The Durango we took to a commercial car wash in Fairbanks. Pookie bought a bumper sticker that says, "I Survived the Alaska Highway", but I told her she couldn't put it on until we get back to the States in Montana. It will definitely have to be scraped off when I decide to sell the trailer. Pookie bought a few postcards that say, "The Alaska Highway, winding in and winding out, One begins to have some doubts, About the lout who built this route, was he going to Hell?, or coming out?" It has pictures of the road with some frost heaves.

Duke is fully recovered. Last nite I spilled my scotch on his rawhide bone that he hasn't chewed in weeks and a few minutes later, he started to chew it like crazy. Pookie watched and said, "The Binky again?" When my boys were babies and were cutting teeth or were especially fussy, I used to take the Binky and dip the nipple in my beer and then stuff it in their mouth. After 3 or 4 dips, they tended to stop fussing as much or even go to sleep. For some unknown reason, I got better results drugging Will than Doyle.

We've enjoyed Fairbanks and are staying another night tomorrow. I know you'll all be salivating at our next experience to take place tomorrow. We're getting up early and taking Alaska Airlines to Barrow, Alaska, the most northerly point in America. There's a large Eskimo community there and tribal activities and wildlife viewing and we stay about 7 hours and then fly back to Fairbanks. To cap it off, we'll have lunch at the furtherest north Mexican restaurant in the world. I was told the lady who runs the restaurant can arrange for me to join the "Polar Bear Club" by jumping into the Artic Ocean, but I'm going to skip that. The cost is about the same as taking Duke to see Dr. Mould 3 more times, but Pookie says she is worth at least as much as Duke's vet. My gal gets the best! Last year I took her to the most easterly point in North America at St. Johns, Newfoundland and to the center of the Australian continent at Ayers Rock near Alice Springs in the Outback and this year to Italy and now Barrow, Alaska. One minor difference may be that we stayed in a 5 star resort at Ayers Rock and in nice hotels in Italy. I hope they've fixed that screw that works the elevators in the tail of the Alaska Airlines jets. If the plane goes down, I'm leaving the trailer keys with the folks at Chena Marina RV Park in Fairbanks and telling them to let Duke out of his pet taxi in the trailer and feed him.

Weirdo Tour Guide

Sent: Tuesday, August 06, 2002 8:03 PM
Subject: Fairbanks & Barrow

Our first day in Fairbanks we took the Durango to Jiffy Lube for new filters, fluids & wiper blades. Everything in Alaska costs more than in the "Outside" as they call the lower 48, since nearly everything has to be brought in by sea, land or air. $78 for Jiffy Lube. Of course, the Durango had about 6500 additional miles on it when we got to Fairbanks from this trip. I guess our detour to the east coast and going around the north shore of Superior and side trips accounted for about 1700 miles, so it was probably 4800 to get here. We had to wait about 1 & 1/2 hours to get it serviced and everyone in the waiting room began to stare at us when Pookie started reading aloud to me from the newspaper. I asked whom she was talking to and she replied to me and that I had taken her away from anyone else whom she could talk to, but at least she quit reading aloud. After lunch, we went to the University of Alaska at Fairbanks State Museum. It's quite well done with the headpieces for narration about the various exhibits. The girl said we could rent just one cassette player and plug in 2 headphones if we wanted to share. I told her that would never work and paid for 2 cassettes and 2 headsets. After the museum, we went to a movie and saw "K-19, The Widowmaker". Don't waste your money. Rent "The Hunt for Red October" or "Das Boot" if you want a submarine movie.

The next morning we did the U. of Alaska Botanical Gardens and Vegetable Farm. The flowers are beautiful and so much more colorful and larger in size than the same species in the Outside. The long daylight and cool temperatures and the angle of the sun in the sky plus the glacial drift soil, which is very high in nitrogen, make the flowers so spectacular. More impressive yet are the huge vegetables. Cabbage with heads bigger than basketballs and lettuce nearly as large and squash plants that are 7 feet across and 4 feet high. The record cabbage head is 69.5 lb. The corn by contrast never gets over 4 1/2 feet high and the tomatoes are puny. They even plant purple cabbage in flowerbeds as a contrast color, but use a variety that doesn't get so large. We then drove to the University Large Animal Research facility and watched the musk ox and reindeer graze in the fields very close to us. Duke tried his best to get at the reindeer, even trying to dig under the chain link fence. He could probably out run them, unlike the whitetail deer he chases at home. I guess you all know that the caribou and the reindeer are the exact same animal, but the reindeer was domesticated about 2,000 years ago as a pack and draft animal and meat source by the Laplanders while the caribou is a wild version. Oh, there is one other small difference also——insert drum roll here————it is that reindeer can fly!

We ate lunch at The Sourdough Cafe as the campground hostess had told me that was where the locals ate. It was around noon and the parking lot was packed, so we tried it. On the menu they had breaded veal cutlets. I haven't seen that on a restaurant menu in at least 30 years, so I tried it. It came with white gravy spread over it and over mashed potatoes. I think I can hold out for another 30 years. After lunch we toured a wildlife preserve that had been the largest Alaska dairy farm for over 75 years before the state bought it. The fields and ponds were full of sandhill cranes and ducks that summer on the property. Next, we drove outside of town to a spot right on the highway to Anchorage where the Alaska pipeline runs alongside the highway. There are a number of exhibits explaining the construction and operation of the pipeline. The pipe is 48 inches in diameter and is elevated about 6 feet off the ground for over half of its 800 mile length and zigzags to keep pressure against the sides of the pipe and for earthquake flexibility. The oil temperature is over 160 degrees Fahrenheit at Prudhoe Bay and drops to about 100 degrees by the time it gets to Valdez, and it is elevated where necessary to keep it from melting the permafrost and has little radiators containing anhydrous ammonia to cool it or heat it wherever necessary. It is built to survive earthquake movements of the land up to 22 feet laterally and 5 feet vertically. There are 554 animal-crossing sites built into the pipeline and the caribou herd has increased from 20,000 animals to 70,000 in the 25 years since construction. The heat from the pipeline makes the lichens, which are a prime food source for the caribou, grow much more profusely. Wonder why the media doesn't report that to the eco-terrorists who oppose all oil development as a spoiler of wildlife? Alaska, or "Seward's Folly" cost us $7.2 million, but 20% of the oil flowing through the pipeline in 1 day covers that cost and it's been running for 25 years. Pretty good return. Better than my 401k which is now a 301k, but still is better off than Paul's 201k.

The retired airline pilot parked next to us in a big motorhome, pulling a Saturn, in Fairbanks had rented a SUV with his wife and driven the 4 day round trip to Prudhoe Bay on the gravel road alongside the pipeline. They had also taken a 6 day round trip by ferry to Dutch Harbor in the Aleutians. Not even I am that crazy, so we decided to go to Barrow instead and do a tour provided by Alaska Airlines. It was a fun and different day. Of course, they told us at the airport that the flight was delayed because the fog was heavy in Barrow and below minimum landing standards. The delay was only about 20 minutes. Flying Alaska Airlines is about like flying Southwest as all the crew and airport staff is friendly and happy and fun and appear to like their jobs and work well together. The Sr. lady agent at the check-in desk was a hoot and fun to talk to. She gave us what she called "hippie medallions" on plastic string to hang around our necks, which said "Top of the World" and "Arctic Tours". Pookie asked if we had to wear them and the lady said sure and began to take them out of the plastic. She asked where we were from, so I did my best Southern Speak. She responded in Southern Speak also and then did New York and Jersey and Brooklyn too.

Bonna met us at the Barrow airport, our late twenties tour guide and a native Eskimo born and raised in Barrow, who was a scream and one of the best we've had. He had lived for a year in Wyoming, but said her name was Leslie and it didn't work out. There were about 40 of us on an old diesel school bus and the temperature was about 45 when we arrived. Bonna told us we had the opportunity to join the Polar Bear Club if we would dive into the Arctic Ocean and said he would go in too if 4 of us agreed. Some guy asked about sticking a foot or arm in and Bonna said there was no Polar Bear Cub Club and it was all or nothing. He had no mike, but talked loud and stopped and faced us when he was talking and always asked for questions. He was talking about the polar bears, which are all teeth and claws and mean, and how there was a year-round polar bear patrol around the perimeter of Barrow as they were not afraid of anything and were extremely dangerous and unpredictable. One guy in the back of the bus asked if a bear got on the bus, would he start feeding at the front of the bus. Bonna didn't miss a beat and replied no, that the bears didn't like dark meat. We stopped at the small Visitor Center where the monument to Wiley Post and Will Rogers was outside next to signposts pointing to LA, NYC, Tokyo, London, etc. Post and Rogers were killed in a plane crash about 20 miles from Barrow on their attempt to fly over the North Pole. Barrow has 4600 people and about 60% are Eskimo. The only concrete in town is the landing strip and there are 52 miles of gravel roads around the area, but no road in and all supplies come by barge from Seattle in summer only or by air. The buildings are wood and very few are painted, as property taxes go up if you paint. Wood lasts forever up here as the air is very dry and no precipitation falls except snow and not much of that.

We rode out on the tundra and saw 5 or 6 snowy owls hunting lemmings. We stopped at a cemetery and he explained that they dug out the permafrost six feet deep and nobody needed embalming, as they stayed frozen forever. The tundra is very wet and the permafrost is about 3 feet down and 3 miles deep. We saw the high school, which cost $74 million and has the best of everything. The satellite receivers for communication are almost as big as the DEW line radarscopes at the edge of town, and are pointed at a 90-degree angle to the earth, barely clearing the horizon, but they get 65 TV channels and high-speed Internet access. Arctic cotton and wildflowers grow all over the tundra, but there is no tree for 300 miles. Seal and caribou meat is hanging in the air on poles to dry until it becomes like jerky.

We did eat lunch at Pepe's, a Mexican-American restaurant next to the Top of the World Hotel. I ate one tortilla chip dipped in the salsa and decided to eat American. After lunch we joined another tour for $60 each extra, and rode out to Point Barrow, 16 miles west of town to the exact furtherest point north in America. We went with a guide in a huge Ford Van converted to 4-wheel drive with 4 others. This guy was like the crocodile hunter you see on TV, except he lived for taking photos of polar bears up close and personal. He even had a hat and jacket like the croc guy. We stopped on the way and had our pictures made standing inside the jaws of a bowhead whale that was killed in 1987 and whose bones are still leaking oil. There is a huge pile of whale bones about 12 miles out on the gravel spit, where the locals butchered 22 whales last Spring and it still attracts bears who scavenge off the smelly remains. The village of Barrow is allowed to kill 34 whales per year because the population of bowheads is increasing. There were lots of bear tracks, but we saw no bears, only jellyfish and birds, although the guide had seen a bear that morning early. He did demonstrate that seawater can produce fresh water ice by breaking off from an ice flow a chunk of ice that we tasted and it had no salt. He could tell by the color of the ice and if it has been under enough pressure, the salt crystals are forced out of the ice.

We caught up with our tour group at the Eskimo Heritage Center and watched a series of Eskimo dances performed by Eskimo children of various ages. I participated in a traditional Eskimo blanket toss where they throw a youngster up in the air about 20 feet, as they needed help from our tour group to do it. The kids are very well educated and speak their native tongue and English. Barrow is part of the North Slope Burrough and has lots of oil money. A schoolteacher makes $65,000 starting pay and a teacher's aide $22 per hour, but prices of everything except natural gas, which is produced locally, are sky high. A gallon of milk is $7 and gasoline is $3.14.

About 5 p.m., we went down to the gravel beach and 12 dummies dove in the Arctic. The temperature had climbed to 68, but the water was 34. The local radio station was there and interviewed the participants who paid $10 for the privilege and received a certificate and a patch. It was a quite interesting experience and flying back over the Brooks Range we could see 2 huge wildfires burning, but nobody is trying to put them out. Pookie took a picture of her favorite bumper sticker from the trip at the Fairbanks airport parking lot. It is red with white letters and says in big print, "Eat Moose". Underneath it says in small print, "12,000 Wolves Can't Be Wrong". Scribe

Sent: Thursday, August 08, 2002 4:34 PM
Subject: Trip Potpourri

1. We saw a video in Elk Island Nat. Park titled "Over Canada". It is aerial photography of all the most interesting sights to see in Canada and starts in Newfoundland and goes west to Yukon Territory. We've tried to find a copy somewhere in Canada, but have been unable to do so. Pookie got depressed and said there is no place left for us to go in the trailer, but I responded that I guessed we'd have to take more overseas trips. She

brightened up and said O.K that she didn't have to cook on those trips.

2. On the Alaska highway we saw deer, elk, bison, caribou, Stone sheep, moose, pine martens, Dall sheep and a huge brown bear that ran back into the woods when we were about 150 yards away, that I believe was a Grizzly. Lots of animal life in British Columbia.

3. We always stay in some unique campgrounds on each trip. In Gaylord, MI one had a "Bark Park" where you walked your dog. In Regina, Saskatchewan our park had a huge round building attached to the side of the office where flea markets were held while we were there. I asked what it was originally and the answer was a dance hall. In Fairbanks, we stayed in a combination marina and RV Park, but not your normal marina. It was not for boats; just float planes or seaplanes, which were tied up to stakes beside the lake with one about 20 yards from our site. They took off and landed all day long and only took about 250 yards to get airborne.

4. Duke has now been in 42 states, DC and 10 territories and provinces of Canada. He missed our first 2 trailer trips or he'd have all 49 continental states. Pookie says he isn't going to Hawaii.

5. The really big trucks up here in AK and in Canada are not 18-wheelers. They range up to 32 wheels and have trailers that are longer and taller than 18-wheelers and may tow 2 or 3 trailers. The standard log truck is 28 wheels.

6. In Denali Nat. Park they "lost" a tourist a few weeks ago who didn't survive the white water raft trip that we took 5 years ago with Tommy & Sue and Gene & Paula. The tourist fell out, or was thrown out of the raft, and forgot the instructions to sit like you are in a chair, with your lifejacket keeping you afloat and float downstream with your feet in front of you and your legs locked. The deceased went downstream backwards and his or her head hit a boulder.

7. We brought a "Dish Network" satellite receiver with us to watch TV. The problem is twofold. One, we don't know how to hook it up correctly and two; it won't work up here anyway. The footprint of the Dish satellites is limited to the lower 48 and just a little way into Canada. Up here you need a larger dish for the Dish Network. Oh well, we'll try again when we get back to the Outside.

8. There is a town named Chicken in AK. It used to be named Ptarmigan, but nobody in town could spell it correctly so they changed the name to Chicken.

9. The Great Plains in Manitoba, Saskatchewan and Alberta are more colorful and varied than in the US. They normally get more

rainfall than in the US and fields of bright yellow canola, which is a genetically modified rapeseed, grow next to fields of flax which has a baby blue flower at the top of the plant and from a distance looks like a blue lake. The rich green wheat is mixed with the yellow and blue and the lighter green of pastures and occasionally the white blooms of potatoes.

10. A restaurant named "The Cinnamon Roll Restaurant" had a unique advertising sign on the highway to Skagway. It was a picture of the rear end of a moose and underneath it said, "Get your Buns In Here". A few hundred feet later another sign said, "If you don't eat with us, we both starve".

11. For all my friends in the Deep South who are suffering from the heat, I would like to advise them that we have run the furnace quite a few mornings and the heater in the Durango a few days. Our low morning temperature has been 38 and today the high was 59. Hang in there!

12. One of Pookie's friends e-mailed and told her that someday she would get to come home and to "stay strong" and it might happen soon.

13. We had a super day today on a 6-hour wildlife and glacier cruise in Kenai Fiords Nat. Park. The Orcas (killer whales) and humpback whales were the best part. Still Heading West, But Running Out Of Land

Sent: Monday, August 12, 2002 4:01 PM
Subject: Denali & Anchorage

We finally saw Mt. McKinley! On our fly/cruise trip we never saw it, despite spending several days in Denali Nat. Park. About 60% of visitors to Alaska never see it as it makes it's own weather and is hidden in clouds most of the time. This time, we stopped in the Park and visited the Visitor Center. We had partially seen the mountain from about 75 miles away to the Northeast as we drove down from Fairbanks, but only saw the top and bottom as clouds hid the middle and it was hazy for the whole view. At the Visitor Center they told us the mountain was "out" if we wanted to take the 7 hour tundra tour or the 4 hour natural history tour, but we declined, as we know they lie. An elderly couple on their first trip to Alaska was standing next to me at the desk talking to the rangerette and kept asking which tour was the best for viewing wildlife. The girl kept saying that they could not guarantee viewing any wildlife on any tour, but 40 pairs of eyes had a better chance of spotting big game animals than did 2 pairs. You can only drive about 12 miles into the park in your own car while the tours in school buses go in about 50 miles with a park service narrator/tour guide on board. I told the elderly couple that we had done the all day tundra tour years ago and only saw 3 or 4 ground squirrels all day long. I did tell them that the poor tour guide got 40 none's and boos, when she asked after the box lunch stop what animals we expected to see in the afternoon. I hit a curb with the trailer driving out of the parking lot, but everything looked all right in the rear view mirror and the trailer kept pulling fine, so we drove on down the highway toward Anchorage, after watching the visitor video and buying patches for Pookie & Kenny.

About 40 miles later, we stopped at a viewing site due east of the mountain and it was totally obscured. At the final viewing site in Denali State Park about 30 miles south of the mountain, it was in full view and is majestic. There is a name for a mountain that rises suddenly out of low foothills, all by itself, like Mt. Rainer in Washington State, but I don't know what it is. McKinley, unlike Rainer is not volcanic and is a granite plug forced up by tectonic plate collision and totally dominates the skyline. On a really clear day, it can be seen from Fairbanks or Anchorage. It is 20,320 feet high, the highest in North America, and still growing about 3/4 inch per year. It has 2 peaks and the southern is the highest and the top 2/3 is covered by snow. Mt. Logan, the highest peak in Canada is slightly lower and only a few hundred miles away from McKinley. Of course, in the Himalayas, McKinley would be considered a foothill. There are 650 mountains in the Himalayas that are higher than McKinley. There are 44 higher peaks in South America.

We stopped for the night about 100 miles south of McKinley and 140 miles north of Anchorage. I noticed after we parked for the night that the rim or wheel on the tire that hit the curb was bent in and the tire itself was concave instead of convex, where the steel rim was pinched in, and the tire had a gash in it, although the trailer pulled fine and the tire still held all its air. The trailer has dual axles and 2 tires on each side. The next day, a Sunday, I found a quick lube place a few miles north of Anchorage that advertised tire service also and was open. The guy looked at my tire and said he couldn't believe it still held air and he didn't have a tool to straighten the rim and could only hammer on it and hope it would still hold air with a new tire. We drove on to Anchorage, a total of 240 miles from where I ruined the wheel and checked into a campground. After we got a site, but before we unhooked the trailer, we tried the phone book and Sears said they had tire service, but no machine to straighten a wheel. Sam's Club was open and had tire service, but nobody would answer the phone. We finally found Johnson's Tires, a chain in Alaska that is a tire store only, sort of like a Firestone or B.F.Goodrich store. We drove over there and the guy said yes, he could straighten a wheel, but he could not sell me only 1 tire, and a pair was the best he could do. I asked why and he said the trailer had passenger car tires on it and I replied that I knew that and that the manufacturer equipped it with passenger car tires when it was built. He said there was too much liability for him to sell me a car tire and I would have to buy a set of trailer tires and mount one on each side behind the passenger tire. The SOB was one of those people who Knows a lot more than he knows. He said the rear trailer tire carried most of the weight and he would put 50lb. of air in the trailer tire and 35 in the passenger tire and that would protect me. I told him the manufacturer suggested 35lb. in all tires and said they all carried equal weight, but he had the wheel straightener and I didn't. I bought 2 trailer tires, drove back to the campground and let air out of the trailer tires and left the SOB a perfectly fine extra tire as I didn't want to carry another spare inside the trailer. I hope he made his sales quota.

The next morning we took Duke and went downtown to the Visitor Center and got the skinny on what to do. We first went to the Performing Art Center and saw the movie, "Alaska—Spirit of the Wild" narrated by Moses, a.k.a. Charlton Heston. It was sad to learn yesterday that he has early stage Alzheimer's, but his statement disclosing it was a class act. The movie is about the climate, topography, seasons and wildlife of Alaska and is quite well done. Next we went to the Public Lands building where all the various state and federal agencies that administer the Alaskan publicly owned facilities have jointly set up operations to assist tourists in planning their Alaskan vacation. The Nat. Park Service, U.S. Forest Service, Alaskan Ferry Service, state and federal wildlife management services, state parks, etc. all have people there to actually help and answer questions. A unique service we haven't found anywhere else. I booked us on a 9 hour ferry trip to Kodiak Island for us and the Durango in 5 days from Homer, Alaska, planning to take Duke and spend a nite in a motel in Kodiak, and tour the island the next day and then return to Homer. It cost $486 roundtrip and we would return at night, but were put on a wait list for a cabin. We then watched the movie, "Aurora—River of Light" shown for free in the building. A total disappointment as it talked all about the medieval and Indian myths about the northern lights and not about how they are created by the earth's magnetic field interacting with the solar wind.

After lunch, we walked Duke and then took an hour-long tour of Anchorage in a trolley with Donna, the tour guide and trolley driver. She was excellent—we really have been fortunate to get some great tour guides on this trip. She is the mother of 5, with 3 in college and teaches drama in high school during the rest of the year. The tip bucket was marked, "college fund". Her kids are 3rd generation Alaskans, which is quite rare, and her husband was a 10 year old during the Good Friday 1964 earthquake, magnitude 9.2 on the Richter scale and the largest ever recorded in North America, which destroyed Anchorage. He was in a dental chair on the third floor of an office building and had just been given Novocain when the quake hit. The dentist and assistant ran out and down the stairs and left him alone. He rode the floor down to ground level and was saved by the dental chair, which kept the roof off his head. He couldn't find his parents in all the confusion and walked home 4 miles. His parents searched the rubble for 20 hours looking for him and finally went home to find him cooking marshmallows in the fireplace. Donna said that marshmallows are still the extent of his culinary skills. There is a statue to 4 mothers who had talked the high school principal into postponing a statewide basketball tournament that was scheduled to begin that day, because it was Good Friday. The high school back then was 2 stories and the gym would have been packed when the quake hit. Donna was vivacious and quite interesting to hear. Earthquake Park where 140 homes were destroyed and buried when the earth sank 15 feet was a stop on our tour.

The next day we went back downtown and left Duke in the trailer. We saw another movie on Alaska in the Experience theatre and then did the earthquake exhibits and the "Earthquake" movie in an old dilapidated movie where the seats shake and rattle as the screen shows the actual film taken during the quake by various parties, including some home movies. There actually was another 4.7 quake while we were in the movie, but we didn't feel it due to the simulation. Alaska has 2% of the world's surface, but has 20% of the world's earthquakes and sits on the "rim of fire" in the north Pacific. A lot of people in the coastal settlements like Valdez and Seward and Kodiak were killed by Tsunami tidal waves after the 1964 quake when they went down to the harbors to see the damage. Ocean freighters were left 1/2 mile inland where they had been tied up at the dock in Valdez. A very interesting series of exhibits. I also went back and canceled the ferry ride to Kodiak and got a full refund. We're too old to stay up all night trying to sleep in a chair and we've done enough ferry rides. To see the brown bears catching salmon, you have to go to Katmai Nat. Park, which is an even longer ferry ride, or charter a plane. The ferries don't run every day to everywhere, so it takes some scheduling to work everything in and I hate schedules anyway. I like the freedom of doing what I want when I want. Pookie is a lot more organized. She says on these trips, the only way she can tell what day it is comes from looking at her pillbox and seeing what day it says.

After lunch, we saw the movie, "My Big Fat Greek Wedding" in a local movie house. A delightful and funny movie, without any profanity or violence, a true rarity today. If it's on near you, go see. Seward Next

Sent: Thursday, August 15, 2002 5:48 PM
Subject: Seward Grand Slam

From Anchorage, we drove down the Seward Highway, about 100 miles to a campground 6 miles north of Seward. I had forgotten how scenic the drive is along the Turnagain Arm of Cook Inlet. We passed the Big Game Nature Farm where we had finally seen all the Alaska big game animals in pens and cages on our motorcoach ride 5 years ago, but we didn't stop again. We got in early, so we went to downtown Seward in the Durango with Duke and visited the Kenai Fjords Nat. Park Visitor Center and saw the video. I walked Duke in the rain and then we went to the Alaska Marine Life Center on the waterfront. It's a combination aquarium, rehabilitation center for injured marine animals and research center for scientists studying marine life. We spent about 2 hours there and they even had TVs showing a Stellar sea lion rookery on an island about 35 miles away. The Stellar sea lion population has been declining rapidly and they can't figure out why. It's now on the endangered species list and fully protected, but continues to decline. They have about 8 theories, but none seem to check out yet, and the closest they can guess is that there has been some change in the winter food supply. The silver salmon were running now and the lions were gorging on them, so it isn't the summer food supply.

The aquarium has tanks holding all kinds of Alaskan marine life for viewing, an open tank for touching all kinds of octopus, squid, crabs, star fish, sea anemones, etc. and both above ground and underwater viewing areas. The harbor seals swimming underwater were cute, but the hit was the tank with a wire cage above ground where the murres and puffins were displayed. They were fed dead fish, which were placed on the bottom of the tank, and you could sit in chairs and watch them fly underwater as they dove down and ate. It's the same wing motion they use flying in the air while they steer with their feet, but much slower underwater. The murres can dive deeper, but the puffins were much more graceful underwater and can hold a lot more in their beaks on each dive. Still raining, so we went back to the trailer and I walked Duke again in the rain. We went up a side road where some old dilapidated houses were, and from about 150 yards away, 3 huge huskies started running toward us barking, growling and showing their teeth. I tried to get Duke to run away with me, but he seemed to think that three 60 pound huskies were just about an even match for a 20 pound Jack Russell and refused to follow me on his leash. The hump that rises up on the back of his shoulders usually indicates that he's ready to fight to the death, so I finally picked him up and backed away, while he explained in dog talk that he would whip their butts if I would put him down. I decided not to walk him in that direction again.

Before we left Anchorage, I had booked us on a wildlife and glacier cruise from Seward with Kenai Fjords Cruises. Yep, they spell fiords with a j and so does the Nat. Park. I chose the 6 hour National Park cruise from a list of 3 different cruises that left at 3 different times as it left first at 8 a.m. and I've always had better luck finding wildlife in the morning. The cruise is kind of expensive at $115 per person, but we got a box lunch with it that had to be worth at least $2, we discovered later. The boat was 95 feet long with 2 enclosed decks and plenty of outside deck space for observation. It was only about half full, so we had plenty of room. As we left the harbor, we saw a single bald eagle sitting on the gravel beach and watching us. It was raining and I had asked if the cruise would be canceled when we got there, but the little girl told me that it was typical Seward weather and that they got 68 inches of rain every year and 80 inches of snow and had only seen the sun on 17 days this year.

About an hour into the cruise, the captain, Leif, said we had just found the fastest animal in the sea and to go out on deck and watch. We were right behind a double pod of Orcas who were tooling along at maybe 3 or 4 knots. The boat got within 10 or 15 yards of them and kept pace. There were maybe 20 odd Orcas who kept surfacing and blowing and diving again. A single pod is 8 to 14 animals, but during the mating season they merge with other pods and can form up to 8 pods combined. They are beautiful animals and the males can get up to 6 tons with a dorsal fin 6 feet high while the females are much smaller. A male Orca will not mate with a female in his own pod, so they join other pods in mating season. This is in direct contrast to some rednecks that think it is an insult to their own family to go outside of it for breeding purposes.

They are highly intelligent animals (Orcas, not rednecks—except for Bill Clinton who is more crafty and clever than intelligent) and speak a distinct dialect to their own pod members, but can also speak a common dialect to other pods. It is a matriarchal society and a grandmother usually leads the pod. Leif even recognized one pod and gave us it's identifying designation, but said the other pod must be a transient pod that had arrived for the salmon run. After about 15 minutes, of us and the Orcas observing each other, the pod dove under the boat and swam away.

About 30 minutes later, Leif said to get your cameras ready and go out on deck again as we had found 2 humpback whales. I went out in front and Pookie had the camera and went out on one side. Just as I got a good view, a huge humpback decided to try and go airborne—-and did! She got her whole body out of the water and did a half roll before crashing back down. It was a lot better than the whale leap you see on TV in the Pacific Life Insurance commercials. Pookie didn't see it, and I didn't have the camera. Leif said not to worry as the other whale was the cow's calf and he would try his stuff too. Sure enough, Junior then tried his leap, but couldn't quite get totally airborne. The cow was about 50 feet long and 50 tons. The calf was about 24 feet and 24 tons. Junior stuck up his pectoral fin to wave at us, and it was about 8 feet long and the scale is 3 times the length of that fin. Leif really knew his animals and announced that Mama would now show us her flukes as he could tell from how her back was arched. She did. He said now Jr. will try it and Jr. did, but again didn't quite have Mama's technique. Then Leif said Jr. is sounding and train your viewfinder about 30 feet to the right of where he went down and in 10 or 12 seconds you can get a picture of an airborne whale. It happened exactly as he predicted. This kept up for 5 minutes and everybody on the boat got 5 or 6 chances to photo the leaps or tail displays from maybe 35 yards distance. Then Leif announced that the whales were going to sleep and they did for 2 or 3 minutes, lying in the water like 2 huge logs. Half of their brains actually do go to sleep. Jr. woke up from the catnap first and again started to show off his skills or lack thereof. The humpbacks migrate to Alaska from Hawaii and the trip takes about 30 days and 1/3 of the calves that are born in Hawaiian waters don't make it to Alaska. Leif announced that for anyone who had used up all his or her film, he was selling it for $75 per roll.

Next we headed up a fjord in the Nat. Park and Leif announced that since we were having a grand slam day, he would take us all the way to the end of the fjord to Aialik Glacier instead of to Holgate Glacier about half way up. We passed Holgate and then Pederson Glacier, a piedmont glacier that doesn't make it all the way to salt water. Ninety % of Kenai Fjords Nat. Park is the Harding Ice Field that covers over 700 square miles and originates lots of glaciers. When we got to the glacier, Leif asked for silence from all aboard so talking would not mess up the sound on the video cameras. We went to within 1/4 mile of the glacier and cut off the engines. Everyone was out on deck watching and listening as the sound of a huge crack, kind of like a shotgun, would go off and then a piece of the glacier would crash into the ocean as it calved into the sea. Actually, we would see the ice fall and then hear the crash as the sound arrived after the event and then later, the wave from the iceberg would hit the boat and rock it. We stayed spellbound for about 20 minutes while a few harbor seals floated on the new icebergs quite near us. Just as we got ready to leave, Leif announced that he thought the left side of a huge ice cave might let go in a few minutes and he would wait and see. Sure enough, it did with the largest iceberg of the day and lots of cameras trained on it. The glacier wasn't as tall at tidewater as those in Glacier Bay, but we were on a lot smaller boat than a cruise ship and were closer to the face of the glacier, so it was quite impressive.

After lunch, we saw 2 sea otters on our way back and then took a detour out into the Gulf of Alaska and pulled up within 50 yards of the sea lion rookery we had seen on TV the day before. We could see the remote controlled TV cameras and their solar panel and windmill generators. A bull Stellar sea lion can get up to 2,000 lb. and will crush a pup by accident if mama lion isn't careful. We also saw lots of bird-life, cormorants, tufted and horned puffins, murres, etc. On the way back, Leif told us what restaurants to choose for pasta, pizza, steak, family style, seafood, etc. He recommended Chinook's for seafood, so we went and got Duke out of his cage and came back for dinner and the sun finally came out. I don't know how much kickback Leif gets from the restaurants, but Chinook's is NOT the best seafood in Alaska. Leif is still a good boat driver/naturalist. I did hold Duke up to smell the silver salmon that were being displayed by the charter boats coming back from a day of fishing. Duke wasn't impressed.

On the way back to the campground, we drove off the road about 8 miles to Exit Glacier. There is a parking lot and a trail about 3/4-mile to the face of the glacier, which originates a stream from its base. In 1951, the trail was about 100 yards from the parking lot. A really fun day and well worth the time and money. We're now back in Canada at Grande Prairie. Just

heard that it snowed 8 inches in Fort Nelson, BC that we drove through yesterday. Glad I skipped Homer, AK and started home. To be continued.
Chronicler

Sent: Wednesday, August 21, 2002 5:59 PM
Subject: Heading Home

About 35 miles heading toward Anchorage from Seward, just north of Moose Pass, the "Milepost" said there was a trail at a pull off on the highway that led to a stream where one could watch salmon spawn in August. We tried to find it on the way to Seward, but it was not marked and traffic was behind us and we passed it before we recognized it. On the way back, I found it and we pulled off the highway, sprayed on the OFF insect repellent, leashed up Duke and took the trail through the forest. We could hear the stream after 50 yards and found it after about 150 yards. There was a small wooden observation deck, right on the water and there were about 45 Sockeye salmon turned red and spawning in the gravel bed of the stream, which was about 20 feet across and maybe 8 to 10 inches deep. A few were splashing around with their backs out of the water and either digging nests for the eggs in the gravel or covering them with the sperm laden milt, but I can't tell the sex so I don't know which. Most of the fish had finished their jobs and were just facing upstream motionless, waiting to die and right at our feet was one already dead. For once, Duke didn't try to attack and just stood still watching the fish. Pookie snapped a few pictures and we watched in silence for about 5 minutes until I commented that I wondered where the bears were. Pookie then decided that she wanted to go back and get in the Durango. I told her we had our bear attack dog to turn loose if necessary, but she still wanted to leave. On the way back, Duke did contribute some nutrients to the ecosystem. In fact, he has contributed nourishments to more ecosystems than maybe any other dog!

In Anchorage, we stopped in a gas station to fill up and the guy pumping in front of me walked back and said, "Are you from Giles County?" He had a pickup with Alaska tags and a piece of heavy machinery in the bed of the pickup that was a welding machine or air compressor or something like that, so I replied, "How did you know?" He replied that he had passed me a few miles back and saw my tag. I stuck out my hand and told him my name and said that we were a long way from home. He said his name was Buck Reed and he lived in Giles County also and was up working for the summer. I don't know him, but it's a small world.

We drove over 1200 miles from Seward to Whitehorse in 3 days, but did detour a few miles south of the Tok cutoff road back to the Alaska Highway, that eliminates going back to Delta Junction, on the road to Valdez, to the Visitor Center of Wrangell-St. Elias Nat. Park and Preserve. (Another tortured Faulkner-like sentence!) Wrangell-St. Elias is our largest Nat Park of them all and is larger than Switzerland and has much higher mountains. It's over 9 million acres and joins Glacier Bay Nat. Park to the south and both of them join the Canadian Nat. Park of Kluane and a British Columbia Provincial Park which when you combine all 4 total over 24 million acres and constitute the largest protected ecosystems in the world. There is a brand new Visitor Center that had been open only 3 weeks. The video on the Park was so impressive, we bought a copy. It's a Park for dedicated back-woodsmen, sport fishermen and sport hunters who get permits and are flown in by float plane with guides and has only 2 old abandoned dirt & gravel roads to old mining ghost towns. The rangers said we could take the Durango on them, but we wouldn't see any of the scenery we saw on the video. We did drive by the side of the Park for about 50 miles back on the Tok cutoff road and the scenery is impressive as is the scenery alongside Kluane Nat Park that we had missed on the way up.

We spent 2 nights in Whitehorse to rest up and restock at Wal-Mart. We went back to the fish ladder and 272 Chinook or King salmon had come up the ladder since July 31, but we didn't see any. There is a wire barrier at the top of the ladder and a glass view port on the chute so each fish is counted and sexed and categorized before it is permitted to finish the chute. 156 so far were males and 68 were fingerlings that had been artificially inseminated and released. They were expecting about 1,000 in all by the first of Sept. when the run would be over.

We drove 985 miles in 2 days on the Alaska Highway to Grande Prairie and that would be a good punishment for anyone who is evil, especially if they had to tow a trailer. I've never done that on an Interstate and the Alaska Highway isn't one. I was sick of rough 2 lane roads and wanted to get off. We spent one night at Toad River, BC with a beaver dam and lodge about 40 yards from us where the owner had put wire screen mesh around all his trees near the pond to protect them. The morning we left Toad River, we spent the first hour and a half dodging moose, caribou and Rocky Mountain Big Horn sheep on the road. Duke loved it and hunted continuously out the windows with verbal alarms to us. We saw a dead caribou on the shoulder and a calf a few hundred yards later that was probably now motherless. On one downhill stretch with very rough asphalt surface, I was going about 45 when a 22 wheeler blew by me at about 60. When his cab got even with me, the van about 100 yards ahead of me jammed on brakes to avoid a 300/400-pound moose calf that had wandered into the highway. I told Pookie to watch as she was about to witness a moose murder as there was no way the trucker could stop in time. He didn't even try and stayed in the left lane and never touched his horn either. At the last possible instant the moose calf strolled into the right lane and escaped. We had seen another van the day before get towed into Toad River with a huge dent in the left side from a moose collision.

After 2 nights in Grande Prairie we drove to Jasper, Alberta through Grande Cache and another large bear ran across the road outside Grande Cache. We stayed one night in Jasper Nat. Park and then drove the Icefields Parkway to Lake Louise in Banff Nat. Park. The drive from Jasper to Banff has to be the most majestic mountain scenery in North America. I spent my birthday at Lake Louise, not a bad place, but it was cold and windy and we had been there before. Yes folks, I know I don't look it or act it, but in one more year I will be eligible for a gummit check. It's been a long time since my last payday. Maybe I will be a little more able to partially afford my lifestyle next August, since I will take Social Security as soon as possible. I've been the oldest male in my family since I was 25, except for Uncle Nelson, who was born retarded and lived into his eighties. Some might say I was born with a few mental problems also, but they would be jesting of course.

We spent one night in Calgary and piddled around that day just relaxing. We saw "Road to Perdition" which wasn't as heavy as Pookie expected and is quite good. I don't think Tom Hanks makes any bad movies. We're now in Casper, Wyoming after a few days driving from Calgary. Congress created another Nat. Park, Great Sand Dunes in southeast Colorado that had previously been a Nat. Monument and we'll swing by it to keep intact our record of visiting all the Nat. Scenic Parks in the 48 contiguous states. We had already been to all the cities in Montana that we've been through and Pookie says it's like the TV commercial where the guy says he's finished the Internet and has nowhere left to go. I however, have a few new ideas for exploring more of North America that I'll mention later.

I told Pookie that I needed to come up with a name for the Durango, as every man needs a name for his truck. I suggested "Big Red" as it's fire engine red in color. I told Pookie Redroots that she could be "Big Red #2", but the suggestion was not well received.
Tome Writer

Sent: Friday, August 23, 2002 6:27 PM
Subject: Casper, Cheyenne & More Potpourri

In Casper we toured the National Historic Trails Interpretive Center. It's brand new, having opened 2 weeks ago, and is a joint project of the City of Casper and the Federal Bureau of Land Management. Four historic trails all come through Casper, the Oregon Trail, The Mormon Trail, The California Trail and the Pony Express. All crossed the North Platte River here and went through the South Pass of the Rockies, which is the only pass gently sloped enough for wagons. The Center is quite well done and worth a visit. The exhibits start with the ancient Indian trails that also used the same route and give examples of all the artifacts found from all over North America that the Indians traded. There are a lot of hands-on exhibits and lots of reconstructed pioneer and emigrant mannequins dressed in period costume and engaged in typical tasks like cooking over a campfire, standing guard at night, riding a wagon or walking beside it, etc. Pookie always goes faster than me in museums, as I read more of the material than she does. I came around a corner and saw her sitting in a reconstructed prairie schooner, on a barrel of flour, with the covered wagon engaged in crossing the North Platte. There was a sign that said if you wanted to really experience how it felt to ford the river, go get a person from the information desk and there was an old geezer with a docent tag standing behind the covered wagon with a handheld gadget hooked to a cord running under the wagon. Right in front of the wagon driver's seat in front of Pookie was an oversized computer screen displaying the rear ends of two oxen pulling the wagon as it crossed the river. In front of the oxen were two men on horseback, fording the river with ropes tied to the ox horns and leading the way and guiding the team of oxen. The whole thing was animated and looked like a movie as the crossing proceeded. The river was flowing by with an occasional piece of driftwood and the wagon was animated too and shook and rocked as a wheel hit a boulder or went into a hole under water. The horsemen were yelling gee or haw and cracking bullwhips and the oxen were protesting with loud noises. The guy standing there said, "Is that your wife in the wagon?" I said my wife was smarter than that and I didn't know that woman. He laughed and said she had told him I would deny her. As the wagon reached the other side and climbed up the bank, I couldn't resist yelling, "Did that ox just fart in your face?" He fell out laughing and Pookie turned around and gave me a dirty look.

We spent a couple of hours in the Center, which also has a multi screen theatre that shows a narrated slide show about the history of all of the trails. Over 600,000 emigrants passed through Wyoming on these trails, the largest non-forced migration in the history of the world. Originally it was a trickle, and then a flood when gold was discovered in CA. The first parties were alone for the whole trip and the latter groups were never out of sight of other parties for the whole length of the trails.

In Cheyenne we toured the State Capitol for an hour or so. Compared to the Midwestern capitols, it's not very impressive and it's a self-guided tour. We also did the Wyoming State Museum across the street from the capitol which is much more interesting. Wyoming is actually a word from the Delaware Indian language that means, "Where the plains are". Wyoming has a lot of unique standings. It is the least populated of any state and is still a place that people pass through more than live. Today, there are 9 tourists every year for every resident of the state. It produces and contains more coal than any other state. It is the home of the first National Park in the entire world, Yellowstone. It was the first self-governed modern day government to grant women the right to vote anywhere in the world. It is the home of more fossils than anywhere else on earth. Both the horse and the camel originated here also. A nice museum to visit.

More Potpourri:

1. Pookie's front passenger window in the Durango wouldn't go down when we left on this trip. She kept complaining about it, so after 5,500 miles when we got to Whitehorse on the way up to Alaska, she said she was taking the Durango to the Dodge dealer if I didn't do something. She really got incensed outside of Whitehorse when she couldn't put it down to take a picture of a moose cow & calf on her side of the road. Under threat of a dealer repair bill, I got out the owner's manual and found out that the power windows were controlled by a circuit breaker in the fuse box. The breaker is an aluminum box plugged into a socket. I couldn't get it out with my fingers, so I jiggled it around and pushed it in hard. Shazam, her window worked! She said thanks very grudgingly and then said that I would have fixed it a lot sooner if it had been the right rear window that Duke hangs out of at low speeds. Of course, Duke would have been a lot more obnoxious about it than Pookie was.
2. We saw on TV the other day where viewers had been given a poll, which asked the question, "Who should play Martha Stewart in the inevitable movie about her stock sale?" The overwhelming choice was the woman the world loves to hate, Kathy Lee Gifford. Even I feel sorry for Frank Gifford.
3. I was thinking last nite about our last visit to Casper. In 1975 we came out the Oregon Trail from Independence, MO in a station wagon pulling the poptop camper with our boys and stopping to see all the sights like Chimney Rock, Scottsbluff, Ft. Laramie etc. on our way to Yellowstone and Grand Teton. When we got to Casper, we checked into a nice motel with a restaurant for 2 nights, which I charged to my bank in Jackson, TN. The next morning after breakfast, Pookie & the boys headed to the swimming pool while I went downtown to a bank in Casper that advertised for sale the software for their Burroughs 500 computer. We used a B-500 in Jackson and were interested in possibly buying their software. I spent a couple of hours looking at all their computer reports and asking a lot of questions. I decided after about 30 minutes that we already owned better software than they had, but stayed longer to be polite and to see if I could learn anything. I turned down an invitation to lunch as I had already acquired free meals at the motel for my family from my bank. I went back to the motel and into the pool with the kids. Hey, it was a lot cheaper for my bank than flying me out to make the same decision. It was a nice break for us from

the campgrounds too, especially for Pookie. She likes bathtubs and not cooking.

4. When we pulled into the first ever KOA campground in Billings, Montana a few days ago, they put us next to two big motorhomes pulling cars with Mississippi State Bulldog bumper stickers all over them and Mississippi tags. While I was unhooking the trailer, Pookie walked over and asked the neighbors sitting outside on a little concrete patio and drinking beer if she needed to sing "Hail Dear Old State". I heard her exclaim, "Of course I know the Fratesi family in Leland!" When I got through and had poured myself a scotch, I went around and joined the group. The older guy asked if I was an Ole Miss graduate too. I replied that I was considered the black sheep of my family because I went to Ole Miss Law School, even though State didn't have a law school. He said, "Couldn't you have found something else to do?" We had a really nice time visiting with them. It was a couple and 2 half couples. One husband and one wife couldn't get off work long enough to take a 3 week trip and the group was going to Calgary where the missing spouses would fly to and join up for the return trip. They were headed to Vancouver after that and then to Portland, OR for the Aug. 31 game between the Oregon Ducks and the Bulldogs. They said they had 2 extra tickets and did we want to meet them in Portland for the game? Pookie asked if I wanted to go, with a tone that indicated that she would like to go. She added that we could visit Arnold & Ginger in OR on the way. Pookie never likes it when I tell her we're heading home and she always pouts for a few days. It's a lot easier to keep up the trailer than the house and she gets to eat out more. I said no thanks, that I had driven over 10,000 miles, I had already seen Oregon and I wasn't heading back west. Besides, I've seen the Dogs play lots of times and if there is a way to lose, they usually find it. They normally have an offensive line that averages 350 pounds and has all the foot speed of a below average sloth. Their other usual attribute is the worst play calling skills on this planet. I would pay a goodly sum to see what Jackie Sherrill writes on that clipboard all during the game. I bet it's all profanity.

5. Pookie had nagged me until I bought the new wiper blades in Fairbanks. The old ones scraped across the windshield constantly. I commented that the new ones were quiet and nice. She replied that I was welcome and I could still indulge my instincts to conserve by continuing to not burn out the turn signal light bulbs. It is such a delight to have a resident driving critic who won't get anywhere near the driver's seat so long as the trailer is hooked up.

Picked Upon Scribe

Sent: Friday, August 30, 2002 5:20 PM
Subject: La Veta, Colorado and Home

I picked out a campground at La Veta, CO because it was only 15 miles west of I-25, while Great Sand Dunes, Nat. Park is 75 miles west of I-25 and at an elevation above 8,000 feet. I didn't want to haul the trailer up that high and I picked a loser. There was a caravan of about 20 RVs in the La Veta campground from Texas and they were all dedicated square dancers, who met there to square dance every night. We had to run the AC to drown out the caller and the music being played in the Mexican Restaurant that was part of the campground. The town was about 400 people and Charlie's was the only grocery store, but it had a soda shop counter and ice cream for 50 cents per scoop. When the Sunday papers are lined up in the window under a sign that says, "Do not pick up a paper with a name or # written on it as those are reserved", you know it's a small town.

Great Sand Dunes Nat. Park and Preserve Act was passed in Nov. 2001 and the dunes became a National Monument and won't become a full scale Nat. Park until they buy some more adjacent land, which is scheduled to happen in a few years if a subsequent Congress appropriates enough money. Would you believe the Nature Conservancy is buying up the adjacent land and will resell it to Congress at a profit? Yes, Virginia, follow the money and you may find out the truth. We approached the Dunes from the east in the morning and you can see them from 15 miles away. They are against a mountain background and look like a painter's palette from a distance. They are up to 750 feet high and are in constant motion from the winds. Most Parks say leave only footprints, but you can't do that here as the winds wipe them out after a short time. They encourage visitors to climb and slide on the dunes, which is in contrast to most Parks. The dunes are estimated to be about 12,000 years old and were created by sand being carried in by the Rio Grande and by streams and the sand became trapped against the mountains by the winds. The Dunes are neither growing nor declining as the sand supply is now constant and just moves around as the wind direction changes. It is a quite unique Park and striking in appearance. We walked a short trail with exhibits near the Visitor Center and watched the video on the Park.

After a picnic lunch where we fed birds by hand and chipmunks, we drove down a road advertised as a 4-wheel drive road that would take us right up to the edge of the dunes. After 1/2 mile, there was a sign that said to let the tire pressure in your tires down to 15 pounds, as the sand ahead was very soft. I paid more attention to the other sign that said the minimum towing fee was $100, and decided to turn around and go back and walk to the dunes from a parking lot. After a few hundred yards walking in the soft sand that was over 100 degrees, we decided that we were close enough and there was no need to climb the dunes. Duke was left in the trailer as it was too hot to leave him in the Durango and he spent the day with AC listening to the PBS station that was the only one we could pick up. As we left the Park to go back to La Veta I asked Pookie how it felt to see her last Nat. Park. She replied very quickly that she still planned to visit 2 more in Hawaii.

On the way to Amarillo to pick up I-40 and go home, we drove within 3 miles of Capulin Volcano Nat. Monument in New Mexico, so we turned off to see it too. It's a cinder cone volcano created about 60,000 years ago during a period of intense volcanic activity in New Mexico. Unlike most volcanoes, it's nearly perfectly shaped as a cone because the lava flowed from the base and never went up the vent that built the volcano. It is heavily forested and I was told I had to unhook the trailer to drive up to the top and then we could walk down into the caldera. It was hot and I didn't want to unhook and rehook the trailer or walk down and then up hill, so we just did the video, ate lunch and left. Can you tell I was ready to go home?

Final Random Ruminations:

1. In Montana on the Interstate, a big white pickup passed us at a high rate of speed. The guy had taken a can of black spray paint and painted on the tailgate in bold black letters, "Osama, Kiss My Red-blooded American Ass!"

2. The more country of the 2 Mississippi State women we talked to in Billings at the campground waited until Pookie went into the trailer to get something and then asked me, "How long you been with her?" I replied that it would be 39 years next month and added that I married her when she was 19. When I later told Pookie, she commented that the woman obviously thought Pookie was my 2nd wife. I asked did she mean my trophy wife. I just got a smile in response.

3. Driving south on I-25 through Denver is like driving across Los Angeles, except L.A. has 6 lanes in each direction and Denver only has 3. Oklahoma on I-40 is almost like the Alaska Highway for road surface roughness and they aren't doing anything about it. No wonder that I-40 Bridge collapsed. Arkansas is no better, but they are working like crazy to resurface there and they've taken down all the Bill Clinton signs, thank God.

4. A rest area on I-40 had a pet walk area with a big sign, City Dogs by a fake fire hydrant and a sign Country Dogs by a tree stump. Duke covered both bases.

We're home now after spending one night on Greer's Ferry Lake near Heber Springs where Barbara fed us a home cooked meal. 12,575 miles on this trip, but there won't be anymore that long. Now I need a little feedback. Plan B would be to upgrade my scooter to a cruising version that could do 60 down the highway all day, and we could take some 1 and 2-day trips on it, but Duke couldn't go. Plan C would be to buy a pontoon type houseboat and see America by inland waterways. I've always thought it would be fun to start in FL in the early Spring and go north 50 miles per day with the Spring as it moves north, all the way up the Intracoastal Waterway to Maine. If you got very adventurous, you could go up the St. Lawrence and home by the Great Lakes and Mississippi and Tennessee rivers. Plan B/C would be to carry the scooter on the pontoon and Duke. What do you think, besides that I'm nuts? My 2 kids don't get a vote, as it's their inheritance I would be spending. Even if they did, it would probably be a tie, with Doyle saying have fun and Will saying what about the grandkids. Let me hear from you. FINIS, Evan

About the Author

The author was born in 1941 in Greenville, Mississippi, the hometown of more than 50 published authors. They say it's the water. As a youngster, he routinely won the annual prize from Greenville's William Alexander Percy (another author) Memorial Library for reading the most books. He earned a BBA degree from Tulane and a JD from Ole Miss. He took early retirement from a banking career at age 55, due to health concerns. Since 1998, he and his wife, Pookie, have traveled 70,000 miles in their travel trailer, all over North America, north of Mexico. This is an informative, entertaining and hilarious account of those travels. They reside just outside the city limits of Pulaski, Tennessee with Duke, their dog.

Made in the USA
Coppell, TX
24 February 2021